Weimar and Now: German Cultural Criticism

Edward Dimendberg, Martin Jay, and Anton Kaes, General Editors

1. *Heritage of Our Times,* by Ernst Bloch

2. *The Nietzsche Legacy in Germany, 1890–1990,* by Steven E. Aschheim

3. *The Weimar Republic Sourcebook,* edited by Anton Kaes, Martin Jay, and Edward Dimendberg

4. *Batteries of Life: On the History of Things and Their Perception in Modernity,* by Christoph Asendorf

5. *Profane Illumination: Walter Benjamin and the Paris of Surrealist Revolution,* by Margaret Cohen

6. *Hollywood in Berlin: American Cinema and Weimar Germany,* by Thomas J. Saunders

7. *Walter Benjamin: An Aesthetic of Redemption,* by Richard Wolin

8. *The New Typography,* by Jan Tschichold, translated by Ruari McLean

9. *The Rule of Law under Siege: Selected Essays of Franz L. Neumann and Otto Kirchheimer,* edited by William E. Scheuerman

10. *The Dialectical Imagination: A History of the Frankfurt School and the Institute of Social Research, 1923–1950,* by Martin Jay

11. *Women in the Metropolis: Gender and Modernity in Weimar Culture,* edited by Katharina von Ankum

12. *Letters of Heinrich and Thomas Mann, 1900–1949,* edited by Hans Wysling, translated by Don Reneau

13. *Empire of Ecstasy: Nudity and Movement in German Body Culture, 1910–1935,* by Karl Toepfer

14. *In the Shadow of Catastrophe: German Intellectuals between Apocalypse and Enlightenment,* by Anson Rabinbach

15. *Walter Benjamin's Other History: Of Stones, Animals, Human Beings, and Angels,* by Beatrice Hanssen

16. *Exiled in Paradise: German Refugee Artists and Intellectuals in America from the 1930s to the Present,* by Anthony Heilbut

Prague Territories

Prague Territories

*National Conflict and Cultural Innovation
in Franz Kafka's Fin de Siècle*

Scott Spector

UNIVERSITY OF CALIFORNIA PRESS
Berkeley · Los Angeles · London

University of California Press
Berkeley and Los Angeles, California

University of California Press, Ltd.
London, England

© 2000 by the Regents of the University of
California

Library of Congress Cataloging-in-Publication Data

Spector, Scott, 1959–
    Prague territories : national conflict and
cultural innovation in Kafka's fin de siècle / by
Scott Spector.
        p.   cm. — (Weimar and now; 21)
    Includes bibliographical references and index.
    ISBN 0-520-21909-0 (alk. paper)
    1. German literature—Czech Republic—
Prague—History and criticism.   2. German
literature—20th century—History and criticism.
3. German literature—Jewish authors—History
and criticism.   4. Kafka, Franz, 1883–1924—
Homes and haunts—Czech Republic—Prague.
5. Prague (Czech Republic)—Intellectual life.
I. Title.   II. Series.
PT3838.5.P7 S64 2000
830.9′943712′09041—dc21   99-041955

Manufactured in the United States of America

08 07 06 05 04 03 02 01 00 99
10 9 8 7 6 5 4 3 2 1

The paper used in this publication meets the
minimum requirements of ANSI/NISO Z39.48-1992
(R 1997) (*Permanence of Paper*).

Eric's.

Contents

Plates follow p. 134.

Preface

What follows is a cultural history of a moment that can only be described as exceptional. Its exceptionality was what drew me to it in the first place; there is something compelling about the extraordinary conditions bearing upon national, ideological, and aesthetic identities that were particular to turn-of-the-century Prague. These circumstances were even more idiosyncratic for the small demographic group that has been my focus: the German-speaking Jews of Franz Kafka's generation. So in the course of telling that history, if not in this preface, I feel compelled to address the question of why an example so unexemplary might be particularly useful to the general project of the study of European modernity. That is one concern. Another arises from the intention to write history while depending to an important degree on literary texts, and on readings of contexts informed by literary studies. Both of these concerns can be expressed as a single question: What is Franz Kafka's "place" in "history"?

This question of placement is closely linked to the heuristic figure I will be describing as "territory," and which is drawn from the persistent reiteration of spatial metaphor in the self-reflexive language of writers of Kafka's generation (a group of whom have come to be known, albeit problematically, as "the Prague circle"). This book is about the emergence of and projected resistances to "territorial ideology"—which I understand as a conceptual system, or naturalized way of looking at one's place in the world, that grounds the sociopolitical claims of nationalism, the cultural claims of national literature, and a peculiarly modern experience of identity. In the introduction to her essays in *Between Past and Future*, Hannah Arendt draws upon Kafka's notebooks to illustrate how spatial metaphor can signal a self-consciousness of historical actors at certain privileged moments that she refers to as odd, "in-between" periods. Not only later historians but the actors themselves seem aware of their own "placement" in a historical moment between an irrecoverable past and an as yet unimaginable future, or between "things that are no longer and [. . .] things that are not yet." The best argument for focusing on the idiosyncratic is that the exposure entailed in this rare condition allowed for conflicts beneath the surface of European modernity more generally to be articulated in exemplary ways.

Kafka's generation, as I will discuss in the introductory chapter and throughout my text, was "in between" in a number of senses. In historical as well as historiographical terms, the Prague circle falls squarely between the Central European fin de siècle and Weimar, bridging a "politics and culture" presumed to be opposed in the aestheticist movements of the century's turn in Austria and, on the other side, the self-consciously politicized culture criticism of the German 1920s. In a stark way, the writers explored here felt themselves to have been in between subject positions or "identities"—national identities, to be sure, but also other sorts of communal identities, aesthetic identities, ideological identities. Again, while each of these sorts of identities was "open" at other critical points of modernity, the irreproducible particularity of the moment explored here meant that the constructedness of selves was not intuited, but experienced in a literal sense.

The ideological break from the past represented by this generation was the abandonment of what in Austria was known as "German liberalism," the imagined line from the Enlightenment to the turn to the twentieth century in which the parents of the Prague circle generation of German-speaking Jews had held so much stock. Much has been said about the famed "father-son conflict" that gave birth to Kafka's best-known letter (the so-called Letter to His Father) and that played a central role in expressionism. At first glance, and at the time, the Austrian ideological landscape seemed to be experiencing an unmistakable break between German liberalism and a number of "antiliberal" movements: the nationalism of the Young Czechs, Zionism, German *völkisch* ideology. The problem with this view, convenient as it is, is that it releases liberalism from responsibility (taken in either the positive or negative sense) for these successive ideologies when, historically speaking, they would each be unimaginable without it. For this reason, "postliberal" is a better way to render these movements. While all the writers examined in this book went through ideological transformations of one kind or another, in each of their various nationalisms, socialisms, Zionisms, and so on, the stamp of their particular position—the Prague circle moment—remains. That is not to say that their cultural products are always subversions of dominant paradigms. Throughout there is a strange cohabitation of subversion and collusion: within an outspoken attack on liberalism, its foundation is refortified; as another ideology is embraced, the tenets of that system are undermined. The strains of discursive resistance and complicity within cultural products cannot be untangled from one another, but they can be grasped.

Implicit in my argument is that the Prague of this period constitutes a privileged site for cultural history because of the special role of the figure of "culture" within political discourse, along with the special function of the figure of "language" in Kafka's Prague. If these theses help justify the suspension of boundaries between culture criticism and historical analysis, they also may begin to suggest the grounds for Arendt's suggestion that Kafka stood at a philosophical moment apart from and yet fused to a lost past and an unresolved historical possibility.

A range of diverse sources has been explored to trace discursive links between the texts and contexts at play in this period. Principal among these have been daily and weekly newspapers (German-liberal and German-Jewish); journals in Austria and Germany that struggled with the emergence of new aesthetic forms; and literary works by Prague circle writers along with (at least as centrally) their essays, diaries, letters, and notes. The first chapter introduces the Prague scene and begins to explore the rhetoric by Praguers on Prague, as well as the critical and historiographical contexts surrounding this book. In chapter 2, the very earliest work of several Prague writers is presented, with a focus on the figure of culture and the notion of the aesthetic as it was imperfectly inherited from the German-liberal generation of their parents. Chapter 3 examines the relationship between language and territory in the Prague context, tracing a line from the German-liberal and nationalist Fritz Mauthner to Franz Kafka, and locating both within the discursive context of the Bohemian language conflict. The collision of the aesthetic and the political is of special interest in chapter 4, which concerns itself with expressionism in Prague, program and practice, and the transformation of the art/life binary during the First World War. The "cultural Zionism" of Hugo Bergmann and the Prague student Zionist organization Bar Kochba is the center of chapter 5; it offers an example of the resistances to the figure of territory even within this venture to imagine a Jewish homeland. Chapter 6 explores the broader turn of these writers to Jewish identity, the identification of this Jewishness with Slavic and Yiddish Eastern Europe, and the important role of gender in this constellation. Chapter 7 considers the Prague German-speaking Jewish writers' crucial role in the translation and mediation of modern Czech literature and opera—activities that inscribed a cultural space or "national literature" of a novel kind.

The only chapter to have been published previously is the fifth, a somewhat different version of which appeared in the January 1999 issue of the *Journal of Contemporary European History* as "Another Zionism: Hugo Bergmann's Circumscription of Spiritual Territory." Individual sections, readings of texts, or fragments of the argument have been included in a number of other articles, including "Beyond the Aesthetic Garden: Politics and Culture on the Margins of *Fin-de-Siècle Vienna*," *Journal of the History of Ideas,* October 1998; "From Big Daddy to Small Literature: On Taking Kafka at His Word," in Linda E. Feldman and Diana Orendi, eds., *Evolving Jewish Identities in German Culture: Borders and Crossings* (Westport, Conn., 1999); "Workshop Nationen: Otto Picks Vermittlungsräume," *Das Jüdische Echo: Zeitschrift für Kultur & Politik* (1996); "Auf der Suche nach der Prager deutschen Kultur: Deutsch-jüdische Dichter in Prag von der Jahrhundertwende bis 1918," in Deutsches Historisches Museum Berlin, ed., *Deutsche im Osten: Geschichte, Kultur, Erinnerungen* (Munich and Berlin, 1994); "Die Konstruktion einer jüdischen Nationalität—die Prager Wochenschrift 'Selbstwehr,'" *brücken: Germanistisches Jahrbuch* (1991/1992). Because of the focus on Germanophone Prague, German versions of street and place names are used most often in this book, with reference to the Czech names where those might be familiar to contemporary readers. The epigraphs introducing each of the chapters are all Kafka's; any faults in the sometimes painful translation of them mine.

The network of debts incurred in the process of researching and writing this book crosses various disciplinary as well as national borders. Only the most important contributions will be mentioned here. To all others who have helped directly or indirectly I express gratitude. For support of the research and writing of the dissertation, thanks are due to the German Academic Exchange Service (DAAD), the Joint Council on Eastern

Europe of the American Council of Learned Societies and the Social Science Research Council, the Wiener Library and Institute for Comparative European History at Tel Aviv University, the Center for German and European Studies at Georgetown University, the History Department of the Johns Hopkins University, and the School of Literature, Science, and the Arts of the University of Michigan. The role these institutions and others like them play in the promotion of new scholarship is hard to exaggerate.

For guidance through the vast terrain of archival and other primary sources thanks are owed to the staffs of the Památník Národního Písemnictví, the State Jewish Museum, the Archives of the Charles University, and the university's Klementinum library, all in Prague; in Berlin, to the manuscript division and general staff of the Staatsbibliothek Preußischer Kulturbesitz, both West and East, and the Academy of Arts; to the German Literature Archive/Schiller National Museum in Marbach am Neckar, and to the Research Center for Prague German Literature and the staff of the new critical Kafka Edition in Wuppertal; in Vienna, to the University and National libraries and the Literatur Haus; in Jerusalem, to the personnel of the Shmuel Hugo Bergman, Felix Weltsch, and Martin Buber archives housed at the Jewish National and University Library, and of the Central Zionist Archives; in Tel Aviv, special gratitude to the staffs of the Wiener Library and the university's Institute for German History, who provided technical assistance along with their personal support. For their intellectual contributions, helpful advice, and friendship I thank Dr. Miroslav Kunštát, Professor Jítka Malečková, and Dr. Oldřich Tůma. Dr. Josef Poláček led me to uncatalogued manuscripts that figure centrally in several chapters, and his scholarly help with regard to the research on Egon Erwin Kisch was offered with warm hospitality. In the United States, acknowledgment is due the staffs of the Library of Congress, the Leo Baeck Institute in New York, and the university libraries at Johns Hopkins, Georgetown, and the University of Michigan.

For guiding the research and writing of this project from its inception I am indebted to my graduate advisors Vernon L. Lidtke, Mack Walker, and Nancy S. Struever. Professor Lidtke has offered attention, advice, and personal support beyond anything that ought reasonably to be expected from a primary advisor. Additional—and indispensable—suggestions were provided by Germanists Sander Gilman, Barbara Hahn, Rainer Nägele, and Liliane Weissberg. With specific regard to the field of Prague German literary studies I am grateful to have benefited from the guidance of Professors Eduard Goldstücker, Wilma Iggers, Georg Iggers, Kurt Krolop, Margarita Pazi, and Hans Dieter Zimmermann. For reading parts or all of the manuscript and offering often lively criticism I thank Mark Anderson, Tommaso Astarita, Roger Chickering, Anne Herrmann, Pieter Judson, Doris Kaufmann, Daniel S. Mattern, Lester Mazor, Rudolf Mrázek, Don Reneau, Richard Selden, and Michael Steinberg. Among other readers I must particularly thank my senior colleagues in German history and literature, Frederick Amrine, Timothy Bahti, Kathleen Canning, and Geoff Eley, each of whom gave me specific guidance on the manuscript and general collegial advice, along with— not least valued—very generous personal support. The text certainly benefited from my contact with colleagues at the University of Michigan's Center for Russian and East European Studies, and at the Frankel Center for Judaic Studies (with particular thanks to Todd Endelman). Finally, I need to acknowledge the contribution of my students and my many additional colleagues in the departments of History and of Germanic Languages and Literatures at the University of Michigan, who offer daily support in the form of scholarly community and example.

My family has offered perpetual encouragement and support for the efforts culminating in this book, and I sincerely thank Natalie and Benjamin Spector, Debra and Thomas Boyce, Rebecca Spector, and Jason McKenney. A huge wolf hybrid named Jed stood, or sat, by me through every word of the first drafting—my most patient interlocutor; a Berner named Burckhardt suffered the revisions. Finally, these acknowledgments would not deserve the name without mentioning Eric Firstenberg, who is as responsible for this book as if he had written it himself.

CHAPTER 1

Prague Circles

Backgrounds and Methods

Prag läßt nicht los. Uns beide nicht. Dieses Mütterchen hat
Krallen. Da muß man sich fügen oder—. An zwei Seiten
müßten wir es anzünden, am Vyšehrad und am Hradschin,
dann wäre es möglich, daß wir loskommen. Vielleicht über-
legst Du es Dir bis zum Karneval.

Prague doesn't let go. Neither one of us. This little mother
has claws. One has only to get used to it, or . . . We would
have to ignite it on two sides, at Vyšehrad and at the
Hradčany, then it would be possible to get loose. Perhaps you
will think it over until Carnival.

letter to Oskar Pollak, 1902

FIN-DE-SIÈCLE PRAGUE: THE POSITION OF THE WRITER

The terms "setting" and "background" are unfortunate, in that they imply the existence of a fixed picture or frame against which a set of similarly stable objects can be understood. Yet contexts are always plural,
and in competition with one another. Where one setting might be confected in which a writer or a work appears to sit comfortably, others are
bound to accommodate less hospitably, to rub against and poke at an object in their midst that belongs to them and remains nonetheless foreign.

The strained relations between texts and contexts are not evenly felt
across time and space. A terse self-consciousness of the tensions between
writer and setting in Prague at the century's turn is already in this letter
from a nineteen-year-old Franz Kafka to his friend Oskar Pollak:

> I sat at my nice writing desk. You don't know it. Why should you. It is in fact
> a good, respectably minded desk, one that educates. In the place where the
> writer's knees generally go, it has two terrifying wooden spikes. And so look
> out. If one seats oneself quietly, carefully, and writes something nice and

Fig. 1. Kafka,
sketch of man at desk. Courtesy of PNP.

respectable, then one is fine. But woe, if one becomes agitated and the body
trembles just a bit, then one unavoidably has the points in the knees, and how
that hurts. I could show you the black and blue marks. And what is that
supposed to mean, but "write nothing agitating and so do not let your body
tremble." [1]

The setting in this representation is animated with as much personality and will as the writer. The desk is beautiful to look at, "nice," "good,"
and, in case the irony was too subtle, "respectable" [*bürgerlich gesinnt*],
but below the surface it is "terrifying." It disciplines the writer and warns
against any agitation; it censors in advance. Kafka lets the reader know
where he stands in this tenuous relationship by baring his bruises.

The passage offers an opening to a discussion of the Prague context,
while also pointing to the way in which the painful confrontation of text
and context at this moment foreshadows the issues at stake for the later
Kafka. Reading the above lines, we are reminded of the ingenious and
writerly torture invented in "In the Penal Colony," where the criminal is
executed by means of a machine that etches the violated law onto his
body; a comparable structure is apparent in Kafka's late and much-
quoted statement that his life was made of literature. Behind much of the
discussion of the following chapters is a fascination with this momentary
subject-object fusion, and with what it had to do with its specific political and social context.[2]

The immediate object of vision here will be the early work of the generation of German-speaking Jewish writers that has become known as
the Prague circle. Since it turns out there never was a Prague literary
circle in the prescriptive sense, it is better to introduce these writers as a
generation of German-speaking Prague Jews. Born between 1882 and
1892, the writers were young men at the century's turn, and experienced

various ideological and aesthetic transformations in the explosive years leading up to World War I. The period between 1900 and 1918 is, therefore, of chief interest, and the mature work of these writers, although it often represents the bulk of their careers, falls with few exceptions outside of this frame. The dissolution of the Habsburg state and the creation of Czechoslovakia are just two of the factors radically altering the state of things we are exploring.

The contributions of this generation range broadly from the literary modernism of Franz Kafka, Franz Werfel, and others to the journalism of the boisterous "roving reporter" and socialist revolutionary Egon Erwin Kisch, the Prague "cultural Zionism" of Hugo Bergmann, the universalist Jewish nationalism of Max Brod, and the efforts of Otto Pick, Rudolf Fuchs, and Max Brod to mediate works of Czech cultural modernism to Western audiences. But what, if any, is the relation of this extraordinarily wide-ranging production to the common social and political context from which it sprang?

The exploration of these issues is organized thematically, but in a way that suggests a historical logic: beginning with the very early signs of young Prague writers' awareness of tensions in the fin-de-siècle German-liberal construction of "culture" and the role of language, continuing to the loud emergences of expressionist and Zionist revolt around the turn of the second decade of the present century, and ending with the eroticized fascination with Slavic and Jewish Eastern Europe that culminates in the creation of bridges from Czech to German culture.

This sort of intertextual analysis owes much to the existence of thorough sociohistorical study of the Prague context. In multiethnic Prague between the late nineteenth-century decline of liberalism and the ideological explosion of World War I, the social and political matrix is so dense and complex that contextual readings would be impossible without the benefit of the outstanding work of several social historians in the last decades.[3] This book is structured so that information on contexts (e.g., imperial language policies, perceptions of Eastern Europe, literary movements in Berlin or Vienna, and Jewish-national and Zionist movements) may be unfolded chapter by chapter. A brief summary of the situation at the turn of the century is a necessary starting point nevertheless.

The Prague philosopher Emil Utitz, a contemporary of the writers discussed here, has described the prewar world of the German-speaking Prague Jews as "a game preserve whose ground was always shrinking ... an iceberg that the surrounding waters slowly eroded."[4] These metaphors are characteristic of German-Jewish Prague of this period; they refer to a circle of territory threatened by the Bohemian nationality conflict and the accompanying expansion of hostile ideologies.

At the turn of the century less than 10 percent of Prague's fewer than half million souls defined themselves as German-speaking, and more than half of these were acculturated Jews.[5] The legal emancipation of Bohemian Jews had been in effect since midcentury, so that the generation before Utitz and Kafka had been nursed on a confident and unshakable commitment to what was known in Prague as "German liberalism."[6] The character of that ideology—insofar as we can identify a single referent for the term, even in one city in a defined period—will be discussed at length later in this chapter and in several of the following chapters. But it is certain that the ideology of the generation before that under study, subscribing to a "liberal" agenda, was manifestly out of step with the sentiments of antiliberal German Bohemia, not to mention the Czech majority of the region.[7] The illusion of an old-fashioned German-liberal dominance was artificially sustained in a city where cultural power remained in the hands of a German population that was, in the majority, Jewish.[8] Yet, the immediate effect of liberal political reform in Prague had been Czech nationalist domination of municipal politics. Faced with a burgeoning racialist *völkisch* ideology on the one side, and a Czech nationalism that was as antisemitic as it was anti-German on the other, the generation under discussion was decentered: it was a postliberal generation without alternatives.

Some sort of crisis of identity for this generation, already implied in this brief summary of its position, is the critical element in the wide-ranging creative production of these writers. But what sort of identity was in crisis—ideological, aesthetic, communal? Or, as Kafka's letter to Pollak seems to indicate, had these identities become impossible to disentangle in the Prague context? Examining this rather small group of German-speaking Jewish Praguers born around the mid- to late 1880s, there appears to be a confusing tension among their positions by the turn of the century: a threatened Jewish minority, which at the same time constituted a majority of the traditionally dominant German population of Prague, a population whose position in turn was threatened by rising illiberal ideologies, but a language group privileged in the monarchy at large. Their self-image commingled with images of the Czech, Slav, or Eastern other, processes that are central to an understanding of their culture-historical role.

These layers of identity trapped the young Prague German-speaking Jews between identities inside and outside of the power structure, so that an analysis of their literary products as representations of "minority culture" is itself problematic.[9] I will argue that it is in the uniquely charged spaces *between* identities—social identities, but also national, spiritual, and political identities—that the creative moment of the Prague circle takes place. James Clifford's assessment of an anthropological predicament raises a provocative point: "one is always, to varying degrees, 'inauthentic': caught between cultures, implicated in others," although clearly in some cases this duplicity is closer to the surface than in others.[10] Utz Riese turns this observation to the Central European (actually East German) case, pointing out that this handicap of inauthenticity, "to be caught between cultural spaces, opens up the possibility of resistance or critique."[11] This definition of inauthenticity, as Clifford's and Riese's spatial metaphors already imply, is closely akin to notions of territory discussed throughout this book. The loss of ground experienced by the Prague Jews writing in German, whether by way of willful abandonment of territory or the force of circumstances, is linked to the critical power of their diverse texts.

Prague Territories seeks to provide a map of complex and rapidly shifting relations of writerly identity, sociopolitical context, and work, for a period in which conventional assumptions about those relations no longer applied. Like any cartographer challenged by a topographical novelty, I will have to invent means of representing this particular landscape in a way that will be most useful to contemporary readers. And like any map, this one will require a legend.

"PRAGUE"

One contributor to a Berlin weekly was astonished: "I can't believe it. I am not from Prague and yet get printed." Conversely, a young tourist in Germany says he is from Prague and is immediately asked, "Oh, and who is your publisher?"[12] The disproportionate literary production of the very small group of Kafka's generation was recognized early; in retrospect it calls the cultural historian's attention like a red flag marking the place where, if anywhere, a historical context provided rich ground for extraordinary texts.[13] Although Otto Rosenfeld reported the above remarks in 1917, he seemed surprisingly to presage Carl Schorske's famous thesis on culture as political surrogate in turn-of-the-century Vienna when he stated of his contemporary Prague: "Literature is trump and the keynote of social dialogue."[14]

But this Prague, the Prague of the retreat into literature, the Prague

where everyone was assumed to be a writer, turns out to have been a mi-
nuscule and remarkably unrepresentative slice of the city at large: it was
not the home of the great majority of the population speaking in Czech,
nor of the German nobility of the Kleinseite palaces, nor of the increasing numbers of students from the German Bohemian provinces, who by
and large eschewed the culturally oriented German-liberal student association in a favor of a new corporation with a *völkisch* orientation and
which increasingly adopted an ethnic, rather than a cultural, definition
of Germanness. The "Prague" spoken of in these quotations was not
only a small part of Prague life, but a shrinking one.

Better known to today's readers is another perception of Prague: the
mythical mysticism of the city, the secrets of the Golem, the ghostly presence of Baroque statues looking down from cornices and along the
Charles Bridge, a magic embedded in Prague work from Meyrink to
Kafka.[15] This, too, was the projection of a certain reading of the city specific to a threatened generation; Czech intellectuals did not share, and
even objected to, this "decadent" image, proceeding so transparently
from a declining class of German bourgeois.[16] But the writers absorbed
with fantastic images of a mysterious city with an inner life of its own,
out of control of its inhabitants, fickle and dangerous, erotic and unpre-
dictable, seem to have been utterly unaware that these images were not
of Prague as it existed for the masses who inhabited it, but of "Prague,"
Utitz's iceberg. The Jewish writer Oskar Wiener introduced a 1919 collection of Prague German writing with an assertion that confirms what
the adjectives above suggest—that "Prague," along with the Czechs and
Slavs generally, was powerfully identified with a female principle, the
oriental other: "Whosoever has looked once into her deep, mysterious
eyes remains subject to the sorceress all the days of his life." [17] From their
position of cultural power, German speakers who came of age in the liberal years of the nineteenth century unreflectively identified their experience of Prague with the idea of Prague generally. This fallacy, the blind
generalization of culturally dominant subjects, is commonplace. But in
Prague in 1919, where the German elite was not only a minority, but
also one whose power had been more than challenged, such assumptions seem to have been monuments to the entrenchment of nineteenth-
century German-liberal smugness.

In Carl Schorske's captivating introduction to the liberal crisis of Vienna, we are led to read the passage from the faith in history to its abandonment in the architecture of the Ringstrasse, the monumental oval
boulevard occupying the space of the old city walls.[18] What do the trans-

formations of Prague in the same period suggest about liberal power and liberal crisis in the city, about the relationship between these images of "Prague" and the changing, physical face of the city? For all its magnificence, one should not forget the provincial character of the "German" city of the earlier nineteenth century. The city's function within the imperial system, as well as its form, were fundamentally different from Vienna's. Of course, both form and function in this case—the sort of place Prague was to be—were profoundly contested issues as the city transformed from a sparkling provincial satellite of German culture to the centerpiece of the Czech nation. This shift is aptly articulated in the transformation of the "horse-market" (Roßmarkt) to the bustling Wenceslaus Square in the course of the nineteenth century. Both Wenceslaus Square and, below it stretching to the bank of the Moldau/Vltava, the avenue named Ferdinand (a name that would give way to the present Národní, or National, boulevard) seemed monuments to a rising Czech Prague; on the latter concourse arose the spectacular modernist Czech National Theater, deliberately dwarfing the two German theaters at the opposite end of Wenceslaus Square; when it was ravaged by fire shortly after its opening, it sprang up again miraculously from its own ashes—a symbol not to be kept down. This was the avenue where Czech national support was demonstrated on the streets, virtually converging with the avenue with the parallel function for the Germans, the elegant boulevard Am Graben (Na přikopě), which had replaced the old city wall. Enclosed within these bounding grand avenues was the Old Town, home to many of Prague's German-speaking Jews, as though they had never strayed very far from the Jewish ghetto (Josefstadt/Josefov, many of its remaining buildings demolished in the last decade of the nineteenth and first decade of the twentieth centuries) nestled in its corner.

But it was with their backs to the ghetto that the German-liberal Jews of Old Town walked to the Graben, to enter the Casino. This was the common designation for the institution of the German House, the umbrella organization for all of Prague's German-liberal free associations and the main organ of German culture in Prague. The author of *The Golem,* Gustav Meyrink, poked fun at the connection of the origins of the German-liberal establishment with the mystical image of Prague, which he himself did much to create: "The German Casino has at its disposal secret and unique powers. The city as is well known stands upon a network of subterranean passages, and one such secret passage connects this center of Prague German life with the distant, but kindred, Jerusalem." A hidden button, pressed at the crucial moment, would

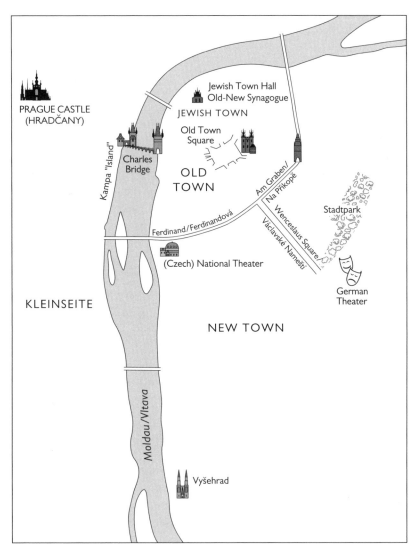

Prague, Quarters and Landmarks.

send a few hundred Maccabees to the rescue, should it be needed, from *völkisch* German fraternities or from Czechs.[19] Even if only in jest, the Christian popularizer of the mystical tales of Rabbi Löw went further than his colleagues (and did so earlier than his critics) in shedding light on the secret links between Prague German culture, the tenuous position of German-Jewish Prague liberals, and the mystical representation of "Prague."

The linkage was imprinted in a more naive and more telling way as early as 1904, in a poem by a teenage Egon Kisch, who had just added "Erwin" to his name and fashioned himself as a writer. I take liberties with the translation of this verse, which is far enough from masterful to sustain the blow:

Futile Remedy

The Moldau's water flows, slipping
In a circle surrounding Prague
Just like a dampened and dripping
Cool headache compress or rag
To soothe the Prague creatures' mania
or this symptom of their disease.
Yet I fear that the ache in their crania
The proudest of currents can't ease.
Not even the wettest and dripping
Cool headache compress or rag.
The Moldau's water flows, slipping,
and futilely, then, about Prague.[20]

If Kisch had been a budding Czech-speaking poet, he might have seen the Vltava as a welling source of creative inspiration for this city, the undisputed center of his nation's remarkable cultural revival. In German translation the same river could not even serve to cool the heads of the burdened Prague patrons. Most unusual and telling in the verse is the uncanny image of the river as a circle—it flows "in a circle surrounding Prague." It does not connect sources and destinations, or pasts and futures; it circumscribes and imprisons its inhabitants. This image of the Prague "island" is a persistent one, as is the corresponding metaphor of the circle. Why a circle? What an unusual course for a river to take.

"BOHEMIA"

The above images of "Prague" inscribe a territory without continuity with other territories, geographical as well as temporal. If history is encoded in Kisch's verse, it is piled up vertically on the burdened necks of the city's inhabitants—or perhaps just some of them. An integral image of a continuous landscape, peopled with a national family, and sharing a common history—the intersection of *Volk,* language, and territory that had become too powerful to ignore—was not accessible to the young Kisch. That was because Prague was the capital of Bohemia, called *Böhmen* or *Čechy,* part of the Czech lands, in Cisleithania, the Austrian half of the Habsburg monarchy.

It is difficult to sort out the notion of "nationality" from the long and complex history of the country called Bohemia. From the second half of the nineteenth century until today, ideas of "nation" have been projected onto that history in ways that have ranged from naively anachronistic to manipulative. More recently, the fluidity of "nationality" in the region has begun to be taken for granted, forcing the focus to shift to the ideological function of national labels.[21] The tendency to read back national identities, allegiances, and conflicts into the defeat of the (Czech) Protestant nobility at White Mountain in 1620, or into pre-Reformation Hussite religious innovation and subversion of (German) imperial power, is difficult to suppress.[22]

On the other side there exists an idealized representation of a pre-1848, supraethnic regional identity that completely obscured national difference.[23] The myth of this ideology of "Bohemism," persisting in certain quarters of Prague even beyond 1848, is in a way more interesting than the phenomenon itself. It was not the favored founding myth of the Czechs (or, as they were called in German and English at the time, the "Böhmen" or "Bohemians"). The ideal of a supranational "Bohemism" seemed even more foreign to the residents of the primarily German areas of western and northern Bohemia, who through the late nineteenth century cultivated a well-articulated resentment of the self-proclaimed spokesmanship of German Bohemia by Prague German liberals. The Jewish origins of German-liberal cultural leaders in the capital was not lost on the non-Jewish and rapidly radicalizing Germans of industrialized northern and western Bohemia and, to a lesser degree, those of the southern Bohemian Wood (Böhmerwald). These tensions led by the end of the century to a formal *Los von Prag* ("Free from Prague") movement.[24] Even if pre-March (or *Vormärz*—the period leading up to the 1848 revolutions) Bohemism existed in some sense, it is certainly a distortion to project onto the period an image of "ethnic harmony and spiritual security" smashed by a capricious, petty, and self-serving Czech national movement.[25] The local patriotic sentiment of Bohemism was one alternative competing with several others in the pre-March, including the similarly supraethnic standpoint of the "Austrianists" (state officials in particular), or the pan-German and pan-Slav movements, each ready respectively to accept Czechs as a distinct ethnic group of Germans, or the German minority as other-speaking Bohemians.[26]

The crescendo moment of Central European nationalist movements in 1848 constituted a crisis in the country of "Bohemia." That year included, after all, the revolts of non-German peoples against Habsburg rule, as well as the liberal nationalist movements in German-speaking Europe that led to the proto-national Frankfurt Parliament. Alfred Meißner offered this analysis in that very year: "What do I say to Bohemia? The finest pan-Slavic revolution is preparing itself there. Every head is hot, every fist turned against Germany."[27] The reference in this description to national conflict is less striking than its provocative geographical innovation. Where was Germany? Where was Bohemia? Every fist in "Bohemia" clearly did not include the fists of the German speakers of Prague or the scattered German language islands of Bohemia, much less those of Germanophone northern and western Bohemia and the Bohemian Wood—thus Meißner's Bohemia (*Böhmen*) shares borders with the Czechs (*die Böhmen*). And those fists were turned neither against Prussia nor against Lower Austria. "Germany" (*Deutschland*) in Meißner's discourse cannot signify a physical territory, but rather "Germandom," either the German-speaking residents of the Czech lands or the German culture they carried—or perhaps even a much more abstract idea.[28] German-speaking delegates from Prague were present at the Frankfurt Parliament, to the chagrin of Czech nationalists, who envisioned a different sort of national liberation to be fruit of the revolution. The Habsburg monarchy remained, no borders were changed, but "Bohemia" was irrevocably altered. Czech was declared a legal lecture language at the university, and at the same time a new organization broke away from the general student union, a liberal and nationalist corporation calling itself the Lese- und Redehalle der Deutschen Studenten in Prag (Reading and Lecture Group of German Students in Prague), or simply the "Halle," to which Max Brod, Franz Kafka, and other writers would belong a half century later.

The academic German nationalist Philipp Knoll quoted Meißner's references to "Bohemia" and "Germany" without a second thought, just as he could frame the question of the Czech cultural claim to the country as "Bohemia, again Bohemian?" and then conclude that, no, history could not be turned back. "Let us just look at a language map. Bohemia lies in the middle of Germany. It is a Slavic enclave in the middle of Germany [. . .]"[29] This construct foreshadows the potential appeal of the pan-German alternative for the German speaker of the northern and western Bohemian edge. It inverted perceptions of center and periphery, as the concerns over a German enclave of Bohemia were instantly exchanged for those over a Bohemian enclave within Germany.

Almost at once, and for the first time, the paradox of the term "German Bohemian" (*Deutschböhme*, or "German-Czech") became appar-

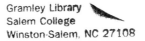

ent: the term *"Sudetendeutsche"* was introduced by the turn of the century; a 1910 book on the national conflict noted that, by calling the Czechs "Bohemians," Habsburg terminology implicitly acknowledged their privileged claim in Bohemia; the "Bohemians" became the Czechs as German-speaking Bohemia gradually became the Sudetenland.[30] Fritz Mauthner put his finger on the problem (as well as the pan-German solution) in the very title of his pamphlet, *Muttersprache und Vaterland* (Mother tongue and fatherland), where he complained that the Czech / Bohemians' "natural" fatherland of the old Bohemian kingdom put to shame the German-speaking Bohemians' artificial, bureaucratic, or "paper" concept of Cisleithania.[31]

Again, shifting conceptions of center and periphery with reference to Bohemia come into play. The rethinking of this region called "the heart of Europe" in terms of ethnicity redefined the ways in which it was placed. The emerging consciousness of Bohemia as the country of the Czechs marginalized the region's Germans, even as they lived in an area both historically and economically central to the Danube monarchy.[32] The "paper" alternative of communal membership offered by the Habsburgs (whose political concessions to Czech leaders in Bohemia were being closely watched by German Bohemians) could hardly compete with the irredentist fantasy of separation and integration into the German Reich. Even the daily *Prager Tagblatt,* the German-liberal organ with a primarily Jewish editorship and readership, announced the concern of the Bohemian question to the German Empire and the Europeans at large. Hoping to motivate the central Austrian government to protect the position of the German Bohemians, the daily cited discussions in the imperial German press, including one from the *Frankfurter Zeitung* where the claim was made that the "slavicization" of Bohemia was not merely an Austrian concern, "but a European one, a strike against all Germandom. It would be the beginning of the end of the *German nation* [. . .]"[33] The question of the periphery itself had become a central issue; the heart of some of Europe's emerging modern problems was to be found at a place that was now suddenly defined as the edge.

The stunning question is not why issues of marginal identity were considered so important, but rather why they had previously been so successfully ignored. To answer that, we would have to offer for contrast another map: a late nineteenth-century German-liberal order that identified Bohemia and especially Prague as realms of German culture, parallel to other significant German cultural "centers" such as Berlin and Munich; Prague as one of the brightest spheres of Central European civilization orbiting about Vienna; the elite, bourgeois, German-speaking, and largely Jewish liberals of Prague as spokespersons for German Bohemia, even for Bohemia at large. It was only after the dissolution of this complex image as German-liberal power declined, after the erosion of the lines of a map measured by a cultural yardstick, that people became aware of the surprisingly different terrain which that projection had concealed.

LIBERAL CULTURE, GERMAN POLITICS

There is a stubborn difficulty surrounding the use of the terms "liberal" and "German-liberal" in this historical context.[34] Close examination reveals that there is no single and stable referent for these terms even in a limited field, such as Prague between the 1880s and World War I. Just as insistent, however, is the appearance of the terms, not only in historiography but in contemporary texts. In other words, people both inside and outside of the place and period in question have continuously identified themselves or others as "German liberals" despite the broad and constantly shifting ideological spectrum they represented. In such a situation, obviously, attempts at definition are bound to fail. It will suffice to focus on the privileged place of "culture" in the context of Prague German liberalism in its many forms, a more limited—at least an apparently more limited—discussion with direct relevance to the questions under exploration.

The conflation of national and socioeconomic concerns is apparent in the nomination "German liberal." In fact, the deployment of terms of national conflict in the playing out of wide-ranging power struggles is coming into increasingly clearer view.[35] The challenge to German-liberal hegemony from 1879 onward coincided with overlapping reassessments of the rationales for the continued leadership of a bourgeois and German-speaking minority in Prague, Bohemia, and the monarchy overall. The liberals identified the interests of this ruling minority with the interests of the Habsburg state, so that, in Bohemia, a generation of German-liberal politicians was willing to accept wholesale refashioning of both rhetoric and policy for the ultimate goal of blocking Czech control over the "Czech lands."[36]

The extraordinary place of humanistic discussions of culture from 1880 onward must be seen in this context of densely interwoven figures of culture and politics. The academic and German-liberal nationalist Philipp Knoll, a good source for examples of the early instrumentalization of culture, described the blossoming Czech civilization as "developed completely on the basis of German [culture]," so that "one might well sooner speak of a reproductive rather than an original culture."[37] This stratification of original (German) and mimetic (Czech) culture is an important one, and one that would survive well into the twentieth century. Even more important to the late nineteenth-century German-liberal position was the special place of German culture in Bohemia and in Prague, a city that, according to Knoll, owed its architectural charm to German artists and craftsmen, a city that "must never cease to be a German cultural abode."[38] Throughout the long fin de siècle, German cultural "work" in Bohemia was identified as national and therefore political work. In the volumes of the journal *Deutsche Arbeit* (German work), as in the essays by the leading Prague literary figures of the Concordia organization or the speeches of the liberal nationalist literary critic August Sauer, Prague is hailed as the center of age-old German Bohemian cultural production, the weighty contributions of generations of poets and artists, scientists and educators, preceding, overwhelming, and dwarfing any trace of Slavic culture in the region.[39]

The authority of cultural representatives in such a setting is already manifest. The official literary organization in the Casino was, as mentioned, the powerful Concordia group, led by the "literary popes" Alfred Klaar, Friedrich Adler, and Hugo Salus.[40] These authors, belonging to the generation of the parents of Kafka and Brod, espoused aesthetic programs that were in step with those in Vienna and farther west on the continent, from neoclassicism to a more decadent new romanticism toward the century's turn. Between these German-liberal giants and the Prague circle stands the transitional generation of the Young Prague movement, the aestheticist secession including Prague German writers Gustav Meyrink, Oskar Wiener, Paul Leppin, and Viktor Hadwiger. This transitional generation was more attractive to the young Prague intellectuals than the haughty Concordia poets, and Leppin, Wiener, and Meyrink were later enthusiastic supporters of the new literature to emerge from German-Jewish Prague. All of these cultural hierarchies, it should be remembered, operated autonomously, apart from (and apparently without awareness of) the growing body of earthy German Bohemian literature coming from the ethnically German areas of Bohemia.

Something not unlike what today are called "focus group" studies is offered in a 1900 text called *Prague German Words*, which contains dozens of individual responses to general questions on Prague German life.[41] The survey was published plainly in the service of a German-liberal agenda, which renders it no less useful as background material. The repeated ironic references to the Jewish character of Prague Germandom are to be noted, but the greatest number of comments by far focus on issues of German culture. Survey respondents attributed the fortification of German interests in Prague to the literary contributions of the aforementioned Concordia, the activities of German clubs under the general auspices of the German Casino, student fraternities, the Wagner cult, and, first and foremost, the German Theater.

The respondents' references to the Wagner cult as well as to the German Theater were alternative ways of praising the work of one man with whom they all were familiar. Angelo Neumann presided over the growing role of the German Theater in Prague German life, and in his person as well as in his program he represented the continuing cultural integration of Prague with German-speaking Europe. He was known to be acquainted with Wagner and other great Central European musical luminaries, he produced the *Ring* to great public enthusiasm, and his contacts led to the arrival of Gustav Mahler as one of the theater's distinguished guest conductors.[42] Neumann's tenure from 1885 through 1910 spans the period from the beginning of German-liberal decline to its last breath; the second decade of the new century saw the dominance of anti- and postliberal ideologies, and "culture" was fast being replaced by the powerful image of "blood."

Neumann was succeeded at the German Theater by another German liberal, Neumann's dramaturg, a journalist and later the editor of the liberal and Jewish *Prager Tagblatt*, Heinrich Teweles. Teweles was a "liberal" of the most nationalist mark, and his moments of influence both at the theater and later at the newspaper corresponded to the increase of illiberal rhetoric in Czech and German Bohemia.

One such voice was that of Ottokar Stauf von der March, a vitriolic anti-Czech, anti-Magyar, and antisemite who in one text sought to redefine the term "cultural book." In contrast to the satirical tones of the leftist press and the Munich *Simplicissimus*, Stauf's "cultural books in the *truest* meaning of the word" carried the grave project of the Germans in Central Europe against their enemies.[43] The books on which Stauf reports are provincial and *völkisch* rather than cosmopolitan, heroic rather than ironic, wrathful rather than witty. He conceives this new sort of cultural work as a self-conscious counter-model not only to the urbane works of modern Germans and especially German-speaking Jews, but mainly to the advances of Czech culture. Wherever the Slavs have demanded "cultural" concessions from the monarchy, Stauf asserts, they have made political inroads. But this idea of culture as an instrument of political power and territorial expansion was neither very new nor particularly Czech. It was more than anything else the inheritance of German liberalism in Prague.

THE BOYS IN THE "HALLE"

A similar ideological progression can be traced in the student organizations in Prague, where schisms and shifts stand as clear markers of national politics: the formation of the German student organization called the Lese- und Redehalle der Deutschen Studenten in Prag (or simply the Halle) as a secession from the general, supraethnic student organization in 1848; its development as a center of Prague German cultural activity in the era of German-liberal dominance; the secession from the Halle of *völkisch*-Aryan and antisemitic-leaning corporations, leading to the formation of the general organization Germania in 1892; the foundation of a small Jewish-national student corporation the following year; and the establishment by the century's turn of student Zionist organizations that competed with the German-liberal Halle for the support of Jewish students. This chronicle could be extended to January 1936, when the Halle abandoned the "foreign" trappings of liberalism altogether and elected a National Socialist student leadership.[44]

If the memoir of Max Brod is to be taken literally, the moment of the formation of the Halle's *Ausschuß,* or executive committee, should be added to the list of ideological transformations. Brod identified the elite committee as "primarily Gentile," allowing only baptized or very wealthy Jews among their ranks, and very few at that. The evidence of the papers left by the executive committee puts to rest any confusion that may arise from the apparent contradiction between Brod's picture of an essentially Aryan Halle leadership and the contemporary and historiographical perception of the German-liberal organization by the first decade of the century as "Jewish in all but name."[45] The records of the executive committee, particularly the logbooks or *Rapportbücher,* in which committee members informally communicated with one another, make clear that Jewish self-perception was a major identification of the German-liberal Halle, including the committee itself.[46] The same sources confirm the elitist self-image of the executive committee members, and a lively ongoing power struggle with the "Literary Section," the organization Brod claims to have created in opposition to the committee:[47]

> We created from within the modest membership of the Halle a center of op-
> position to the executive committee, the "Section for Literature and Art,"
> which pursued entirely different goals than the rich little noble sons with
> their dance amusements and banquets. We thirsted for cultural achievement,
> we wanted to invite the great poets of Germany to lecture [. . .][48]

Even in this retrospective formulation, the coincidence of cultural
and political power is naively reproduced. The "Section for Literature
and Art," the branch of the Halle in which Brod would meet Kafka along
with most of the other Prague circle writers,[49] set itself up as a competing elite, an elite that was cultivated and intellectual, the true heir of
high German civilization in Prague. The point of resistance against the
increasing German nationalism that was marginalizing these German-
liberal sons even in their own student organization was found within
German culture.

PRAGUE CIRCLES?

As one may infer from the above paragraphs, the idea of the Halle or its
Literary Section as an incubator for the future "Prague circle," with
more or less the same "members" and bursting with nascent creative talent, is a fiction of Max Brod's. The idea of a "Prague circle" altogether
is a creation of Brod's circulated in another memoir, *Der Prager Kreis,* in
which the author's ideological and personal agendas in historicizing the
notion are transparent.[50] In fact we cannot really speak of the existence
of a "Prague circle" of German-Jewish literati, at least not in the prescriptive sense in which the term is usually understood from Brod's own
writings and certain secondary sources citing them. There, the "Prague
circle" is a constellation of great writers revolving around and agreeing
with the "central" figure of Brod himself. But there were many "circles,"
many orbits in which Prague German-speaking Jews of this generation
came into contact with one another, influenced or disagreed with one
another, and contributed to each other's work. There was the philosophical salon at the home of Bertha Fanta, where Brod and Kafka were
secondary participants after the more philosophically oriented Hugo
Bergmann, Emil Utitz, and Felix Weltsch; there was the circle of friends,
Kafka, Brod, and Felix Weltsch among them, reading their work aloud
to the blind colleague Oskar Baum; there was the Literary Section of the
Halle that Brod mentioned, but also the Bar Kochba student Zionist organization; the regulars at the cafés Louvre, Continental, and, most fa-

mously, the Arco (hence Karl Kraus's biting references to the Prague writers around Brod and Werfel as the "Arconauts"); the group of young
Jewish writers contributing to the Prague journal *Herder-Blätter* (1911–
1912) under the editorship of Willy Haas, or those who following this
venture created the journal *Arkadia* (1913) with Max Brod. To this Venn
diagram of subsets of a single generation of creative people we might add
those inscribed historiographically: Zionist Prague circles in Brod's work
and reiterated in the work of the Israeli scholar Margarita Pazi; socialist circles emphasizing the contributions of Egon Erwin Kisch and Rudolf Fuchs, and including writers of later generations that seem to follow
in their footsteps; Slavic-oriented Prague circles that would incorporate
Czech writers, including Gentile Czechs; and finally the circles inscribed
in the vast body of Kafka scholarship, attaching the literary production
of Prague's greatest writer to circles Czech, Jewish, anarchist, socialist,
aestheticist, expressionist.[51]

While none of these prescriptions serves to define a programmatic
Prague circle, and even as the people weaving in and out of these various activities battled with each other over matters both political and aesthetic, a core of writers coming out of this generation were often in contact with one another, aware of each others' activities, and, most of all,
seemed despite the tremendous diversity among their works to parry
around a similar kernel of issues that was not as sharply in focus for
those beyond them temporally, socially, or geographically. Why those
directly involved in these activities were all men is an interesting question, since gender has a central place in the way identity issues were inscribed in territorial terms for these writers.[52] Perhaps there was a certain inevitability in the grouping of these young men in configurations
of various circles; in any case, the projection of a circle onto such writers had already begun in the period under study. Critic Josef Körner in
1917 reported on a circle of Prague writers in which he included Kafka,
Brod, Baum, Werfel, Fuchs, and Otto Pick, and mentioned Egon Erwin
Kisch—almost precisely the "circle" inscribed in the chapters that follow.[53] Several years earlier, Czech intellectual and Kafka classmate Rudolf Illový had defined a "circle of writers" in German Prague whose
sympathy for the Slavs was breaking away from chauvinist German
Bohemian tradition. He included in the group Kafka, Brod, Werfel,
Fuchs, Baum, and Kisch, along with Meyrink and Leppin, two who were
clearly supporters of and contributors to the others' efforts, although
neither was Jewish and both belonged to the half generation before Brod
and Kafka.[54] One cannot resist noting that Max Brod responded to the

attention at the time petulantly, insisting that there was no such thing as a Prague school of writers, that the "coarse visible association" of these writers in Prague was insignificant compared with their differences, and that Brod himself was closer to writers abroad than to those in his home city.[55]

With all of these circles to choose from, how is a "Prague circle" to be defined, and what is the value of perpetuating the term at all? I have self-consciously employed the term not in order to preserve the notion of a literary clique of more or less fixed membership and common program, but because it is apparent that the image of the "circle" had a particular power in this context, invading the rhetoric of those both living in and talking about it. The rhetorical form of the circle has a number of functions. The first is the quality of circumscription, a gesture that at once effects a charting of inclusion and of exclusion, a dichotomy of internality and externality. Also implicit in this structure are the notions of center and periphery, which relate directly to the problem complex of the geographic and ideological positions of Prague in the context of Bohemia, the Habsburg monarchy, and Judaism in exile. The circle, however, is also the formation representing the interpretive process itself. When observers posit a circumscribed group of objects in order to speak of them together, it is not surprising if the configuration of these objects confirms the analysts' hypotheses. This is what is known as the hermeneutic circle. Seen in this light, the early, even contemporary attempts to posit a Prague circle, as well as the resistances to the circumscriptive gesture, are to be watched closely. The deployment of "circular" rhetoric in each of these functions is inseparable from metaphors of *territory*: ideological, spiritual, and physical turf inscribed by discourses of inclusion and exclusion.

These metaphors in turn are kin to the recurring image of the Prague "island," another territorial metaphor with a similar operation. A very clear articulation of this image appeared in a dedication of 1959 by Norbert Frýd:

> Prague contains in its heart several small islands [. . .] but the one I want to report on today is not included among them. It has disappeared [. . .] Its misfortune was that that which surrounded it was a completely different Prague, the living, fighting, forward-looking Prague of the Czech people; while the Prague of German literature was the lordly Prague of yesterday, stubbornly concerned with transforming its untenable position into a lasting one.[56]

With these images my own text, like the river surrounding the city, comes full circle back around to "Prague." What I would like to suggest—what I hope I have been suggesting all through this discussion of backgrounds historical, ideological, literary, and rhetorical—is that the Prague circle island floated between the two banks described above, one of a German hegemony being eroded and another of rising Czech power. It belonged no longer to the past, and could find no place for itself in the future; it was no longer liberal, and found no grounding in the postliberal alternatives available to its neighbors. Centered on a map of universalist and hegemonic German high culture, earlier generations did not imagine their existence to be insular; the "island" occupied by German-speaking Jewish Prague was visible only from without—by its attackers, and from the retrospect of history. The Prague circle writers opened their eyes to see themselves precariously suspended between territories, with no firm ground beneath their feet, and grasped at the air.

WALKING AROUND . . . A TRICKY HISTORY

In opening this chapter with Kafka's letter to his friend Oskar Pollak, the question of the links between "circles" of friends and creative production was opened, if not yet addressed. For if the story of the disciplining desk invoked the tenuousness of the Prague setting, it is primarily a comment on the experience of writing. A return to the youthful Kafka's correspondence with Pollak in 1902 and 1903 is one way to begin to discuss how kneaded into one another were these discourses on writing, writerly identity, and writerly contexts; at the same time, it offers an example of the way readings of such texts can be placed within a historical inquiry. How were the interrelations among articulations of self, circles of friends, and writerly identities conceived, and how did they move in tandem with the historical shifts we have been describing? A nineteen-year-old Franz Kafka writes to his best friend, Oskar Pollak:

> While I was walking with you [*mit Dir ging*] on Saturday it became clear to me what we need. Yet I write you just today, for such things need to lie and stretch themselves out.[57]

The first letter that survives of this friendship in letters opens with an association of the friendship with the trope of walking around—a recurring figure in Kafka's letters to Pollak. In opposition to this wandering through the streets of Prague, Kafka offers the image of writing from the confinement of his desk, the same desk that opened this chapter. The "things" that were unclear during the friends' walking also need to lie down, to stretch themselves out. The walking metaphor continues

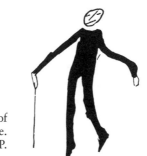

Fig. 2. Kafka, sketch of
man walking with cane.
Courtesy of PNP.

throughout Kafka's description of the limitations of the close friends'
discussions:

> When we talk with one another: the words are hard, one walks over them as
> over bad pavement. The most delicate things are trodden by clumsy feet and
> we cannot do anything about it. We are almost in each other's way, I bump
> into [*stoßen*] you, and you—I dare not, and you—. When we come to things
> that are not exactly cobblestones or [the journal] "Kunstwart" [. . .] we
> suddenly become sad and tired. Have you ever been so tired with anyone as
> with me?[58]

Kafka seems at first to differentiate between speech and writing, yet
then the written text of the letter constantly reiterates the awkward stroll
of the two friends, "trodden by clumsy feet," as the sentences get into
each other's way, and dashes poke (*stoßen*) the personal pronouns
("you—I dare not, and you—"). The topics of their discussions are
"come to" as things one encounters on an aimless walk through the old
city. The sadness and exhaustion upon walking in these circles through
Prague belong to that particular perception of Prague discussed earlier:
the sleepy and morose ruminations of the two friends, young as they are,
contrast with the enthusiasm and vitality inherent in a term like "cultural Renaissance," a common identification of the resurgence of Czech
language and literature since the early nineteenth century. Kafka's description of the walk becomes cranky; as Pollak becomes practically ill,
Kafka pities him; both become silent and then again tired; ashamed,
fearful of one another, they yawn, become disappointed, morose, hide
their yawns with words. A space in the letter once again reproduces this
yawning.

All of this misery is after all comical and meant to be so, like the
black comedy of "The Metamorphosis" and much of Kafka's more well-
known work. The misery and hostility never threaten to dissolve the

friendship, which is taken for granted, and which throughout the correspondence is identified with the writer himself and his writing, in turn
identified with the prison of the writing desk and the city Prague. The intellectual dialogue of the two friends is thus figured as a dialogue with the
writerly self, their intercourse an enclosed and decadent self-absorption.
The erotic charge of this activity—the homosexual tension within the
correspondence—is not far below the surface of the letters, and as I have
indicated is closely linked to an image of writing that evokes the enclosure of self-pollution.[59] Gender and sexuality are important elements of
much Prague circle production, as we will see, and they intersect with a
poetics of territoriality that can be seen in this early letter: an unhealthy
("ill"), cramped insularity is associated with the enclosure of Prague,
the writing desk, and endogamous intercourse; the figure of woman lies
beyond this narrow circle, an other both of deterritorialized existence
and of the creative activity that is its companion. Thus there is another
kind of walking or going that appears in this first letter; rather than the
dizzying circling around narrow Prague streets, or confinement within
incommunicative language, Pollak sometimes speaks "not just in order to speak," and goes to a destination instead of walking around. He
goes "out":

> We have been talking three years with one another, in certain respects one
> cannot distinguish the mine and yours. Often I could not say what comes
> from me or from you, and perhaps it's the same for you, too. Anyway I am
> wonderfully glad that you are going [umgehst] with that girl. [. . .] You talk
> with her a lot, not just to talk. You go [gehst] with her somewhere here or
> there or to Rostok, and I sit at my writing desk at home. [. . .] I sit at my
> desk at home and yawn. It's already gone [gegangen] that way with me.
> Would we never get away from one another? Is it not strange? Are we ene-
> mies? I am very fond of you.[60]

The radicalized ambivalence of the relationship with Pollak coincides
with the pain associated with writing and with being in Prague, even
while both of these, as will become apparent with the readings of Prague
cultural texts to unfold in these pages, are identified as primary sites of
identity. The association of the intercourse (Umgang) with woman as a
step onto firm ground and an escape from the circularity of writing and
identity is persistent, and it will return in many different sorts of texts.[61]
These dynamics peak with Kafka's failed engagement with Felice Bauer,
represented once again in a lengthy and dense collection of letters between Prague and Berlin.

The escape onto terra firma, or (conversely) away from the isolation of Prague, is not merely an object of irony for the young Kafka, nor for his fellows (nearly all of whom left Prague for long periods of their careers). The letter to Pollak of August 24, 1902, which opens with the image of the policing desk, ends with the disclosure that Kafka's hopes of escaping Prague to work somehow for the "Madrid uncle" have been dashed.[62] In the last letter to Pollak of 1902 this problematic is articulated in this way:

> Prague doesn't let go. Neither one of us. This little mother has claws. One has only to get used to it, or . . . We would have to ignite it on two sides, at Vyšehrad and at the Hradčany, then it would be possible to get loose. Perhaps you will think it over until Carnival.[63]

This is the most frequently quoted passage of the brief correspondence with Pollak, where it is usually noted that "little mother" is a direct translation of the Czech nickname for Prague, "*matička*." It is an extraordinary passage in its very early and explicit articulation of an ambivalence as well as a violence within Kafka's work that is usually ignored in favor of a more univocal image of a victimized "K." In this passage, the release from the imprisonment of the city entails the complicity of the friend who is closely identified with Kafka's experience of the city. The escape from Prague for both parties would be an escape from each other (they need to light the fire on opposite banks of the Moldau and escape in opposite directions). The flight is in this case dependent on the same figure from which flight is taken—just as the despised imprisonment is policed by a powerful attraction or love (of Prague, of writing, of Pollak: "Will we never get away from each other? Are we enemies? I am very fond of you [*Ich habe Dich sehr lieb*]"). Reminding oneself that this belonging, or flight, or this destruction—these "territorializations" and "deterritorializations"—must take place within writing only complicates these relations further. As a later letter explains, Kafka feels he cannot write when he is out of Prague: all the words are too "wildly scattered," so that he cannot confine or capture (*einfangen*) them into sentences.[64]

The vicious circles of dependency and rebellion among the writer Kafka, the friend Pollak, writing, and Prague circulate throughout the letters, and spill out after the Carnival passage into a story, the earliest sustained example of the macabre sort of tale for which Kafka would become best known. He introduces it as "the tricky story of Shamefaced Lanky and the Impure in His Heart," which in the context of the correspondence and framed by the Carnival passage seems to address the vexed friendship. The suggestion, at any rate, is posited in the description of the characters, with Kafka's self-perception as tall and thin, and his suggestions in these letters that Pollak is less honest about their troubled relationship. *Schamhaft* means "withdrawn" or "bashful," but the translation "shamefaced" retains the crucial element of shame in the word. Philosopher Peter Sloterdijk offers a bridge from shame to withdrawal and at the same time to a consciousness of self in a reading of "the origin of human self-consciousness via shame."[65] It is not Kafka but the story of the expulsion from Paradise that leads Sloterdijk to this description of shame, which is provocatively appropriate to a discussion of Kafka and the Kafkaesque:

> From then on, shame, along with feelings of guilt and of separation, would become the oldest and most powerful instance of self-referentiality through which the individual "makes an image" of himself. The deepest traces of Being as an extant shortcoming are inscribed in this image.[66]

The constricting setting for Kafka's tale more than resembles the "Prague" experienced by the two friends, as Kafka describes in these letters: "[. . .] an old village among low little houses and narrow alleys. So narrow were the lanes that when two people walked together they had to friend-neighborly brush against one another [. . .]"

Without providing a reading of the complex [*vertrackt*] text, which descends into a familiarly refined and otherworldly sadism, the place of this text within the Carnival letter and within the circle of Prague friendship is clear. After the agonizing visit of the Impure in His Heart, Shamefaced Lanky is left crying in his cramped space.

> His heart pained him and he could tell no one. But ill questions crawled up him from his legs up into his soul.
> Why did he come to me? Because I am lanky? No, because I . . . ?
> Do I weep out of pity for me or for him?
> Am I fond of him, finally, or do I hate him?
> Is he sent by my God or my devil?
> The question marks throttled Shamefaced Lanky.

By the end of the letter, the source of the pain of the central character is not locatable in the single agent of the friend/enemy, but is associated throughout with the eerily cramped spaces of the town and the house, which is too small for such a tall man to stretch out in, as well as with the written language, as he is choked by his own question marks. No one is really held responsible for the pain, which is above all a masochism of Shamefaced Lanky, knitting stockings rather than writing, the knitting needles, instruments of his creative activity, also instruments of torture. The letter ends on this note, as the story ends, and Kafka recapitulates to his friend the theme with which he began, as if it might now be understood better or taken more seriously:

> The question marks throttled Shamefaced Lanky.
>   Again he took the stockings before him. He nearly bored the knitting needles into his eyes. For it was even darker.
>
>   So think it over until Carnival.
>
> Your Franz[67]

GENEALOGIES: CULTURAL HISTORY, MINOR LITERATURE, AND "TERRITORY"

The "map" I have begun to lay out here already indicates the potential depth and the difficulty of a committed interdisciplinary approach to fin-de-siècle Central European politics and culture. Such an approach is admittedly ambitious, necessarily eclectic, and frankly open to skepticism from the perspectives of the critical traditions from which it draws. The promise of a cultural history grounded in several critical traditions, however, is that certain pitfalls of each of these can be avoided, that a novel mode of understanding these texts and this period might emerge, and that a self-consciousness of the relevance of this new material will be enabled. To generate a limited set of coordinates that will help define the place of such a method in intellectual historical scholarship, I want briefly to discuss three of my own methodological sources, focusing on the way they deploy the notion of territory. The first is Carl E. Schorske's pathbreaking cultural history, *Fin-de-Siècle Vienna: Politics and Culture,* with its manifest relevance to a study of turn-of-the-century Prague. The second is the study of Kafka by Gilles Deleuze and Félix Guattari, which has been centrally important to contemporary critical conceptualizations of minority culture and "minor literature." Finally, I want to consider the recent attention paid in critical social theory to questions of territoriality, space, and place as a way of defining more precisely the relevance of these rhetorics to contemporary scholarship and to the contemporary world.

In Schorske's justly famous *Fin-de-Siècle Vienna* we have a very important model of one way cultural historians might negotiate these terrains. In several significant respects, history and literary studies have converged in the years since Schorske's study. In the last decade or so in particular, intellectual history has been transformed by more rigorous

textual approaches, just as literary scholarship has turned increasingly to
the reading of historico-political contexts.[68] All this should make it easier to write a history of the Prague circle that takes the textual or aesthetic
life of the literary works seriously. Yet, any such effort is bound to encounter a resistance, a tension between the historical/contextual and the
aesthetic/textual—the very resistance that is thematized in Schorske's
work itself. It is worth a closer look at the structure of Schorske's argument to lay out the disciplinary dimensions of what might provisionally
be called the "aestheticist hypothesis"—shorthand for the complicated
critical/historiographical diagnosis of a territory of art removed from
historical consciousness and political engagement.

Schorske's studies of the Central European turn of the century depended in their own right on a rhetoric of territory and spatiality. In the
first place, he represented the context of an evolution of political liberalism from historicism through to the abandonment of historicism in
terms of the transformation of the urban landscape: the Ringstrasse circumscribes the relations of culture to social place and political salience
that remain at the center of each of the essays. Second, Schorske's deceptively simple thesis throughout *Fin-de-Siècle Vienna*—the claim that
modern culture emerged as political surrogate for a marginalized liberal
bourgeoisie—is mapped by a series of highly evocative, constantly re-
surfacing dichotomies: political engagement versus the aesthetic "garden" of modern art; history versus "the fortress of the psyche"; politics
versus culture. The realm of the "aesthetic" for Schorske, whether in the
form of artistic innovation or psychic epiphenomena, is an insular refuge from the continuity of traditions and an escape from the embattled
ground of political engagement. Elsewhere I have dealt with the possibility of reading the Central European and even Viennese fin de siècle in
a way that differs from Schorske's, but for our purposes here, two major
issues are of note.[69] The first, which these pages have begun to broach
and which will be pursued throughout the book, has to do with the idio-
syncrasy of the Prague case; the second, with the different historical moments in which Schorske's history and my own have been written.

Schorske published his Vienna essays together with an introduction
that is no less than remarkable for its extreme and explicit sensitivity to
a dialogic relationship between critical text and object, long before that
relationship was commonly recognized.[70] This frank self-reflexivity casts
a different light on Schorske's almost nostalgic preoccupation with the
high liberalism that comes under such attack in the course of his story.
Likewise, it provides a context for the author's barely disguised sugges-

tion that something, perhaps even everything, might have been spared if only the liberals could have had the generosity to appease the growing, sometimes unreasonable, if not irrational, demands raised by national minorities and working classes. Schorske's liberal historical reconstruction thus reiterates, albeit in revised form, the fantasy of the German liberals to represent class and national interests that did not feel represented by them. At the same time, as Michael Roth has deftly shown, the real power of Schorske's influential book lies in the way it performs or enacts the tension between historicism (or contextuality) and aestheticism (or textuality), reflecting, at the same time, on the contemporary political charge of doing so.[71]

There is a point to be made that is crucial to the shift to be undertaken here from Schorske's Vienna to the Prague circle. Schorske's sharp dichotomy of grounded history or politics on the one side, and a precious, dégagé aesthetic domain on the other, belies the radical potential of the turn to the aesthetic, at times even the explicitly political intentions of its agents. Even Freud's liberation of the unconscious becomes for Schorske a repression of history and politics, and the "explosion" of Kokoshka and Schoenberg can only be an explosion "in the garden." These examples in particular raise a question about the aestheticist hypothesis that will not go away: Is the "aestheticist" gesture, the move demarcating a discrete territory for the aesthetic apart from history and politics, inscribed in fin-de-siècle cultural practices, or first in our readings of them?

One has to look beyond Schorske's history to get to a treatment of "politics and culture" (his subtitle) that does not represent them as oppositional poles, even—or especially—in the "aestheticist" fin de siècle. The aestheticist hypothesis cannot really assimilate the notion of "cultural work," or the idea of the material labor performed by language or within aesthetic systems. This sense of the "work" of the artwork is shared by literary critical language in the late twentieth century and the politicized discourse on culture of the last turn of the century (recall the 1900 cultural journal mentioned earlier, entitled *Deutsche Arbeit* [German work]). Here, again, the specific and unique condition of the hegemonic German-speaking minority in Bohemia points to a feature of the fin de siècle that is crucial and yet, in the Vienna context, understated and easier to ignore. It is therefore not accidental that the seminal contemporary study of the notion of literary "deterritorialization" and the field of "minor literature"—particular ways in which literature does political work—focuses on Prague in this period. That study is a single,

slim volume on Kafka by the French critics Gilles Deleuze and Félix
Guattari entitled *Kafka: Toward a Minor Literature*.[72] It is there that
they establish, on the basis of apparently scanty evidence, the structure of the political content of Kafka's writing: basing their analysis
on Kafka's famous diary entry on "minor literatures" of December 25,
1911, they define his Prague German as a "deterritorialized language,
appropriate for strange and minor uses." This notion of "deterritorialization," of the subversion of the major language, discourse, or culture
from within, marking a line of escape from the majority discourse,
single-handedly opened a new field of inquiry of minor literature studies.[73] In spite of this enormous impact (and in part in reaction against
it), the 1990s have brought with them a note of skepticism toward this
critical legacy. If such skepticism is scrutinized, in its various forms, the
relationship to the aestheticist hypothesis is unmistakable. At our own
fin de siècle, the claim of a political operation of art is apparently untenable. And yet there are better reasons to hold on to Deleuze and Guattari's model of the interplay of work and setting than to let it go. What
Kafka enables is a critical reading of a specific potential political operation of literature, or the ways in which writing works with and against
history. The analysis offers the opportunity to read political effects of
works without identifying revolutionary (rather than aesthetic) authorial
intention. Minor literature is precisely not a multicultural absorption of
marginality into a cultural canon, but instead posits an indigestible par-
ticle into the core of territorialized language, the concord of artist, work,
and setting. Stanley Corngold has critiqued Deleuze and Guattari in a
way that defends Kafka's writing against a particular misuse of the notion of minor literature, since that writing is certainly not to be read as
"a kind of polemical ideolect aimed against high German literature"—
say, the "major literature" of the "semi-divine" figure of Goethe.[74] It is
Deleuze and Guattari's intention to show, after all, that the minor use
can take place only within the major language/literature/tradition. Oskar Pollak's pilgrimage to the Goethe National Museum elicited a letter
from Kafka in which the use of the word "national" is described as "the
most delicate, miraculously delicate irony."[75] The letter beginning with
Kafka's punishing writing desk is the one that leads to Goethe's, the central object in the sanctum sanctorum of the Goethe house. And then
comes another irony:

> But do you know what the all-holiest is that we can have of Goethe's as com-
> memoration . . . the footsteps of his lonesome walks [*Gänge*] through the

country . . . it would be those. And then comes a joke, a really splendid one, which makes the beloved Lord cry bitterly and hell get hellish laughing cramps: we cannot ever have the all-holiest of someone else [eines Fremden], only our own; that is a joke, a really splendid one.[76]

The territory inscribed by the great writer's footprints is an unshareable country; the steps are traces [Spuren] inaccessible to those who would walk with him. To turn Kafka's delicate deterritorializations into a univocal subversion narrative directed against German literature would obviously miss the point. The historical circumstances in which Kafka found himself allowed for a uniquely nuanced and complex web of territorial relations to be articulated, including strands of collusion as well as resistance, breaking away as well as digging in one's heels.

In Kafka, Deleuze and Guattari dismiss the production of the rest of the Prague writers who benefited from the same rare contextual and linguistic condition. The others (only Meyrink and Brod are given brief mention) Deleuze and Guattari assume to have resorted to artificial means of "reterritorialization," such as mysticism or symbolism, to avert territorial crisis. Attentive readings of the actual works, however, reveal the complexity of the aesthetic and political projects of Kafka's fellow Prague writers, and the kinship of their projects to his.[77] It is urgent to explore the different ways in which these other writers of Kafka's generation share a space with him, precisely because their less self-conscious cultural production sheds a different kind of light on the Prague historical context. For this reason, literary specialists may wonder why so many of the following pages concern themselves with virtually unknown authors and often utterly unknown texts. These texts do not merely shed light on the contexts that inform our understanding of a great author such as Kafka (although I hope they do that, too); they project figures of territory, identity, and ideology in different ways from him and from each other.

The figure of territory foregrounds the political aspect of cultural production, since, according to Deleuze and Guattari, the "cramped space" of a minority literature forces the immediate connection of everything in it to the political. Surely a reading of Kafka's famous letter to his father is enough to make this point. This process distinguishes itself from the operation of self-consciously politicized literature in that the spaces of aesthetic and political articulation naturally coincide. This cozy cohabitation, though, like the friend-neighborly closeness enforced by Kafka's village's narrow streets, is far from an easy solution to a difficult dilemma; in other words, it is the product of a "tricky history" (*vertrakte Geschichte*). Hence the intensely personal manner in which the relation between the aesthetic and the political was experienced not only by Kafka, already sophisticated enough to problematize it, but also—and strongly—by Max Brod throughout his career, by Egon Erwin Kisch, by the expressionists, the Zionists, and the Czech-to-German translators of this generation. Similarly, these writers took for granted the congruity of the circles of personal, group, and universal human experience, and without visible hesitation identified the crisis of self inherent in their obviously atypical condition with the broad cultural dilemma leading up to the world wars. The few texts cited thus far should already make clear the special place reserved for territorial metaphor in the language of the Prague Germans from the end of the last century through the First World War.

Yet, the focus on territorial metaphor seems salient in ways that may have as much to do with our own intellectual historical setting as with turn-of-the-century Prague. The violent return of repressed ethnoterritorial visions of east central Europe since the 1989 collapse is less a cause than a symptom of a contemporary focus on territory not unrelated to that experienced by the Prague circle, as I will argue. Contemporary anglophone critical thought, particularly that branch of left-wing critical writing described as "social theory," has been experiencing an apparently irresistible gravitational pull toward questions of space and power, and toward metaphors of spatiality and territoriality.[78] While many different sources of this intellectual turn could be identified, of indisputable influence has been the work of French philosopher Henri Lefebvre, culminating in his pivotal study *The Production of Space*.[79] This work contains the foundation of a critical thinking that takes account of the way space is much rhetorically invoked and little critically interrogated; Lefebvre takes seriously "space" as a discursive system *and* as a matrix of socially produced relations, instead of merely as a set of physically delimiting factors. His work seeks to move beyond an assumption of space as an ideologically neutral and given grid, or as a passive geometry. This project has proven to be particularly attractive to a group of Marxist (or what are today cryptically called post-Marxist) geographers or social theorists strongly influenced by geography: David Harvey in his important statement on the "postmodern condition"; Edward Soja, whose review of "the reassertion of space in critical social theory" posits the spatial turn as a postmodern alternative to historicist thinking; Doreen Massey, who introduced feminism into the equation in a serious and productive way, and whose differential treatment of space and place has been widely influential; and others.[80]

All of these works are urgently engaged with the relationship of the production of social space, with its palpably concrete and often violent ramifications, with the discourse on space, spatial metaphor, or representation. This central concern can be described as a variant of the question of aestheticism, or, more familiarly for these (post-)Marxist writers, the base-superstructure discussion. Hence they are all concerned with the political valence of space: the way sovereignty inscribes space (or space implies sovereignty), and the way the authority of space can impose or oppose power differently from, say, the claim of time or history.[81]

In a concise article entitled "Sovereignty without Territoriality," Arjun Appadurai has offered a succinct history of the constitution and deterioration of normative territoriality in the West.[82] While one must take issue with the accuracy of such a compressed account, its force lies in its ability to streamline the trajectory of "ethnoterritorial thinking" from its presumed inception (after the Peace of Westphalia, in 1648) through to its acute present crisis. Appadurai's elegant passing definition of this ideological construct is: "The isomorphism of people, territory, and legitimate sovereignty that constitutes the normative charter of the modern nation-state." Elsewhere Appadurai has written about the more generalized crisis of the nation-state, indeed the necessary contradiction inherent in the dually constructed term. The disjuncture of nation and state (which were assumed in their high modern form to have been coterminous), the fissures among categories meant, at least ideally, to be coextensive (such as citizenship, ethnos, nationhood, and territoriality), are characteristic of a postmodern age where territorial tropes of cultural coherence persist even after the conditions supporting such fictions have dissipated. "Since states, territories and ideas of national ethnic singularity are always complicated historical coproductions," Appadurai writes, "diasporic pluralism tends to embarrass all narratives that attempt to naturalize such histories."

The least persuasive part of this argument is the novelty of the crisis of territory it describes.[83] Narratives distinguishing a radical shift from high modern to postmodern are often fraught, it seems; but in the particular case of the high modern setting of fin-de-siècle Prague, Appadurai's description of crisis and reaction is startlingly apt. The diagnosis of an intensification of nationalisms at the precise moment that their foundation is "embarrassed"—that is, revealed to be fictive—is worth keeping in mind. The common sense of the nation as isomorphic coincidence of ethnos (even "blood"), language (and "culture"), citizenship, and territory exceeds the empirical fact, now in plain sight, that the boundaries of these imagined entities do not naturally coincide. Appadurai understandably assumes that the exposure of these contradictions within the ethnoterritorial prototype is recent, as though the myth of isomorphism were built on the foundation of a past where populations were or seemed to be nonplural, where identities were or seemed to be stable, where centers were centers and peripheries were peripheries. But as we have already seen in our review of turn-of-the-century Prague and Bohemia, such is not the case—nor is the degree of self-consciousness so often assumed to be "postmodern" unique to the late twentieth century. Prague may be privileged as a site where the fissures plaguing modern models of who and where one is were plainly exposed, but this atypical condition was nonetheless symptomatic of wider-reaching fault lines in the terrain of European identity.

In invoking "identity" I come around to another recurring theme within the contemporary literature on space, place, and territory. These figures in social theory have been practically inseparable from the boom cultural studies field of identity politics and/or "identitarianism." It would be easy to posit that a study of Prague nationality and culture in this period might belong to this growing body of theoretical literature, and yet I am inclined to suggest at the outset that I hope my research brushes against the grain of much of this work. Walter Benn Michaels has attacked the currently fashionable "identitarian" position most directly in his article "Race into Culture," where he traces the insoluble links and resemblances between intended constructivist notions of identity and the essentialist categories they were meant to supplant.[84] In several of the sources mentioned above there is a consciousness of the problematic nature of appropriating territorial or spatial metaphor, and the same can be said of the embrace of "minority," "hybrid," or "othered" identities.[85] Neil Smith and Cindi Katz warn that the explosion of spatial metaphorics in radical social theory can have the effect, through the very mechanics of metaphor, of positing the hegemonic notion of "absolute space" as natural. The radical distinction of here and there, or of self and other, and the unproblematic stability and integrity of each of these opposed entities, are ironically refortified in these repeated deployments of territorial discourse. Sara Suleri has been exceptionally sensitive to this issue in her rhetorical analysis of imperial India, pointing out that the celebration of otherness or "alterity" in much contemporary work "entrenches rather than displaces the rigidity of the self/other binarism already governing traditional colonial discourses."[86] This raises a complicated problem that goes beyond the naive celebration of difference for difference's sake—for the invocation of hegemonic discourses does have the tendency to reassert them in unintended and uncontrollable ways. This phenomenon has its double in the historical texts themselves, where, as we have already seen, even challenges to dominant discourses on nation, language, and race can buttress their foundations. What defines a discourse as hegemonic is the degree to which it becomes a lingua franca among those it marginalizes as well as those it empowers; the degree to which it is taken as given, or mistaken as nature. In this sense, to the degree discourses that subvert territoriality (Deleuze and Guattari's "deterritorialization") are possible, they are so only within the discursive realm they are meant to attack. The historian or critic's quandary is no different. For to fail to engage the discourse under study is to misread—or fail to read—the historical object.

My own method in the pages that follow powerfully depends upon a close analysis of rhetorical figures that appear in comparable ways in the Prague circle writers' literary works, polemics, diaries, and letters, as well as in the discourses of their political, aesthetic, and social contexts. If it becomes clear that discursive resemblances between texts of, say, *völkisch* German nationalism, Zionism, and expressionism exceed comfortable levels, this should only accentuate the deceptive aspect of the kind of history of ideas that erases these original marks from the "arguments" distilled from texts. Our aversion to this language is after all the product of a certain censorship by the dominant discourse of our own time, which recognizes in the revolutionary antiliberalism of the years surrounding the Great War a deadly enemy.

By the same mechanism, historians of the last several decades have discussed the circle of Prague German-speaking Jews in an involuntarily revisionist way. Looking at the activity of this circle—their contact with the Czech artistic community, their valiant and successful attempts to translate the literature of the Czech Renaissance and to mediate production of Czech plays and operas in the West, their persistent return to the idea of universalism in their expressionist, Zionist, or socialist works— looking at this cultural production, historians of our own period have projected onto this slim segment of the Bohemian population a face of liberal humanism.[87] They have identified in their work the pleading voice of liberal reason and tolerance—in other words, their own voice, the voice they would like to have had if they themselves were transported back to the epoch when competing illiberal ideologies were barreling toward disaster. This historiographical ventriloquism takes place in bold defiance of a glaring common feature of the wide-ranging work of the Prague circle. For each and every one of the "humanists" of the Prague circle, while diverging from one another in every other way conceivable, set himself in opposition to the liberalism he saw to be at the root of his contemporary dilemma.

The distortion (albeit, at least at times and in part, unintentional) of this "liberal historiography" of the Prague circle is possible only through, first of all, the claim of nonideological objectivity, and, second, the *translation* of the discourse represented in the rhetoric of the actual texts into ostensibly neutral language. One way to avoid this fallacy, it seems to me, is to "save the text." Primarily this involves the generous presentation of texts and the patience to break them apart and observe how they work, rather than to extract essential arguments from them. There is also in my secondary text a replication of the rhetorical forms that are found in the primary sources—a trick that escapes the trap of speaking in an apparently neutral but in fact ideological voice. In surrendering this very particular ideal of neutrality, the partisan element in the original texts and in my readings of them is exposed, with inner contradictions intact. The particular competence of this strategy for this specific subject matter (replication of the discourse of more distant periods, for instance, might render an analysis illegible) depends upon a premise toward which these introductory comments have been moving, and which will be returned to as this book unfolds: the territories created by the Prague circle functioned as various and radical solutions to a contemporary crisis from which we have not yet emerged.

Such a historiographical direction moves toward the erosion of walls between secondary text, primary text, and context. In this regard, the discussions of Hayden White and Fredric Jameson on the narrativity of history seem less relevant than the judgment of Rainer Nägele, who has focused on the "radical difference" between history and interpretation, the "stubborn presence of the text and the irrevocable absence of past life that history would like to recapture." [88] The "text and context" debates are themselves recent representations of the modern struggle with a binary opposition that recurs throughout the texts under study in the following pages. The current culture-historical task of defining a method in a way that evades the presentist inheritance of nineteenth-century historicism is not unlike the various projects of the Catholic-spiritualist-expressionist Franz Werfel, the Zionist Hugo Bergmann and his teacher Martin Buber, and other Prague writers in their efforts to rediscover immanence, and to bridge an intolerable fragmentation characteristic of modern life. Georg Lukács's provocatively comparable situation as a Budapest Jew writing in German comes to mind when we look at the 1911 collection *Die Seele und die Formen,* a group of literary critical essays with the very same object in mind. His remarkable introduction to the collection is a self-reflexive piece called "On the Nature and Form of the Essay." There he writes of the confrontation of the essayist with the critical object itself as a ritual unification of an inexorable dichotomy:

> Das Schicksalsmoment des Kritikers ist also jenes, wo die Dinge zu Formen werden; der Augenblick, wenn alle Gefühle und Erlebnisse, die diesseits und jenseits der Form waren, eine Form bekommen, sich zur Form verschmelzen und verdichten. Es ist der mystische Augenblick der Vereinigung des Außen und des Innen, der Seele und der Form.

> The critic's moment of truth is that where "things" become "forms"; the moment when all feelings and experiences that used to be on this and that side of "form" receive a form themselves, fuse and condense into form. It is the mystical moment of union of the outside and the inside, of the soul and of form.

CHAPTER 2

Where's the Difference?

Culture, Ideology, and the
Aesthetics of Nationality

Weißt Du aber, was das Allerheiligste ist, das wir überhaupt
von Goethe haben können, als Andenken ... die Fußspuren
seiner einsamen Gänge durch das Land ... die wären es. Und
nun kommt ein Witz ... das Allerheiligste eines Fremden
können wir niemals haben, nur das eigene—das ist ein Witz,
ein ganz vortrefflicher.

But do you know what the all-holiest is that we can have of
Goethe's as commemoration ... the footsteps of his lonesome
walks through the country ... it would be those. And then
comes a joke ... we cannot ever have the all-holiest of another, only our own—that is a joke, a really splendid one.

letter to Oskar Pollak, 1902

THE CULTURE OF HEGEMONY

In the Prague of 1900 it would have been difficult to say which could
sooner do without the other: Prague German culture, or the city's German-speaking Jewish population. For German culture was as central to
bourgeois Jewish life in Prague as Jews seemed to be to its production,
funding, and appreciation.[1] The Prague Jews had a stake in German cultural life, as Felix Weltsch (1884–1964) reveals in his description of the
typical paterfamilias reading aloud from the morning paper about the
German Theater, rather than from the front page. To this scene Weltsch
adds the comment:

> It was certainly an idyllic time—for the Jews and also for the world in gen-
> eral—those years at the turn of the century. But they were also years marked
> by a strange aloofness from reality, by a surprising lack of consciousness of
> the past and of history, especially amongst the Jews.[2]

This "idyllic" scenario is reminiscent of Stefan Zweig's Austrian memoir, *The World of Yesterday*,[3] with its evocation of a bygone "world of security."[4] But this image stands in marked contrast to historical representations of 1900 as the culmination of two decades of popular and political antisemitism in Prague, Bohemia, and the Habsburg monarchy more generally.

One way to understand this inconsistency is within the framework of Carl Schorske's thesis that in fin-de-siècle Vienna, at least, culture functioned as a retreat from an untenable political world.[5] Yet, such a conclusion would assume that the cultural sphere was (or at least was imagined to be) separate from the sphere of political conflict in turn-of-the-century Prague, when in fact just the opposite was supposed. In this sense—and not only in this sense—culture in this central-marginal space within the Habsburg realm operated more as it does for Edward Said's British Empire: culture was inseparable from national fantasies; it represented a combative site of identity construction and defense, and operated as an instrument of power over those outside the privileged national/cultural circle.[6] Further, in German-liberal Prague, these mechanisms connecting cultural to political projects were remarkably overt in comparison with Said's and other cases. The relative exposure of these mechanisms left a different kind of legacy for the Prague circle generation.

The phrase "the culture of hegemony" is meant to suggest several interrelated components of this legacy: the assumption, first of all, of the superiority and dominance of one culture over others; the understanding that cultural "lordship" implied, and at the same time justified, political control; and not least, that hegemony in the multiethnic environment itself constituted a kind of culture, necessitating the production and circulation of all of the formations that the word "culture" connotes. Yet, by the end of the nineteenth century, neither greater cultural nor political power could be taken for granted by German Prague. We will begin by examining the ways in which this ideology of cultural and political power was sustained by the generation of Prague German liberals preceding the Prague circle—that is, these writers' parents. From there, we will move on to the way in which that same rhetorical structure was inherited by the young Praguers (albeit imperfectly) in the first years of this century. Cracks in the foundation of the German-liberal rhetorical edifice, invisible to the parents' generation, broke through to the surface in the early reiterations of this generation, and these fissures belong im-

portantly to the German liberal legacy. At the same time that the young
Franz Kafka and Oskar Pollak mused about the ironies of Goethe's
traces and the notion of a national literary legacy, others of their generation were working through comparable questions, in different ways,
and with varying degrees of self-consciousness. Here the focus will be
on three central writers of the generation who knew and were in contact with one another, and who ended up in very different places: Felix
Weltsch, one of Kafka's closest friends, later to become an active Zionist and political theorist; Egon Erwin Kisch, the innovative journalist and
later socialist activist; and Max Brod, the best integrated of the three
into the literary-aesthetic life of Central Europe, and who would also become a Jewish nationalist. An examination of the early works of these
writers will allow us to trace a line from the "foundational" German-
liberal outlook into which they were born, through the early signs of
rupture within that view, and on to the aesthetic experimentation undertaken by Kisch and Brod in the first decade of the century. The great
differences between Kisch and Brod highlight the variability of forms to
rise from the earth of German liberalism in decline—or rather, from the
fault lines of the ground of German liberalism itself. For the ruptures
within the ideology had been little concealed in the years leading up to
the century's turn.

In and of itself it is not surprising that the German-speaking Jews of
Prague, as elsewhere in the monarchy, identified themselves in the main
with German-liberal ideology and politics, even as German-liberal hegemony had begun to wane. After all, they owed their social position to
that ideology, and the fates of liberal politics and Jewish integration
seemed to many of them to be inextricable from one another.[7] So it was
that Prague Jewish writers of the last part of the nineteenth century engaged in a cultural program that was linked to the reinforcement of
German-liberal power. As Brod says of Fritz Mauthner, the author of
the nationalist "border novel" *The Last German of Blatna* (1913),

> [he] belonged to that precise generation of Jews that counted themselves
> as Germans without a second thought, and that fanatically participated in a
> pugnacious Germanism.[8]

Mauthner's autobiography, however, with its significant reflections
on his Jewishness, suggests that he and other staunchly nationalist German liberals of his confession gave more thought to their nationality
than is superficially apparent.[9] One might also take a second look at Felix Weltsch's father, who at the breakfast table read aloud on the latest

production at the German Theater, and in the evenings wrote nostalgic poetry about Jewish tradition.[10] It is not that these or other acculturated Jews of their generation "felt themselves to be German"; it would take substantial space to puzzle out what that assertion might mean. As cultural representatives of German-liberal ideology, they had a stake in glossing over any difference between German and German Jew, Prague German and Viennese German, or, in some cases, even Austrian German and imperial German. Fritz Mauthner (1849–1923) and Alfred Klaar (1848–1927), like their successors in Concordia (the cultural organ of the Prague German literary establishment) Friedrich Adler (1857–1938) and Hugo Salus (1866–1929), were guardians of a cultural and ideological frontier: Prague German culture was an outpost of civilization, charged with remaining as pure and as strong as German culture in the heartland. As Emil Utitz writes of Salus and Adler:

> Both acknowledged Jews, they nevertheless felt themselves to be the authentic representatives of all Germans in Bohemia, as well as further afield. Those Germans wanted little to do with Prague in any case, and least of all with its Jews. But Salus and Adler were liberals of the old stamp.[11]

The "stamp" of liberalism brought together German-speaking Jews, German Bohemians, Prague Germans, and the Germans of upper and lower Austria into one imagined cultural community. But the main feature of the liberal stamp of the Concordia generation was the focus on culture itself. "Culture" served to authorize German rule in a multinational empire.

In the late nineteenth century, as the advance of Czech-national municipal and regional policy challenged the status of Prague as a German cultural capital, German-liberal ideologues such as the Charles University professor Philipp Knoll went on the defensive. Knoll's lectures and scholarly essays on the German art and architecture of the city, on its German historical roots and on the German origins [sic] of the Charles University did not stop short of drawing an explicit contrast between the Germans and their "cultureless" Czech neighbors.[12]

There was an urgent purpose behind this insistence on German culture's *unique* status as authentic Bohemian culture, as opposed, for example, to more modest claims of cultural superiority or greater maturity. In late nineteenth-century Bohemia the "liberal" component of German liberalism, the commitment to democratic politics, had undermined the "German" component. If German hegemony was to be preserved in some form, the discourse that privileged the Germans as the unique Central European *Kulturnation* had to be recovered and reinforced. Further, there was a need to address the conflict between a German claim to power, legitimated by "culture," and the competing Czech claim, legitimated by liberal "politics."[13] The establishment of the primacy of culture, then, became more important than ever.

Knoll's account of the history of the Charles University, "the oldest university of Germany,"[14] calls upon the authority of a centuries-old German culture to defend itself against very recent and, according to his logic, fleeting political tendencies:

> [I]t seems to me indispensable to secure a long-standing center of German culture against the changing circumstances of political life, and to return to it the peace and quiet that are essential to intellectual production.[15]

Knoll depends on a German discourse setting culture against politics, one that had currency far beyond Bohemian borders and would continue well into the twentieth century. In the Bohemian context, however, "culture" became identified with the Germans, over against a capricious parliamentary "politics" identified with the Czechs. The not unfamiliar notion that culture requires protection from politics had, in this case, very particular national (hence political) implications. As the most recent and exciting sociohistorical research on the Habsburg state is demonstrating, the categories of "nation" and "ethnicity," "culture" and "politics," were never really distinct from one another in this discursive context. Pieter Judson in particular has shown how transethnic class interests were represented by the figure of "German culture"; conversely, the Czech national challenge shook things up well beyond the sphere of ethnic relations.[16]

Ideologues armed with academic credentials were on the front lines of this Bohemian *Kulturkampf,* regularly publishing scholarly evidence of German cultural uniqueness in the Prague German-liberal press all the way through to the First World War. *Deutsche Arbeit* (German work), a new journal devoted to Bohemian German culture, began to appear in 1901; by then, the fine line had been crossed between culture as rationale for hegemony and culture as defense against "czechization." Culture, in other words, was maintained as the cornerstone of the German-liberal offensive as well as defensive strategies.[17] It would remain fundamental even as German-liberal rhetoric evolved: a 1912 advertisement for *Deutsche Arbeit* headed "National Struggle and Cultural Work" asserted that "*völkisch* work is cultural work in its highest sense, and vice versa." The advertisement alluded to the "considerable tasks" incumbent upon German Austrians, the fulfillment of which was their "historical destiny." [18] This last represented a defensive attempt to recover a strand of what had been the dominant discourse on culture until the mid–nineteenth century: that the Germans belonged to a privileged group of "world-historical" peoples, bearers of civilization capable of producing culture of universal significance.[19] The division of world-historical and nonhistorical peoples was parallel to discussions of German as the unique "culture-language" in Central Europe, the only language in the region in which a literature of universal value could be written.

So culture was the weapon of choice on this battleground of nationality and ideology, as it was defined by the German-liberal ideologues. It was a game designed to give unique advantage to the Germans, which, however, did not prevent the Czechs from mastering the rules. In 1817, the discovery of alleged medieval Czech illuminated manuscripts at two sites (Dvůr Králové and Zelená hora) had cast into question the presumed German monopoly on culture in the Central European arena. An anonymous challenge to their authenticity in a German-liberal daily a half century later sparked a debate and a libel case, both of which were ideological to the core.[20] In fact, the documents were forgeries, but neither the German-liberal (and Jewish) editor charged with libel nor his accusers undertook to locate any actual evidence bearing on the forgery or authenticity of the documents. The libel case took place in the 1860s, well into the Czech offensive against German hegemony in Bohemia, as the Germans were forced to defend the dogma of their unique status in the region. On the Czech side, even accepting the challenge to the sources by investigating the authenticity of the manuscripts seemed to imply an acceptance of the (unique) authority of the Germans to judge or identify true culture. Thus, the claim raised by the young academic named Tomáš Masaryk, that a secure nation must be willing to put the Czech national irons to the fire, had to some the ring of treason.[21] The stalemate of two intransigent positions, winning the day over Masaryk's call for a cool and secure empiricism, was symptomatic of the German and Czech attitudes toward culture at the height of the national conflict; it also illustrates how much was at stake in this time and place when the term "culture" was invoked.

Masaryk had confidence enough to test the German challenge to the manuscript forgeries since the issue arose at a time when Czech culture, with or without the Dvůr Králové and Zelená hora artifacts, had come into its own. The Czechs had been the most successful of the Habsburg Slavs in establishing a modern and autonomous national literary and musical tradition. Instead of rejecting the German-liberal skewed standard of judging the viability of a nation by its high culture, the Czechs absorbed it, and lived up to its requirements. Czech literary and musical giants enjoyed the status of national heroes—as Germans in Prague heroized Goethe and Schiller. The simplest and in fact most common way for the Prague German-liberal establishment to cope with the Czech cultural renascence was to ignore it. Prague German memoirs amply document these cultivated Praguers' relative ignorance of the explosion of Czech music, art, and theater centered chiefly in their own city. Prague German academics elaborated systems of evaluation proving that Czech culture was not only "behind" German culture, but in a different class—mimetic rather than original.[22]

The earliest manifestations of an aesthetic of the Prague circle must be understood within this context. It has often been remarked that the Prague circle figures began from a position of unproblematic self-identification as German nationals. Other historians have sought to locate them primarily as Jews, resisting what may only be external German-liberal appearances. There are even voices to appropriate them, or some of them, into the canon of a Czech national literature. Part of the problem resides in the question itself, which unapologetically ascribes a stasis and fixity to nationality that is ontologically naive as well as anachronistic. The focus ought not to be on what the national identifications of these young people were, but instead on *how* such identifications—and resistances to them—actually operated.

Kafka's letter to Oskar Pollak of August 1902 is one of the very earliest Kafka texts on record—the actual letter has been lost—and it was written in the period focused upon in this chapter. The young Kafka's play with the notion of a "Goethe National Museum" in Weimar sets the tone for readings of the early texts of others of his cohort. Worthy of note right from the outset is the tension in the letter between a powerful veneration for the towering figure of Goethe on the one hand, and, on the other, the skepticism about any inheritable legacy that such a figure could offer; hence the "irony" of thinking of him in "national" terms. Kafka here, and apparently Pollak as well, held fast to a certain exaltation of culture that characterized the German-liberal values of their parents' generation, while at the same time finding the project of a national museum in Goethe's honor ridiculous. Kafka's "joke"—that there is nothing to "possess" of our cultural forebears except their lonesome footsteps through the country, now swept away and therefore unshareable—performs this tension; an unreconstructed acceptance of the centrality of the figure of "culture" cohabits with the naked consciousness of the atomization of the contiguous and stable cultural commonwealth of German-liberal fantasy.

The title of this chapter asks, "Where's the difference?" This question returns to the issue of specificity of location, in the first place, since it is that very specificity—the idiosyncratic position of Prague at this moment of national self-definition—that was obscured by the image of the city as a solidly grounded center of high German culture. That image obscured as well what we would today call a consciousness of "difference" among its bourgeois German-speaking class (since a self-identification of elite status is not the same thing as marginal consciousness). A Prague German poet born at midcentury was still able to take for granted a host of assumptions that would prove problematic for those born in the 1880s: that he shared a cultural space with German poets across central and northern Europe, but not with the majority of residents in his own city; that German culture was de facto superior to any other Central European culture, and German language uniquely suited among Central European languages to the creation of great literature; that high culture was superior, indeed incomparable, to folk culture; and that any mark of the local degraded literature from its universalist aspirations. These assumptions took the form of lessons handed down to the Prague circle generation, but like all lessons, their content was altered by the lens of readers who found themselves in a very different position by the century's turn. The early texts of such figures as Max Brod, Egon Erwin Kisch, and Felix Weltsch, which have not otherwise merited scholarly attention, in fact reveal the extraordinary complexity of their feelings about nationality and its relationship to creativity and, conversely, the role of culture in the life of a nation. In the reconfiguration of these problems, borrowed, as they were, from the special brand of German liberalism native to fin-de-siècle Prague, we can begin to map a cultural-political topography in flux.

FOLK AND SONG

In 1900 the sixteen-year-old Felix Weltsch wrote a final essay titled "The German Folk Song" for his rhetoric class.[23] It is telling that he inserted the qualifying adjective "German" as an afterthought in the title of his draft, which had originally been called "The Folk Song," even though the specificity of the analysis to the German case was never in question. Persistent references in the Prague German-liberal press of the time demonstrate the fundamental assumption that "culture" in Prague could refer only to German culture. What is curious in this case, however, is that such an assumption could be applied so hastily to folk culture, the one particular kind of national culture that even the most chauvinist Germans had to concede was accessible even to those peoples not deemed to be *Kulturvölker*. Thus, in Weltsch's title, "The (German) Folk Song," there already appears a powerful tension that is characteristic of the whole text. On the surface, the essay seems unambiguously celebratory of German culture, plainly deploying nationalist rhetoric typical of the period. In some ways, the essay is no more than a rote repetition of certain German-liberal pieties about culture and nation. And yet throughout, the text is subconsciously and relentlessly engaged in issues beyond the sight of the German-liberal gaze of the previous generation; its model of the relationship between folk art and *Volk* betrays an awareness of the dilemma of the Prague German-speaking Jewish writer that is utterly absent in the artistic identity of Concordia giants Hugo Salus and Friedrich Adler.

The Czech-nationalist revival of folk culture, the call for its academic study and claims of its usefulness as a source for modern national culture, had been successful, and indeed was a model for nascent national revivals in other parts of Central Europe. One German-liberal response to this cultural strategy was to judge the focus on folk culture as a measure of primitivity, as in the argument that the integration of folk themes in symphonic music represented an early stage in the development of a national musical culture, reached by the Germans over three centuries earlier.[24] The paternalistic lens through which Czech culture could be viewed as primitive depended upon a dogmatic distinction between high and low culture. This is precisely the distinction revised by the young Weltsch in his attempt to confer artistic status on the German folk song, calling upon Jacob Grimm's definition of poetry as "the life of man himself, grasped with purity and contained within the magic of language." The power to achieve true art, then, is accessible not only to a "career poet," postulates Weltsch, "but also men of the people [*aus dem Volke*], simple people who think and feel, strive and reflect as the *Volk* itself [. . .]"[25]

There was nothing radical in this claim, as witnessed by Weltsch's citations of Grimm, Herder, and others. Yet, the conventional German-romantic valorization of the "Volk"—of the songs and legends of the simple folk of the nation, and of their special status in the true art of a nation—presented a particular problem to the German-speaking student studying Grimm in Prague in much the same way that Grimm was being studied in Leipzig or Vienna. The Prague German poets, whether they were writing at the century's turn or in the late nineteenth century, could not pretend to a relationship to a German "Volk" in their locale. The earlier Concordia poets were radically separated from the thoughts, feelings, dreams, and reflections of any popular entity, be it the Czech proletariat of Prague (which they studiously ignored), the Germans of rural or industrial Bohemia (from whom they were not only culturally but also geographically separated), or the folk culture of distant alpine Austria or Saxony. As for the popular culture of the rural Czechs of the Bohemian environs (and those moving to Prague in ever greater numbers), the literati of nineteenth-century Prague never gave it a nod.

This is the context in which to situate Weltsch's claim that authentic poetry lives "in the ear of the *Volk*, on the lips and the harps of living singers [. . .]" Such singers were simply not to be found in German Prague. And so it was to the songs of remote times and lands, to a holistic fantasy of a German past, that the future Zionist turned to find the genuine soul of his nation:

> In [these folk songs] we feel the heartbeat of the German *Volk*. Here German wrath thunders, here is German scorn, here the kiss of German love; here is the sparkle of true German wine and true German tears.

The *Volk* informs the poet's song; its voice is channeled through the artist, especially the folk artist, an authentic mouthpiece of the people, to take form in the work of art. Nor does representation exhaust the function of the artwork. In every generation it serves as a source of national inspiration, it goads readers to carry on the torch of the national project, always defined as creative:

> So much for the poet. But we may, long into the future, not only delight and find true amusement in the fountain of youth of German poetry and folk song, with their eternal and inexhaustible richness; from their love and enthusiasm we may also create for our German nation, whose sons we feel ourselves to be, through thick and thin, until the end of our very lives.

If Weltsch's belated insertion of the qualifying "German" into the
title of his essay points to the Prague German-liberal tendency to regard
the terms "culture" and "German culture" as synonymous, the background of the Czech national revival nonetheless colors the text in every
paragraph. The choice of the folk song as theme and the attack on the
distinction between high and low culture bore connotations in Prague
that they would not have in German lands proper. The image of traditional folk culture as a "fountain of youth" calls to mind Czech-national
rhetoric, which turned German paternalism on its head by contrasting
Czech cultural youth and vibrancy to a senile German decadence. At the
same time, however, this passage represents a call for German cultural
renewal; it envisions an activist epoch of creativity inspired by a vital
past. It is an intensely nationalist message, to be sure, but one that is simultaneously responsive to and mimetic of the Czech cultural revival,
which every good German chauvinist had been trained to ignore.

The young Weltsch, along with some of his classmates, already sensed
an internal crisis in Prague German culture that ran deeper than the attacks levied from the outside by a Czech-dominated municipal government. In a 1901 essay (written for the same class the following year),
Weltsch tackled the problem of comparing the literary genres of epic and
drama. He chose as examples the epic *Nibelungenlied* and Hebbel's
drama *Die Nibelungen,* once again identifying the relation between
people and culture as the central theme, buttressed by the concept of
epochs of national vitality and decadence:

> [. . .] happy the *Volk* that is in the process of activity and ascent, for this rise
> upward is health, joy, and strength [. . .] and truly, happy is our German
> *Volk;* for it has twice struggled to the heights in vital triumph, twice has its
> literature marvelously blossomed, bearing sublime fruits [. . .] [26]

The obvious tension here is between the first axiom, happy the people
in the process of cultural rebirth and ascendancy (read: Czechs), and the
second, asserting that the Germans *had* possessed that happiness, in the
twelfth and eighteenth centuries. The emphasis on culturally ascendant
peoples as not only happy but also possessing "health" and "strength"
has parallels not only in the contemporary rhetoric of Czech nationalists, but in the Zionism that Weltsch would embrace before the decade's
end. Weltsch identifies two periods of German cultural blossoming: the
first between 450 and 1250, and the second from 1748 through 1831.
Significantly, Weltsch's thesis is that the second ascendancy has its source

in the first. That he chose the *Nibelungenlied* and the Hebbel work it inspired as his examples would seem to open the possibility that a third creative epoch had begun, heralded by Wagner's *Ring*. But Weltsch flatly avoids the claim that German culture has entered a new creative period. Echoing his earlier essay, he lets past glories stand as a challenge to the present generation. They are eternal works that inform and nourish the *Volk* in future generations, give it pride and define it, and finally drive it to further creation. Weltsch doesn't term these works an inspiration, but rather a "*Mahnung*"—which can be read either as a "reminder" or a "warning."

These two apparently celebratory texts on German culture represent the uneasy cohabitation of conflicting instincts in Weltsch's generation of Prague German-speaking Jews: we encounter in his essays certain of the values of an inherited German liberalism—such as a paternalistic view of cultural development and an intense German chauvinism—coupled however with a cultural pessimism that was decidedly not on the German-liberal curriculum. Likewise foreign to the generation of Weltsch's parents were the subtextual indications of a powerful sympathy with the discourse of the burgeoning Czech-national movement. Weltsch's essays appeared at a moment when the ideology that had justified the social existence of that previous generation was already in some sense obsolete, but was sustained in Prague for lack of any accessible alternative.

The contradictions of the Prague German-liberal world find a voice even in these very early lines of one of its true sons. It is a voice that, in its plea to salvage that world, forebodes a crisis through which the old ideology would not survive. To what degree, however, would German liberalism—or more precisely the contradictions within Prague German liberalism—inform the very alternatives the postliberal generation would seek? By 1907 Weltsch was committed to Jewish-national identity and politics, in what seemed to him an utter reversal of the sentiments expressed in these essays. But these commitments, as we will see, could themselves not be seen apart from the ideological complex emerging from the constellation of terms peculiar to Prague.[27] But if it is strange to note the persistence of traces of Prague territoriality in the formations designed to escape it, it is no less striking to find the fractures within Prague German-liberal ideology articulated throughout these early writings, in which Weltsch intended nothing so much as to reproduce the pieties of that ideology. Six years after composing it, Weltsch reread the essay on the German folk song, ending with the mission of creativity "for our German nation, whose sons we feel ourselves to be, through thick and thin, until the end of our very lives," and scratched below, "*I revoke everything.*"[28]

SINGERS AND SAVIORS

The early German-liberal identification of Egon Erwin Kisch (1885–1948), who would go on to make his mark as a revolutionary activist and socialist journalist after the First World War, has not been lost on historians and literary critics. The bulk of the Kisch scholarship has appeared in the Communist countries of the former German Democratic Republic and Czechoslovakian Socialist Republic, but the general contours of the views elaborated there curiously resemble those of the liberal historiography in a number of important aspects. In both Communist and Western liberal versions, we find the story of shifting allegiances: Kisch begins as a young German nationalist of the bourgeois-liberal stamp, who is even a member for some time of a liberal-nationalist student corporation; he then vies for entry into the liberal establishment press, only to find his sympathies shifting to a pro-Czech position and, ultimately and most significantly, toward socialism, culminating in party membership and revolutionary activity.

Such a view betrays an extraordinary methodological investment in the transformation from one view of the relationships of nation, culture, and politics to a different alignment of those same terms. An alternative method might find it constructive to accept and focus on the inherent tensions within the early texts, rather than to reduce them to unproblematic reiterations of German-liberal ideology—to unpack them rather than package them—and in so doing to reveal the uncomfortably discordant ingredients of later ideological and aesthetic innovation.

In the earliest extant examples of Kisch's creative work, pieces from satirical student newspapers he and a friend began writing and editing as of the first month of the new century, it is easy to identify a complicity with the fin-de-siècle Teutonic style that Richard Hamann and Jost Hermand have described as a "*volkhaft-nationalistisch*" tendency.[29] Complementary imagery of the writer as a Gothic knight is found in the roughly contemporary texts collected in Kisch's notebooks, the drafts of poems he would publish in 1904 under the title *Vom Blütenzweig der Jugend* (From the blossoming branch of youth).[30] In these texts, drafted by a seventeen-year-old in the first German *Oberrealschule* in Prague, the budding ambivalence of a new generation found its most articulate early expression.

In the long poem to be entitled "Meine Heimat" (My homeland) Kisch provides our most detailed charting of the relations of nationality and culture as read by a Prague German-liberal son.[31] The opening lines of the poem establish a foundation of conflict between two terms, headings under which a row of other presumably synonymous terms fall:

> But us? We have singers
> And we have a homeland;
> But these two stand, foreign,
> Stark as opponents of one another.
> Our poets sing songs
> Of the Spanish bullfights,
> Of toreros, matadors,
> Of Italy's glowing skies
> And forget those of *their* country.

The original drafts of the poem are revealing, because they include several corrections that, while clearly motivated by the needs of poetic meter and to avoid repetition, offer crucial clues to the terms he considered interchangeable: "homeland" (*Heimat*) and "Volk," then "Volk" and "Czechs"—thus the Bohemian homeland and Czech *Volk* are a single figure in the poem, opposed to another set of figures hostile to it. This is a representation of conflict between two principles, like the "two" nations of Prague, German and Czech; as in Weltsch's early essays, there is no consciousness here of the Jews as a third group, or even as a subgroup of one or both of the nationalities. Since the two principles map onto the central art/life binary—German poets at odds with the real life of Czechs—the poem asserts an anti-aestheticist position at the same time as it attacks the national divide. Recall that nationalism in the modern Bohemian context depended upon a construct of three major terms that were seen to be ethically and metaphysically bound to one another: "nation" ("Volk," "people"), "language" ("literature," "culture"), and "territory" ("country," "homeland"). But here, Kisch opens with the discord between the terms "singers" and "homeland," foreign and adversarial figures, in a tragic relation that mocks the healthy, organic interplay of folk and song constructed in Weltsch's 1900 essay. A tracking of these terms through the poem reveals a remarkable dichotomy, a vivisection of an organic whole into two parts that can be kept alive only by artificial means. National poets without a nation (the German poets remaining deliberately out of touch with Czech life: "Our poets say with cowardice / 'We are not chauvinists / But the national struggle demands / That we remain silent about the Homeland / Which we hold as our enemy'") are in opposition to rather than concord with a rich (if voiceless) Bohemian homeland. On the one side of this dichotomy Kisch inscribes the figures "We," "singers," "poets," "chauvinists," "Germans"; on the other the terms "homeland," "*their* [the poets'] country," "Volk," "Bohemian people," "Fatherland Bohemia," and "Czechs." This calls to mind the problematic status of the words "Bohemia" and "Bohemian," which by 1900 had developed the uncomfortable feature of simultaneously including and excluding the German-speaking population of the region. But Kisch's "Bohemia" is neither the mythical German folk landscape of writers Carl Hans Strobl and Fritz Mauthner, nor the cultureless Czech-Bohemia of the nationalist German-liberal scholar Philipp Knoll, but rather the vital Czech nation, the authentic Bohemian *Volk,* the Czech homeland, which is the only possible earth from which an authentic Bohemian (including German-Bohemian) culture can blossom.

The only references to coexistence, the allusions to a world not shuttled into either side of the dichotomy, are represented in the terms "the same, steady sphere" (cohabited by German poets and Czech *Volk*) and "the same battleground." This shared space is no potential ground for culture, merely "battle," "mockery," and "racial conflict." These stand as pathetic miscarriages of a union of poet (German) and *Volk* (Czech) that could have borne art. If Kisch on the surface places all blame on the side of the Germans, the poets who steadfastly refuse to be inspired by their native environment, the text is grounded in the German-liberal paternalism of those poets. Foreshadowing the seemingly insurmountable obstacle of the later Prague German-Jewish literature, the young Kisch sings praises of a simple and tough, pure and loving Czech *Volk;* the poet, singer, and ultimate savior in the text hails from the nation of poets and thinkers.

This theme is taken to another level in Kisch's novella *Dragotin Podravič, der Slovene,* published less than two years after the poem.[32] The Slovene soldier Dragotin feels ethically superior to the decadent German Austrians of his platoon, often bragging to his German comrade about the uncorrupted simplicity of the Slovene people, to whom he has dedicated his life. The contrast between German civilization, cultivation, mannered hypocrisy, and decadent morals on the one hand, and Slavic earthiness, folksy simplicity, and purity on the other, is the central point of this morality play: Dragotin's life is shattered when he learns that a girl from his hometown has been seduced into prostitution by his German commanding officer. The young Wida's fall, and even worse, her parents' complicity, force Dragotin to a painful reassessment of his people. Consider the deployment of the term "culture" in Dragotin's climactic confession:

> The Slovenes are a pious and simple people [. . .] because they could never of their own accord come to the idea of making their life more comfortable, or to change it at all, because they are culturally backward. But when bearers of a new culture come, eloquent and persuasive, then they will take on that culture, and with it its burdens, falsehood, lies, deception, dishonesty, sin. Culture will not be a blessing to them, but a curse; the Slovenes will be brought to the same low level as the other peoples, they will end up like Wida.[33]

The patronizing tone of this treatment was not so visible to Germans of their day as it may be to us. One reviewer found that the most remarkable aspect of the story was that it had been written by a German.[34] The reviewer's confusion is produced by Kisch's rearrangement of the elements of a Prague German-liberal cultural paradigm to the (apparent) favor of the Slavs; but the grounding in that patriarchal paradigm is itself evidence of the author's origins.[35] Dragotin is not, however, the narrative spokesman for the author Kisch;[36] the protagonist is instead a kind of Slavic mirror image of the writer of "Meine Heimat"; he is the antipoet, the would-be savior of an anticultural Slovene *Volk*.

The hero of Kisch's poem "My Homeland," its invisible protagonist, is a bearer of culture; he is the authentic, messianic "singer" whose absence Kisch proclaims:

> Oh, if *I* could! Could I sing
> Of the hundred-towered homeland
> Of the castle, of the palaces,
> Of the fortresses, of the sagas
> Of the ramparts and bastions
> A thousandfold echo I would awaken
> With the songs of the homeland!
> But [oh!] out of each verse
> Stares the impotence, a stark grimace,
> Rejoicing at my misery
> The feeling of envy, or sympathy
> And of impotence
> Let me just spit out the question:
> Country, when will your savior come?
> And the answer I can stammer:
> When your first singer comes!

The future poet, cultural (national?) savior, is identified in the poem as Kisch himself. Throughout the poem, Kisch projects himself into the phantasmagoric figure behind the text, the mythical singer that *could*, *would want to*, and finally *will* unite text and context, poetry and homeland, the German and the Czech, song and folk. His answer to the question, "Country! When will your savior come?," is "When your first singer comes!" That final line itself raises a question to which Kisch waits posed as the answer. In Kisch's second notebook, containing more poems to appear in *Blütenzweig* and further pieces of "Meine Heimat," the following appears:

I Am a Knight
I am a knight, nobility
A coat of arms entire
The pen, that is my weaponry
The verse, it is my squire.[37]

It is a pitiful strophe, but significant in that it makes explicit what had been the omnipresent subtext of the longer poem. Kisch casts himself in the role of the medieval knight-minstrel, subject and object of folk song; he takes the task of the savior onto his own generation. The notebooks themselves (as the published version of *Blütenzweig der Jugend*) represent an attempt to take on this heroic poetic role. This conclusion can be drawn by simple deduction, since Kisch chose to express the impossibility of Prague-German poetry in a poem. But it is explicit as well in portions of the above draft ("If only I could sing of . . . "), as well as in further drafts of the poem, where he adds imagery from the city that foreshadow his later Prague reportage. Further on in the notebooks, we find a poem replete with cascading references to Bohemian kings, Prague's mythical Czech mother Libussa, the ancient castle Vyšehrad, and the Hussite wars.[38] So it is clear that Kisch did not wish to take on the role of singer-savior at some future time, but that he hoped to do it in the above poem itself. It is a poem, then, in which Kisch is doing what he claims he cannot: he sings out about his inability to sing, poetically expresses the inaccessibility of poetic expression, voices his voicelessness with as much eloquence as he can muster.[39]

The German-liberal deification of high culture was passed on to the new generation of Prague German-speaking Jews with writerly ambition, but in their hands it took a different shape. The disturbances that were most repressed in the age of "high" Prague liberalism returned with a vengeance; even in the earliest, clumsily articulated creative products of

Kisch and Felix Weltsch, the inherent discordance of the German-liberal vision of culture in the context of the German-speaking Jewish writer in Prague was not silenced, as it had been by the Concordia poets, but shouted out. That is not to say that the new generation was at once comfortable with discord, with difference—in a word, with their own dilemma. They were merely conscious of the inevitability of at least a confrontation with their condition, in a way that their parents had not been. They still dreamed of a heroic escape from the crisis they sensed, and it is noteworthy that they looked to culture, the fulcrum of German-liberal ideology, for that hope. The bearers of that redemptive culture were to be themselves: the one point in Kisch's poem in which the discordant terms from opposite sides of his dichotomy are put together in a harmonious way is in the title itself, with the possessive pronoun of a German subject united with a homeland that has been coded as Czech—the title itself a German translation of Smetana's 1879 Czech national classic *Má vlast: My Homeland*.

THE REPORTER'S NEW CLOTHES

Kisch is in many ways atypical of the Prague circle writers, even while in other ways he may be seen as a prototypical exponent of later Prague German-Jewish cultural production.[40] He left Prague earlier than did others; he did not study (excepting one semester) at the Charles University, and consequently was not involved in the Lese- und Redehalle; he wrote fiction and poetry, but made his fame in journalism, rather than belles lettres; and finally, because of his central role in the revolution of 1918 and his later radical activity, his name is seemingly inextricably connected to the socialist movement. At the same time, however, each of these divergences from what might appear to be the pattern of the Prague circle writers can also be viewed as remarkably early, well-articulated responses to the contextual problematic behind the work of all of the writers under discussion here. In many senses, "the roving reporter" Kisch would never escape from the discursive prescriptions of culture and nationality of Prague.

Egon Kisch had begun using the pen name Egon Erwin Kisch while still in the *Oberrealschule* where, as we have seen, he developed the ambition to become a writer. Moreover, he fashioned himself as a Prague writer, an artist whose work came out of and in turn fed into the life of his homeland. What he had difficulty deciding was which genre was best suited to this purpose; he tried his hand at poetry and prose, and maintained his early interest in journalism. In his conceptions of each of these, Kisch had in mind a new understanding of the rubric "Prague-German literature."

One way to characterize the transition of Prague-German literature from the Concordia group, by way of the *Jung-Prag* aesthetes, to Kisch's own generation is as a shift of emphasis from the "German" in the term to "Prague." The aim of the German-liberal aesthetic of the latter half of the nineteenth century, I have maintained, was to supersede the inherent tensions in the Prague German context through an artificial reterritorialization to the safe ground of high German culture; the same strategy is apparent in the neoclassicist poetry of the late nineteenth century and the new romantic and aestheticist trends of the fin de siècle. Kisch did not seek to recover the "Bohemism" of Adalbert Stifter; he ignored the possibility of a harmonious, multinational *Landespatriotismus* in an age in which such an aesthetic strategy would have been manifestly anachronistic.[41] Instead, Kisch took pride in his own "marked local patriotism," focusing on the discord and multiplicity within his home city.[42] Prague is the theater for *Aus Prager Gassen und Nächten* (From Prague streets and nights; 1912), Kisch's first collection of reportage; for *Prager Kinder* (Children of Prague; 1913), the stories of the Prague underclasses that had been so studiously ignored in the earlier Prague-*German* literature; for his only novel, *Der Mädchenhirt* (The shepherd of girls; 1914), a naturalist attempt to capture the sociopsychological background of Prague prostitution; Prague provides justification for socialist ideology in his first memoir, *Die Abenteuer in Prag* (Adventures in Prague; 1920), and he once admitted that his later and better-known memoir, *Marktplatz der Sensationen* (Marketplace of the sensations; 1942), could really have been called "Memories of Prague."[43] F. C. Weiskopf, the Prague German-Jewish critic whom socialist historiography proclaimed Kisch's successor, described it this way:

> What is the Prague element in Kisch's work? It is the connectedness to old history; it is an understanding of the vicious and fruitful tension found in regions of mixed nationality; it is the recognition and proper appraisal of the Slavic role in past and present; it is a trace of old Jewish legend and a droplet of Hussite rebellion and a hint of Bohemian baroque; [. . .] it is coffeehouse anecdote and naive folk song; it is curiosity for the wide world and unquenchable nostalgia for home; it is early knowledge of the strength of a minor people's desire for freedom and of the invincibility of truth.[44]

These are precisely the elements that Prague-German literature prior to Kisch's generation sought to cloak behind a facade of high culture.

But subversive as the themes that interested Kisch appear to have been to German-liberal ideology, a distinction must be drawn between subversion of the "classical" German-liberal view of literature and a conscious rejection of the ideology as a whole. Clearly, Kisch's ideological stance from the beginning of his journalistic career in 1906 through to the war could be identified either as bourgeois German-liberal or as anticipatory of his later pro-Czech and socialist position, depending on the historiographical construction. If on the one hand he showed early and consistent sympathy with Czech culture and the life of the Prague underclass, it remained his main professional goal to secure for himself a place in the establishment Prague German-liberal press. While the precise details of his *Burschenschaft* (nationalist fraternity) activity may be obscure, he clearly had a sympathy for the German-liberal Saxonia, a dueling fraternity, more aggressively nationalist and less sophisticated than the Lese- und Redehalle.[45] In any case, Egon's long correspondence with his powerfully German-nationalist brother, Kafka's classmate Paul, reveals that he took the chauvinist aspects of the German-liberal program with rather a large dose of salt.[46]

More interesting than these hints of nationalist sentiment, but not unrelated to them, is Kisch's early and lasting enthusiasm for the emerging chauvinist writer Carl Hans Strobl (1877–1946), whose student novel *Die Vaclavbude* (1902) convinced Kisch that, finally, a true "Prague novel" had been written.[47] The cohabitation within Kisch's sphere of interest of the nationalist ardor of the German student on the one hand, and the vitality of Czech daily life on the other, is harder for the historian looking for ideological trajectory to reconcile than it was for Kisch. The living Prague encompassed both of these elements; he saw them less as mutual enemies than as animated sources of a vibrant *Heimatkunst* powerful enough to replace moribund German-liberal culture. His correspondence with Paul about participation in the new nationalist student journal, *Deutsche Hochschule*, shows an impatience with the journal's (and Paul's) chauvinist rhetoric at the same time that it affirms his enthusiasm to contribute something "student-ish," "Prague-ish," or "national."[48] Egon's reservations about the *Deutsche Hochschule* project come out full force only after the publication of the first issue. In a letter to Paul attacking the programmatic thrust of the journal, Egon claims:

> There really had to be a student novella in there instead—by Carl Hans Strobl, if at all possible—a chatty piece about fraternity loyalty, the first duel and such. Without feuilleton material the thing is just not worthwhile.[49]

Kisch's real commitment was never to the chauvinist ideology behind German-national student life; it was to an authentic homeland art that found solid ground equally in the Czech tavern and on the fraternity dueling field.[50] Inasmuch as Prague German student life was an organic source for literature, Kisch again sought to stress rather than suppress the intricacies of national difference that gave student life its substance. In this spirit, he insisted on making corrections to his essay on dueling sites to locate the conflicting factions nationally and ideologically: the reference to the fraternity Germania was to be qualified *"völkisch"*; the neutral Josefstadt replaced with its former name, the Jewish ghetto (Judenstadt); the setting of a "noble hotel" changed to "noble German hotel." [51]

The pieces collected in *Aus Prager Gassen und Nächten,* then, had a certain appeal to the German-nationalist readers of the *Deutsche Hochschule*. In its intimacy with Prague's deepest and darkest corners, its German author seemed to be reclaiming lost national territory. The journal's editor saw the collection as a monument to the claim that the Germans were "on firm ground and at home" in Prague, and "that they love this their old and beautiful homeland, and know how to appreciate it better than the Czech, who did not come here until much later." [52] Kisch had his own, somewhat different ideas for how his book might appeal to a nationalist student audience. He drafted a review of his own work for *Deutsche Hochschule,* intended to promote the book. Kisch's call to student nationalists does not so much focus on privileging the "German" over the "Czech," but on the work's accomplishment as *Heimatkunst:*

> The young people in German Bohemia should be given the book *Aus Prager Gassen und Nächten* to read. Homeland art! But not petty and philistine, but to the contrary, exuberant and brisk. [. . .] Well, enthusiasm: this first homeland book by a Prague German in decades is of effervescent temperament, drawn from an uncanny familiarity with the Prague streets and nights, in glittering style, everything personally heard, felt, seen, and experienced.[53]

Kisch's prospectus of his own work celebrates the victory of a vital "national" literature over the narrow and lifeless German-Bohemian culture of the old ("petty and philistine") mark. It is symptomatic that Kisch locates the innovative creation of an authentic Prague *Heimatbuch* with the author's personal knowledge of, even identification with, the city he is writing about. In the new Prague German art, as Kisch understands it, the relations among artwork, artist, and *Volk* have undergone a radical transformation.

It is no coincidence that Kisch's contribution went beyond a reconsideration of subject matter in favor of a primary focus on generic innovation. A commitment to the "invincibility of truth" required the disclosure of the tensions within Prague life, the Slavic presence in the contemporary and historical life of the city, and the unsightly aspects of urban underclass life. In his single novel, Kisch displayed a naturalist literary tendency à la Zola.[54] But the shift in subject matter was also closely linked to an attack on the distinctions between high literature and reportage. The reporter Kisch self-consciously identifies himself with the folk singer, the singer of truth, as we see in Kisch's description of the ballads of the blind Czech street singer Methodius:

> His repertoire consists throughout of incidents that all more or less were history, are history, or will be history: ballads. [. . .] Why are he and his kind reproached for primitiveness, naivety, and lack of form, when all these are considered advantages of the folk song, as long as it only expresses feelings? Why should those ballads of Gottfried August Bürger and Edgar Allan Poe be the most highly valued, when they depict neither a single real-life occurrence nor a possible one, but just spooks? Why does the ballad-poet Friedrich Schiller preach irreality? The answer is: a concrete statement is dangerous, particularly in literature, for every truth contains potential criticism and resistance.[55]

In this way Kisch senses a linkage between poetic irreality and high literary forms, both poised against relevance. In the same gesture, he privileges folk ballad and historical subject matter over poetry and fiction. Indeed, Methodius's repertoire mirrors Kisch's own; he sings of the betrayal of Prague by the German officer Windischgrätz, the legendary highwayman Babinsky, the medieval manuscript forgeries, and the Hilsner ritual murder case—all topics that appear in Kisch's writings.[56] The Hilsner case had special meaning for Kisch, as it must have for all of the Jewish Praguers of his generation; the murder of a young girl near the Bohemian town of Polná had catalyzed popular antisemitic sentiments in the country when Kisch, Kafka, and Brod were at impressionable ages. The verse of Methodius, "Hilsner, you wicked one / in the Březina wood what have you done?" echoed Kisch's memory of the taunting of Jewish children on their way to school, as well as other popular verses of the time, such as "Buy from the Jew not anymore / coffee, sugar, wares / the Jews, they've gone and slaughtered / a baby girl of ours." Kisch recalls

hearing these and other "folk songs" and coming upon the idea of uti-
lizing his toy print kit "to publish a newspaper for the enlightenment of
the masses."[57] This powerfully anti-aestheticist construction identifies
grim reality as the immediate inspiration of writing, and writing as po-
tentially redemptive for the masses.

The didactic role of reportage casts Kisch's partiality for folk art in a
different light. Kisch's reportage is, first of all, a search for truth; that
truth has the ring of authenticity when it is voiced from a man of the
people, or from the *Volk* itself—when it is report rather than fiction. In
Kisch's first encounter with hard journalism, his report of a mill fire, he
was faced with the difficulty of recovering and reproducing in text form
the "stone of truth."[58] He concludes, "I defined for myself what a news
report actually represents. It is a form of expression, perhaps even an art
form, although just a minor one." This admission, adorned with (false)
modesty, is more than a reaffirmation of Kisch's role in raising reportage
to the level of art. While professing the "minor" artistic status of reportage, Kisch actually raises it above other literary forms, which depend
upon the author's fantasy. The reporter, in contrast, is the poet of truth.

Thus the claim that reportage is "only a minor" art form is necessary
to its legitimation as relevant, "real," or "true." An author of belles lettres is omnipresent behind the fictive text; with every fantastic turn of
his pen we are conscious of his function as creator, and marvel at his
imagination. The reader of the report, however, must be convinced of
the authority of the chronicle over that of the author; the reporter's skill
is exhausted in his ability to collect the truth. So even the mature Kisch
of the memoirs (and he was by no measure a modest man) retreats from
taking credit as a great writer. He sees himself rather as a great reporter,
even the first great reporter; he is the protean figure who is capable of
inserting himself into every aspect of Prague life on which he reports. He
is at home in the Prague underworld, as a day laborer, in a transient
shelter, in the workingmen's taverns, in commerce with prostitutes. His
voice is not that of a privileged German-Jewish bourgeois from the heart
of the old city, but rather a polyglot bridge to the "other" Prague, the
"Volk." Kisch revels in his own transformation into the other, as in this
description of the end of a three-week stint as an agricultural laborer:

> In Saaz I stop off at a tavern and allow myself a goulash—after all, I have
> earned good money with my hands and have seen no meat for a long time.
> The waiter brings it, and I am already at it with my fork. But then: "Pay up
> front, please." His suspicion is justified; my clothing is tattered, street filth
> clings to my trousers and stockings, and stalks of straw to my jacket.[59]

The reader is given a provocative glimpse of Kisch's cross-dressing before several of these episodes in the realm of the other. Kisch transvests to redress the presumably irrevocable divides between classes and between nations in Prague; the reporter appears in the text itself to resolve what cannot be touched from without. The ironic turn in Kisch's radical anti-aestheticist program is this: the reporter, eschewing the poet's distance from the gritty everyday, transforms himself into aesthetic object.

Kisch's modest remarks on the less artful nature of reportage are, therefore, disingenuous, for his reportorial strategy is not to mask the face of the author behind the authoritative text of the chronicle. On the contrary, the reader is consistently aware of the reporter's presence; his reports, collected by now in various volumes, have the flavor of a traveler's personal adventures.[60] Behind his single-handed identification of the murderer of a tavern keeper are his erotic contacts with Czech working-class women; his exposé of a home for wayward girls is undermined when the reporter himself is exposed by the inmates as their intimate associate; everywhere we find the fusion and confusion of the strands of truth of the cases reported and the frays of the life of the reporter.

Where Kisch personally is not the central figure of the text, he is hiding within the text, as in his survey of representations of bears on Prague houses.[61] An erudite reader of the feuilleton, mistaking Kisch for an outside observer like himself, remarked that the author had missed one of the city's most splendid examples, the two golden bears in the heart of the city, guarding a doorway on the Melantrichgasse (see plate 10). Kisch's response was indignant: of course the house "Zu den zwei goldenen Bären" was his birthplace and home throughout his youth. The episode betrays the way that Kisch does not speak, as does his presumptuous reader, from the perspective of a knowledgeable Prague hobbyist, but from a position of special authority in relation to the nooks and crannies of Prague. Kisch's answer, in essence, scolds his critic: you are right that I do not know the golden bears on the Melantrichgasse, prominent as they are, sir; I am those bears.

Kisch's reportage moves toward erasing the borders between literary text, authorial subject, and context; the perusal of the *Bohemia* Sunday feuilleton became a reading of the person of Kisch at the same time that it made legible the diversity and multiplicity of the life of Prague. In this way, the new genre enabled the young Prague German-Jewish bourgeois to cross out of his shrinking island into the wide world, while offering itself at the same time as a solution to the cultural dilemma facing Prague (at least from the perspective of Kisch and his classmates): his reportage broke down the distinctions between high art and folk song, auteur and *Volk*, German and Czech. In an innovative figuration of the "reporter," then, Kisch confected the national poet-savior of Prague whose absence he had lamented as a youth.

THE "DIFFERENCE" IN "INDIFFERENTISM"

Max Brod (1884–1968) was the first of the Prague circle generation to establish himself in the literary world.[62] While Kisch's early collection of poetry was published at his family's expense by a vanity press, Brod's work was being published, both in Prague and abroad, in such journals as *Der Amethyst, Deutsche Arbeit, Die Gegenwart, Das Leben, Österreichische Rundschau,* and others. The trajectory ultimately traced by Brod's career would in some ways prove more compelling than his work; as early as 1923, Franz Rosenzweig identified this trajectory as *der Lebensweg einer Erkenntnis,* the life path of an idea.[63] It is, to be sure, a different "idea" from Kisch's, or even Weltsch's, and yet there, too, we noted the tendency by historians and critics to reduce lives to ideologies, and texts to illustrations of these. In the case of Brod, the author's own autobiographical work contributes to the image of his life as a sort of conversion narrative.[64] Felix Weltsch's cousin Robert, expanding on Rosenzweig's assessment, summarizes this construction:

> A highly sophisticated and versatile Jewish intellectual, he moved from an almost exclusive and deliberate preoccupation with aesthetic aspects to complete identification with the Jewish people. [. . .] [H]is life proceeded on two tracks [. . .] in this case novel-writing and Jewish engagement.[65]

It would be futile to deny the major transformation evident in Brod's thinking and writing between the first decade of the century and the second, and any such shift merits a certain kind of analysis. Yet, there is a particular ideological effect to the representation of Brod's development as in the above passage, in Rosenzweig's quotable phrase, in Brod's memoirs, and in a considerable segment of Brod scholarship.[66] This compact passage is exemplary in its replication of a dualism with which Brod and his cohort were intensely involved; it reinforces the antinomy that their most innovative cultural products seem to sabotage. In the lines of Robert Weltsch cited above, Brod "moves" from the realm of the aesthetic to the living world, from a fetishist "preoccupation" with the minute field of art to a "complete" national identification. Brod's life journey for Robert Weltsch and others can be represented as the victory of a holistic Jewish "engagement" over a dégagé aesthetic.

A careful consideration of the relationship between the aesthetic text and the national context in Brod's work destabilizes this position, and at the same time allows for a more differentiated discussion of Brod's work both before and after his turn to Jewishness. While Brod's earliest writing is in a manner aestheticist, it is a brand of aestheticism that is more deliberately engineered to confront the difficulties of the Prague national and political context than its more conventionally aestheticist counterparts in the earlier *Jung-Prag* movement and in Vienna, for example.[67] It is also possible to examine more closely the second half of Weltsch's two-track formula, exposing Brod's turn to Judaism as a form of aesthetic engagement, or underscoring the way that Jewishness provides for Brod an avenue for the aestheticization of life.[68] Such readings of the compendious products of the struggle with an art/life dualism challenge the reduction of Brod's literary path to the growing recognition of the primacy of national identification over narrow artistic concerns, or of Zionist ideology over literary assimilationism.

The young Brod fashioned his first published works to conform to an ethico-aesthetic philosophy he called "indifferentism." Brod and those in his cohort thought of Schopenhauer as a source for this "philosophy."[69] Yet, although Brod and others self-consciously selected philosophical and literary models for their early enterprises, it is fallacious to look back to these sources as if they were keys to Prague German culture; what Brod claimed was inspired by Schopenhauer, Bernhard Bolzano, and the Brentanist philosophers of contemporary Austria, or French writers Jules Laforgue and Flaubert, had generally very little to do with the original works. The claimed models were chosen for transparently aesthetic reasons, dictated alternatively by fashion and academic or literary-critical authority. To treat them as sources, in the sense of building blocks for a history of ideas, can be misleading or worse.[70] Brod drew from Schopenhauer a coarse notion of the arbitrary role of destiny, but Brod's indifferentism is optimistic, even lighthearted, beside Schopenhauer.[71]

Brod's indifferentism manifested itself in a naive delight in all things, amounting at the end of the day to an acceptance of the random quality of destiny. Clearly, such a standpoint is related to the more general movement of aestheticism; Brod's delight in all things is an aesthetic and aestheticist epicureanism. But inasmuch as aestheticism itself implies programmatic commitment, indifferentism was intended to stand above it, as little Lo, the child-hero of Brod's emblematic story "Indifferentism," explains:

> I consider everything of equal value, one never needs to strike any particular tune. Every quality of man is human, that is my simple wisdom. [. . .] If I should name this perspective [. . .] then I should like to call it "indifferentism." [72]

Instead of inscribing an aesthetic realm discrete from a nonaesthetic world, a domain that ignores ideology, politics, ethics, and nationality, Brod's indifferentism would subsume all of these into a neutralizing discourse of equanimity and indifference. [73] It might have the optimistic tone it takes on in the figure of Lo, who, mildly crippled, finds an aesthete's pleasure in all things from the vantage of his favorite place, his bed. A more pessimistic brand of indifferentism is found in Brod's second paradigmatic indifferentist hero, Walter Nornepygge, whose recognition of the senselessness of life leads him to contemplate suicide. [74]

Above and beyond "indifferentism," the more conventional aestheticism of the *Jung-Prag* movement and of the French aesthetes held the attention of Brod and others, including, despite himself, Egon Erwin Kisch. [75] Brod's early poetry in particular is clearly derivative of French aestheticist models. There Brod dwells on the erotic moment as an avenue of escape into the realm of the sensual-aesthetic. In a letter to Herwarth Walden, Brod announced his ideal to "present the erotic [. . .] internally," without external trace, in the manner inaugurated by Flaubert. [76]

Around the same time that he was producing his early erotic poems, Brod wrote a series of reviews that in their language as well as choice of subject matter betray an aestheticist agenda. [77] He espoused a critical strategy focused on the internal aspects of the work alone, attacking literary criticism that made use of biographical material and, worst of all, the writer's ideology. [78] He lashed out at *Pan* editor Alfred Kerr when a manuscript was rejected for being too literary, and greeted Walden's new journal with enthusiasm, raving, "finally an independent journal, *only art, without secondary goals* [. . .]" [79] In this respect, the stated program of the *Jung-Prag* writer Paul Leppin's journal *Wir,* to which Brod contributed, is not far removed from Brod's in the first issue of *Arkadia*. [80]

Indifferentism offered Brod an escape from ideology by declaring political, national, social, and even aesthetic identities arbitrary. [81] The Vienna critic Otto Zoff identified "indifferentism" as an aestheticist phase of naturalism, parallel to a similar evolution toward aesthetic equanimity in Renaissance painting.[82] Yet, already in these early reviews of the indifferentist work, Zoff wondered about the "difference" within indifferentism. It may be a coincidence that the primary representative of this literary trend was from Prague, he offered, but then, on the other hand "Prague Jews could be regarded as the prototypes of indifferent people. Raised between Slavism and Germandom [. . .] they strive for political and national neutrality [. . .] which all too often ends in complete passivity."[83] Of course, neither Brod nor any of his cohort could be considered "passive" in that they did each break radically from the aesthetic and the ideology of their parents. The young Brod's innovation was not passive—although it was, in a manner, escapist. Instead of seeking to inscribe a territory for himself, he vowed indifference to any particular territory, and disavowed any claim to one. The creative Lo fashions an alpine landscape out of household objects, a magnificent project that impresses the story's narrator, who is shocked to find its creator's apathy when it is accidentally destroyed.[84]

The radically individualized position of the indifferentist artist has the effect of not overcoming but overlooking, and begging others to overlook, the painful issue of difference, the brand that was fast marginalizing Brod and his generation. In contrast to what is typically characterized as an aestheticist program, where the justification for a pure art divorced from the social and political context is taken for granted, the consciousness of national, social, and ideological difference permeates Brod's early writings. This crucial distinction is encoded within the nomination "indifferentism" itself, which betrays the fact that the first interest was not the concentration on art for itself ("aesthetic"-ism), but rather the calculated indifference to a complex of "differences" that had become impossible to ignore. Brod's sleepy aesthetic indifferentism was not disturbed by the murmurs of Prague history or the clamor of national conflict—it was born out of that milieu.

Prague was the home of indifferentism. It is therefore ironic that, as the "pure" indifferentism of *Tod den Toten!* (Death to the dead!) and *Schloß Nornepygge* (Nornepygge castle) began to seem inadequate, Brod depicted Prague as indifferentism's antidote. In the 1909 novel *Ein tschechisches Dienstmädchen* (A Czech servant girl), the indifferent Wilhelm Schurhaft is sent from Vienna to Prague by his father, who hopes to shake him out of his condition:

> You will get to Prague and your indifference to the outside world and to everything that doesn't take place within yourself will vanish for good. Nothing else is possible in a city where history forces itself on one, and where at

the same time something so strange is becoming history before our eyes, the battle of the two nations. The statues of saints and church towers will invade your eyes, you will encounter baroque facades, touch ancient spires and cannonballs, hear a foreign tongue and the shattering of windowpanes. Your sense of reality will finally awaken.[85]

But Wilhelm Schurhaft at first continues to take little notice of the world outside of himself, as startling as his father imagined it would be to him. The antidote to his sleepy and self-absorbed indifference proved to be not the Prague environment, but the Prague other; he is awakened to the outside world, to the world itself, through the mediation of love. The isolated and insulated Prague aesthete's redemption is made possible by the novel's title figure, a Czech servant girl.

EROTIC SYMBIOSIS I

From the publication of *Ein tschechisches Dienstmädchen* onward, Brod's position toward the aestheticist island became increasingly self-consciously problematized. While he continued to insist upon the criticism of artworks according to more purely aesthetic criteria, and while his attachment to the French aesthetes went on past the century's second decade, these points were balanced by an implied acceptance of the impossibility of living in the insulated world of the aesthete. We are more apt now to find in Brod's work a nostalgia for a world where aestheticism is possible, as in the 1912 essay "Panorama,"[86] or in the following piece, with its longing for the manageability of the old Prague "island":

> Well, since this morning I have been wishing for an island.
> An island to order.
> A love of order is my most secret and truest quality, please do not doubt that. [. . .]
> The Infinite and Context. Now I have named the triumphant enemies of my love of order. [. . .] I am going to go to a government and ask it to give me an island, just a little island to order.[87]

Brod's island is simply "something closed off, my own kingdom," but when the writer sits down to order his own desk, it expands into the world, beyond his capacity to reconcile.

As in *Ein tschechisches Dienstmädchen,* Brod's window to the outside world and instrument of redemption there is love, the same element that dominated his self-contained aestheticist poetry. The poet Else Lasker-Schüler could not remember the names of the works she heard at a reading of Brod's, "but it was always love that came over his lips," she wrote. "Max Brod is a love poet." [88]

There may be some truth in Lasker-Schüler's overall diagnosis:

> I think one can only write love poems in "Prague," where there are so many curves and ramparts; and pure gray figures emerge from the old houses— stone ghosts push the startled hearts to one another. [89]

In any case, if it was love that embraced all things equally in his indifferentist works, it was love that would bring him into the world of action, and into the world of spirit. By 1912, after having heard the Prague lectures of Martin Buber, and with indifferentism behind him, Brod speaks through his character Anton Tätzl:

> I believe in a redemption; in something monstrous behind everything we know something about. I have become pious in a certain way and I have always been, actually [. . .] I will be effusively rewarded one day by something, I think, an experience or an inner transformation. These torments just can't be the last of all goals; one day yet, with my last breaths, I will storm the enemy castle . . . [90]

These lines, published in 1912, promise an ecstatic redemption that the early Brod would have rejected. Yet, Tätzl's redemption in *Der Bräutigam* (The bridegroom) comes by way of his recuperation of a lost passion, and it is that moment of love, the lovers' plan to surrender everything and run off together, that he wishes to preserve. Once the promise is made and the moment achieved, Tätzl shoots himself.

When the eminent literary historian Peter Demetz makes the argument that the element of erotic redemption is present even in Brod's early work, it is no coincidence that he skips over the true indifferentist works and looks to *Ein tschechisches Dienstmädchen:*

> [. . .] even Max Brod's early novels betray much of the instinctive effort to escape from the [Prague] "island," if nowhere else than into the embrace of a Czech plebeian girl. That embrace was the redemption of the fictive hero, but not him alone; it also meant the redemption of the "Volk," overall, a general redemption. [91]

Demetz identifies this literary function as corresponding to the mediating role that Prague circle literary production prescribed for itself; the link between the Czech and Western cultural worlds that Brod and the translators of the Prague circle would form has an analogue in the "erotic symbiosis" of Brod's fiction. [92]

The element of love comes forth in the very early works of Brod as an aesthete's love, an aesthetic moment captured and conserved within the artwork. The erotic symbiosis begun in *Ein tschechisches Dienstmäd-chen* is a key to Brod's later attempts to bridge the cultures of the Prague German-Jewish cultural island and the surrounding Czech culture, as well as his construction of a Jewish nationalism that would serve a cause of universal redemption. Eroticism transforms in Brod's work from a re-treat from ideology into an ideological vehicle. Brod's love remained the center of a circle that began as the isolated aestheticist self and expanded in ever widening ripples, until it circumscribed humanity. Heinz Politzer notes:

> Brod's humanism embraces humanity in social structure and in social need; sympathy, compassion opens itself from the origin of love, storms over into the family, raises itself up and blesses the *Volk* and humanity![93]

These early aesthetic strategies of Brod's, in a completely different and yet parallel manner to Kisch's experimentation with reportage, point up the ways in which the breaches between nations and those between writ-ing and life seemed to be fused into an aesthetic problem. The Kafka texts to be read alongside these examples would be those fragments col-lected in *Betrachtung* (Meditation), with their florid aesthetic style evok-ing fin-de-siècle French models, as did Brod's early poetic work. Mark Anderson, in *Kafka's Clothes,* has already provided a stunning reading of this and the other early Kafka work, and it is a reading that bears sa-liently on these questions of aestheticism.[94] The opening words of *Be-trachtung* serve to launch Anderson's argument:

> Und die Menschen gehn in Kleidern
> Schwankend auf dem Kies spazieren
>
> And people stroll about in clothes
> Swaying on the gravel pathways[95]

This couplet connects Anderson's privileged trope of clothing to the territorial figure of walking we have observed in Kafka's roughly con-temporary correspondence with Oskar Pollak. In both figures, a world of surfaces, interactions, spectacle, and commerce is identified with the universe of the fathers—"clothes" in Anderson's Kafka refer back to Hermann's fancy-goods business. But *Kafka's Clothes* also recuperates Kafka the aesthete: Franz's own fixation on fashion, and his own metic-ulous self-fashioning. Anderson's reading of these dynamics in Kafka from the earliest texts through to his last story unsettles the master nar-rative favored by the Kafka industry, which tends to discount the aestheticist work as undeveloped and contrary to the crystalline, "stripped-down" style of the work after the 1912 "breakthrough." [96] With Kafka, as with less talented members of his cohort, the emergence of modernist literary innovation should not be divorced from its roots in an aesthetic moment that was particularly self-conscious. In Prague, part of the clothing one donned when one went out into the public sphere was one's nationality, and one's language. The performative character of national-ity and language, a feature that seemed to be in conflict with the ro-mantic claims of these to be deeply rooted in immutable subjectivities, was part of these Praguers' daily lives.

The generation of Franz Kafka, Felix Weltsch, Egon Erwin Kisch, and Max Brod grew into an awareness of the dilemma of culture and nation in Prague that the generations before them had been able to repress. Their early explorations of the constellation of issues attached to artistic pro-duction in postliberal Prague point to a tension between aesthetics and politics, art and life, text and context—in other words, the specific pathology of their very particular condition in this time and place put them in a privileged position vis-à-vis a set of issues at the center of the Modern. [97] It remained for them, in the coming decade, to find new ways of coming to terms with life and with art. In doing so, they were never to wander too far from the realm of culture; when they thought about the nature of their crisis and the means of its resolution, it seemed to them that they were thinking about language.

The Territory of Language

From Art to Politics

Die Sprache kann für alles außerhalb der sinnlichen Welt nur andeutungsweise, aber niemals auch nur annähernd vergleichsweise gebraucht werden, da sie entsprechend der sinnlichen Welt, nur vom Besitz und seinen Beziehungen handelt.

For everything outside of the sensory world, language can be employed only allusively but never even with any degree of approximation, since it, with respect to the sensory world, deals only with property and property relations.

aphorism, early 1918

THE STATE OF LANGUAGE

In the first year of the new century, Kafka wrote an entry in a friend's memory album that begins with these lines:

> How many words in this book! Meant for remembrance! As if words could bear remembrance!
> For words make poor mountaineers and poor miners. They carry no treasures from the mountain peaks and none from the mountain depths.[1]

At seventeen years old, Kafka used the metaphor of the mountain to suggest the incompetence of language to delve, to transport, to bear. These words engage territorial imagery to evoke a skepticism about words familiar to those who have read other language skeptics of the late Habsburg empire such as Ludwig Wittgenstein and his less famed predecessor Fritz Mauthner. The fin-de-siècle Habsburg preoccupation with language and its relationship to the material world ranged broadly, but its predominance is unmistakable.

The relation of a proliferation of philosophical and literary reconsiderations of the status of language to the context of a multiethnic empire vexed by language troubles is unlikely to be casual.[2] On the other hand, to posit such a relation does not yet begin to answer the question of how "language" as a figure functioned in these spheres. In the Vienna context, Joseph Peter Stern identifies language as a fortress of "shelter and solace" from a crisis of values, venturing that the compulsion toward thought about language had "all attributes of an ideology except for one: what is fully lacking here is political power."[3] A close reading of Prague texts and contexts at the fin de siècle calls into question this sharp disjuncture of the realms of language and of politics. Strangely, an unprecedented skepticism about the representational capacity of language went hand in hand with the coupling of language with material concepts such as property and power. In this time and this place, the assumptions that language bears meaning and reflects reality fell prey to two emerging and apparently contradictory notions: that language was an artifice that could refer only to itself, and that it did not reflect as much as it constituted power, possession, or "territory."

Fritz Mauthner was a Jewish novelist from Bohemia, a zealous German nationalist, and the philosopher who wrote *Contributions to a Critique of Language*. The links among his multiple identifications began to occupy Mauthner when he wrote his memoirs. Looking back at his youth, he reflected, in an unfortunately quotable phrase, that the nineteenth-century Bohemian landscape had "predestined" him to turn to thought about language.[4] Thus a few lines in Mauthner's 1918 reminiscences would launch a historiographical tradition in the way cultural production in Bohemia was regarded: as the fruit of a terrain torn asunder by a national conflict, which in turn was framed by a heightened consciousness of language.

But this retrospective reflection of Mauthner's ought to be revised. For the preoccupation of the literature of the period is no more striking than the fact that a discussion of language had become the exclusive figure of political discourse in Prague. Speech was no mere vehicle of ideological debate; it occupied the whole space of "politics," carving out territories of sovereignty for the full spectrum of potential ideological interests. There is a serious problem, therefore, in reducing the role of language in Prague politics and culture in the way it has been in Mauthner's lines and by many of his readers—namely, to a vulgar, reflexive relation that identifies in Kafka's work the depiction of an essential "language conflict" taking place around him.

In the case of Kafka, the constellation of writer, literature, and nation discussed in the previous chapter is particularly complex. We find traces in his work of Jewish identification coupled with a powerful ambivalence, not only toward Jewish nationalism or Zionism, as has often been noted, but toward identification with any community whatsoever. "What do I have in common with Jews?" he noted in his diary in early 1918. "I have hardly anything in common with myself [. . .]" [5] Still, the most striking moment in Kafka's extant writings with regard to the problem of the self, culture, and national community may be an earlier diary passage, of December 25, 1911. This is the five-page essay on the literature of minor nations such as the Yiddish theater and the Czech cultural revival. The passage is the centerpiece for Deleuze and Guattari's discussion of the politics of Kafka's work, the power of which they locate in the particular linguistic operation called "deterritorialization." Kafka's diary entry and the two theorists' critique of it thus provide a bridge from the aesthetic dilemma we have seen facing Weltsch, Kisch, and Brod to the possibility of a political engagement, mediated by way of a reassessment of language. Nor is it mere coincidence that the terminology Deleuze and Guattari coin for this politicizing function of language revolves around metaphors of territory: "deterritorialization," "reterritorialization," "territoriality."

A return to Mauthner's Bohemia is needed to reveal the ways in which the discursive parameters of Prague irresistibly politicized the writing we are exploring. Rather than elaborating intricate strategic links between aesthetic text and political territory, the Prague German-speaking Jewish writers of this generation took for granted the shared terrain of language and politics. The question with which to begin, therefore, is how, in Kafka's Prague, "language" and "territory" had come to be mutually inextricable.

THE LANGUAGE OF STATE

The Bohemian "language conflict" had taken shape in the nineteenth century, operating almost from the start as a signifier for broad and complex processes of political transformation. The image of German as the natural language of state for the Habsburg monarchy, as having grown organically into that role since the early modern period, only to encounter a challenge to its authority rather suddenly in the nineteenth century, was a myth constructed in response to that very challenge. It is easy to forget that the legal status of German as the principal language under the monarchy was established as a deliberate program, and moreover that it was technically the official state language only before 1848; thereafter it became a "regional language" [*Landsprache*], albeit obviously a privileged one.[6] But it was still later in the nineteenth century that the language conflict came into its own, becoming shorthand for a general cultural and political crisis.

With Czechs in control of the Prague municipal government after 1861, the language of instruction in the city schools came almost immediately to debate.[7] Since the German liberals maintained political control at the regional level until the end of the 1870s, the turning point in the legal battle for the status of particular languages in Bohemia at large was not until the spring of 1880, with the Stremayr Language Ordinances for Bohemia and Moravia. This legislation gave co-official status to Czech in the Czech lands, along with German. They were nonetheless understood to be anti-German measures, since educated Czechs would know German while the reverse would not necessarily be the case, and the provincial civil service, it was feared, would be passed into Czech hands. This prospect led nationalists to think increasingly about carving mixed-language areas into smaller, more arguably monolingual districts. By the time the crucial question of language at the famed Charles University came to a head in 1881, leading to a total division of the institution into autonomous Czech and German units, the pattern for a long-term power struggle that would outlive the Habsburg state had been set.[8]

The Czechs at first favored the strategy of dual official languages in Prague and Bohemia, a policy tellingly designated *Utraquismus*, a term with the veneer of neutral Latin but inextricably associated with the Hussite tradition.[9] From the first, residents of the predominantly German parts of Bohemia, who only rarely understood Czech at all, perceived this to be a hostile policy.[10] From the vantage point of the German liberals in Czech lands, the language conflict more generally was an aggressive attack from the side of the newly empowered Czech majority, with the German-speaking community mounting justifiable defensive maneuvers in response. Within a few decades, many of those living in majority German areas contiguous to Saxony and Lower Austria would become the most enthusiastic supporters of *völkisch* nationalist ideology, and, more rarely, even of political union with the German Reich. The German liberals, in contrast, were obliged to stand both for the Habsburg legacy and for the protection of Germans in Bohemia and Moravia.

Thus, there was a conflation in German-liberal discourse of German interests and the general interests of the state; German nationalism was called upon to hold the state together after other nationalisms had threatened to tear it apart; a single "duty as Germans and as Austrian patriots" manifested itself in the two-pronged goal of "protection of the Germans and state order."[11]

This conflation of the interests of one linguistic community and the universal interests of the state was predictably expressed as an issue of language. The challenge to the primacy of the German language in Austrian crown lands was immediately recognized as an attack on the state, since any solution to the problem required a discussion not only of what the state language (*Staatssprache*) was or should be, but of what a "state language" was, what it could mean for a state to "have" a language. The Bohemian German-liberal politician Ernst von Plener attacked an 1884 proposal on the language question for raising this dangerous issue:

> You go [too far] and it seems, when you say in your address that you don't know what a state language is, it also follows from this resolution that you no longer know what the [a] state is [*daß Sie nicht mehr wissen, was der Staat ist*] [. . .][12]

The ambiguity of "der Staat" in the above sentence, which could refer either to the specific state of the Habsburg monarchy or the general concept of the state, suggests that this challenge of traditional assumptions represents an action both treasonous and anarchistic. In fact, it was neither, since the proposals represented a reorientation of the model of a Habsburg state that was to remain in place. But for politicians like Plener, a rethinking of the centralist, German-led state must be defined both as anti-Austrian and as a challenge to order as such. The liberals were those most sensitive to the potential of the language conflict in the Habsburg monarchy to lead to questions of the existence of the state.

The use of the language question as a code for a contest of nationalities, which in turn contained complex and explosive rethinking of class relations and ideology, took place on various levels of discourse. The state itself sponsored that coding, refusing in the 1869 census to allow any national, ethnic, or linguistic category to be entered, but in censuses after 1880 providing a space for "everyday language" (*Umgangssprache/ obcovací řeč*). This category was explicitly defined as linguistic rather than national.[13] Of course, the effort on the part of the government to deflect national conflict by speaking only of linguistic difference was ill fated; for language was to turn out to be the most politically charged issue of all in those peripheral spheres of declining German power.

LINGUISTIC BORDERS

> He had to walk all the way to the Karmeliterstraße to the German school, such a long way into the completely strange and foreign realm, and the Czech school was so nearby [...][14]

Egon Erwin Kisch reproduces the way territory in his Prague was carved out by language, here from the viewpoint of a Czech boy sent by his mother to the German school. By the first decade of the new century, with Czechs in control of the Bohemian Diet, as well as the Prague Municipality and local delegations to the Reichsrat, it was incumbent upon German communities all over Bohemia and Moravia aggressively to assert their presence and the status of their residences as German or as mixed areas. Census returns provided data for a new mapping of the country according to the "everyday language" of the respondents. This mapping process, as we see in the text above, took place within Prague itself, with necessarily more complex results than in the monolingual regions.

In the contiguous and predominantly German areas of northern and western Bohemia (hardly yet known as the Sudetenland), the issue was simpler: the definition of a linguistic border between the predominantly German-speaking parts of Bohemia and all the rest. Even this border proved difficult to define, and raised rather than solved the question of what to do with this implicitly new-defined territory. It could be monolingual, along with the purely Czech areas of the country; there were some radical voices, increasing in numbers, to separate from Bohemia and join the German Empire; and even its German-liberal representatives gradually came to a proposal of segregation of Czech- and German-speaking administrative units within Habsburg Bohemia.[15] Proposals like these naturally inflamed the mania for linguistic-border drawing and increased the insecurity of German speakers in isolated or mixed communities.

German-liberal newspapers such as *Bohemia* watched the border closely, reporting jubilantly at the opening of a new German linguistic-border school [*Sprachgrenzschule*] or, more often, lamenting that another had closed.[16] Everywhere we find this rhetoric identifying language with territory, linguistic borders to be defended by fortresses in the form of German-language schools or community centers. Attacks on German minorities, whether in the form of legal action limiting German-language use or persecution by the Czech populace, were routinely represented as the acts of marauding barbarians (a not unfamiliar chord in German-liberal discourse).[17] *Bohemia* even scoldingly reported when property [*Besitz*] passed from German to Czech hands, as if the border were slipping from house to house.[18] The term *Besitz* or "property" also directly implies territory, as an estate. As imagined borders were shifted according to census results and elections, with very real effects, the term *Nationalbesitzstand* (state of national property) came into currency, suggesting a calculable sum of national wealth and especially land held.[19] In a discourse where territory was represented by language, property loss meant the erosion of a territorial border, as well as a diminution of (German) language within Bohemia. As threatened German minorities of the Bohemian and Moravian hinterland fled their shrinking "language islands," there was felt a simultaneous degeneration of coterminous figures of land and of language.

The language-territory equation was often articulated in the protest over the "*Tschechischerklärung*" (designation as Czech) of towns of long-standing mixed language, such as Pilsen/Plzeň, where a pronouncement of Czech-language identity was set against a historically justified right of "*Bodenständigkeit*," attachment to soil or to "*Heimat*."[20] Largely symbolic gestures such as these were correctly assessed to signal the beginning of a fatal crisis for German minorities of the Bohemian and Moravian hinterland, as well as for towns of mixed populations, even Prague. The Prague German community was called upon for financial support for the "fortresses" of German culture in remote outposts.[21]

It is not surprising that the language of street signs in Prague would become critical markers in a battle for symbols.[22] By adding Czech translations below the German street names, the aldermen meant to acknowledge the Czech community in the city. When the Czech-controlled municipality later eliminated the German superscripts, and then declared the untranslatability of the Czech names back into German, they meant these signs to serve as victory banners. Street signs, as well as the Czech-language shop signs required even on German businesses operating out of city-owned buildings, along with the numerous Czech-language theaters and community centers, all staked out the jewel of the Moldau as Czech territory. German Praguers took these symbols as seriously as they did more concrete campaigns to do the German community financial harm.[23] The "czechization" [*Tschechisierung*] of institutions in the city—

and it should be stressed again that the term referred to the exclusive imposition of the Czech language, rather than to the transfer of control to ethnic Czechs—became synonymous in the German press with the collapse of the city into "anarchy."[24] As engaged as *Bohemia* was in this battle of territorial metaphor, it was surely cynical of the newspaper to mock the aldermen's efforts to change the order of the German-Czech notices in train stations, as though it were a petty issue.[25]

Gestures on the part of the Czech administration with regard to public language policy were not meant to aggravate or even damage the German-speaking community, as the German-liberal press claimed. Rather, they were designed to shatter the German-liberal image of a Prague and a Bohemia that were culturally and historically integrated into German territory. The reterritorializing gesture of German-liberal high culture, which for centuries had maintained Prague's position along the axis defined by Vienna, Weimar, Munich, and other great German "centers," no longer seemed viable. With that German-liberal fiction annulled, the act of speaking German in Prague and other parts of the Czech lands was no longer the same.

POSSESSING GERMAN IN PRAGUE

It was to be expected that the image of the German spoken in Prague would change with the emergence of this powerful discourse of language and territory. Up until a certain point in time, *Prager Deutsch,* or Prague German, was thought to be exemplary, and the Prague Germans themselves exaggerated the claim, regarding themselves as speakers of the "best" or "purest" High German of all German-speaking lands.[26] They attributed this result to the educational level of the Prague German elite and its insulation from any lower-class dialect. But this image of Prague German had changed radically by 1893, when the phoneticist Augustin Ritschel took a second look at it from his seat in the relatively new-founded German Reich:

> If, in the "pre-March period" [before 1848] and still in the fifties and sixties, many educated Praguers prided themselves on the "purity" of theirs, the "best" German pronunciation, then this was either because of their ignorance of actual German phonetics, or else because they did not employ common Prague German speech, but rather a deliberately selected pronunciation that was learned at school or, more likely, from the stage. This appears affected to the natural speaker.[27]

Ritschel himself significantly (albeit without explanation) designated the nationalist revolutions of 1848 as the pivotal point in the evolution of this image of Prague German. It appears that the pre-March view, whereby insulation from contamination by the dialect of a German *Volk* was thought to have positive effects, had given way to the view that the isolation of *Prager Deutsch* represented a linguistic pathology.[28] The crystalline High German that Praguers were thought to have spoken seemed suddenly an outrageous, artificial creation, a stage German, a theater prop, with no relation to the *real* spoken German. Ritschel regarded the stilted affect of Prague German to be obvious "especially to any German from the 'Reich,'"[29] the homeland of the living *Volk*. From the perspective of a "natural" condition of a German on German soil, Ritschel and his compatriots were, according to this account, sensitive to the artifice of a language divorced from German earth. It is easy to imagine an older Praguer reading this article and wondering how such an indictment had come to replace the praise for the clean purity of Prague German. By the next decade, a young writer like Egon Erwin Kisch would begin to rebel against the eloquent High German poetry of the Concordia poets and turn his gaze to the particularity of Prague.

Later in his essay, Ritschel took a bird-watcher's interest in the rare and endangered species of authentic *Prager Deutsch,* relating its heyday to a bygone age of friendly interaction of Czechs and Germans in Bohemian mixed-language urban centers. At that time, Ritschel claimed, since German was the accepted lingua franca of educated classes of both Czech and German background, and since even native German speakers were from childhood exposed to a German pronunciation with a strong Czech influence, a curious Slavo-Germanic phonetic hybrid was in widespread use. Here the linguist recognized an organic and authentic idiom, informed from a Czech *Volk* and resulting from a healthy interaction of High German and surrogate dialect. The recent "social division" resulting from the "sharpening of national oppositions" was the cause of an unnatural distancing of the German elite from Czech influences and its attempts to affect "a pronunciation as close as possible to stage German."[30] This new interpretation of the language of the Germans of Prague, based on metaphors of degenerate isolation rather than of salutary insulation, is the one that would prevail after the century's turn, and actually outlive *Prager Deutsch* itself.

From the late nineteenth century through the considerations of *Prager Deutsch* by Kafka scholars in the 1960s, there is an apparent disagreement not only on the character and quality of the language, but also on which language was actually under discussion. Is it the German spoken by native speakers in Prague, or in Bohemia at large, or in those parts of Bohemia and Moravia in which Germans were in the minority?[31]

Egon Erwin Kisch took an early interest in the study of *Prager Deutsch,* producing two witty pieces of journalism, "Prager Deutsch" and "Vom Kleinseitner Deutsch und vom Prager Schmock,"[32] which celebrate the particularities of a German blessed with the benefit of an accessible Slavic and even Yiddish syntax, vocabulary, and idiom. The essays offer an alternative both to the pre-March image of an insulated, elite High German and to the diagnosis of an atrophied island German. For Kisch, contact with Czech and with Yiddish is a source of enrichment for *Prager Deutsch* (by which he means the German spoken in Prague itself); it is a remnant of a linguistic and cultural symbiosis. In some cases, as in the word for "closet" (Prague German *Almer,* Czech *almara*), one can no longer trace which language has informed the other. This last point was developed by Kisch in response to a rebuttal to his original *Bohemia* feuilleton by an angry scholar who would sooner recognize any number of technical linguistic explanations for Prague German particularity over "enrichment" from the Czech, in this case noting the probable dissimulation from the Latin word *armarium.*[33] The professor's rebuttal calls upon general linguistic laws throughout to deflect the uncomfortable local patriotism implicit in Kisch's collection of "Praguisms."

Although Kisch actually ended his first essay with a warning about the threat of "localisms" to German in Prague, representing an "internal" decay more ominous than the "external" national threat, the conclusion seems tacked on at best, and vanishes in a later version. The placement of the essay in *Die Abenteuer in Prag* and the enthusiasm with which Kisch collected "Praguisms" in his notebooks and presented them in the essays implies that, on the question of Prague German, he stood closer to the German-liberal champion Heinrich Teweles. A week later, writing in the same journal, Teweles expressed his "pride" in the idiosyncrasies of the local language; as would be the case for any dialect, such local peculiarities only fortified the case for the authenticity of German *Volkstum* in the city.[34]

The literary historians of the 1960s and after relied neither on the obscure article by Ritschel nor on Kisch's essays in their consideration of *Prager Deutsch.*[35] In fact the most consistently cited text in the secondary literature seeking links between *Prager Deutsch* and the litera-

ture of Kafka and his contemporaries is the confession of Fritz Mauthner, who in 1918 wrote in his memoir:

> As a young man [I] was filled with plans to be a writer. And for the art of
> words I lacked the living word of an idiom of my own [*fehlte mir das leben-
> dige Wort einer eigenen Mundart*]. [. . .] In my inner linguistic life I do not
> possess the strength and the beauty of an idiom. And if someone should tell
> me: without an idiom, one is not in possession of a true mother language—
> then I could perhaps cry out even today, as in my youth, but I could not call
> him a liar. The Germans that live close together in the Bohemian border re-
> gions, the Germans of northeast, northwest, and western Bohemia, have their
> beloved and true dialects. The German from the Bohemian interior, sur-
> rounded by a Czech rural population, speaks no German idiom, he speaks a
> paper German, as long as his ear and mouth have not oriented themselves on
> a Slavic pronunciation altogether. There is a lack of the fullness of earth-
> grown expression, there is a lack of fullness of idiomatic forms. The language
> is poor. And with the fullness of idiom, the melody of idiom is lost as well. It
> is characteristic of this that a person does not have any distance from his own
> language, either: the German Bohemians delude themselves and say at every
> opportunity that they speak the purest German. The poor souls! As if dialects
> were impure![36]

Mauthner, the German nationalist founder of the "linguistic-border-
land novel" genre, was deeply involved in the discourse that identified
language with territory. Mauthner's rhetoric reflects the alliance of language-territory metaphors with a *völkisch* (or *Blut und Boden*) discourse
setting an organic space of linguistic and territorial wholeness against
fragmentation, artifice, and lifelessness. Standing between him and his
dreams to become a poet was the lack of "the living word" of "an idiom
of [his] own." "His own" does not quite reproduce the territorial aspect
of "*eigen*," which in noun form is synonymous with "*Besitz*": possession, property, lordship, territory. Returning to an organic metaphor,
Mauthner declares that in his "inner linguistic life" he does not possess
("*besitze*") a true idiom. The deprivation of an organic German *Volk*
around him and true German ground under his feet has robbed Mauthner of the "*Besitz*" of that to which everyone should be entitled: a mother
tongue.

Mauthner's text instructs us that within the borders of Bohemia, a
German's geometry must reverse Euclid's: the periphery is centered, and
the central regions marginalized. Mauthner envies the living German
communities of the periphery, where German speakers are planted
thickly [*dicht beieinander*] as the trees of the *Böhmerwald*, and speak
with thick accents; the journey to the interior is a voyage into the desert,

where German speakers are fewer and farther between. Dialect disappears in a linguistic landscape that is like a blank sheet of paper. *Prager Deutsch* is a paper language, desolate and impoverished, lacking roots and any organic ("earth-grown") expressiveness (*erdgewachsener Ausdruck*). If "language" was recognized by German Bohemians as well as their Czech adversaries as having the power to inscribe borders of political control, Mauthner asserts a sinister corollary: the loss of territorial control for Germans meant the surrender of their own voices.

MOTHER TONGUE AND FATHERLAND

Reading Mauthner, or the bits and pieces of his text cited by most critics reflecting on Prague language, it is easy to believe that the constellation of linguistic and territorial identities in Prague revolved around two national poles: "German" and "Czech." It is just as easy to forget that Mauthner, this thoroughly "pugnacious" German nationalist, was himself never forgetful of the particular ambivalence of his position as a Jew. His remarks on the burdens of an aspiring writer in his childhood milieu are introduced in fact with the complaint that

> I had to consider not only German, but also Czech and Hebrew, as the languages of my "forefathers" [. . .] I had the corpses of three languages to drag around with me, in my own words.

Later on in his memoir, Mauthner goes further to describe the role he feels his Judaism has played in interfering with the realization of his aspirations as a German writer:

> As a Jew in a bilingual country, just as I possessed no proper native language, I also had no native religion, as the son of a completely religionless Jewish family. Just as I did not precisely share in common the building stones (words) with my people (the Germans), we also did not share a common house—the Church. [. . .] Precisely because the Church is so through and through human, earthly, thus it is a poetic loss not to stand from the start on this common ground. [. . .] My poetic language [lacked] the highest and deepest: the earth.[37]

In contrast to what is often said about the German-liberal Jews of the presumed golden age of assimilation before the Prague circle, Mauthner makes it clear, here and in other writings, that he saw Jewishness to be at the root of his feeling of rootlessness. He lacked access to poetry, not only because of the fissure between the language available to him in a Bohemian country town and the linguistic grounding of German territory proper, but because his Judaism, in the confessional sense, prevented him from compensating for that fissure and from recovering a German space for himself as a poet. The Church (which church, it might legitimately be asked) is the "house" of the German people. In Mauthner's metaphor it seems to be constructed from the building blocks [*Werksteine*] of German words, "stones" of German earth. The church is "earthly" and offers a "ground" to its members [*irdisch, Boden*]. Mauthner, a Jewish German living among Czechs, is homeless twice over.

These revelations are remarkable primarily because they hail from Fritz Mauthner, that supposed paragon of German-Jewish assimilation and German-liberal chauvinism, the man who perhaps best exemplified, in Max Brod's words, "that precise generation of Jews who counted themselves as Germans almost completely unproblematically, without a second thought, and who fanatically engaged in a pugnacious Germanism."[38] Part of the reason that these excerpts from Mauthner's memoir seem to contradict this image of his "unproblematic" German identity relates to a problem of retrospective sources: Mauthner's memoir was published in 1918, in a context more receptive to Brod's view of nationality, language, and culture than that portrayed in Mauthner's earlier novels. A Jewish-national review of Mauthner's memoir, published in the same year, had nothing but praise for Mauthner's washed-out description of German-Jewish assimilation—"without mother tongue, without native faith," a generation to be replaced by youthful Jewish strength, an old-new mother tongue, and an old-new motherland.[39] Mauthner's memoir was at once useful for such readings, in a way that could not have been possible had he been born in Berlin.

Germanophone Jewish writers in Prague had been engaged in a provocative rethinking of these issues even earlier in the decade, one example being Brod's essay entitled "The Jewish Poet of German Tongue."[40] By 1913, when Brod published the piece in the Zionist student organization's seminal anthology *Vom Judentum,* there was a more general recognition of the tensions inherent in the Prague German-Jewish writer's relationship to a national literature that had been intuited by Kisch and Weltsch a decade earlier. Brod wrote of the general denial on the part of "modern theoreticians" of the possibility of Jewish access either to "great poetic development" on the one hand, or to "naive feeling" on the other. This distinction echoes Kisch's dualism between poetic literature and naive folk song, which, as discussed above, was a code for the German and Czech nations, respectively. Brod, in a formulation in which the German and Czech models remain coded but are not made explicit, contrasts the dilemma of the Jewish poet in a Western setting with Jewish access to both poetry and folk culture through other languages and "national" literatures. There was high national poetry in biblical and post-biblical Hebrew, and authentic Jewish folk culture in contemporary East European Yiddish. Brod found himself caught between East and West, in a sense: positioned to look upon but not to touch either Hebrew (or German) "heroic power" and "biblical [classical] greatness," or Yiddish (or Czech) "folksy naivety" and "Eastern Jewish [Slavic] simplicity."[41]

Brod was out to resolve a specific problem with this construction: the essential alienation of the Jewish writer from the instrument of German language, a lexicon "pulsating" with German (i.e., alien) sentiment (*mit dem von deutscher Gefühlsarbeit durchpulsten Wortschatz*). The reference to "pulse" reminds the reader of the image evoked in the title of the essay: the body of the poet, its substance and essence, is "Jewish," while only his tongue is "German." The "pulse" of his language is foreign to him, an image that is kin to the *völkisch*-racialist figure of "blood." The German language, claims Brod, is not "the inheritance of his ancestors." The German-Jewish poet is alien to German; he holds it as "foreign property" (*fremder Besitz*).[42] Brod, like Mauthner, confirms his simultaneous disenfranchisement from language and territory. Yet Brod seeks a reterritorialization via the legacy of grounded Hebraic and East European language that Mauthner never identified. The window to Brod's reterritorializing gesture is opened by the poet's immersion in Jewish national identity, through which, by analogy, he can approach the relationship between the German language and *Volkstum* from which he would otherwise be excluded:

> It is my opinion that, on the path to a deep Jewish national sensibility, access to the true German folk spirit is opened for the first time to the Jewish poet of German tongue [. . .] The joy of one's own *Volkstum* is closer to the joy of a foreign *Volkstum* than is the attempted contrivance of a foreign *Volkstum* [. . .] for [the Jewish nationalist] has "Volk" within him.[43]

Brod's designation of the German-speaking Jew's own language as "foreign property" is not unusual, as evidenced by the comparable rhetoric of Mauthner and others. The typically Brodian solution represented in the above citation lies in the promise of a recovery of authenticity through the medium of "analogy." The notion that folkdoms are mutually translatable and the faith in the redemptive power of an abstracted, universalist "Volk" each represent typical ways in which Brod finds refuge from the tensions he and others identify in their situations. Brod would later coin the term *Distanzliebe* to describe the alien and some-how privileged love of German by the German-Jewish writer.[44] But these attempts to leap over the grain of the conflict that had come to the sur-face of Prague German-Jewish writing, just as Brod's earlier indifferen-tist and erotic-symbiotic solutions, were not the strategies adopted by others in his position.

CONTRADICTIO IN ADIECTO

Max Brod was sensitive to a shifting discourse that was severing the Ger-man tongue from the body of the German-Jewish writer in Central Eu-rope. His desire to gloss over that irretractable rupture, even to turn it to his advantage as a grounded German poet, stands in sharp contrast to the thinking of his friends Hugo Bergmann and Franz Kafka. Re-viewing a volume of poems by the Jewish writer Alfred Wolfenstein in 1918, Brod marveled that the poet had created "a Jewish mode of lin-guistic expression within the German language, as paradoxical as that sounds."[45] This was precisely the "paradox" from which there was no escape for those German-Jewish Praguers who likewise identified the rupture, but who did not see in it a way back to a grounded German literature. As early as 1913 Brod had puzzled out the irrevocable rift within the Prague German-speaking Jewish poet, while somehow re-coiling from what would seem to be its necessary consequences.

The emerging sense of a disparity between an essential self and its in-strument of expression was evident very early in the circle of Prague Zionists, assembled in the student organization Bar Kochba. In the writ-ings of their most creative and articulate exponent, Hugo Bergmann (1883–1975), this estrangement is represented to take place simulta-neously on the levels of the individual self and the Jewish community, and, finally, to be symptomatic of a universal modern condition. For Bergmann, the deterritorialized self stands at the center of a crisis mov-ing outward in concentric circles.[46] Given the specific function of the no-tion of language, as we have identified it so far, it is not surprising that the young Bergmann fixed on language as a primary concern of a Zion-ist. The absorption of Hebrew language was the central element of the program he drew out for the Prague student Zionist group. As early as 1901, upon accepting Bar Kochba leadership, Bergmann declared that "a Zionist student without knowledge of Hebrew is a *contradictio in adjecto!*"[47]

This maxim is all that remains of Bergmann's acceptance speech as recalled by Bar Kochba alumni as they recorded the organization's history a half century later on another continent. It was memorable perhaps for its formulaic simplicity, for its identification of a personal task incumbent upon every Prague student committed to the Zionist project. Or perhaps what stuck in the mind was the style of this student Zionist commandment, which escapes in a breath from its own programmatic German into a universalist Latin—but not into Hebrew.

In the decade that followed Bergmann's acceptance speech, the slogan was transformed into eloquent arguments in his articles.[48] With a kind of ritualist persistence, he repeated his emphasis on absorbing Hebrew. The texts themselves stand as representations of the same self-conscious condition that Brod described as the schism felt by the Jewish writer of German tongue. The more creative Bergmann became in constructing his German essays, the more convinced he became that this language kept him prisoner, binding him to foreign territory, hindering his creative powers. We must look back again to the power of the term "language" in the Prague context if we are to understand what circumstances brought Bergmann to this recurring act—what drove him to question, repeatedly, in eloquently assertive German, the possibility of speaking German.

Bergmann's vision of the role of Hebrew as an instrument of liberation from this Promethean condition is expressed in his 1904 essay "On the Meaning of Hebrew for Jewish Students." Here he maintained that a language normally thought of as dead and antiquarian should be a source for the future, a "bearer of a new, burgeoning life [. . .]" Hebrew would serve this end first of all as a means of self-knowledge, which Bergmann interestingly described as knowledge of the other:

> If you want to know the Jewish people, if you want to participate in discussions of issues that determine its life, then—first learn to understand its language![49]

This imperative reminded the acculturated readers that they were yet strangers to the "Jewish people," even as Bergmann's texts share Brod's fantasy that German was inherently alien to its Jewish speakers. The Hebrew curriculum for the Prague cultural Zionists entailed a recognition of the alienation of Western Jews from a language of their own as the first step of a self-conscious attempt to recover that loss, to unite themselves with their own Judaism and the Judaism of the rest of the world and of history. They were to create a Jewish territory, again, synonymous with language, in exile. Hebrew would be the instrument of a "unification movement," which was in fact a kind of solution to the same dilemma of estrangement identified by Brod. The project amounted to no less than the creation of a new Judaism:

> We must think of the unfolding of this [new] Jewish character [*Eigenart*] as a great synthesis: *a synthesis of the national spirit of our people with European culture.* Both must work together, completing one another, growing into one another.[50]

The "synthesis" unites spirit and culture, Jewish and European identities, *Hebrew and German*. In Bergmann's messianic-Zionist moment of fusion, an internal Jewishness was joined to the instrument of German language and culture—the Jewish writer with his German tongue, content with form. Biblical Hebrew, packed with Jewish spirituality, was the vehicle through which juxtaposed elements could grow into and complete one another, merging in erotic fulfillment. For Bergmann, as for other Zionists of his time, modern Hebrew represented the inscription of a new and living Jewish space for a revived Jewish people. This Zionist proposition had particular gravity for a writer in Bergmann's position. As we have seen in Brod's essay, general assertions made in Prague about the relationships of languages, literatures, and peoples were automatically sorted into structures resembling the familiar Czech-German constellation. Just as Brod evokes "German" and "Czech" when he means to speak of "Hebrew" and "Yiddish," so does Bergmann's biblical Hebrew resemble classical German: rich and eternal, but not the language of a living *Volk*. He is therefore delighted by Bialik's technique of informing his modern Hebrew poetry with the content of Yiddish folk songs: reminiscent of the early Kisch's longing for a union of the German poet and Czech folk, Bergmann wished for a synthesis and the creation of a new "Hebrew."[51] Need it be reasserted that, in Prague, the creation of a new language cleared a political space, inscribed a new territory? Rather than seek a way back to the territory lost by the disjuncture of Jewish self and German language, as Brod had done, Bergmann—in Zionist fashion—dreamed of a new haven for the disenfranchised self.

Between Brod's and Bergmann's imagined future territories of language, there remained the potential course of the writer that might remain in the conflicted nonterritory from which they sought escape. Either by choice, or because he failed to perceive any possibility of choosing, that writer would find himself at home in the space of disjuncture from which Brod and Bergmann tried to flee. From within the "major language," he would produce, in Deleuze and Guattari's words, a "minor literature." These were Kafka's words as well, as he reflected on literature after experiencing the Yiddish theater.

JEW TALK

In the years leading up to World War I, the status of Yiddish and Eastern European Jewry was becoming a matter of poignant interest for German-speaking Prague Jews. Bergmann and others were beginning to view the Yiddish world differently from those emancipated Jews who shunned it as a bleak reminder of their own uncivilized past. The Eastern Jewish community began to be seen by many Western Jews as an authentic, organic folk culture, and this was thought to have been related to the fact that the East European Jews lived in a majority culture, among themselves, with a language of their own within definable territorial borders stretching from the Baltic to the Black Sea. This view was allied with Nathan Birnbaum's reassessment of the distinctly anti-Yiddish view of Max Nordau, which had previously been the dominant Zionist representation.[52] The image of an organic, "territorialized" Jewry held incredible power for intellectuals situated in the Prague context: Bergmann took an immediate interest in the study of Yiddish and in contact with Eastern Jewry, and Kafka's similar interests have been well documented.[53] In ways strikingly parallel to their attitudes toward the Czechs, the German-Jewish Praguers' fascination with Yiddish and its speakers was a strange amalgam of romantic glorification, envy, and condescension. But beyond these judgments, what was the relationship of the shifting image of Yiddish to the language-territory discourse in Prague?

In an essay in the Prague Jewish-national weekly *Selbstwehr*, the journalist Abraham Kohane drew a telling distinction between contemporary East European Yiddish and the Yiddish formerly spoken in Prague.[54] The latter was a "distorted German," a product of the particular and limited social function of the pre-emancipated Jewish minority within Prague, full of "gaps" that needed to be filled in with Hebrew vocabulary. "It was neither Jewish nor German nor Hebrew, but rather an inharmonious amalgamation of these elements, which must not have seemed very aesthetic [. . .]"[55]

As in the assessment of *Prager Deutsch,* here an unnatural social and national condition yields a deformed language, a freak that pathetically parodies healthy language. The author compares this pitiful "hermaphrodite" to contemporary East European Yiddish, a viable [*lebensfähig*]

language that has expelled most of the foreign elements (such as Hebrew!) from its vocabulary. While the relationship of this rhetoric to *völkisch* nationalist discourse is compelling, the point that touches on the
Prague question is the association of linguistic health and territorial integrity. In the same way that the exemplarity of Prague German began
to be questioned at the precise moment that the foundation for the hegemony of the Prague Germans was shaken, so was the recognition of a
circumscribed, majority-Jewish territory in East Europe a necessary prerequisite for the legitimation of Yiddish language and culture.

This image of a healthy Yiddish language is not precisely the one
with which Kafka was working when he produced the texts on Yitzhak
Löwy's Yiddish theater, the "Introductory Talk on the Yiddish Language," and the essay on minor literatures. Kafka's initial enthusiasm
toward Yiddish culture was clearly grounded in his identification of
"Jews of a particularly pure kind," the sort that accepts its Jewishness
unreflectively, without self-consciousness as the non-Christian other—
in other words, a territorialized Jewry.[56] To be found in these texts as
well, however, is an extraordinary tension between references to the self-
sufficient Jewish language described above and another sort of Yiddish,
inherently different from other national languages, more subversive to
the model of territorialized language than mimetic of it. Mark Anderson
has astutely estimated as a "flagrant but insightful misreading" Deleuze
and Guattari's conflation of Kafka's discussion of a minor literature (i.e.,
the culture of a small nation, the Yiddish theater in particular) with
Kafka's own subversive literary constructions within the "major" language of German.[57] I would add to Anderson's judgment the suggestion
that Deleuze and Guattari's manipulation is justified by the presence of
that very "misreading," or conflation, within Kafka's writings themselves. His identification with Yiddish derives more from a longing for
an unproblematic, territorialized national and linguistic existence than it
does from a sense of the power of Yiddish to dismember that construct;
Kafka blurs the lines between his discussions of an authentic Jewish national literature and the provocative political defiance of "Jew talk."
Even at their most subversive moments, these moves work within the
system of language and territory or property that we have been exploring in Prague discourse. Language, Kafka noted, never deals with anything beyond property, or territory, and its relations ("nur vom Besitz
und seinen Beziehungen handelt").[58]

Kafka's brilliant and subtle "Introductory Talk on the Yiddish Language," delivered in early 1912 as an introduction to a presentation of

Yiddish dramatic readings by his friend Yitzhak Löwy, rests upon and, at the same time, pulls the rug out from under the notions of what we have been discussing as cultural "groundedness."[59] The structure of the address performance itself already introduces a provisional dichotomy. The expectation is that Kafka's talk will mediate mutually incomprehensible entities before and behind him: the spectators he faces in the audience (assimilated Prague Jews) and the Yiddish they cannot understand (Jewish language and the Polish actor Löwy) behind him on the stage. He thus literally occupies the space between a Yiddish-speaking, communal and territorialized past constructed in this historical context as the authentic counterpart of the less primitive and vulgar, yet inauthentic, identity of the Prague present. Kafka opens by naming this distance between spectator and spectacle as one created by the assimilated Jews themselves because of their comprehensible "dread" of Yiddish, rather than by its inherent foreignness. Thus Kafka opens with the wish "just to say something about how much more Yiddish you understand than you think," and ends with the promise (and threat) that, if the audience will let it, Yiddish will "take hold" of them, they will find themselves "in the midst" (hence at the center) of the territory defined by Yiddish. This displacement is what the audience most fears, quite naturally preferring the illusion of centeredness offered since emancipation by enlightened, German-liberal ideology:

> Our western European conditions, if we glance at them only in a deliberately superficial way, appear so well ordered; everything takes its quiet course. We live in positively cheerful concord, understanding each other whenever necessary, getting along without each other whenever it suits us and understanding each other even then. From within such an order of things who could possibly understand the tangle of Yiddish—indeed, who would even care to do so?

Kafka's description is a faintly ironic replication of the representation of assimilated Western Jewish life known from the memoirs of Weltsch and Zweig. Of course the irony in Kafka's lines, and the sense of looming danger behind the meticulously ordered facade, must have been manifest even to an audience that had never read *The Trial* or *Amerika*. Still, this passionless order of life is "understandable" if one considers the alternative, "the tangle of Yiddish."

Kafka has immediately established the coterminous status of national language and the territory of national life; he achieves this by setting parallel a description of western European conditions on the one side against the condition of East European Jewish language on the other. It is easy to imagine reversing this process, with the precision and order of the German language contrasted to the "tangle" or chaos of life in the Pale of Settlement. Throughout the essay, Kafka's depiction of "Yiddish" is a depiction of Jewishness—not just of East European Jewish life, but of the Jewishness of the spectator masked behind assimilated cultivation. But the condition of Yiddish (versus "our western European conditions") is not merely the authentic condition of Jews; Yiddish does not offer a space of integral territoriality so much as it brandishes the terrible prospect of a liberation of language from the cozy imprisonment of territory.

> [Yiddish] has not yet developed any linguistic forms of lucidity such as we need. Its idiom is brief and rapid.
>
> No grammars of the language exist. Devotees of the language try to write grammars, but Yiddish remains a spoken language that is in continuous flux. The people will not leave it to the grammarians.
>
> It consists solely of foreign words. But these words are not firmly rooted in it, they retain the speed and liveliness with which they were adopted. Great migrations move through Yiddish, from one end to the other. All this German, Hebrew, French, English, Slavonic, Dutch, Romanian, and even Latin, is seized with curiosity and frivolity once it is contained within Yiddish, and it takes a good deal of strength to hold all these languages together in this state. And this, too, is why no sensible person thinks of making Yiddish into an international language, obvious though the idea might seem.

Kafka's description of Yiddish is silently but constantly juxtaposed to the *Prager Deutsch* in which he speaks. In lucid and precise German, he declares that Yiddish lacks such lucidity; the Yiddish idiom is "brief and rapid," a brief phrase that quickly follows, performing the naive brevity of Yiddish. An open identification with the function of language he describes as "Yiddish" is detectable throughout the talk, and this position is explicitly opposed to the one he projects upon an imagined assimilated audience, which feels centered within German language and culture, and is alien to the Polish Jewish language about to be heard on the stage. Thus the "staged" position of the Yiddish performer and his German-speaking Jewish double supersedes the passive and depoliticized role of the German-Jewish bourgeois audience. The contrast of assimilated German-speaking and Polish Yiddish-speaking Jews recalls the dualism of Kisch's and Weltsch's early texts, where a lucid but somehow moribund, sterilized language of classical German literature was counterposed to the vitality and roughness of folk song. There is one great difference here, however: the vibrancy of Yiddish does not spring from its grounding in a territorialized *Volk*, but in the mercurial flight of its

stolen vocabulary. It has no grammatical structure or any uniquely circumscribed lexicon, but is pieced and strung together; in contrast to the
High German of Prague, Yiddish "as a whole consists solely of dialect."

The Praguers were particularly sensitive to the discourse linking the
essence of the *Volk* simultaneously with a language and a territory. It is
therefore understandable that what Kafka saw in Yiddish was not the
representation of a stable and grounded people, as many of his contemporaries who admired Yiddish saw, but rather the remnants of eternal
migrations, deterritorializations. The notion of territoriality—or the
"normal" alignment of nation, language, and ground—comes forth in
Kafka's address in the figure of "rest" (*Ruhe*). In the superficial order of
Western Jewish life, everything takes its quiet course (*seinen ruhigen
Lauf*). The opposite of this condition is the Yiddish language, which is
in continuous flux, never coming to rest (*kommt nicht zur Ruhe*). Its
words are all imported, and themselves do not sit still within the language (*Diese ruhen aber nicht in ihm* . . .).[60]

The Yiddish "whirl of language" is for Kafka an escape from "language" in the ordinary sense, just as "Jewish nationality" is a contrived
expression for a state of nationlessness. Yiddish is not, as it might seem,
an international language, representing an embrace of all nations. In
fact, it represents the opposite: this nationlessness, the lack of hold on
any specific territory. Where the poet of Kisch's and Weltsch's imaginings
finds strength in the language of a territorialized *Volk*, the Yiddish language lives off of the energy of its user: "it takes a great deal of strength
to hold all these languages together in this state." Without the support
of embracing borders and firm ground beneath it, it must be held together by the poet's act of will.

Since all language inscribes some sort of territory, it would be most
correct to define the circle of Yiddish, "in the midst" of which the receptive spectator will find himself, as an "anti-territory," the space from
which reterritorialization (à la Brod or Bergmann, for instance) is no
longer accessible. Kafka stresses this point after driving Yiddish away
from anything that might be taken for groundedness, declaring that the
audience will in fact come to feel "the true unity of Yiddish," a path that
stimulates a different kind of fear than the dread of Yiddish with which
he began his speech. It is a fear of oneself, rather than of Yiddish, toler-
able only because it is accompanied by a unique "self-confidence" that
Yiddish bestows upon the speaker, unknown to German-speaking Jews.

The power of this language of deterritorialization that is manifest in
Kafka's text is the strand picked up by Deleuze and Guattari when they

allow a slippage in their discussion from Yiddish to Kafka's German. In case the argument that the slippage takes place already in Kafka's diary entry and talk on the Yiddish language has not been convincing, we may briefly examine a more explicit example from a letter to Max Brod written in a somewhat later period. Before looking closely at Kafka's fascinating discussion of *das Mauscheln*, it is useful to take a brief look at what is loaded up in that word.

Mauschel (or the verb *mauscheln*, or *das Mauscheln*), like *Prager Deutsch*, is a term with an ambiguous referent: now it is a Bohemian form of Yiddish, now a Germanized Yiddish, now a Yiddishized German. In all of its uses, it carried a distinctly derogatory flavor, which we might capture with the pejorative phrase "Jew talk." Sander Gilman has offered a concise genealogy of the term, which was synonymous with usury (in other words, Jewish-like action) until the nineteenth century, when it became associated with language. Gilman demonstrates that the notion of a Jewish defacement of German took on this name at the moment when Jews were perceived to overstep the boundaries of their difference; thus social emancipation and integration were linked with the Jews' assimilation of the majority language, and the inauthenticity or impurity of their language reflected the effrontery of their entrance into society. The idea of "*Mauschel*," with its connotation of annexation and distortion of language, is thus a creation of an antisemitic German discourse, which, of course, is shared by German-speaking Jews.[61]

The Prague German liberal Heinrich Teweles provides a demonstration of the process described here in an essay in which he asserts that *Mauschel*, like *Prager Deutsch*, cannot be considered a dialect: "These are not simply alterations proceeding from the German linguistic spirit [*Sprachgeist*], but rather it is the influence of a foreign linguistic spirit that generates the laws of *Mauschel*."[62] From this distance, the comic aspect of this sentence is lost. Teweles meant to amuse his readers with the absurd comparison of the Jewish corruption of language with an authentic idiom. When reproached by a reader defending the integrity of Jewish language, Teweles clarified himself by stressing that he was not referring to *Mauschel* in the sense of East European Yiddish, but the language used or known by all West European German-speaking Jews, which he named (comically, again) "Modern High *Mauschel*."[63]

Here Teweles struck a chord familiar to Fritz Mauthner, who identified in the language Teweles described as "common or known to all German Jews" the obstruction to true German nationality. In Mauthner's most famous work, the *Contributions to a Critique of Language*, he claims that the German Jew "will become a full German only when *Mauschel* expressions become a foreign language or when he no longer understands them."[64] Mauthner thus reverses the customary paradigm by assuming that the Jew's internal essence follows from his language; more interestingly, both Mauthner and Teweles make no distinction between employing Jewish language and simply understanding it. A German text by a Jewish author is thus always "Jew talk," "even if," as Kafka writes, "not the slightest linguistic error could be demonstrated." Kafka illustrates the point in reference to Karl Kraus:

> [Kraus's] wit is primarily *das Mauscheln;* no one can *mauscheln* like Kraus, although one can hardly do anything else but *mauscheln* in this German-Jewish world. That is, *mauscheln* taken in its broadest sense (in the only sense it should ever be taken)—namely, as the flagrant, or dead-silent, or self-pitying usurpation of foreign property [*eines fremden Besitzes*] that has not been earned, but stolen with a (relatively) fleeting grip, and that remains foreign property [. . .][65]

Here the gesture of deterritorialization takes place within German, although the description closely follows the outlines of the earlier description of Yiddish: the foreign vocabulary, "stolen property" (*Besitz*), held with a light grasp, slippery and fleeting.[66] Smug, sneaky, or guilty, the German-Jewish writer cannot avoid this language use, and it operates independently of his attitude toward it. With a Praguer's eye Kafka spies upon the writers of his generation, commenting as an outsider, in the past tense:

> They lived between three impossibilities (which I arbitrarily name linguistic impossibilities, since that is easiest, but they could be named otherwise): the impossibility of not writing, the impossibility of writing German, the impossibility of writing differently [. . .] thus it was a literature impossible from all sides. It was a gypsy literature that had stolen the German babe from the cradle and trained it some way or other in great haste, since someone had to dance the tightrope.[67]

The "gypsy literature" of the German-speaking Jewish writers of Kafka's generation, like gypsy Yiddish, has no language of its own, and no territory. The words, held loosely with a thief's hand, are mobilized; the writer causes the German language to "take flight on a line of escape."[68]

Just as they were caught between languages, caught between nations, the Prague German-Jewish writers were trapped between literary impossibilities (to the three listed above, Kafka adds a fourth: the impossibility of writing). It is in these charged spaces between possibilities, iden-

tities, and territories, as I have argued, that the creative moment of the
Prague circle takes place. Kafka declares this himself as he introduces the
above complex with the problem of the generational conflict and Jewishness: the writers wanted to write German, "but with their hind legs
they were stuck to the Judaism of their fathers, and with their flailing
forelegs they found no new ground [*keinen freien Boden*]. The despair
over this was their inspiration." [69] This dilemma at the root of Kafka's
generation's inspiration was at once a dilemma of identity, language, and
territory—a tension, as Kafka writes, between desires for lost and new
ground.

The subversive role of *das Mauscheln,* Yiddish, and Prague circle literature is not condemned in Kafka's letter; that role is the salvation of
Prager Deutsch, for in German only the dialects or the most classical
High German "really lives," while all the rest—"the linguistic middle
class—is nothing but ashes that can be stirred up to a semblance of life
only by the rummaging of surviving Jewish hands." [70] Beauty and nature
are brought out of sterile Prague German by the gesticulation of the
Jewish poet-usurper. But this condition of German is not necessarily
particular to Prague; after all, Kafka was writing about German and
German literature, not *Prager Deutsch.* Certainly it is not unreasonable
to assume, as Deleuze and Guattari do, that Kafka's meaning could be
applied much further afield, in minor and minority literatures elsewhere.

Kafka's "theft of the German babe from the cradle," this dispossession
of the major language from its territory, is the salvation of literature—seen here from the unique perspective of a German-speaking Jewish writer in Prague. "Jew talk" and "the rummaging of Jewish hands"
have universal functions, and operate in a full spectrum of ways "in this
German-Jewish world" in which one can scarcely do otherwise—that is,
can hardly justify any territorialization of language. Kafka's language,
which he identified as closely coupled with his Jewishness, begins to take
apart the perilous construct of language, nation, culture, and territory
that held so much power in Prague.

CHAPTER 4

Encircling Humanity

Expressionist Universalism and Revolution

Wie kann man sich über die Welt freuen, außer wenn
man zu ihr flüchtet.

How can one rejoice at the world, other than when one
flees to it.

Octavo Heft G, mid-November, 1917

PRAGUE AND EXPRESSIONISM

In the decade in which the First World War was to begin and end, sig-
naling the breadth and gravity of a modern cultural crisis to which the
Prague writers held a privileged view, a new literary movement emerged
in Central Europe. Many of the Prague writers discussed in this study
have been counted as German expressionists: Max Brod and Oskar
Baum, the translators and poets Otto Pick and Rudolf Fuchs, and even
Franz Kafka, in spite of his own aversion to the new style.[1] The Praguer
Hans Janowitz cowrote the screenplay of the pathbreaking expressionist film *The Cabinet of Dr. Caligari,* and there is little doubt that his
brother, the talented poet Franz Janowitz, would be considered an important contributor to the movement had he produced more work before his untimely death at the front.[2] All this aside, however, the two
Praguers most important to expressionism, albeit for different reasons,
were Franz Werfel (1890–1945) and Paul Kornfeld (1889–1941). Considerably younger than Brod and his classmates, these two would prove
to be the most sensitive to the potential of the expressionist vision for
opening up an escape from their specific Prague territoriality.

Retrospective attempts to situate Prague German expressionism
within the larger cultural context have been plagued by two persistent
literary-historical myths. The first of these I have already discussed. This
is the liberal-humanist interpretation that would identify the universal-

ist image of a brotherhood of man in the work of Werfel, Kornfeld, and others as a tolerant and humane—let us say a "liberal"—alternative to the antiliberal ideologies competing with it. In fact, however, Prague expressionist discourse assigned itself the violent task of overthrowing the "earthly" life it identified first and foremost as the property of the German-liberal generation preceding it. In rhetorical terms, the attack mounted by the expressionists approximates that of the German *völkisch* movement rather more closely than liberal historians are comfortable recognizing.

The second myth has to do with a traditional distinction in the scholarly literature between "activist" and "contemplative" expressionists, an analytical maneuver that would have us regarding the Prague writers as more "metaphysically" oriented, and therefore less revolutionary, than their counterparts in the German Empire especially.[3] Both Kornfeld and Werfel in their own time were struggling for a revolution that sought above all to overcome the dichotomy represented in this very distinction. That the distinction can be so glibly reproduced in retrospect indicates nothing quite so much as the failure of that revolution, and the resolute and permanent reinforcement of "borders" that the Praguers more than any other expressionists had a stake in destroying.

Viewed through the distortions of our postwar vantage, none of this can make much sense. To understand how the vision of expressionist revolution operated, as well as to grasp its relevance to the Prague context, we must go back to the moment of expressionism—indeed, to the moment it was born.

WORLD FRIENDS WITHOUT A COUNTRY

> Mein einziger Wunsch ist, Dir, o Mensch verwandt zu sein!
>
> My only wish, O Man, is to be kin to thee!

With these words, composed by a very young Franz Werfel and recited by Max Brod in Berlin, German literary expressionism is presumed to have begun.[4] The poem, entitled "An den Leser" (To the reader),[5] is typical of Werfel's earliest work. It appeared in *Der Weltfreund* (Friend of the world), the young poet's first book, and it ably represents the brand of expressionist work that would come to be labeled, after the above line, "O Man" poetry. The book caused a sensation among young Prague German-Jewish writers, a description authoritatively, if not impartially, attested to in Brod's memoirs.[6] But the implications contained in the above line, to say nothing of the rest of the poem and the anthology's title, are more complex than they at first appear.

The resonance of these stanzas from the vantage of Berlin, as well as from our retrospective point of view, is one of "humanism"; they appeal for a brotherhood of man. Why, though, was it left to a Praguer to claim membership in a circle of humanity that transcended birthplace and class? The poet sings of a "memory" that transcends his personal experience, for he "knows" the experience of the poor, of exploited workers, and (above all) of "timid governesses in the foreign family circle." It cannot but be significant that this boy from the exclusive *Stadtpark* quarter, a member of the wealthiest stratum of the Prague bourgeois elite, who, among the writers discussed here, had the weakest command of Czech language, should be the first to formulate the appeal "Thus I belong to you and to all!" The poem closes on this note, ornamented by the quietly desperate plea "Please, do not wish to resist me! / Oh, that it could once come to pass, / That we, Brother, fall into one another's arms!"[7]

For the writer in young Werfel's position, the referents of concepts of "belonging" and "foreignness," "homeland" and "abroad," or even "self" and "other," had shadings altogether lacking for the Berlin expressionists he would inspire. "Wo ist . . . " (Where is . . .), another poem from the collection *Der Weltfreund,* casts this predicament in a somewhat starker light:

Where Is . . .
I carry much within myself.
The past of earlier lives,
Buried regions,
With faint traces of starshine.
Often I am beneath the surface,
Immersed in foreign regions am I.

I am homesick.
O remnants, remains! o passed past!
As I am for childhood, homesick,
As for the baby's high chair, homesick,
As for forgotten friends, homesick.
Homesick,
As I am for the lost tenderness of people
Who look coldly at me
And no longer pinch my cheeks.[8]

The poem's title, as Eduard Goldstücker first noted, alludes to the Czech nationalist song (and future anthem), "Where Is My Home?"[9]

Just as the image of a lost homeland is the center of the piece, the consciousness of a territorialized Czech nation around the author surely informed that image by way of contrast. The poem explores that "memory" beyond personal experience claimed in "An den Leser" as the site of a fuller experience "carried" deep within the self. This rich ground, the "buried regions" of other lives, constitutes for Werfel a more authentic collective existence than the shallow categories of the national and the social. Werfel affirms that he often finds himself beneath the "surface." Banished from the chart of any national territory, the author and his kind have been driven below the superficies of form, to a deeper realm within. "Sunk into others' regions am I" (*Hinabgetaucht in die fremdeigenen Gegenden bin ich*) is a critical avowal of the piece, establishing a space that is at once "foreign" and "home." Even within the single qualifier "*fremdeigen*" (*fremd* meaning "foreign" or "strange," and *eigen* suggestive of belonging and the ownership of territory), we find the cohabitation of possession and dispossession.

The homesickness expressed in the second half of the poem could appeal to other German expressionists. It seemed to refer to a nostalgia for a primordial unity and a discomfort with a cold and fragmented modernity, which is a major theme of expressionist works more generally. Yet it took a poet in Franz Werfel's position, a newcomer to young adulthood in his native city and in the house of his parents, to identify this profound "homesickness" that possesses one while one is at home.

Werfel continues these themes throughout this and his other early poetry collections, significantly entitled *Wir sind* (We are)[10] and *Einander* (One another). The poem "The Wise Man to His Enemies"[11] can be read as a Christian consideration of the Prague German-Jewish dilemma; similarly, Werfel is peculiarly sensitive to universal conditions such as that expressed in "Fremde sind wir auf der Erde alle" (Strangers are we all on earth).[12] In that piece, human hostilities, patriotic chatter, and other "earthly" matters are depicted as meaningless: "All lands will become but waters, / Beneath your very feet the places melt away." Possession and territory are the objects of Werfel's irony: "The sturdiest falls fleeting before our eyes," "What we hold is at once no longer to be held," "Whoever says 'his' and 'mine' is deceived"; in the last stanza, our mothers, houses, and very heartbeats are borrowed, temporal, and fleeting, and we are united with each other only in our mortality. This illusory condition of the territorial and of our common alienation on earth were themes about which the Prague poet had special insight. Assessing both his talent and his project, the young Werfel declared, "Being foreign is my craft." [13]

The attack on the territorial and its implications are illuminated in the few essay pieces Werfel composed in the same period as the early poems. In his afterword to the collection *Wir sind,* for instance, Werfel demarcates the battleground, complaining of "this mess of an earth teleology" [*Erdenteleologie*] into which we are thrust, forgetting Being, the colossal human experience. "If a single heart that has been crushed by that most horrible curse of earthly work [*Erdenarbeit*] can be brought closer to the world through these poems," he writes, "then I am content." [14]

It is worthwhile wading through this murky rhetoric because it reveals the societal critique underpinning Werfel's Christian-spiritualist message. The term "earth" (in *Erdenteleologie* and *Erdenarbeit,* as well as throughout such poems as "Fremde sind wir auf Erde alle") is the watchword for what I have described as the "territorial": for Werfel it is the mark of spiritless modern politics and society. Werfel's heaven-earth dichotomy allows him to accept true pain and essential human lonesomeness among the heights of human experience, the way out of the "earth" and toward "paradise." [15] The "world" of the *Weltfreund* stands in direct opposition to this earth, as it does in the above hope that the poems will bring readers away from the curse of "earth" and nearer to the "world" (a vocabulary, incidentally, that rather remarkably foreshadows Heidegger's). [16] Thus the world friendship, or radical humanism, that is often noted in these early works ought to be seen as it was conceived and presented: in conscious opposition to a contemptible "earth."

Contemporary reviews of these early poetic works were already aware of the way they operate: the universalist message certainly focuses on "love," "community," "world feeling," and "hope," but what Julius Bab finds most notable in the *Weltfreund* was that "it was no *everyday* book. It overran the petty little things of the everyday." [17] The "everyday" (*Alltag*), signifying the material condition also denoted by "earth," was to become the primary target of both Werfel's and Paul Kornfeld's violent attacks on contemporary life.

A prewar essay expresses most clearly of all the relationship of this rhetorical apparatus to the conflict of nationalities. In "Wenn die Russen tanzen, wenn Battistini singt" (When the Russians dance, when Battistini sings; dated 23 January 1912), Werfel praises the universalist and spiritual culture of the Russian ballet and Italian opera, in contrast to the civilization of nation-states motivated by business, finance, and politics.[18] He attacks the movers and shakers of such a civilization who *"have not the least idea of the most colossal miracle that things are!"* The pessimism of a civilization left wondering why life is worth living "is a sign that we are not yet awakened to a new humanity, *the first current and first emblem of which we hold the Italian opera and the Russian ballet to be."* The dualism set forth in the essay is one of individualism against spirit; economic organization against the seeing of stars; modern rationalism, political do-gooders, and dogmatism against . . . one Italian singer and a Russian dance. These are moments of national culture that transcend nation: a "fantastic un-nationality" within national culture, a mad "being-beyond-oneself" [*Außersichsein*] or turning away from one's outer form [*Entformtsein*]. This experience of the Russian ballet is not described by Werfel as an aesthetic effect, but rather as a symbol of a new humanity. The space filled by the tenor and the ballet dancers represents an antinational idea. In Werfel's text it becomes an escape from the constraints of form, as the constraining borders of the map. This deformation is liberating, for "form" in this sense is at odds with the new, spiritual humanity. This tension duplicates the strain identified in "Wo ist . . . " between the surface and the foreign region beneath it. It represents a battle between nationalism and expressionist universalism as well as the traditional Christian struggle of the spirit against the flesh. This is no asceticism, however: all emotion races to the newly opened space of the spirit, to the "being-in-the-world," to the feast.

Thus, for the young poet Werfel, the revolution at hand would throw off the burden of territoriality and liberate the realm of the spirit. The political implications of this program, already implicit in these early texts, mature in the wartime writings with which this chapter closes. First, we further open these questions of spirit and politics with the writings of the young Paul Kornfeld, who, like Werfel, was more than willing to surrender claim to a circle of earth in order to join the circle of humanity.

INSCRIBING INFINITUDE

It was Paul Kornfeld's fate to be remembered for his few, powerful programmatic writings more than for his dramas, despite the success of the latter in his lifetime.[19] If he lacked the literary talent of certain better-known expressionists such as Georg Kaiser, Walter Hasenclever, and Fritz Unruh, he was somehow in the position to articulate most clearly the spiritual mission of expressionism. Continuing with the notion of fate, we might call upon the generations of rabbinical tradition in Kornfeld's ancestry, or upon the untimely death of his brother—the moment that gave birth to his writerly ambition and production—or we might reflect on Kornfeld's own fate in the concentration camp at Lodz. There is a way in which each of these destinies, past and future, remains buried within Kornfeld's texts.

A lesser-known text, appearing at the end of our period, sets the frame for Kornfeld's earlier work. The rhetoric of the passage which opens the fragment "Gerechtigkeit" (Justice) is so dense that it deserves to stand on its own here:

> Happy the man who takes part in all that is living, beyond that which is his own calling; wonderful the man who, further beyond it, is kind and involved, sympathetic with the poor and victimized and who helps them where he can, for he considers his own property [*Besitz*] as nothing and his own well-being; and how sublime the man that sees on the one hand how little he can do for the poor from within his own narrow circle [*in seinem eigenen engen Kreis*], on the other hand though is mindful of the infinitely many poor and victimized whom he cannot reach, and so, to help them, steps completely out of his circle and makes his new circle of the whole world.[20]

This passage opens an essay that represents and simultaneously advocates one kind of "justice" against another, and one sort of "circle" over another. Through its biblical style, a device Kornfeld uses generously elsewhere, this ideal justice is characterized as heavenly, in contrast to a spiritless, earth-bound, and material law. That stylistic device also makes it seem like a contextless metaphysical speculation, but it addressed a very specific context. The catastrophe of World War I ended with a socialist revolution in Central Europe, the "November Revolution" of 1918, which by early 1919 had been co-opted. The target of this essay is actually the socialist revolutionary, for Kornfeld a hypocritical figure who has sought to change the external face of society from within his own narrow circle. The similarity of the adjacent words "own" and "narrow" ("*eigenen*" and "*engen*") foregrounds the necessity of narrowness entailed in the possession of a circle of one's "own." Focusing on material well-being and justice in a mere judicial sense, by focusing in fact on "politics," the socialists spoiled the hope of a true and spiritual revolution of humanity.

In a piece of the same period, "Prayer for a Miracle" (another prose-poem in a style encouraging critics to remind readers of his rabbinic heritage), Kornfeld contrasts the finite quality of God's laws to His immeasurable power.[21] His prayer is that the limited and limiting rules of earthly existence be destroyed in an unleashing of that limitless, engulfing spiritual force. The issue at hand is described with the territorial metaphor of borders [*Grenzen*]: constricting rules [*begrenzende Regeln*] versus infinite or "boundless" power [*unbegrenzte Macht*]. The metaphor of boundaries — of boundedness and boundlessness — allowed both Kornfeld and Werfel to evoke time just as they evoked space, and to focus intensely on an overdetermined condition of constriction in order to imply the possibility of freedom.

Kornfeld, as the passage from "Gerechtigkeit" demonstrates, is intensely aware of the two conflicting qualities of the circle: the first is enclosure, the limiting function of the circumference and the constriction of form; the second is the engulfing function of the circle, its potential ability to hold together disparate things. The former is the earthly inscription of territorial boundaries, social classes, and political interests; the latter is the spiritual embrace of the whole world sphere. Similarly, in an extension of the thesis with which he ends the essay, the first kind of circle represents the present, the limitations of the moment, and of what one perceives as reality. The alternative choice is the future, which opens the door not to tomorrow but to the everlasting way of humanity. Again Kornfeld contrasts the circumscription of the material moment to the encirclement of eternity. That watchword of expressionism that is known as *Aufbruch* ("breaking out") was, for Kornfeld, the breaking open of the earthly circle, releasing a collective soul of humanity that would encompass the globe.

The expressionist attack on materialism had a particular function within the logic of Prague territoriality. The whole of Kornfeld's serialized novella *Legende* can be summarized as the struggle between a lord and his servant to escape from the imprisonment of ownership. In a series of didactic events and confessions, the reader is made tiresomely aware of the enlightenment of the two characters, each wanting the estate to belong to the other and thereby to free himself of the anguish of property.[22]

Here, again, we see that the rhetoric of borders and the infinite, of social conflict and humanity, earth and paradise, all had a very particular relevance in Prague. What it found in the movement of German expressionism more generally was a convenient vehicle. In Kornfeld's short contribution to the important anthology *Das jüdische Prag,* he depicts a brief encounter in Venice between the soul-searching protagonist and a poor flower vendor in which the former's attempt to overpay for the flowers is rejected with contempt.[23] The hero despairs over the distance separating them while "her destiny stands on the same earth as mine! It is our common homeland, and my neighbor suffers and weeps!" The incident may be one that would inspire sympathy in a broad assortment of readers, but the Praguer had privileged access to relations characterized by paternalism, pity, difference, and contempt among "neighbors" in a "common homeland." What the piece is really about is that by now familiar tension between dream and reality, heaven and earth, and the transcendence of territory:

> Today I was in hell! Or was it in me [. . .] Or did I just see hell because I saw the earth? Or do I just think I saw it, because I sense paradise? Oh, Miss, infinite [*grenzenlos*] is—what is infinite? Is it the world, and I its reflection, or is it me, and the world a shadow?

In an ecstatic moment of love—an expressionist erotic symbiosis to which we will turn in a moment—dream and reality trade places. The finite breaks through its territorial borders, leaving the lovers to sense the "radiation of a thousand foreign lives and the shadow of every destiny." The boundless paradise of spirit, with its general expressionist appeal, is a dream in which the Prague poet had a vital stake. We recall the recurrent references to the shrinking Prague "island" in every Prague circle memoir as Kornfeld's hero looks into the quarters of his dying mother, her spirit leaving the cramped confines of her body and the little room transforming into a garden, which dramatically expands in turn into an "infinite landscape."

INSIDE THE FAMILY CIRCLE

The model for this "brotherhood of man," as the metaphor implies, is the family circle. The Prague expressionists dwelled upon the metaphor of family, which after all holds a powerful place in German expressionism generally.[24] In the expressionist context, the family circle provides an image of primordial closeness that has been lost through the modern perversion of society. At the same time, the revolutionary attack on this atomized, alienated, soulless society was represented as a radical generational hostility—the famed "father-son conflict"—hence a struggle within the family circle. In Prague, both sides of this coin had special currency. The collapse of an imagined premodern organic community was as strongly felt in the city of national conflict as it was elsewhere in Central Europe. Yet, in Prague it was impossible to separate the sense of a hostile social environment attributable to "modernity" from the hostility attributable to class and national conflict in daily life. Indeed, as Werfel's poems make clear, class and national consciousness belonged to the alienating modernity expressionism rejected. As for the salience of the generational (or "father-son") conflict, in other centers of expressionism the revolt against the father was a strike against materialism and bourgeois respectability. In German-Jewish Prague *above all,* however, the intensely liberal and assimilated generation of the expressionists' parents was perceived as the sponsor of a fragmented and untenable society.[25] Opening literary expressionism with the hope to transcend that condition and approach a more organic humanism, Werfel called upon the family metaphor—"O, Man, to be *kin* [*verwandt*] to thee!"

The diaries of the sixteen-year-old Kornfeld chart the formation of a writerly identity within the family circle. Paul's first attempts at writing —in fact, what seem to be his first thoughts about becoming a writer— coincide exactly with the sudden death of his older brother Richard. His diary entries of this period, somewhat awkwardly striving toward literary eloquence, center first and foremost around this loss of his closest family member. As he becomes obsessed with his new identity as a poet, he consciously seeks out a new circle (which he describes sometimes as *Kreis,* or circle, sometimes as a circle of friends, *Bekanntenkreis*), just as in the entries we detect a search for a style of his own.[26] That the lost brother Richard had been the writer of the family, his first publication appearing posthumously in the *Deutsche Arbeit,* complicated matters considerably. His father was enraged by his attempts to mimic the lost poet-brother, and this father-son conflict rapidly possessed the notebooks.[27] One moment of that conflict, described in the entry of July 20, 1907, where Paul and his father battle over whether the son should work in a factory, rather astonishingly resembles the more famous battle between the Prague father and son named Kafka.

The generational conflict so clearly articulated in the cases of Kornfeld and Kafka must be seen within the frame not only of the expressionist "revolt of the son," but also of the more general "postliberal" revolt of the time.[28] Mary Gluck succinctly characterizes the struggle as one pitting Victorian moralism, utilitarian ambition, and rationality against spontaneity, instinct, and spirituality.[29] Kornfeld's translation of these oppositions in his diary into a hostile confrontation between everyday work on the one hand, and the pursuit of art on the other, is reproduced almost to the letter in Brod's account of the 1911 crisis in the Kafka family.[30] The resistance to any compromise on this issue emerges clearly in a letter from Kafka to Brod. Upon being directed to look after a factory on his father's behalf for a two-week period, Kafka writes, "I saw perfectly that I had only the alternatives of either waiting until everyone had gone to bed and then jumping out of the window, or of going every day to the factory [. . .] for the next fourteen days."[31] Brod, "gripped by cold horror," begged Kafka's mother to intervene for the sake of her son's life, and the three together conspired to deceive the father. The paradigm that set the liberal values of respectable industriousness against a life worth living was, in an almost absurd sense, taken literally.

The struggle within the family circle was violent precisely because of the assumption that the bonds among embattled factions were insoluble. Ernst Weiß, a contemporary often ascribed to the Prague circle, had just this model in mind for his novel *Die Galeere*.[32] In a letter to Martin Buber, Weiß describes the grounding idea of his novel as "a sort of circle closed within itself," like a ring of molecules. "There are people bound together to one another, mother and father, mother and son. The son to the beloved, the beloved to her sister. That is the convention. This convention entails obligation."[33] It is useless to try to discuss the evident tensions within the family circle (Kornfeld's and Kafka's encounters with their fathers, for instance) outside the context of this "convention," the naturalized and unquestioned, intimate bonds obliging hostile elements to one another.

The family circle was a figure that was compelling in its dual representation of conflict and unity, or of a utopian projection of human bondedness inextricable from the discord and pain entailed in those bonds. In fact, the dual and conflicting functions of the family metaphor should not be unfamiliar, for they are parallel to the dialectical tensions within the figures of the circle (inclusion/exclusion) and of territory (possession/dispossession). It is easy to argue that the family is the central metaphor of nationalism; but it is also linguistically available to antinational or supranational discourse (the "family" or "brotherhood" of man/humanity). Revolutionary revolt and primordial unity were not as much diametric oppositions as they were mutually necessary, in dialectical tension with one another. That is why it is the idealized memory of childhood within the family circle that served the Prague expressionists as an image of the lost primordial community of humanity, and as a utopian image of the shape of a future humanity. This is the force behind the obsession with childhood images in the earliest Werfel poetry. In a poem like "Father and Son," which touched such a nerve that it was published in three anthologies of its time, the familial relation highlights both that promise of human harmony and that hostility between father and son that were emblematic for Werfel's generation. The first line of the poem was thus given a page to itself to introduce a section of *Wir sind*. Here is how it went:

> How we once in boundless [*grenzenlos*] love
> pursued the amusements of the everlasting . . . [34]

FROM BIG DADDY TO SMALL LITERATURE

Kafka's famous undelivered letter to his father, written in the expressionist decade, offers rich source material for a survey of the terrain inscribed by the family circle, as well as the possibilities of trespass into aesthetic and political realms. It is an unwieldy text, which we might better get a grasp on by focusing on the trope of size and, in particular, of size anxiety. The theme is addressed explicitly in the letter, and it also relates directly to Deleuze and Guattari's reading of the political function of Kafka's literature.

It is possible to speak in this context about the father-son conflict on three discrete, while intimately intertwined, levels. The first and most obvious is the personal, which would seem almost inevitably, although misleadingly, to lead to a diagnosis of an Oedipal conflict in the Kafka home. Any such conclusion would be misleading in the first instance because it forgets that Franz Kafka was perfectly familiar with Freud. He quotes him frequently, sometimes in parody, sometimes as a trap.[35] The second level of the father-son conflict is historico-political. The ideological valence of generational conflict in Prague at the time has to do with the revolt of young writers against a worldview that was powerfully identified with the preceding generation (Hermann Kafka's generation). Here we come directly to the issue of the relations between the personal and the political in "minor literatures," as pointed out by Deleuze and Guattari:

> [E]verything in [minor or "small" literatures] is political. In major [large—*großen*] literatures, in contrast, the individual concern (familial, marital, and so on) joins with other no less individual concerns, the social milieu serving as a mere environment or a background; this is so much the case that none of these Oedipal intrigues are specifically indispensable or absolutely necessary but all become as one in a large space. Minor literature is completely different; its cramped space forces each individual intrigue to connect immediately to politics. The individual concern thus becomes all the more necessary, indispensable, *magnified* because a whole other story is vibrating within it.

In this way the family triangle connects to other triangles—commercial, economic, bureaucratic, juridical—that determine its values. When Kafka indicates that one of the goals of a minor literature is the "purification of the conflict that opposes father and son and the possibility of discussing that conflict," it isn't a question of an Oedipal phantasm but of a political program.[36]

Of particular note for our purposes here is the inversion of valuations relating to images of size. These come straight out of Kafka and are directly applicable to a reading of the letter, as I will trace in a moment. The theoretical statement offered by Deleuze and Guattari brings us to the final level on which the father-son drama was played out in Prague, this one historiographical or methodological. This issue will be returned to later on, but for now it will suffice to warn against looking at the social milieu as "a mere environment or background," as the "big picture" in which to understand the littler picture of Kafka's life and his own representations. We are identifying here a mode of interpretation that favors the position of the father, a liberal interpretation for a liberal generation. This analytical mode preserves Hermann's size advantage. Another potential reading rescues the son from these forces larger than him or, better said, records Kafka's own self-rescue.

Franz's letter was inspired by Hermann's question of why a son would fear his father. At the moment the question was posed, Franz was unable to answer, "in part just because of the fear I have of you, and in part because so many little parts [*Einzelnheiten,* or details] belong to the grounding of this fear that I cannot hold them at all together in speech." [37] Even in writing he knows his explanation will be partial or incomplete (*unvollständig*), crippled by fear and "simply because the mass of the material [*Größe des Stoffs*] goes far beyond my memory and my understanding." Already in the contrast between Hermann's booming question and the writer's ability to respond, between critical faculties and "material," there is the suggestion of size anxiety.

Very early in the long letter, Franz describes himself, already shrinking in anticipation of the comparison with Hermann, as "weak," "frightened," "restless" [*unruhig*]—with the figure of rest, as in the introductory talk on Yiddish discussed in chapter 3, opposing the mobile subject who finds no ground. But the bald comparison of the two men's bodies comes a few pages later with the emblem of the size–anxiety trope, the memory of the two Kafka men in the changing room:

> I was already oppressed by your plain corporeality. I can still remember for instance how we used to undress together in a changing room. Me skinny, weak, delicate, you strong, big, broad.

This comparison was the source for Franz's early recognition of his wretchedness, not in relation to the father, but "to the whole world, for you were for me the measure of all things." The trap Franz lays throughout for the reader (whether the father and addressee, the mother who holds the letter and could never deliver it, or the literary public for which it has been salvaged) is to read this comparison as an inferiority complex; to forget that "world" and "things" might not represent the neutral ground of a stable reality, but values that only seem self-evident and incontestable to the generation of the father.

From the perspective of the value system of his father, Franz is willing to concede everything: Hermann worked hard his whole life; he has done everything for his children, whereas Franz had the "freedom to study what I wanted." This, too, belongs to the letter's taxonomy of size, as the heavy substance of the bourgeois life, responsibility, and worries is opposed to the light, fleeting, fairly insubstantial figure of Franz's writing. Faced with the father's enormous, massive, and weighty generosity, the son's reaction is withdrawal: "I have drawn away [*verkrochen*] from you." He *shrinks* from the father (*"verkriechen"*), as a tortoise into a shell. "Neben ihm kannst du dich verkriechen," in the German phrase: you can never measure up to him. Franz identifies the world of books and ideas as an escape, in this sense of *verkriechen*, from the world of Hermann.

So this notion of shrinking is identified with escape, and explicitly tied to this realm of thinking and reading. Yet, it is an incautious reading (a "confident" reading, one that someone like Hermann might engage in) to see this shrinking as submission. The trap Kafka lays for a certain reader, perhaps for the intended reader, lies in the assumption of the valence of these terms of self-deprecation—"Weakness," for instance, in "me skinny, weak, delicate, you strong, big, broad." "Weak" (*schwach*) must have seemed to Hermann to be a simple enough term to judge—a negative term. To be weak was disgusting to him. But in Franz's short text "Eleven Sons," where the narrator position is occupied by the father, a more complex function of weakness is disclosed:

> My eleventh son is delicate, probably the weakest of my sons; but deceptive in his weakness; he can be at times powerful and determined, although even then is weakness somehow fundamental. However, it is not a shameful weakness but rather something that only on our earthly ground [*Erdboden*] appears as weakness. Isn't for instance readiness to flight weakness, since it is after all wavering and indetermination? My son displays something like that. Such qualities are naturally not pleasing to a father; they obviously take off

from the destruction of the family. Sometimes he looks at me as if he wanted to tell me: "I will take you with me, father." Then I think: "You are the last one I would trust myself to." And his gaze seems again to say: "Let me then at least be the last one."[38]

The grounded earth of "ours," "*Erdboden*," is the sphere of the everyday and of pedestrian valuations from which the deterritorializing gesture escapes. This passage offers a legend of the way the same set of terms is mapped in the letter: what appears to the father as weakness can be experienced as flight, creativity, liberation. Whether understood as flight or as weakness, the gesture emerges from the hostile dynamics of the family circle—and the father here recognizes that its victory will mean "the destruction of the family."

By now we are at the point where we can clearly generalize the principles of "Ich" and "Du" in terms of generations. The boundary between these generations, as in Mary Gluck's previously cited definition, is a clash of class values. But also this idea of mass versus flight: the bigness of Hermann's will to life, business, conquest ("Lebens-, Geschäfts-, Eroberungswillen"). Franz is fighting for his life against this monstrous will, and it is a struggle to the death:

> In any case we were so different from one another, and in this differentness so dangerous to one another [. . .] one could have assumed that you will simply stamp me out until nothing is left of me.

The bigger they come, the harder they fall. Franz makes a sly reference to a Hermann who was once "younger, therefore fresher, wilder," whom he contrasts implicitly to a more decrepit Hermann posed to receive the deadly letter. We recall "big" Prague German liberalism, the German-Jewish ruling class that fancied itself the cultural center of Bohemia, a cultural power closely associated with sociopolitical hegemony. These illusions had been utterly shattered by World War I.

"I did not have your strength, not your appetite," writes Franz. "Your self-confidence was so great [*groß*]," while Franz trades this self-confidence for "a boundless sense of guilt" [*ein grenzenloses Schuldbewußtsein*]. Guilt and shame are the product of the father's "education" of the son, and when Franz compliments Hermann as a good father for having educated or "raised" the children well, he calls him "*ein guter Erzieher.*" Earlier in the year in which the letter was written, Kafka explored this notion of "Erziehung" through the sadistic military figure at the center of the story "In the Penal Colony." The confident father and shameful son complement each other; the torturer leads the object of his sadism to understanding, shame paring away at the mass of the body to reach toward the core of existence. The profit of the industrious father is paid for with the guilt of the son (the letter puns with the words for "guilt" [Schuld] and "debt" [Schulden]). Thus the hardy gourmand gives way to the Hunger Artist; the "greatness" of the former's confidence collapses before a shame that no borders can contain [grenzenloses Schuldbewußtsein].

This play of terms devastates optimistic misreadings of the frequent and exalting references to family that litter Kafka's notes and letters. "Marriage is the greatest of all," and if Franz could only marry, he could become Hermann's son. This is precisely because marriage belongs to the substantive, material, territorial world that the father represents for the son. The territorial is explicitly invoked in the letter:

> Sometimes I imagine the map laid out before me with you stretched out over it. And then it seems to me as if the only regions that would come into question for my life would be either those that you do not cover or those that do not lie within your reach. And in light of the image I have of your size, those are not many and not very satisfying regions [. . .]

Of course there is nothing left—nothing earthly. Hence the escape, the deterritorializing gesture, the mercurial flight, which, destroying territoriality along the way, opens new horizons. The value judgment that this flight is superior to mass is really only barely concealed; the text protects itself against a reading that would identify in Kafka the assimilation of the discourses marginalizing him. Thus the generational conflict represented the struggle against those really very "big" discourses of territory that exceeded the value system of the bourgeois life, covering essential assumptions about nation and race, borders and political power, identity and the body. The creative moment is not that in which Kafka is defeated in the face of dangerous, colossal, insurmountable discourse, but rather the construction of a text that is a very cautiously and deliberately engineered instrument, a technology developed to provide a way out of the confines of the body.

UNCIVIL WARS

It is not hard to see where the liberal-humanist assessment of the cultural contribution of the Prague circle comes from. Modifying that wishful assessment by giving the longing for a renewal of a primordial family of humanity circumscribed by spiritualist love a new name, such as radical humanism, only partially succeeds in differentiating it from that other humanism. Perhaps surprisingly, the liberal-humanist interpretation of the Prague contribution is not the exclusive property of western European and American scholars. It has marked writing about the Prague circle from the Communist regimes of the former eastern European republics, even if the latter stopped short of claiming, as one popular treatment has concluded, that the Prague "humanists" were "anti-ideological."[39] And yet, as the title of the Czech anthology *Weltfreunde* implies, something like a liberal-humanist image of the Prague circle tempted scholars of varying ideological stripes.

While it is necessary to differentiate what was called "German liberalism" in fin-de-siècle Prague from contemporary "liberalism"—indeed to resist the notion that the term ever had a single, static, and consistent referent—the contemporary term does have some relation to its nineteenth-century counterpart. Contemporary liberal historians consistently betray a sympathy with certain aspects of the German-liberal program of the period, and deploy an apparently shared vocabulary of tolerance, emancipation, representative governance, socioeconomic mobility, and, above all, rationalism. Even if we stress that these terms carried with them extremely different baggage in 1910 than they do today, we must recognize a family resemblance between these values of the generation of Werfel's and Kornfeld's parents and our broadest general notions of liberalism today.

It is here that the liberal representation of Prague circle humanism collides with the projects of the Prague writers themselves. For the battleground they inhabited was not one of enlightened rationalism against irrationalism, or of modern liberty against authoritarianism. Despite their contempt for the rising *völkisch* movement and mistrust of the most radical directions of the Czech nationalist movement, neither of these was ever the primary enemy inscribed in these writers' texts. In the expressionist work above all, the objects of ultimate scorn were always materialism, earthly politics, and lifeless reality, identified as products of modern liberal society. The generational conflict was central because the blame for the modern dilemma was placed on the liberal values of the fathers' generation.

A superficial concentration on gestures toward "world friendship" and the "family of man" has the further pitfall of deflecting attention from the violent quality of these texts. The Prague expressionists did not take up the liberal appeal for civility in this period of manifest national and ideological conflict (an appeal that, it is often ignored, served and serves the ideological interests of certain empowered classes over all others). The desire to "break open" the discrete circles of a modern, fragmentary existence contained within it an explosive revolutionary element.

The expressionist battle in the Prague context represented two kinds of civil war, then: the first, the attack on the figure of petty liberal complacency symbolized by the father; and the second, a war within the self, the struggle to release the dormant spirit from within the comfortable but constrictive confines of the body. So the protagonist of Kornfeld's first play, *Die Verführung* (The seduction; written 1913), opens the drama with a mood of dreary despondence arising from the tension between his explosive anger at the earth and his ever-willingness to embrace the world:

> [. . .] And my hatred for it all, which however—oh, God!—is unfaithful enough to be ever ready to transform itself into an embrace of the world, with these arms that are faithless enough to clench their fists.[40]

Even while this passage is cited to illustrate the cohabitation of contempt for the earth and the desire to embrace all the world, it is clear which of the two impulses is stronger in the aptly named personage of Bitterlich. He delivers this monologue after an attempt to flee the earth through suicide has failed, and while he still has plans to try again. And when a moment of erotic insight leads him to abandon surrender and to return to the battlefield, the first act he undertakes is the strangulation of a complete stranger, whose mere appearance seems an emblem of the times:

> That nose! That mouth! How common you look! [. . .] And then a yellow vest over that belly. All you need to do now is to set a golden blond toupee on that bald head! [. . .] I am seeing him now for the first time—and yet I have seen him a thousand times before! He populates the world! Just look at the horror of him![41]

The tragedy of the play is not the capricious murder of a fellow human being; we recall from the previous excerpt that Bitterlich does not see such entities as humans nor even as beings. Rather, the tragic injustice lies in the custody of Bitterlich's fate within that dominant and false brand of "justice" that is allied with the murderer and his values. The public prosecutor, mistakenly assuming that Bitterlich has killed for love, facilitates the criminal's escape. He, too, identifies a truer and more spiritual justice beyond an external, legal justice that awaits the hero:

I know that you are innocent; I know your life and your fate; I understand you. But what will the others understand? Only what has *happened!* Therefore . . . flee! [42]

Here, again, the "truth" of inner life and destiny is contrasted to the external sham of what appears to have happened. The prosecutor privileges his true understanding of the essential Bitterlich ("I know *you*") over a superficial narrative of events, and Bitterlich's spiritual righteousness over the transgression of a soulless law. True justice, then, consists in the triumph of the internal spirit over the external superficies. The term "expressionist" itself evokes this promise of an outward propulsion of *"das Innerliche."*

In Kornfeld's ongoing career in Frankfurt, he developed this attack on externality into an expressionist theory of drama. Just as the style of the expressionist drama as literature violated the conventions of naturalist dramatic language, Kornfeld's prescription for the role of the actor seeks to release the player from the confines of realistic portrayal; the actor's job is to represent not a natural man, but rather the essence of a man:

> [H]e does not have to conform himself to reality, but rather reality to him. With his personality, with his tone, his movement, he has to create something new: namely, the reality, the tone, and the movement of that world in which man is his own essence, the sum of himself. That is the productive performer, in contrast to the analytical one [. . .] [43]

The antinaturalist performance of the expressionist actor is not mere external affect (or superficial "style"). It represents the outward expression of inner truth. Through this radical act of expression, the actor lays claim to the territory of the stage, and transforms it, in a relationship that exactly parallels the attack on the surface of "reality" outside the theater via the spiritual revolution of humanity. The jarring destruction of naturalist convention corresponds to the rupture of conventions of reality in the world outside, and both revolutions are effected through an outward propulsion of spiritual essence.

The dualism of the "productive" versus the "analytic" player is a new one in this discussion; it at first deceptively appears to parallel the historiographical distinction between "activist" and "contemplative" expressionism. But "analysis" for Kornfeld represents an only apparently internal act, which in fact dwells upon the surface of a lifeless and earthly mechanics. "Productivity" here is not measured by an external mass of product, but is defined rather as the departure from externality and identified with the revolutionary activity involved in releasing the soul. This reversal of identifications of within and without, a typical gesture of Prague texts of all sorts, is at the heart of this uncivil battle of spirit against matter.

PSYCHOLOGY AND SOUL

The relationship between the actor's strategy and the two kinds of circles mentioned in the Kornfeld text opening this chapter becomes even more apparent in the essay "Worte an den Schauspieler" ("A word to the actor").[44] The function of acting as "embodiment" of spiritual truth calls for the exaggeration of gesture, the generous enlargement of pathos, the abandonment of naturalism. As in the dual function of the circle, the body is not invoked for the sake of its pedestrian function of enclosing the spirit, but as a vehicle for the embodiment of the soul and its transmission outward. In the dichotomy Kornfeld sets up in his advice to thespians; he offers an artistic possibility in the place of what he perceives as a reality of life, a spiritual function versus a material function, eternity instead of the present moment, and an engulfing gesture rather than circumscription. Thus the note to the player becomes an integral part of Kornfeld's major programmatic piece, the essay presented in installments in the journal *Das junge Deutschland* that would become a central manifesto of expressionism: "Der beseelte und der psychologische Mensch" (Spiritualized and psychological man).[45]

In this complex and exhaustive essay, the rhetorical figures identified so far are brought together in the service of a self-conscious, politicized program that ultimately endows art with a revolutionary function. The figure of the circle and its counterpart, the body, appear from the beginning. Man, says Kornfeld, is the *middle point* of the world sphere, the mediator of the earthly and the divine.[46] Inherent in man is a certain dualism. He possesses a soul and a character: the soul is a vessel of wisdom, love, goodness, faith, piety, while the character is the shelter of a thousand qualities—cleverness, bravery, humanity, spite, envy, and so on. These two may be in harmony with one another, fused together into one, in men that are perfect—that is, whole—forms (*vollkommene Gestalten*). More usually, the two are at odds. To reach that perfection, the character must be subordinated:

> Let us leave it to the everyday to have character, and let us be nothing but soul in greater hour. For the soul is heaven's, and character all too earthly.[47]

The character is external, sublunary, and everyday, while the soul promises both the divine without and the eternal within. We cannot fully renounce the character and overcome the material, for

> [i]t is the fate of man that his essential essence is trapped within a blood-filled, urge-driven body, in a conglomerate of characteristics and abilities and understandings that can serve his everyday needs, as his body does. It is the misfortune of man that he, once conscious of this disharmony, cannot complacently be fully earthly anymore, nor perhaps can he ever become fully spiritual.[48]

This dualistic curse of humankind can be negotiated, but never completely overcome. Only in the work of art can freedom from duality be won. The "humanistic" desire to overcome this painful condition through earthly reform is a great sin; its proponents are the most shameless, primitive, and banal humans of all, for they have condemned themselves to pure earthliness. The contemporary crisis, in Kornfeld's view, is one in which "humanist" interests such as social democracy and Catholicism, perceiving themselves to represent a truth beyond borders, in fact recognize the legitimacy of territorial borders and earthly political interests. These proponents are as foul fruit that has fallen from the tree of humanity. Kornfeld contrasts the political goal of mass politics to the only valuable struggle:

> The only means the individual has to change the world is that of changing himself. [. . .] And so let the unpolitical man be the final goal, for the issue is not to improve but rather to overcome the state.[49]

The way to this redemption is the turning back into the self, to consciousness and conscience, to the soul, whence man emerged and which distinguished him from the animals. Kornfeld's dialectic, then, begins in a state of unproblematic spiritual nature (as does Marx's primitive communism), an age without ideas and ideals, and without consciousness and conscience. It then moves into a sphere of competing interests and lifeless principles—a segregated existence, where isolation is effected at once in mankind and in the individual man. The final messianic-dialectical move is toward within, toward the soul of the individual through the work of art, where the spirit of mankind can be reconciled with his earthliness and the divine promise of humanity reclaimed.

It has been argued that Kornfeld's radical resistance to the everyday, to external and territorial "politics," led to his demise. His despondent retreat into himself in the face of the advance of National Socialist Germany prevented him from "acting," from engaging in the practical and manifestly necessary motions that would have afforded him escape from his Prague retreat. "If he had engaged himself with the despised, political everyday [. . .] perhaps he would have saved himself," notes Margarita Pazi.[50] Most of those close to him did so. But what flight could have saved Paul Kornfeld from the fate of the territorial? His "escape," like the metaphorical escape from earthly reality in so many of his own works, was death, in Lodz in 1941.

Kornfeld's work was programmatic, setting a tone for expressionism at the same time that it mapped a plan of action (for the actor, for the artist, for the political subject), and that program was grounded in binary oppositions such as "political engagement" and "aesthetic flight." The reversal of valuations that leads to a reassessment of which of the realms constitutes real life is not unique to Kornfeld: the play with oppositional terms such as "life" and "lifelessness," "reality" and "irreality," and so on marks the work of Max Brod in this period and even before. Focusing on Brod's essay "On the Beauty of Ugly Pictures," the Praguer Hermann Grab has noted a reversal of the conventional understandings of these terms; the powerful dichotomy of external world versus spiritual reality; the jarring images of modern (expressionist) art, which shatter the naive assumption of external reflection of internal essences.[51] If impressionism was for Brod the last moment of a naive view of world beauty, expressionism marked the destruction of that world. But even before his apparent appreciation of expressionism, Brod's work demonstrated his sympathy with the figure of the divine, artistic, spiritual man in opposition to politics and materiality. In "The Pilgrimage to Orazio" he not only elaborates this dichotomy, but also specifies the particular function of art to save man from his terrestrial purposiveness and to bring him closer to God.[52] Brod's "aestheticist" concerns that art was being vilified through its use as a political medium and that critics were "psychologizing" the spiritual relation between artist and work were very closely tied to the view of the world painted by Kornfeld.[53] It will be recalled that Brod decried the critic's analysis of the psyche of the author, rather than focusing on the soul to be found in the work of art.

Clearly the dualism articulated in Kornfeld's major essay is grounded in (or even defines) the antirationalism classified under the rubric *Lebensphilosophie* or "vitalism."[54] Walter Sokel links the essay to Buber's prewar *Ecstatic Confessions* (1911), and, provocatively, to Heidegger's *Being and Time* (1927).[55] Heidegger's magnum opus, according to Sokel, may be seen as "a tremendous elaboration of Kornfeld's thesis"; or, in reverse motion, one may read back onto Kornfeld's texts the Heideggerian dichotomy of "authentic" and "inauthentic" existence.[56] Surely, as a mere glance at the index of *Being and Time* will verify, that term is at the heart of the work.[57] Its relation to the territorial paradigm becomes clearer when we consider that "authentic" is used to translate *"eigentlich,"* with its connotations of property or ownership that the English term lacks. Moreover, Kornfeld's treatment of a moment of art in which the earth is embraced by the world and the dualism overcome is at the heart of Heidegger's 1934 essay "The Origin of the Work of Art."[58]

It is Buber, however, and particularly the mystical Buber of the influential *Ecstatic Confessions,* whose presence was directly felt by Kornfeld and Werfel, and who would so strongly affect other Prague Jews. Buber's construction of futurity is provocatively comparable to Kornfeld's vision, in that it is both "humanistic" (in striving toward a spiritual universalism) and at the same time antiliberal (in rejecting contemporary Jewish assimilationism). The language of these attacks on liberalism often approaches the language of *völkisch* antisemitism contemporary with it, and the attempts to neutralize that language by paraphrasing the "humanistic" goals of the expressionists and other Praguers are misguided and misleading. Sokel's points of reference in Buber and Heidegger point to discursive rather than causal relations of thought. Such an approach allows for an apprehension of connections that the rationalist reduction of arguments renders invisible.

THE COMPLICITY OF DISCOURSE

A good place to begin an exploration of the rhetorics of the new Prague "humanism"—to investigate where it identified its enemies, and where it laid its hopes—is Werfel's 1914 essay entitled "Glosse zu einer Wedekind-Feier" (Gloss on a Wedekind celebration).[59] The "Gloss" is a true program piece of the period, turning at once from a discussion of a cultural event to a violent confrontation with the generational conflict on the one hand, and the national conflict on the other. While a superficial glance might support a liberal thesis that the young Praguers' hope to overcome the national conflict was a manifestation of liberal humanism, an actual reading of the essay more clearly defines their internationalism. The "Gloss" remarks upon the translation and production in a Czech theater of the German author Frank Wedekind's *Lulu,* which Werfel recognizes as one of several "wholesome flashes" beginning to overcome the "black abyss between the nations in Prague" in the last years. Werfel refers of course to the spirited revolt of his own generation between 1910 and 1914, a "new will and spirited youth" in Prague, set in contrast to "the blunt and cynical matter (*Materie*) that with the same insipid mass of understanding is born and dies and exists only to pursue the business and values of the father." While it is true that Werfel condemns nationalist intolerance in these lines, the rhetorical strategy of his condemnation is aimed steadfastly at the German-liberal establishment. Not unlike the texts of both the Young Czech and *völkisch* German movements, Werfel's discourse revolves around the principal opposition of an old, materialist, pedestrian, and obsolete order ("tepid national liberalism and senile enlightenment, which even now believes its humanism [*Humanität*] to be a translation of humanity [*Menschlichkeit*]"), against a new will (a "stronger and more genuine decisiveness"), a spirited and spiritual youth, and a revolutionary movement. Werfel reverses the pedestrian notion of "real life," which in his imagined revolutionary moment is shifting from the practical sphere of the material world (what he calls the "fictive life of the average Prague German") to "the will to a real life" within the spirit of this more authentic generation. The expressionist revolt of son against father had this application in Werfel's Prague: the new will of a spirited, universalist youth would strike dead the decrepit doctrine of chauvinist German liberalism: "The value of youth it seems to me lies in the strength of its revolutionary instincts: a youth that does not desire to strike the establishment dead ought to be struck dead itself . . . " This youthful revolt is not nationalist, but is intensely loyal to Prague, and uniquely prescient of their danger of losing it:

> But we, who love Prague with all of the force of childhood and who really fancy ourselves patriots, see only this: the Prague German minority must put an end to the exclusion to which it condemns itself, more than to which it is condemned. [. . .] *We want to take part in Prague again*, and can perceive only that after another half century of this attitude we will be Praguers no more!

How is one to read this expressionist discourse in relation to the language of the contemporary antiliberal movements that are seen as its opponents? In a concrete sense, the violent antisemitic movements of Czech and German Bohemia were the greatest threats to the members of the Prague circle, while the hegemony of German liberalism had by this time quite obviously passed. It would be shallow and misleading to point out discursive similarities of these movements with the texts of Werfel and others as evidence that expressionist universalism was in fact proto-fascist or racist. Yet, it is no less misleading purposefully to overlook the way the texts position themselves rhetorically in order to recover from them a precursor to late twentieth-century liberalism.

The phenomenon we can identify in these texts, which often appear all-too-dangerously to approach the language of competing ideologies, can be called "the complicity of discourse." It is possible to refer to a *völkisch* "discourse" in opposition to other specific ideological discourses that were in currency at the same time. But it is also possible to employ the term "discourse" in the way that it is used without an article and always in the singular. The conceptual lexicon and grammar that are shared by ideological opponents at moments of pregnant historical crisis can be more revealing than the programs that set them against one another. The competing ideological systems of the prewar period were all engaged in and fighting for control of discourse itself, together writing a page left blank by the discursive collapse of liberalism. This moment is a concrete representation of Foucault's declaration that discourse "is [both] that *with which* and *for which* is fought." [60]

It is therefore no surprise to find an antisemitic note in Werfel's "Gloss," even though it was published for a German-speaking Jewish readership: he lays the primary blame for the current situation on a figure that is clearly a stereotype of the Central European Jew: "The freak we have to thank for it is the omnipresent schmuck, the typical Prague neurotic, quivering, loud, and vain, who has to reaffirm his pitiful existence everywhere he goes." An even more fascinating tension is contained in the complicity of his radically antinationalist discourse with chauvinist liberalism itself. The German minority is to be blamed for its own self-isolation in Prague, but the Czech nation for its own part "strikes itself the bitterest wound through [national] hatred. For it is a fact that Czech culture can only be a child of the German culture in the midst of which it lives. [. . .] And in the bold moment in which this people, forgetting all historical necessity, boasts a sudden independence, it will also have lost its own remarkable cultural possibilities and, despite recent European fashion, be barbarians." The revolutionary youth is suddenly in the same camp as the German patriciate, tending the Slavic child. The castigation of the Czechs for their arrogance culminates in one of the most steadfast and insipid of German-liberal prejudices, the identification of the Slavs as "barbarians." But first and foremost, the piece

allies itself with that massive array of German-language antiliberal cri-
tiques that range from the misogynous antisemitism of Otto Weininger
through to the ideologues of what would become National Socialism.

In light of this rhetorical complicity, the various historiographical
Prague circles are strikingly consistent in their inexplicable omission of
a certain Max Steiner, the best student in the class of Max Brod and Felix Weltsch at the Piarist grade school where Werfel was also a pupil.[61]
But where in the postwar discussions of the great humanists of the Prague
circle is there room for Max Steiner, so revered by his friends and readers as a kind of Prague double of Otto Weininger, down to the detail of
his suicide?

In his major work, *Die Rückständigkeit des modernen Freidenkertums* (The backwardness of modern freethinking), Steiner accuses the
liberals (or "freethinkers") of greater fanaticism and intolerance than
any religious sect might show.[62] Forging a line through his avowed pre-
cursors Kant, Schopenhauer, Nietzsche, and Weininger, Steiner shapes a
critique of modern society that is radically antimaterialist, antiscientist,
and laced with misogyny. The current view of the way of modernity is
simple, he says: "*Atheism, Materialism, and Darwinism; Democracy,
Social Reform, Women's-Libbery . . .* " The day of the freethinkers has
arrived.[63] They are the vanguard of a detestable mass politics, betrayers
of the elite legacy of Kant and Socrates.

Steiner's worldview is a close relative of the social critique elaborated
by the Prague expressionist sons. Surely there is a compelling resemblance between Kornfeld's view of history as we have discussed it and
Steiner's history of philosophy. The dialectic gets under way with folksy
or naive religion, moves then to "natural science–atheism," and finally
arrives at a synthesis that, as in Kornfeld's version, seems to the writer
just to have begun: the recognition of the emptiness of human science,
the return to faith, but this time to a faith that is personal (Kornfeld
again) and nonsuperstitious.[64]

It would be difficult to overestimate the importance of this neglected
"flip side" (which is sometimes the same side) of the dichotomy under
examination. Weininger himself was certainly and seriously read by all
of the Prague writers; his influence on the very young Paul Kornfeld, for
instance, is manifest in the seventeen-year-old's diary.[65] More significant
than Kornfeld's early attempt to mimic what he (correctly) identified as
current intellectual fashion is the opposition in his diary entry of the
modern female to the "natural," her "lifeless" quality. This is the figu-

ration of woman into the dichotomy that would be so richly developed in his later writings. Weininger's Mann-Weib (or M/W) dualism appears in force as well in the writings of Max Brod, Oskar Baum, and Franz Werfel.

The central issue of the function of art in many of these writings is gendered according to the Weiningerian model. Brod's *The Pilgrimage to Oratio,* cited above, is representative in its bold elitism, with the frank opposition of the godlike artist to the "mob." [66] Inscribed within this model is the dualism of "creator" (Weininger's M) and "creation" of nature and of art (Weininger's W).[67] The same model comes forth in the greater part of Oskar Baum's fiction. What happens in Baum's texts more than in Brod's is the curious reconstellation of Weiningerian elements to produce an anti-Weiningerian—arguably even a feminist—result. The remarkable feature of the complicity of discourse is this durability of rhetorical features on all sides of ideological struggle.

In much the same way, Franz Werfel explicitly rejected what he called Weininger's theory of "transcendental racial inferiority" at the same time that he was speaking of Judaism in terms lifted directly from the most notorious chapter of Weininger's *Sex and Character.* Werfel depicted Judaism not as "the particularity of a particular people or race, but a quality that is in some degree within all individuals." The opposition of Jew-Aryan was for Werfel at the center of a metaphysical conflict of the future.[68] Of course, Werfel's relationship to Judaism was nothing if not idiosyncratic. Typical, however, was his failure to escape from Weiningerian categories even while pretending to refute them. His most successful moment at gaining control of the discourse, of engaging in it fully and undermining its effects, was in the pacifist essay written on the front in the midst of the war (1916). Entitled "Fragment against the Masculine Gender," the piece engaged in the by now familiar reversal of notions of reality and irreality, always within a gendered dichotomy.[69] The girl playing with her doll is not playing, since she becomes an emblem of love and nurturing; at that moment she is motherhood, a real (essential or spiritual) entity. In contrast, the boy playing soldier is not the emblem of the masculine role; on the contrary, the soldier is the emblem of unreal boyhood. Similarly, the apparent heavy reality of "science" (along with Weininger, Werfel accepts this as a purely masculine element) masks its true essence of "play." The deepest secrets of nature, the heights of true experience, and access to an organic life are closed off to the man. Rather than challenging Weininger's iron categories of M

and *W,* Werfel leaves them intact and changes only their valuation. Man is still the essence of science, war, creativity, battle, and knowledge—only none of it is real.

This "playful" turn of Werfel's can be seen as an application of the potential turn theorized by a more recent Central European thinker, Slavoj Žižek, in *Metastases of Enjoyment.*[70] The Weiningerian maxim "Woman is nothing," the antithesis of subjectivity, ironically provides for Žižek the only possible space for a self-conscious and therefore more "authentic" claim to subjectivity. If the Enlightenment (Weininger, like Steiner, starts with Kant) is the source for identifying the Jew as "shapeless" rather than disfigured, qualified by a lack of substance rather than any positive feature, this move may ironically privilege woman/Jew to transcend form. Hegel's description of subjectivity as something *"angezogen,"* worn, as a mask or a costume, is thus most "authentic" in this playful feminine moment of masquerade. The feminist critique that Žižek's generous gesture toward the female vessel all but escapes the closed circle of masculine subjectivity is similarly applicable to Werfel's discourse.

Woman's potential to transcend her own irreality, to realize the spiritual essence of herself, is a hope for Werfel. This is the secret of his dependence on the erotic relationship for the continuation of his artistic existence. This is the kernel of his attachment to Alma: "Alma is a reality [. . .] She stands before me not as an image of sweetness conjured up in a dream [. . .]—she stands before me as a human being who has more of the vital properties of life, more stability, more direction, than I myself have [. . .]"[71] Woman opens the artist's road from the sham reality of territory to a more authentic existence—a life at rest within itself [*das in sich geschlossene und ruhende Leben*]. This positive role of *W* takes place within the categories of Weininger's misogynist model: the masculine artist is still the dreamer, the creator of this new world; woman is the dream itself, his inspiration, the stuff from which he creates his work.

EROTIC SYMBIOSIS II

"Erotic symbiosis" is central to many Prague German-Jewish writers, beyond the way it operates in Brod's aestheticist texts.[72] Just as Werfel's relationship with the dreamlike Alma provides access for him to a new "reality," the redemption his heroes experience is most often triggered through an encounter with the feminine other. The place where the two meet is the new ground from which the artistic/spiritual revelation arises. In *Der Besuch aus dem Elysium,* the protagonist tells the object of his unrequited love that she "elevated [my] common existence to the eternal" and taught him "to renounce material happiness."

> *You* were the meaning of my waking and slumbering breath, so eternally one with my every word and deed, secret content of my most minor agitation, so that I soon forgot your earthly image, which had melted into the aimless ruminations and endless states of my self. How in vain I taxed my eyes to recall your image! Unreachable, you existed unknown, you wandered through my daydreams, you negotiated within my essence, and I knew nothing of the color of your hair, I had hardly a sense of your gait or your speech.
>
> And yet, what is this feeling? *You are in the world!* Somewhere, a condensation of tender ether, a product of primordial matter, lovely mass, a form!!![73]

The passage is dense with blinding alternations of material and spiritual imagery. The ephemeral desire awakened in the artist-hero ("Desire! That desire which strays from its center") becomes independent of its object. The spiritual is manifest, not in the woman, but in the desire she awakens in the man's soul. The symbiosis in this text does not take place in the union of M and W, but rather in the space created by their irreconcilable disunion. The true symbiosis of matter and spirit begins within the person of the male artist: "My love could never have found such fulfillment through mutual love and the gift of contentment . . . " Requited love could never have borne this synthesis.

The earthly image of this female object of the hero's desire melts into his words and deeds, thoughts and dreams, and becomes one with his own being. She remains within him, engaging [*handeln*, as in trade] with his Being, corporeally walking [*gehen*] through his unearthly daydreams. The woman in this image is earthbound, as she is in the Weiningerian model, and, also following the model, dreams remain the realm of M. Reflection on that "product of primordial matter," the purest of forms, lifts only the masculine spirit to its potential.

In his play *Die Verführung* (The seduction), Kornfeld too ties redemption to an erotic symbiosis sought in three different female characters, finally finding it in Ruth.[74] Symbiosis is a recurrent theme in the poetry of the Prague expressionist and translator of Czech verse Rudolf Fuchs as well.[75] It is nonetheless in Kafka's friend the brilliant poet Franz Janowitz that the relationship of this erotic symbiosis to expressionist universalism takes its most emphatic shape. Janowitz's contribution to the 1911 *Herder-Blätter* is entitled "Weltverwandtschaft" (World affinity):

> Bin ein ankerloses Schiff,
> Bist du das Meer, das es bewegt,
> Das mich von Stern zum Sterne trägt
> Auf Bahnen, die ich nie begriff.
>
> Doch bin ich bloß ein schwankes Licht
> Bist du der Wind, der froh es neckt
> Der mich bald liebt und bald erschreckt,
> Bis mich ein Finger bricht.
>
> Vertausendfacht liegt in der Welt,
> Was dich und mich zusammenhält.
> Und Lust und Leid von tausend Ich
> Umfaßt mein Herz, infaßt es dich.[76]

Man remains the subject throughout in these stanzas, breaking out of the finitude of the self by way of the infinite worldly correspondences inspired by the model of erotic symbiosis. He is an anchorless ship or an unsteady light—both images of finite, contained, and manmade products of civilization. She is the ocean carrying him from star to star, the wind stretching the flame. She is the natural motor of the created—the inspiration of art; but she is also the limitless spirit imbuing the finite. The final juxtaposition between the prepositions "*um*" and "*in*" ("surrounding" and "into") effects a sexual metaphor that simultaneously refers us back to the rhetoric of the circle. Her function is engulfing; it represents a spiritual encirclement that offers a path to the universal. Here it is the unity with all things.

Certainly these gendered projections of the dichotomy so well represented in Kornfeld's programmatic texts and so typical of other Prague writers have profound national implications. Weininger's own text articulates these to a significant degree, with its discussions of Jewish and Aryan culture and the relative masculinity or femininity of peoples. What we are beginning to see here are the ways in which a modern complex of the gendered metaphorics of artistic production took on more specific and exceedingly complex meanings within the Prague scene. As we will see in detail in our readings of both the "turn to Jewishness" among these German-language Prague writers and their parallel interest in the translation of Czech literature,[77] the peculiar gender codes of the nationality conflict itself inflected images of erotic symbiosis in ways that unsettled the gendered relationship of male artistic subject and female artistic object. The discourse identifying woman with the earth and man with the spirit had specific salience in the context of Prague's "deterritorialized" cultural production. Yet, as we will increasingly see, the more deeply such dichotomies are entrenched by these texts, the more their contingency, even their illusory nature, is exposed. The boundaries segregating such gendered spheres as spirit and earth (or art and politics) would be radically retrenched—and at the same time provocatively opened—as these poets went off to war.[78]

THE WAR AGAINST WORLD

With the declaration of war in 1914, Werfel's attention turned to the essay genre, and at the same time to the problem of a political resolution to the crisis of humanity. In a score of essays written between 1914 and 1918, either from the field or at the War Press Bureau, Werfel worked through the problems he had laid out in his prewar writings and ruminated on how they could be reconciled with a horrifically unreal "real" world.

The initial task, more modest than the ultimate goal of finding a solution to the crisis, was to diagnose the state of the world at the moment war was declared. In a 1914 article printed in the expressionist journal *Die Aktion,* he listed "multiplicity, confusion, [and] insolubility" as symptoms of a more general and quite apparent "formlessness" of his time. Since the specific aim of the essay is to oppose the outlines of states, external action, and the state as such, this concentration on the issue of form is interesting. All of these things he might have identified as "forms." The dissociation of the activity of daily life from the unity offered by soulful purpose is the "formlessness" Werfel identified. The Modern has followed a course that has no relation either to the soul of the individual actors or to the spiritual needs of the community of man.

> Who of all of us born around the turn of this time has not felt a little like a ghost!? [. . .] We stand powerless against the detail, which makes no gesture toward unity; it seems that the "and" between things has rebelled, everything lies unrecoverable in a heap, and a new and appalling aloneness makes life mute.[79]

The profound spiritual crisis in modern civilization that Werfel saw behind the declaration of war had philosophical roots that he thought he could trace back through occidental intellectual history. Yet, rereading this paragraph with "in Prague" inserted into the first line shows how closely Werfel's description of the general crisis of humanity resembles the specific situation from which he sprang. Now set this text against his answer to a 1922 newspaper survey asking Prague-born artists abroad why they had left the city. He answered that the Czechs had a vital capital city in Prague that meant for them "life," "health," "culture"—nothing ghostlike at all. In contrast:

> For the non-Czech, it seems to me, this city has no reality. For him she is a daydream that offers no experience, a crippling ghetto without even the poor life relations of a ghetto, a dull world from which no activity or only sham activity can originate.[80]

Asked specifically about Prague life, Werfel, perhaps hastily, identified the fissure between spiritual reality and external life, between community and the life of the individual, as one emerging from the "sick" condition of the non-Czech Praguer (read: Jew). Writing in 1914, this writer from the city of ghosts had privileged access to the sensibility he identified at the root of the crisis of modernity.

In this respect Werfel's position toward the war differed from that of other German-speaking intellectuals—including Prague Jews—who saw Austria and Germany as defenders of the spirit battling the powers of modern materialism. Thomas Mann's *Reflections of a Nonpolitical Man* is the best-known articulation of that position, which the Praguer Oskar Baum laid out in similar terms.[81] For Werfel, the war appeared as the destiny of a world in crisis, both symptom and result of the despicable condition of modernity, and from that perspective he could identify the war in general and the bureaucracy driving it in particular as the enemies of spirit. This position is sometimes veiled in the wartime essays, which Werfel knew were subject to the censor, but it emerges less subtly in the lengthy and rich correspondence left to us from the romance with a certain Gertrude Spirk.

In a moment of particular unabashedness, for example, Werfel excoriates the "arch-bureaucrat Pilate" who could be found everywhere,

> washing his hands in innocence.—By the way, are you following the parliament?—Don't you find the Germans to be the most miserable scum of humanity? Without any human charm, spiritless in body and word, cruel as the principle of unproductivity, informants, deceitful and vain, void of beauty and goodwill—an abomination! If you don't believe me, just read the German representatives' speeches.[82]

It is of more than incidental interest that the "scum" in question were the German Bohemian representatives, with whom Werfel felt no commonality beyond the German language, "whose mortal enemies they are." For Werfel, the real opponents and genuine comrades in this war stood on both sides of the front. Werfel conveys the violence of his personal war experience, with almost no exception, as the "eternal, gray indifference" of endless hours of "the company of strangers [*Fremden*], who hurt you and grate on the nerves. The rape of the soul, involuntary togetherness with the lifeless, wretched, common, lustful, pedantic, pitiful, talentless man!"[83] Not unlike Kornfeld's bitter protagonist Bitterlich, Werfel's rage against spiritless existence is aimed at everyday men. His diagnosis of the significance of the war developed by 1916 into the hope that it would mark the beginning of a newly awakened humanity. The resemblance of Werfel's redemptive projection to the Marxist view of the war as the long-awaited crisis of capitalism from which the revolution would arise is provocative. His cautious avoidance of any explicit declaration of the coincidence of these visions, and the lack of any specific denunciation of the Communists, clearly left the relationship open. In another letter, a few months later in 1916, he writes:

> A time will come [. . .] when the days will take on meaning, even for the deepest skeptic. I know but little for certain yet, but I sense the beginning of a great, raging passion over all lands. [. . .] I prophesy that this war was just a little fly who boldly set himself on the sleeper's nose. We have no idea what movement is—until he awakens and sets loose.[84]

REVOLUTIONARY POETICS, POETIC REVOLUTIONARIES

Werfel's description of expressionist *Aufbruch* may seem to resemble Marxist revolution, and his vision of truer hostile divisions within the ranks of each army may evoke Jean Renoir's film *The Grand Illusion*, but Werfel's language avoided the issue of class. The materiality of social class set it plainly on the side of Werfel's adversaries, and he never deigned to take up such a material cause. From the start, the vanguard in Werfel's spiritual revolution was the artist; the politician-bureaucrat was his archenemy. Thus, Werfel's stance in the wartime essays is difficult to locate within the political spectrum of his time, although his program was by definition political (i.e., radical and in fact revolutionary). The painful negotiation of how he could best engage that program while remaining on the side of spirit against "politics" is a story that is difficult to follow, and easy to misread. By 1916, he understood the com-

plexity of his own situation clearly, as he was to articulate in an essay
ironically published in Kurt Hiller's "activist" journal *Das Ziel.* In "Letter to a Statesman," Werfel spells it out:

> You developed the dream of a new state, and you were even so kind as to go
> into the creative role of poetry in this state. You appealed for the establish-
> ment of a purpose for poetry within the state, and at the same time for a sub-
> lime bureaucracy of poets. [. . .] The *action directe,* though, that you wish
> of literature (and it is mainly to this point that I wanted to speak) seems to
> me to be all too artificial, all too theoretical. [. . .] All poetry represents a
> transformation: the transformation of reality into truth, of sinfulness into re-
> demption, of the world into [. . .] paradise. [. . .]
>   Oh, how impossible it is for me to express to you clearly how contradic-
> tory these terms "poetry" and "politics" are for me![85]

All of this conforms well with the image of Werfel's vision present already in his prewar work. This essay, however, develops with extraordinary precision a theme that will run through his essays all the way up to
the fateful moment when he would be forced to "take a side." He subtly reverses the valences of the art/life dichotomy. The political vision
here is the one that seems to him to be "constructed," "theoretical," and
above all "abstract." By removing politics from the sphere of real action,
or from "reality" altogether, he neutralizes the statesman's adventurous
claims about art performing an *action directe* in the service of politics.

This reversal becomes increasingly explicit as the essay continues. The
politician, with his impossibly abstract conceptions of society, is crip-
plingly deceived by them. That supposed paragon of realists is really the
most intoxicated utopian, incapable of seeing anything beyond ludicrous
abstractions (such as classes and nations). The poet, on the other hand,
is incapable of understanding these abstractions. He cannot see this at-
mospheric medium that is the foundation of the state; he can only see
through it. The politician, then, is the one who conceives and constructs
fleeting fictions, while the artist, the supreme realist, sees. The artist is
not a mediator for Werfel. His vision is based in a move toward immanence and spirit, toward the unmediated experience of faith within the
self. The origin of all human misery is the fissure between *being* and *expression,* Werfel stressed in the philosophical essay "Ex abrupto," which
appeared in 1916 in *Die Aktion.*[86] In this way, the problem of the artist
stands in for what Werfel defines as an eternal crisis of humankind.

Werfel began to develop his vision of an anarchic and an artistic revolt against political forms as a response to the call for a concrete political program to fulfill the promise of his earlier poetry. Leading that call

was the Berlin Jewish leftist Kurt Hiller, calling this more engaged branch of expressionism "activism." But the charge against the contemplative direction of Werfel's work came from Prague as well, leveled by none other than Max Brod, who had by the war's outbreak become a committed Zionist. More interesting than the contrary position Werfel charts out in response to these charges, however, is the fact that a common language is being spoken by the expressionist socialist Hiller, the Prague Zionist Brod, and the "antipolitical" Werfel. It is a language that proceeds from a moment of a highly self-reflexive Central European culture in crisis, a foreign language that is lost in the translation into a present-day literary-historical representation that divides contemplation from political action.

A glimpse of this language begins to come through in an essay Werfel sent to Gertrude Spirk in 1916 and later revised to be included in an anthology, *The Future of the German Stage*.[87] In both the draft and published versions, Werfel begins by resolving firmly that the state, or any instrument of power, exists in direct opposition to the spirit. The present state—he has in mind the German Empire, but not only—has demonstrated its determination to consign the spirit to the service of abomination. Werfel immediately transforms the opposition of power and spirit to one of politics and art, explaining how the work of art can survive in the social and political context of the national stage. In this and other essays Werfel seems to echo that aestheticist credo of Brod's, which Brod imported into his political engagement: that the holy work of art is profaned by contact with ideological instrumentality.[88] Other correspondences emerge in Werfel's description of a light at the end of this dark tunnel of modern politicized life and art:

> Yet, there remains a glimpse of hope even here. Tens of thousands, hundreds of thousands seeing, knowing, feeling—have become human. Perhaps a new exodus is signaling us! And from the hundred thousand will rise a people [*Volk*] and a poetry—two things that have been lost to 70 million since the founding of the [German] Empire.

The potent reversal of valuations in this passage lies in the assumptions about *Volkstum* and art explored in chapter 2, assumptions that were shared by contemporaries across the ideological spectrum. Seventy million Germans have lost their *Volkstum*, their culture, and their access to the spirit at the moment when they acquired and embraced a territory. The revolutionary *Volk* Werfel imagines is scattered among the peoples, on both sides of the military front; it is Kornfeld's "we, the feeling," those who have opened their hearts, who will create a nation of artists. The model for this authentic *Volk* is clearly the Jewish people, circumscribed by no territory but rather scattered in the Diaspora, awaiting the messianic moment.

As a metaphor for the revolution Werfel chooses the Jewish Exodus (the same image is at the center of the Zionism of Hugo Bergmann as well as in the ruminations of Franz Kafka, as we will see). The foundation of the German Empire [*Reichsgründung*] has not grounded a *Volk* and a basis for poetry, but rather has cast the spirit in chains and done away with the possibility of art. Werfel's exodus is a departure from the notion of "state" altogether. It promises the birth of new poetry that will transcend the limits of national literatures.

Werfel's major essay on the correspondence of the transformation of the political world with the emergence of a new poetics is "Substantiv und Verbum" (Noun and verb), published in *Die Aktion* in 1917.[89] Werfel extends the familiar polarity to the dichotomy of prose and poetry, or (respectively) noun and verb. Here again the presumed "realism" of the prose word is in fact the abstracted "expression" decried in *Ex abrupto;* the word of verse (the "verb") offers the essential relation of things, rather than their relations. The poem escapes the territorial rigidity of prosaic grammar and harbors a revolutionary promise:

> I believe in the birth of a new verse poetry that will be completely free of the scholastic symmetry of previous architecture [. . .][90]

Even within poetry, Werfel seeks to escape the model of architecture—the most material of art forms—to get at a truer spiritual essence. His new model is alluded to in a separate essay, an open letter to Fritz Mauthner on the issue of the educational system, where he declares that the goal of pedagogy ought to be to make man more "musical."[91] Thus the valuation of the essential realism of things is again reversed. Furthermore, in emphasizing the verb over the noun, Werfel apparently underscores the element of "action" within a discourse at odds with the initiative that identified itself as "activism."

The most important text in which Werfel exposes the structure of that conflict appeared in 1917 in *Die neue Rundschau* under the title "The Christian Mission: An Open Letter to Kurt Hiller."[92] Here Werfel is direct and explicit in his rejection of "activism" with its emphasis on the omnipresent buzzword "deed" [*"Tat"*], naming as his opponents not only Hiller and his fellow German-Jewish radical essayist Ludwig

Rubiner, but the activism "in another [Zionist] direction" of Max Brod.[93] These activisms, Werfel argues, are alike in espousing

> a program whose main goal could be called the *politicization of literature,* or even better the *politicization of the whole youth.* It is not a system, but a battle cry that demands that everyone come out of his isolation, interrupt the work of his soul (which is egocentric, mean and heartless work) and apply every bit of his time and energy to the work of social betterment. Every pleasure is despised [. . .] all passion cursed, and above all the passion for higher things, for art and individual fulfillment, and only one may count and remain: the passion for politics. "Become politicians," cries the activist [. . .]

The essay represents one of the most explicit elaborations of the dichotomy we have been exploring in this chapter, as it goes on to set politics not merely against art but against Werfel's peculiar understanding of "Christianity," based upon the work of Dostoyevsky. This movement toward the revelation of the individual spirit, which in turn revives and imbues passion into a prosaic and fragmented existence, is at once a kind of reformation and counterreformation. In this text as in some of those we have already presented, Werfel's Christian vision is radically anti-ascetic: it resists traditional Christian asceticism in the same gesture with which it rejects the secularized asceticism of modern life. In this sense, the revolutionary moment at hand represents a dialectical return to true faith, such as Max Steiner had foreseen in his critique of modern thought.

Politics for Werfel is an impossible faith because it has nothing but a social abstraction for grounding, rather than being moored in the solid earth of true faith (the faith of the individual moving toward redemption). Similarly, the modern flight into the social construction of the cities represents for Werfel the loss of faith and of reality. Social relations have replaced human consciousness, parties overcome community, the political manifesto takes precedence over Christian example. The formal implications of this movement are the most telling: the political moves in the direction of above to below, whereas the Christian moves from below to above; politics represents an impulse from without, whereas Werfel's Christian revolution moves from the center to the periphery. It is an abundantly ramified position for a Prague German Jew. After Werfel's constellation, it is clear that the move toward faith and toward art, away from party politics and social engagement, was indeed a self-consciously political program. It represented a radical initiative to seize and disperse centralized power.

Yet, the tension between this revolutionary program and Werfel's orthodox resistance to external political engagement moved headlong into crisis as the war moved on. The Bolshevik Revolution in Russia was a turning point for Central European artists and intellectuals whose hopes for a radical transformation of society would emerge from the war experience. By the spring of 1918, left sentiment and exhaustion with war were being transformed into a revolutionary movement all over Central Europe, which would spill out into the famed, if ill-fated, November Revolution. Werfel's tentativeness toward the political led to a break with Egon Erwin Kisch, who (along with no less prominent writers than Hugo von Hofmannsthal and Rainer Maria Rilke) was engaged with Werfel at the War Press Bureau in Vienna. In mid-1918, with the hope of revolution at hand, Kisch characteristically did not hesitate to get his hands dirty and emerged as a leader of the Vienna Red Guard. Werfel for his part seems to have had a moment of hope that this revolutionary transformation could indeed yield the fruit he had longed for in his antipolitical reflections.

On tour in Switzerland in the service of the propaganda office, Werfel used the occasion of a scheduled reading to workers in Davos to deliver instead an unapproved speech, which was understandably interpreted at the time as a sign that he had joined the revolutionary ranks. It is easy to see the discontinuity between this address—laden with the rhetoric of revolutionary socialism, expressing explicit admiration for Soviet Russia—and his attack on Kurt Hiller. The opening words seem to stake out a new position, but they also show that Werfel has not discarded the rhetorical foundations of his previous, "antipolitical" program:

> Comrades!
> I appear today before men that know the real work of the earth, that grave and honest work on which parasitically rests all that fraudulent activity that calls itself culture.[94]

True to form, Werfel goes on to reverse the values he takes as givens in the above lines, and by the end of the address has endowed the poet with the unique role of spiritual mediator. He contrasts the absurd and parasitic Central European artist to the writer in Russia, where there is no abyss

> between spirit, poetry, and socialism [. . .] And only because in Russia spirit and socialism are melded into one, because the battle for realization of human love, because religion is the issue of heart for millions, could the revolution triumph.

It is certainly apparent that Werfel's deployment of "Christianity" in the Hiller letter and "religion" here are totally removed from the conventional definitions. The artist's function of spiritual intermediary is a priestly one. Nevertheless, the socialist and even Bolshevik rhetoric of the speech is easier to reconcile with Werfel's previous position than is this issue of mediation itself. For, however "anarchic" he hoped the revolution would be, however he hoped the revolution could disperse the centrally held spiritual authority of organized religion and the political power of the state, the entrance into the realm of earthly politics and the acceptance of the poetic role of mediation are in direct conflict with the earlier texts.

Of course, there remains the possibility that Werfel's apparent gesture toward the revolution was opportunistic. If he was convinced, as anyone might have been, that the moment of socialist revolution was surely spreading westward, it would not have been ignoble to claim an early stake in it with the hope of changing its course in a more heavenly direction. More likely, I think, is the possibility that the revolution did what Hiller and Brod could never do: it forced Werfel to confront the difficult issue of how his spiritual revolution was to take place without any profaning contact of the physical, the social, the territorial. The purity of Werfel's earlier doctrine was no longer an available discourse; he needed to confront the necessity of boundaries he had dreamed the artist could (and must) overcome. Here is his disquieted confession from the same year:

> I have painfully recognized that I am an individual, an individualist! Listen: Indivi-Dualist. [. . .] Listen how they make fun of us in Latin. They say "inseparable and divided" in one word.[95]

Whatever his personal reconciliation of these complex issues, the address at Davos fed alarmed press reports that the cultural elite was betraying the country, lining up behind Kisch in the ranks of the Red Guard. Seeing his position reduced to this irreducibly political gesture must have been more than the torn Werfel could stand. An urgent telegram to Spirk from late 1918 reads in full: "ALL RUMORS & NEWS REPORTS ABOUT ME UNTRUE WILL WRITE AGAIN WHEN MY HEAD IS CALMER LOVE FRANZ." [96]

He did write again, the letter evading the censor through the hand of his friend Otto Pick, the expressionist poet and translator of Czech literature. Behind Werfel's usual polemical and arrogant epistolary style, one senses the deep humility of apology in this letter. On the surface

Werfel lashes out at the enthused revolutionaries, at the charismatic but ineffective Kisch, at the timid and ignorant bourgeoisie, at the vicious press, while he searches for a rationalization for his own action—or inaction. In fact it is far less transparent whether Werfel regrets his gesture toward the revolution or his inability to truly engage in it:

> Certainly, I remain more radical today than before! I am a Bolshevik as far as my actual program is concerned: for the final overthrow, for the absolute dissolution of the bourgeois class (spirit of possession [*Besitz*] & of flight from life) [. . .] and for the newly erected just relation between work and life, something that has always been the motive of my production.
>
> I will therefore identify myself today on the most extreme side, as I always have [. . .] [but]—my work is not that of a politician.[97]

It was easier for Werfel to conform his program to Marxist rhetoric than himself to the revolution. Absurdly calling himself a Bolshevik, he compiled a list of qualifying convictions: he is for the final overthrow, not just of this state or of capitalism, but of the state and politics altogether; he favors the destruction of the bourgeoisie, if the term is taken to mean materialism and *Besitz* as a concept; he denounces the opposition of bourgeois life and real life, desiring instead a new relation of work and life, taking into account once again some rather idiosyncratic definitions of terms. Thus he is more "radical" than ever, yet no "politician."

For Kisch, on the other hand, socialism in the concrete was a grand solution to the morass of nationalities, classes, and cultures in which he had immersed himself in the service of a German-liberal newspaper. In the war "diary" published in 1922, as well as in the first of his major memoirs where he reflects on his early journalistic career, Kisch sees all of his diverse and apparently contradictory experience moving toward this political universalism. His most famous reporting experience, the exposé on the Austrian officer and spy Redl, was not excepted from this rereading. This was Kisch's personal Dreyfus affair, for he had a stake in attacking the image of a national collective threatened by a foreign element within; he favored the myth of a corrupt state universally distrusted by a suspicious and united common people.[98] Similarly, he sees popular antisemitism in Serbia (as perhaps in any other place for different reasons) as explicable within a particular sociopolitical context;[99] here, again, the promise of socialist universalism seemed to obliterate the borders closing around the threatened Prague island.

From one perspective the socialist solution conformed more readily to the populist Kisch, who had sought an art form that would dissolve the line between high culture and folk song, than to the elite individualism of Werfel, who dreamed of a folk of enlightened artists. Seen another way, Werfel's more sophisticated vision did not allow him the delusion that political change could provide an escape from the metaphysical dilemma of modernity. Both Prague writers were wrestling with the same angel: they were fighting for their lives and for unity.

ECSTASY

Werfel was more pessimistic than Kisch in part due to his recognition of an abyss between being and expression and the terrestrial impossibility of bridging it. The differences between the two men could be attributed, if simplistically, to type: Werfel, the elite *Stadtpark* son with the weaker command of Czech, whose contact with the common people was limited to their role as his servants; and Kisch, the roamer of Prague's back streets, fluent in Czech and the social language of the underclass. Yet, a close look at Werfel's wartime texts reveals a growing presentiment that the fragmentation of modernity was represented not only in the polarity of self and other, or essence and mediation. Werfel, as Kornfeld, was increasingly aware of the despised dualism within himself. "I am not a unity against the world," he wrote to Spirk in 1916, "I am a unity against myself and the world." [100]

The incompetence of language to mediate spiritual experience, the will to unity, the dualism of self and other, and also within the self, can all be found in the work of Martin Buber, whose influence was felt strongly in the expressionist movement. Werfel's vision of Christian-spiritual revolution, on close reading, aligns perfectly with Buber's redemptive renewal, whereby redemption would take place within the individual soul and simultaneously effect a renewal of Judaism and humanity. [101] Of the very few books we know Werfel to have been reading at the time of the essays, he reported enthusiastically on Buber's two early collections of Hasidic tales, which he had received from the author. [102] But the text that best reveals the correspondence of the two thinkers, the one that is most often counted among the sources of expressionism, is Buber's *Ecstatic Confessions:*

> Of all experiences of which one says, in order to indicate their incomparability, that they cannot be communicated, ecstasy alone is by nature the most inexpressible. That is because the person who experiences it has become a unity into which no division can enter anymore. [. . .] Thus are the contents

of his experience and the subject of his experience—thus are world and
self—joined together. [. . .]

   As soon as they spoke [of their ecstasy], even to themselves, they were
immediately back in the chain, within the borders; the boundless does not
even speak to himself, within himself, for there are no borders within him either: no multiplicity, no dualism, no Thou and I anymore. As soon as they
speak, they are ruined by a language that is suited to everything but the foundation of experience, unity. As soon as they utter, they have already uttered
the other.[103]

The consciousness of a deep-seated dualism that could be overcome
only by a messianic moment of revelation ran through the programmatic
expressionist writings of Paul Kornfeld and the struggle with politics of
Franz Werfel into the circle of Praguers who had begun to think about
their Judaism in a different way than their parents had done. Even Werfel's formula for Christian revelation/revolution had roots in what Buber and Werfel both regarded as the privileged position of the Jewish self
with respect to this universal polarity.[104] Buber may thus be seen as a
kind of link between this discussion of expressionist universalism and
other young Prague Jews, whose thought took forms hauntingly reminiscent of their compatriot expressionists.[105] Searching for ecstatic revolution, for a simultaneous escape from the European crisis and their particular territorial dilemma in Prague, the Zionists of the Prague circle, as
if following Kornfeld's and Werfel's prescriptions, looked into themselves
for access to the universal.

Plates 1 and 2. "The Moldau's water goes slipping / In a circle surrounding Prague." Prague Germans imagined the city as an island whose ground seemed to be shrinking. Courtesy of Archiv hlavního města Prahy [Archive of the capital city Prague].

Plates 3 and 4. The transformation of the early nineteenth-century Roßmarkt or horse market (1830, TOP) into Wenceslaus Square (c. 1910, ABOVE) embodies the passage of Prague from one of the provincial spheres of German culture orbiting about Vienna to the metropolitan center of the Czech nation. Plate 3 courtesy of Archiv für Kunst und Geschichte, Berlin (engraving signed Smidt, after C. Würbs); plate 4 courtesy of Památník Národního Písemnictví, Literární Archiv [Memorial for National Literature, Literary Archives], Prague-Strahov [hereafter PNP].

Plate 5. Years after the emancipation of the Prague Jews and the removal of the Jewish ghetto wall, the Old-New Synagogue and Jewish community hall were paces away from Kafka's home at Old Town Square. Virtually none of the Prague Jews could decipher the time from the backward-running clock with Hebrew letters on its face. Courtesy of PNP.

Plates 6 and 7. TOP: Class picture of the Old Town Square
Gymnasium, 1898. Franz Kafka is second from left on the top row;
beside him on the right is Egon's German nationalist brother, Paul
Kisch; Kafka's closest friend and early correspondent Oskar Pollak
is second from left on the next row down; Hugo Bergmann is
third from left on the second row from bottom. Courtesy of PNP.
ABOVE: The Kinsky Palace at the Old Town Square housed both Kafka's
Gymnasium and his father's fancy-goods business (storefront on
bottom right). Courtesy of Bildarchiv Preussischer Kulturbesitz, Berlin.

Plate 8. From the logbook of the steering committee of the Halle. A *völkisch* man-in-the-mountain (smoking a pipe labeled "1848") overlooks a bucolic landscape. Committee leaders have scrawled in ironic references to territorial contest: "Bathing is prohibited to Jews"; the main farmhouses are labeled property of the Halle, the distant farm the realm of the *völkisch* Germania; a small shed in the foreground labeled "ZDE / HIER" ("here") is reserved for Czechs. Photograph taken by Jan Smit. Courtesy of Ústav Dějin Univerzity Karlovy, Archiv Univerzity Karlovy, Prague (carton B611 IIB29, *Rapportbuch* 9.7.1911–22.2.1912, p. 876).

Plates 9 and 10. ABOVE: Egon Erwin Kisch fashioned himself as an adopted member of the Prague underworld. This mug shot was likely taken by a friend on the police force as a joke in the spirit of this self-fashioning. Courtesy of PNP. RIGHT: Portal of the "House of the Two Golden Bears," 475 Melantrichová, childhood home of Egon Kisch. Kisch's essay surveying bears in Prague architecture was self-referential. Reprinted from Oskar Schürer, *Prag: Kultur—Kunst—Geschichte* (Munich, 1930).

Plates 11 and 12. LEFT: Max
Brod in Dresden in 1914.
BELOW: Photograph portrait
of Brod by Hugo Erfurth,
1918. Brod was by far the
most prominent writer of his
generation in German Prague.
In these photographs he
retains something of the
habitus of a fin-de-siècle
aesthete. Both courtesy of
Deutsches Literaturarchiv—
Schiller-Nationalmuseum,
Marbach am Neckar,
Germany [hereafter DLSN].

Plates 13 and 14. ABOVE: The view over the Moldau from the aristocratic Kleinseite ("little quarter"), c. 1860 (lithograph, artist unknown). Emil Utitz described German Prague as "a game preserve whose ground was always shrinking." Courtesy of Archiv für Kunst und Geschichte, Berlin. RIGHT: In 1892 the city's aldermen ordered that Prague street signs be changed from Czech and German to exclusively Czech, a symbolic move that incensed the city's German residents. Courtesy of PNP.

Plates 15, 16, and 17. The two major collaborative projects of Prague circle authors were the journals *Herder-Blätter* and *Arkadia*. After Axel Juncker, the next publisher to take on innovative and increasingly fashionable Prague German-Jewish writers was Kurt Wolff, whose advertisement "Three Prague Writers" appears above. All courtesy of PNP.

Plate 18. Franz Kafka as a young man (1906). Courtesy of PNP.

Plates 19 and 20.
ABOVE: The German-liberal daily *Bohemia* published Kafka and other Prague writers, especially Kisch, in feuilletons (here Kafka's early "The Aeroplanes of Brescia"). Courtesy of PNP.
RIGHT: Kurt Wolff's publication of Kafka's *The Stoker* (the first part of what we know as *Amerika*).

Plates 21 and 22. ABOVE: Werfel was a celebrated expressionist poet in his early twenties. This photograph (Leipzig, 1911 or 1912) with expressionist dramatist Walter Hasenclever on the left, Werfel at center, and editor of the pathbreaking *Menschheitsdämmerung* Kurt Pinthus at right, attests to his early integration into the literary establishment. Courtesy of DLSN. RIGHT: A sketch of the Prague expressionist essayist and dramatist Paul Kornfeld. Courtesy of PNP.

Plates 23 and 24. LEFT: After the war, in 1919, Werfel fell in love with Alma Mahler, with whom he would remain for the rest of his life. "Alma stands before me as a reality . . . " Courtesy of Bildarchiv Preussischer Kulturbesitz, Berlin. BELOW: Egon Erwin Kisch in uniform, in a photograph taken during military service before World War I. During the war he served on the front and (with Werfel) in the War Press Bureau; in 1918 he joined the Communist Party and became co-leader of the Red Guard in Vienna. From the personal collection of Josef Poláček, Prague.

Plates 25, 26, and 27. TOP LEFT: Hugo Bergmann as a young man (detail of a group photograph). Courtesy of Shmuel Hugo Bergman archive, manuscript division, Jewish National and University Library, Jerusalem [hereafter JNUL]. TOP RIGHT: Bergmann's Jewish Correspondence Bureau press identification for a trip to Palestine after the war (1921). Courtesy of Shmuel Hugo Bergman archive, manuscript division, JNUL. ABOVE: The Bar Kochba student association in the period of Martin Buber's Prague lectures. Courtesy of the Central Zionist Archives, Jerusalem.

Plate 28. Souvenir photograph from a visit to Vienna, at the Prater, 1913. Kafka is at left; second from right is Otto Pick, Prague expressionist poet and translator of Czech literature. The others are Albert Ehrenstein and Lise Kaznelson. Courtesy of PNP.

Plates 29 and 30. TOP, a Kafka portrait of 1917. ABOVE, Milena Jesenská. Both courtesy of PNP.

CHAPTER 5

Circumscribing Spiritual Territory

Inside Prague's Cultural Zionism

Die Sehnsucht nach dem Land? Es ist nicht gewiß. Das Land
schlägt die Sehnsucht an, die unendliche.

Desire for the country? It is not certain. The country calls
forth desire, desire eternal.

diary, 19 January 1922

ROOTED FLIGHT

Among the startling creative products of the very small group of friends
known in retrospect as the "Prague circle," the particular brand of "cultural Zionism" associated foremost with Kafka's classmate Hugo Bergmann (1883–1975) seems to have been forgotten. His early activities in
the student organization Bar Kochba and his prewar writings on Judaism
are little known nowadays.[1] It may be the case that this early and creative Zionism is now dated; by the end of the First World War, it had
slipped away from Bergmann himself, as if it could survive only in the
unique and unstable environment of a Prague that was soon to disappear.

Bergmann was a classmate of Kafka's, and the first of his friends to
turn to Jewish nationalism. While a turn to Jewish self-identifications—
of different sorts, as we will see—was to become typical of German-
speaking Jewish writers of this generation, for most this would be experienced in the watershed period from 1910 through to the outbreak of
the war. Bergmann identified himself as a Zionist as a much younger
man. This identification interested Kafka enough to ask about it, and
thus the earliest recorded expression of Bergmann's Zionism is in a letter to Kafka from 1902:

> Why have I become a Zionist? [. . .] I should almost stop wondering, and
> yet again and again I have to wonder why you, who [. . .] were my class-

mate for so long, do not understand my Zionism. If I saw a madman before
me and he had an idée fixe, I would not laugh at him, because his idea is a piece
of life for him. You think Zionism is also an "idée fixe" of mine. You surely
do not know that it is perhaps also a piece of my life, yet it is so. It is perhaps more for me. It is pieced together and patched together from the shreds
of my self.[2]

Bergmann's response begins with the repeated "wondering" about
why the opening question should be a question for him at all, for his
Zionism was inextricably connected to the circle of classmates and their
common condition. The positions of Kafka and Bergmann were perhaps
not as foreign to one another as they seemed.

Bergmann's Zionism was from the outset constructed in a complex
way that can be seen as a model for all that is to come. An "idée fixe" is
in one gesture transformed to something very material in Bergmann's
letter, with the awkward and persistent appearance of the term "piece"
(*Stück*). So adherence to an external ideology here has an immanent
source: it is a "piece" of Bergmann's "life," with all the ring of authenticity and essentiality that the term "*Leben*" had in the early twentieth
century. But this "piece" of life is itself "pieced" together from "shreds
of self." This reflexive relation, conflating and then again subdividing
subject-predicate definitions, scrambles the terms necessary to construct
a simple relation between self and community. And of course that relation is at the heart of the step that Bergmann has taken. The letter
continues:

I have searched and searched [. . .] I did not have the strength to stand alone,
like you. [. . .] Don't think that it was sympathy that made me a Zionist. My
Zion is a good piece of selfishness. I sense that I would like to fly, I would like
to create and cannot; I no longer have the strength. And yet I also sense that
I might have the strength under other circumstances, that the innate ability
doesn't abandon me at all. I only lack the strength. [. . .] Perhaps we will in
fact overcome this weakness once more, and stand sturdily once more on our
own ground instead of waving unrooted like a reed; perhaps, perhaps I will
even find my strength again . . . Sometimes I feel that I might be able to fly,
but then my strength is broken and my wings are lame. I would like to stand
for once on our own ground and not be rootless. Maybe then my strength
will return to me, too.

The lamed and powerless modern self, then, seeks a reconstitution of
strength through rooting itself in a community. The individual alone is
defeated by what Bergmann elsewhere in this letter calls "raw reality."
However, there is a slippage in the text from the declaration of "my" loss

of strength to "our" weakness; the strength does not return with inclusion in the community, for the community itself is impotent outside of its rootedness to a territory.

The element of strength (*Kraft*) seems at first to be manifestly in step with the Zionism of this period, with its stress on reversing the qualifiers associated with Diaspora Jewishness. Despite this similarity, Bergmann does not faithfully reproduce a discourse where a positive "strength," physicality, and power are juxtaposed to a negated intellect, or an ephemeral spiritualism. For what Bergmann seeks in this circle of community that fast becomes a territory is the power to dream; it is the strength to stand ground, but only in order to escape from "raw reality." This paradox—Bergmann's need to be "rooted" in order to "fly"—already suggests the extraordinary ambivalence of his relationship to the notion of territory.

Another interesting tension with the pedestrian notions of the face-off between Zionism and assimilationism is in the phrase "I did not have the strength to stand alone, like you," ascribing a strength to noncommunally identified Diaspora Jews who were more commonly figured as weak in Zionist discourse. Indeed, Kafka, for his part, might wonder how his lack of faith in a communal circle could be read as an expression of strength. In a more resigned despair over powerlessness, Kafka stands in an open-ended and unstable territory for one, sooner characterized as an angle (*Winkel*) than as a circle, and writes:

> What have I in common with Jews? I have hardly anything in common with myself and should stand very quietly in a corner [*Winkel*], content that I can breathe.[3]

THE ZIONIST REAL

The elision of Bergmann's images of rootedness (to territory) and flight (of spirit) are not merely the mixed metaphors of a confused teen. This creative play with territorial metaphor foreshadows Bergmann's most serious philosophical and political work from his university years until his departure from Prague after World War I. Implicit in these images is the binary opposition of reality/ideality—an opposition sustained by a set of powerful assumptions that Bergmann's Zionism attacked head-on.

When Bergmann entered university and joined the Zionist student association Bar Kochba in 1901, the organization was ripe for revitalization. In its short history, the only Jewish-national student association had not maintained a stable membership or a consistent program.[4] Even during Bergmann's tenure, only a very small minority of Jewish students chose to join Bar Kochba rather than the German-liberal Lese- und Redehalle der deutschen Studenten in Prag.[5] Yet, Bar Kochba can be said to have represented the focus of Bohemian Zionism in the prewar period,[6] and the birthplace of the peculiar stamp of Zionism that was particular to Prague.[7]

By all accounts, the original direction Bar Kochba took in the first years of the twentieth century can be directly attributed to the activity of Hugo Bergmann. What was that direction, how did it engage young Jewish people at the time? A former Bar Kochba member recounts:

> At that time, a community was created that took pains to spread the idea of a Judaism of life and of the future [. . .] The realization [*Verwirklichung*] of Jewish life did not simply serve an externally directed program [. . .] it stressed the necessity that a member take up Jewish culture in himself [. . .][8]

This passage reads like a catechism, with the terms learned by rote remembered years later by the devoted pupil. The contents of this catechism, the discourse constituted by the elements of "life," "future," "realization," "external/internal," and so on, are at the heart of the project the Prague student adherents preferred to call "cultural Zionism."[9]

The concrete program of Bar Kochba was decidedly intellectual; it stressed the study of Hebrew, Jewish history, and even Yiddish, while the public social activities typical of most student associations were replaced by public addresses and discussions on Jewish topics. Yet it is important to keep in mind, as the citation above stresses, that the significance of this program was not conceived as an externally directed, didactic one. The activities were designed as a route out of a foreign cultural circle (*Kulturkreis*) into the circle of Judaism.[10] This transformation was presented as the solemn, personal task of each member of Bar Kochba, and its ultimate goal was the general cultural regeneration of Judaism. Viktor Freud claims that the students' Jewishness may have previously been represented as an object of "love" or "passion," but it now took on the urgency of a more active "task": the realization of Judaism.[11] Thus Bergmann described the role of Hebrew as specifically noninstrumental— that is, as a key neither to understanding the Bible nor to an aestheticist appreciation of its beauty. The "serious Jew" recognizes that taking Hebrew into himself or herself is an "irrefutable necessity," offering a "new, swelling life."[12]

The achievement of Zionist youth in learning Hebrew was no less than the recovery of a continuity in Judaism, represented in two and a half millennia of religious writing. Bergmann's own intensive study of the liturgical canon testifies to its importance in this view of Zionism. The religious texts were seen as the key to Judaism's essential spiritual mission in universal history: from the attack on paganism through the "Jewish" revolutions of Christianity and Islam, Judaism brings history to the moment of messianic revolution, a transformation of the mature world opened by the French Revolution.[13] Bergmann, therefore, could not imagine a Zionism that could be separated from an essential religiousness rooted in scripture; even the impulse of nonbelieving Jews to go to Palestine must be "religious." None of this could be changed by Herzl and Nordau's "politicization" of Zionism, which attempted to privatize spiritual questions, as in liberalism or socialism.[14]

This spiritual Zionism, influenced by the modern Hebrew essayist Ahad Ha'am and especially Martin Buber, who had spoken in Prague in 1903, opposed itself not only to the "dogmatic" or "political" Zionism of Herzl and Nordau, but to any tendency that did not seem to spring directly from "within" the mystical circle of Judaism it sought to create. Herzl himself advocated Jewish abstention and noninvolvement in the Bohemian nationality conflict, but on tactical grounds that Bergmann might have rejected.[15] The Bar Kochba group eschewed Herzlian tactics for the same reason that it sought to distance itself from the nationality conflict: both represented profane and foreign forms, irrelevant to a spiritualist Jewish renewal. By identifying the necessarily religious, messianic, and revolutionary character of Zionism, Bergmann put into question the authenticity of a Zionism based on diplomacy and party politics. His political engagement undermined the secular realm of Jewish "politics": it challenged Zionist youth to join in a spiritual transformation of self that would change the "political" world. But this strict heavenly diet was predictably not to everyone's taste.

In the year that Bergmann became chairman of Bar Kochba, a group of members made the proposal that a faction of the association take a more "fighting" stance in Prague student life: wearing colors, entering duels, and taking on the form and function of more typical Austro-German fraternities. In Prague, this included the regular boisterous marching on the boulevard Am Graben (Na příkopě), where, upon the marchers meeting rival Czech student groups doing the same on the adjacent Czech corso Ferdinandová, it predictably came to fists.

The group wished to remain a faction within Bar Kochba, but the suggestion that only a section of the circle of Zionists would go in this direction was naturally no appeasement for Bergmann and the members committed to his uncompromisable vision. When the dissatisfied students formed their own corporation called Barissia, with the fighting motto "Wort und Wehr für Judas Ehr," Bergmann was insistent on a rule forbidding Bar Kochba members from participation in any of its activities.[16] The vehemence with which the Bar Kochba leadership rejected Barissia—they even attempted to have it barred from the Austrian and World Zionist Organizations[17]—foregrounds the fact that Barissia was not a mere rival to them; it was founded on principles irreconcilably opposed to Bar Kochba's. Years later, with calm retrospect, a cohort of Bergmann concludes that

> "Barissia," with a conscious appropriation of foreign forms, fought an *outward* [*nach außen*] battle against assimilation in order to more easily win over Jewish *society*. "Bar Kochba" searched for the way *inward* [*nach innen*]; it immersed itself in the problem of Jewishness [. . .] On the one side a battle for Jewish *society* to be won over to Zionism, on the other a struggle for Jewish *spirituality* [. . .][18]

This neat chart of oppositions, which are anything but complementary, could have served as a model for the critique at the heart of the Bar Kochba program.

DE-CENTERING ZIONISM

Bar Kochba's search "for the way *inward*" is related not only to the cultural Zionism of Ahad Ha'am, but also to the policy that came to be known as *Gegenwartsarbeit,* or "present-work."[19] *Gegenwartsarbeit* was the catchphrase for a Zionist policy that focused on conditions of Jewry in the Diaspora, a position rejected by the political Zionists. While it was usually associated with the alleviation of conditions of strife in the Pale of Settlement, Bar Kochba stressed the amelioration of the state of cultural destitution of Western Jewry on their home turf.

The proposed reevaluation of priorities represented a shift of focus from a Zionism oriented outward, aimed at the establishment of a Jewish state through external means, to the issue of cultural renewal within the Jewish circle. By the time of the Tenth Zionist Congress, it had become clear that early hopes for a quick acquisition of territory via a diplomatic windfall or magnanimous Jewish patronage had been unrealistic. Bergmann declared that this fact returned the focus from Palestine to the work of every small and local Zionist organization. If "Zionism is Judaism on the road to self-liberation," Bergmann insisted, "all of us, whether we live in Palestine or here, are on this road."[20]

There is a note of relief in the fact that the failure of political Zionism had laid to rest the illusion that Judaism could be redeemed from without. For Herzlian diplomacy had been doomed to fail even if it had established a Jewish state; the Jewish people must first find their homeland in themselves. The error of the Zionist organizations was their faith in a Jewish Palestine's power to redeem world Jewry from without, and their affirmation of their own role as peripheral. In Bergmann's text, the individual organization becomes a center for local "Judaization work" (*"das Zentrum der gesamten Judaisierungsarbeit seiner Stadt"*). This is the necessary work to be done, if Palestine is to become the cultural center (*Kulturzentrum*) of Judaism.[21] Further, the role of the organization is merely instrumental for the real work that must be done, the active self-liberation that must take place in "all of us."

If the road to self-liberation must be found within the individual, and yet this search itself is part of a communal gesture with universal consequences, the structure of political center and periphery is necessarily disfigured. Bergmann's use of the center-periphery model in the reconstruction of these relations seems self-canceling; it appears to subvert itself. The ease with which the center-periphery structure is used to represent ideas that break it apart betrays Bergmann's intimate familiarity with it. We recall the discourse of German (-Jewish) liberalism in Prague, with its self-authorization as center of Bohemian culture and politics;[22] or the marginalization of the Jewish majority of German Prague through the rise of a *völkisch* German circle centered in an Aryan mythology; the currents of ideology and politics that pushed the Prague of Bergmann's parents straight out of the constellation of German cultural spheres revolving around Vienna. The language of center and periphery was native to the Prague Zionists; they employed it with fluency, and undermined it from within.

The spiritual Zionism embraced by Bar Kochba found its revolutionary character in the stance that a movement of self-liberation can take place only within the self. Thus it saw the diplomatic maneuvers cheered by mainstream Zionists to be counterproductive. In this, again, Bergmann was representing a minority faction of Zionists who felt that spiritual issues, or the "cultural question," were as important as, or even prerequisite to, the territorial question.[23] In his 1913 speech to the Bohemian Zionist District Assembly, Bergmann differentiated Zionism from

other Jewish perspectives through its active engagement with Jewish destiny, an engagement that eternally separates slaves from free beings, or
those that "choose" from those that "let happen."[24] Deploying the revolutionary rhetoric of the Central European youth of this period, which
as Mosse has pointed out is as connected to *völkisch* thought as it is to
Lebensphilosophie or "vitalism," Bergmann condemned the political
Zionist approach for being mechanical: it becomes carried away with
the machine of politics and leaves behind the organic, spiritual Jewish
Volk. The stress on culture, he explained, was because culture is what is
most intrinsically (*am innigsten*) bound to true Zionism, which is not
the instrument of a party (or machine), but the expression of a people
(*Volk*). A *Volk* does not have abstract goals, it *lives*. "Cultural work"
would "fulfill the Jewish community with real life."[25]

   Bar Kochba's program of lectures and discussions, Hebrew lessons,
and readings in Jewish history and literature was seen as intimately connected to a revolutionary project to renew modern Judaism. The modernity under attack—mechanical and lifeless—was clearly not unique
to the Jewish community; in the rhetoric of the above passage it is impossible to ignore the tones of a particular German-language culture critique running through the late nineteenth and early twentieth centuries.
Hence this attack on the modern Jewish condition, the modern condition par excellence, was figured as a spiritual struggle. "Zionism" for
Bergmann and the Bar Kochba Association was the name of this ethe-
real battle for an alternate "reality," even as their program focused on
the practical tasks encompassed by *Gegenwartsarbeit*. The sage of this
spiritual venture for a new reality was to be Martin Buber, who would
return to Prague to deliver a series of influential lectures from 1909 to
1911. Kafka retained a skeptical interest in the Bar Kochba activities,
and subscribed to the Prague Zionist weekly, *Selbstwehr*. Yet, his most
profound investment in the Zionist project of *Gegenwartsarbeit* took
form first during the war, and was not focused on the program of the
Prague Bar Kochba Association at all, but on the Berlin Jewish woman
named Felice.

FELICE, OR, "ANY REALITY, HOWEVER SMALL"

In view of the array of oblique and apparently contradictory references
to "Zionism" in Kafka's notebooks and letters, the question of Kafka's
relationship to Zionism has been recognized as a difficult one. Early assertions by Brod, Bergmann, and Felix Weltsch that Kafka eventually

came to be a fully committed Zionist have been revised to allow for a more complicated picture. Yet, the general image of a gradual but steady conversion to Zionist ideology is by and large reinforced by these revisions.[26] There is much to speak for this assumption: Kafka's alienation from Brod over the latter's insistent Zionism around 1913 gives way to more positive references to Zionism in Kafka's notebooks of 1916; a list of self-identifications in Kafka's diary includes, in sequence, "anti-Zionism, Zionism . . . "; there appears to be a chronological transition in the Kafka diaries from the intense interest in Yiddish and Yiddish theater in the early teens of the century to the Hebrew exercises that dominate the last extant notebook of Kafka's life; and, finally, there is Kafka's stated plan to move to Palestine with Dora Dymant and to work there as a bookbinder or a waiter. Yet, it cannot be overlooked that each of these pieces of potential evidence is a narrative construction, and never remotely a political engagement—even, as it turns out, the plan to move to Palestine, materializing only very far into Kafka's illness, when it was certain that such a journey could be imagined but never executed. To describe these narrative constructions even as an ideological "sympathy" would require a much more careful exploration of "Zionism" as a figure in Kafka's texts than we have tended to see in Kafka scholarship.

A similar (and, as I will argue, closely related) problem arises when we try to determine Kafka's position toward bachelordom and marriage. Presented with often obscure and persistently contradictory statements in the Kafka ephemera, one is easily led to the pathetic image of a lonesome Kafka wishing desperately for marriage. Critics are tempted to take at face value Kafka's assessment of marriage and children as "the only thing that matters," without looking at the terms "bachelor" and "marriage" as the same sort of complex literary figures they examine in his fiction.

The figures of "Zionism" and "marriage" run through much of Kafka's letters and diaries, as well as through the literary work itself, however elusively. But these figures come together in a revealing way in the course of his correspondence with Felice Bauer between 1912 and 1916. Of these two figures, "marriage" has received substantial attention in the critical literature, because scholars have been able to connect it to what Kafka himself identified as a breakthrough in his writing: the deferral of "happiness," or of physical union with the beloved Felice, is linked within the correspondence itself to the pain and solitude of writing. But the nature of that link is not as simple as it seems; Kafka's figuration of Zionism and his relationship to it is no less complex.

The association of Felice and Zionism is established at the very beginning of Kafka's correspondence with her. In his description of their first encounter at a dinner party, Kafka mentions that in the course of conversation "it transpired that you are a Zionist, and this suited me very well." Kafka then offered Felice a copy of the Viennese Zionist journal *Palästina*, which he happened to have along, and the two discussed taking a trip together to Palestine. It was this casual conversation that Kafka recalled to Felice in order to inaugurate the correspondence, thus linking their relationship to each other and to Palestine in a way that would never entirely vanish from his letters to her. Following this inaugural move in their relationship, Kafka made several attempts to put Felice in contact with Yitzhak Löwy's troupe of Yiddish actors when they performed in Berlin. But the most direct identification of Felice with Zionism emerges in the correspondence in 1916, as Eastern European Jewish refugees arrived in Berlin in large numbers. From this point onward, Kafka developed an intense investment in Felice's involvement in the Zionist *Gegenwartsarbeit* project of a Berlin Jewish Home. Felice did volunteer at the Jewish Home upon Kafka's repeated insistence, and his letters to her thereafter attest to his continued obsession with her involvement, as he just as insistently policed her reports to him of her activities there. So while the letters may be taken to provide evidence of Kafka's Zionist "sympathies," they do so only through Felice: Kafka repeatedly asserts that he himself would be incapable of such an engagement.

A third figure that is associated with Felice—and hence with Zionism—is that of "health," and here again it is contrasted to the writer's own ill health. We now recall the dynamics of Kafka's early correspondence with Oskar Pollak, where, as we reviewed in chapter 1, woman and the intercourse with women were identified with "going out," with escaping from the self-polluted and "ill" atmosphere evoked in the Kafka-Pollak correspondence and associated with isolation, with writing, and with the homoerotic correspondence with Pollak itself. In the decade between Kafka's letters to Pollak and the initiation of his correspondence with Felice, his perception of his own weakness and ill health had become much more developed—in spite of the fact that he was not to be diagnosed with tuberculosis until the very end of his correspondence with Felice, in 1917. Early in the exchange of letters, though, Kafka articulates the dichotomy that has long been discussed in relation to the correspondence: namely, that between health and happiness, marriage and children, on the one side, and solitude and illness, Prague and writing, on the other. Thus already on November 11, 1912, he explains that he does not heroically leap onto a train to join his beloved because "My health is only just good enough for myself alone, not good enough for marriage, let alone fatherhood."[27] One does not need to rehearse very long that which is well known: that Kafka's letters describe what he calls an "inner battle" for Felice, which he describes as a conflict between happiness with her, a happiness associated with "reality," with groundedness and health, and on the other side his illness, his solitude, and his writing. But what must be remembered and often is not is that this is not a simple matter of a battle between opposing terms. What Kafka specialists call the "breakthrough"—the single night in September 1912 in which Kafka composed the story "The Judgment" from beginning to end, and after which followed in rapid succession much of the major Kafka fiction—is justifiably associated with the relationship to Felice (hence Kafka's dedication of the story to her). While both writing and illness were self-identifications for Kafka before meeting Felice, neither of these took really concrete form, or came into their own, until his epistolary relationship with her. The "reality" represented by Felice is thus inseparable from the becoming-real of this writing, and of this illness, even as these are figured to be in opposition to the life and health she embodies. The "inner battle" Kafka thematizes in the letters is thus not simply a struggle between two life choices, but rather describes an intensely painful dialectical process through which the writerly Kafka is to emerge. What if—in keeping with the association of Felice and Zion established in the correspondence—we were to think of Kafka's relationship to Zionism in the same way?

To do so, we would have to take as a starting point the construction of Zionism in Kafka's text as a figure of unqualified strength, youth, vigor, territory; one that is diametrically opposed to the figure of the assimilated *Westjude*.[28] In a particularly difficult passage of Kafka's diary, in 1922, there is an elliptical reference to the relation of this latter condition and the production of literature: Kafka writes obliquely of a "hunt" that he says can also be called "the storming of the last earthly border" (*"Ansturm gegen die letzte irdische Grenze"*). In a reworking of this passage, Kafka writes

> This entire literature is a storming of the borders and it would have—if only Zionism had not gotten in the way—easily been able to develop into a new secret teaching, a Cabala.[29]

Here the territorial ideology of Zionism blocks the creation of a new spiritual language, represented by the metaphor of Jewish mysticism. So we see again what *appears* to be a clear opposition (of Zionism against writing, territoriality against deterritorialization). This binary seems to be reinforced in Kafka's letters to Felice: even as he directs her to volunteer at the Jewish Home, it is she that becomes identified with the figure of "Zionism" in his letters, while he stands on the other side. The Zionist bank of this apparent chasm is the one charged with "reality":

> Only the reality of the [Jewish] Home can teach you anything of importance—any reality, however small. [. . .] As far as I am concerned, please consider that this work removes you to some extent from me, since—in any case at present, and I am not thinking of my state of health in this connection—I wouldn't be capable of doing this kind of work; I would lack the necessary dedication.[30]

It may seem a cruel joke for a lover to have lured Felice into the Jewish Home to please him, only to declare that the engagement will contribute to the gulf between them. Yet, as this letter of September 12, 1916 demonstrates most clearly of all, the distance from Kafka created by this grounding in "reality" (however small) is a necessary step in the overcoming of that distance, as he continues:

> On the whole I can think of no closer spiritual bond between us than that created by this work. I shall live on every small thing you do, on every difficulty you shoulder . . . I shall live on every one of these things, as on your last letter. As far as I can see, *it is positively the only path, or threshold to it, that can lead to spiritual liberation.*[31]

Felice (or "Zionism") does not represent a territorialized existence in stark opposition to Kafka's ephemeral one as much as she/it offers the promise of a bridge to "spiritual liberation." The East European pupils, of course, are not the beneficiaries of this liberation, but rather effect it in their bourgeois Western Jewish teachers (or "helpers," as Kafka consistently refers to them). The *Gegenwartsarbeit* or charitable work of the Berlin Home is precisely this work of *opening up the possibility* of some kind of spiritual transformation. This function of "Zionism" was alluded to in a postcard to Felice from Kafka the previous month, on August 2, where he stated that Felice need not worry about her commitment to Zionism itself before getting involved in the home:

> Through the Jewish Home other forces, much nearer to my heart, are set in motion and take effect. Zionism, accessible to most Jews of today, at least in its outer fringes, is but an entrance to something far more important.[32]

Zionism is not the impossible dream, but rather something fully accessible—only it is itself not the ultimate object, but the "entrance" to something far less accessible but more important. As he would write in the September 12 letter, it is itself not the path to liberation as much as the "threshold" to it. Both these images evoke the famous threshold or entrance to the law in one of the most well known Kafka writings, the fragment from *The Trial* known as "Before the Law." The law itself is never glimpsed in the parable, which itself, belonging to "the introductory writings to the law," stands before—or at the threshold of—a fully inaccessible text. Kafka identified the Zionist kernel of the Jewish Home in its "youthful vigorous method, youthful vigor generally," in the same breath as he confessed that he might not be a Zionist, upon "examination." And yet it is necessary to embrace Zionism, or to wish to embrace it, to wish powerfully for redemption through it: to come straight through Zionist ideology and come out in a place far away from territory. Surely this complex set of relations is best described as dialectical. In the last analysis, neither are Kafka's Zionism and Kafka's Felice objects of identification/desire nor are they figured in diametrical opposition to a writerly Kafka. They are figures to which Kafka was powerfully and painfully drawn, but which he would never fully grasp; they would come to represent necessary passages to something beyond themselves.

LECTURING IN CIRCLES

The relationship of Martin Buber to the Prague circle of Zionists was, by all accounts, a special one. Bergmann had long been influenced by him, and had invited him as guest speaker at Bar Kochba's first *Festabend* in 1903. But the real engagement between Bar Kochba and Buber began with a series of three lectures sponsored by Bar Kochba between 1909 and 1911. Max Brod attended the lectures as "guest and opponent," and came out a Zionist.[33] Interestingly enough, the experience also left its mark on Buber himself. He found in the young Prague intellectuals a certain attachment, a family resemblance of sorts,[34] and he was to maintain contact with some of them for the rest of his life.[35]

So it was that, when his lectures were published more or less verbatim, Buber admitted his embarrassment, as if some convention of intimacy were being violated:

> I hesitated [to publish the lectures], because it remained very much in my
> mind how they originated: spoken from a Jew to Jews, particularly aimed at

a circle of young people, out of the inspiration of the most subjective coexperience, and in a sphere of the most direct response.[36]

The suggestion that address is specific to the nature of the circle in which it is produced is familiar. More notable in this paragraph is that the receptive "circle" described by Buber reduces itself with astonishing velocity, from a macroscopic to a microscopic lens view. From an audience assumed to be not—essentially—Jewish, Buber remembers his lecture as, first of all, a discussion within a national community, then as taking place in a smaller circle of "young people," not without a suggestion of revolt;[37] from there Buber enters an even smaller circle, the realm of "subjective coexperience," the dialogue between subjects, and finally straight into the "sphere" where direct response is effected—into the subject itself. The structure that is set up in Buber's introductory apology is diagrammatic for the text that follows. His analysis hinges on a rhetorical structure of concentric circles, where an essential conflict can be traced from the heart of a universal crisis to the condition of Judaism, and finally to a struggle within the individual self.

"Why do we call ourselves Jews?" is Buber's framing question in his first lecture, "Judaism and the Jews."[38] It is important to him that the question be defined not as an *abstraction,* but as something very "real":

> I want to speak to you not about an abstraction, but of your actual life, of our actual life. And not of its external machinery, but of this life's inner justification and essence [*Recht und Wesen*]. [. . .] I am not asking about the formation of external life, but about its internal reality. Judaism has as much meaning for the Jews as it has inner reality.

If the title of this lecture had not already announced that its primary concern was internal to the community of Judaism, these opening lines certainly did so. By deploying the singular "life" with the plural pronouns "your" ["*Ihr*"] and then "our," Buber closes a circle around a collective "life" that must be defined from within. The *inner/outer* dichotomy, implicit in the rhetorical structure of the circle, takes on ethical significance in Buber's essays. We should also note at the outset the character of those terms relegated to the "inside"—"*Leben,*" "essence," "reality"—with their organic connotations, as against an external machinery capable only of abstraction.

So the structure of the question determines the fundamental heresy of an answer that defines Jewishness according to the relationship to the non-Jewish [*außerjüdischen*] world. "How can [the individual] feel his people not just around him, but inside himself?" ("... nicht bloß um sich: daß er es in sich fühlt?")[39] The differentiation is defined by the hostile relation of the prepositions "*um*" and "*in*"—which define a circle from without (around) and within (inside). "*Umwelt*" and "*Innenwelt*" introduce the list of contents of a dichotomy that is at the center of Jewish (i.e., also universal, also individual) existence—a life-critical choice

> between environment and inner world [*Umwelt und Innenwelt*], between the world of impressions and of substance, between atmosphere and blood, between memory of one's life span and memory of millennia, between the purposes presented by society and the task of redeeming one's own power.[40]

The process of redemption—personal, communal, and universal—is clearly the subject of the three lectures. The first step toward the "sanctification" of the circle is the ritual suggested in the above choice. For the way to redemption is a journey toward unity, toward the destruction of the "deep schism of existence" described above. "Judaism and the Jews" defined analogous circles of nation (Buber: "*Menschenkreis*") and of the individual subject. Buber's construction of the question of identity itself invites the sanctifying gesture of unity through the replication of the contents within the two analogous circles. It will come to the moment when a Jew will think of his/her people (*Volk*) and feel:

> I don't have compassion with them, but they are my passion. My soul is not with my people, but rather my people is my soul. And in this same sense, every one of us will feel the future of Judaism, and will feel: I want to continue living, I want my future, want a new, whole life, a life for me, for the people within me, for me within my people.[41]

This vision cannot be reduced to an argument for membership in a national community. Much more is implied in this discursive axis, which sets self and *Volk* in perfect alignment. The borders of the nation are in turn analogized by the outline of the body, circumscribing the self. It is within this single circle that the question of personal Jewish identity coincides with the "Jewish question."[42]

Buber's internal identity issue is closer to the externally defined "*Judenfrage*" than it appears. The relation of the Jewish self and community to the larger circle, the analogy of the crisis in Judaism to the crisis of modernity, is made explicit in Buber's second lecture, "Judaism and Mankind." Having established that Judaism is above all a "polar phenomenon," defined by its inherent sets of oppositions, Buber slips easily

to the claim that the Jew has an extreme and unique "duality consciousness." The struggle of Judaism in all of its creative periods has been

> [t]he striving toward unity. Toward unity within the individual person, to-
> ward unity between parts of the people, between peoples, between mankind
> and every living thing. Toward unity between God and the world.[43]

We are not surprised when Buber calls on the historical examples of
monotheism and the notion of universal justice, or of early Christianity
and universal love, or even of the element of synthesis in Spinoza and in
Marx. The privileged position of Judaism with regard to the redemption
of humanity is based on its privileged relation to that from which humanity must be redeemed: the will to unity is bred into Judaism because
of its inbred dualistic and fragmented nature. If Judaism is to save mankind from degeneration, it is because degeneration is essential to Judaism.[44] This is the dark secret behind Buber's promise of a mystical coincidence of redemption fixing together the circles of the self, of Judaism,
and of humanity.

> And so this is and remains the basic significance of Judaism for mankind.
> Aware as no other in its innermost being of this originary dualism, knowing
> it and representing it as no other, that it proclaims a world in which it is ex-
> pulsed: a world of God, which wants to be realized in the life of the individ-
> ual as well as in the life of the whole: the world of unity.[45]

The aspect of purification (*Reinigung*) within Judaism is therefore a
fundamental element within the promise of Buber's third lecture, "The
Renewal of Judaism." Unity is one of three ideas whose realization stands
at the center of the historical mission of Judaism; it is the idea that characterizes the goal of that mission. The other two ideas—"Deed" (*Tat*)
and "Future" (*Zukunft*)—foreground the revolutionary germ that acti-
vates the periodic "renewal" of the unifying mission. The three ideas are
not "abstract concepts" but, to the contrary, "natural tendencies" in Judaism that must be *realized*. A unification of spirit and matter is already
implicit, then, in what is defined as a spiritual struggle for reification:

> The spiritual process of Judaism is carried out in the form of a *spiritual
> struggle,* an eternally renewed inner struggle for the pure fulfillment of the
> tendencies of the people [*Volkstendenzen*].[46]

For the degeneration within Judaism is actually the impurity of the
Jewish circle—the confusion of the outside with the inside, the projection of foreign forms onto native essences. The circumscription of a puri-

fied and discrete territory for Judaism in itself begins a process of activation of the natural tendencies unity, future, and deed.

This more purely Jewish sphere is a place where concepts take on a character that Hugo Bergmann describes as "fundamentally distinct from [those] known to us through the conceptual world of our cultural circle [*Kulturkreis*]."[47] So it was that in the lectures sponsored by Bar Kochba, Martin Buber inscribed an imaginative space reserved for authentic Judaism. The circle of young Prague Jews listened, and thought of how they could occupy that space, and make it holy.

KIDDUSH HASHEM

The fusion of spirit and matter is the task of Judaism that Bergmann finds in the strange notion called "Kiddush Hashem," "the sanctification of the name."[48] In this term, which Bergmann chooses for the title of what will become his most important essay on Judaism, one can identify an active process intended to spiritualize ("sanctify") matter ("name"). But the "strangeness" of this concept lies in its reversal of the valences of a simple spirit-matter (or "heaven and earth") dichotomy, where the deity is not holy in and of itself, but is made holy by the human act:

> Neither shall ye profane my holy name; but I will be hallowed among the children of Israel: I am the Lord which hallow you . . .[49]

The circle of Judaism is not, then, merely a physical community chosen and blessed from an external spiritual realm; it is in the center of this circle ("among the Israelites": "in der Mitte *der Kinder Israels*") that God is hallowed. Bergmann accepts Buber's proposition that a certain fundamental dualism is essential in Judaism; the dualism, however, like the conception of the relationship between creator and creation, is astonishingly *dynamic*.

We will take the wind out of Bergmann's sails by revealing where his biblical exegesis leads: the Jewish deed (or "act") is set up as eternally bound to this law of holiness, so that even compromise, fragmentation, assimilation, and opportunism all become "covered by the Holy Name." That is, God is not sanctified in the middle of the children of Israel, but profaned within an impure circle. The old sense and function of the term can be recovered only by a Buberian renewal of Judaism: "Zionism is our Kiddush Hashem."

This somewhat undramatic disclosure of Bergmann's argument has the advantage of allowing us to focus on what is more remarkable in the essay: for the "dynamism" Bergmann sees in the Jewish conception of God soon consumes a whole discourse that has been based on the existence of an inexorable dichotomy. The concept of God itself no longer stands unequivocally on the side of heaven; in the declaration "YHWH Elohim" Bergmann sees a union of the principle of creation (in "Elohim" or God) and the divine sustainer of the world (in Jehovah, the true name); in "Elohim" itself he sees the manifest "elh" ("this") combined with the unsubstantiated subject of the world "mi" ("who"); finally, in the principle of the "name" itself, with its various layers, Bergmann loses track completely. In despair, he writes to Buber:

> The concept "Name" is hard. In my lecture I thought it could be understood as the expression of God comprehended as *object*. Then *the true name* would be the God that is *spoken* of by the *non*-God-united, the God still merely conceived *from without*, but *not realized within* [. . .] Inasmuch as we *speak* of God, we do not actually speak of him, but rather of the Name. Perhaps that would explain why the high priest on Yom Kippur, standing to a certain degree in unity, calls on God with his *real* name, whereas the congregation answers merely: Baruch shem [Blessed the Name]. The true Name, that is YHWH, and the germ that must be reified ("sanctified," "unified") in order to become YHWH. But then as to what could be meant by the difference between God and his true Name, for example when it is said that before creation only God and his Name existed, I am completely at a loss.[50]

This dense passage discloses a complex field of relations effected by a dynamic and mystical view, where terms weave in and out of the spirit-matter dichotomy, rather than being shuffled into place under a rigid binary structure. The earthly community is divided (into those "united" with God and those comprehending God from "without"); the division "God" and "the Name of God" is undermined by further divisions: the spiritual "true Name" (YHWH) against the material "Name" (*Shem*), recalling the former duplicity of a subject-God, who sanctifies, and an object-God, to be sanctified.

A key to the puzzle of these alternations is found in the parenthetical clarification claiming synonymous status for the terms "reified," "sanctified," and "unified." It is symptomatic of Bergmann's elastic categories that the material Name must be made "real" (*verwirklicht*) to cross over into the realm of the spiritual. The earthly and the divine become one in the charged space between these two worlds, exactly where the firmament defining the dichotomy used to exist. The effect of this rhetorical cross-dressing is to jumble the original rhetorical edifice to a point where the speaker can call upon terms such as "real," "politics," and "Zionism," to define a program that could also be described with the terms "holy," "faith," and "humanity."

Looking back, the seeds of this gesture are detectable in Buber's original lectures, where the dualism structure, as something by definition unwhole, stands on one side of itself. While an exhaustingly long "present" has been characterized by schism, the primal past and the messianic future are whole. To Bergmann's confused question about the primal existence of the dual "God and His Name," Buber responds that

> as long as unity is conceived not as a goal, but as an origin, it can no longer be conceived as pure unity. For we can all comprehend the creative function merely as polarization, as the expression of an immanent duality.[51]

Buber finds it significant that the Oneness over all disunity, God, is continually penetrated (*wird durchsetzt*) with duality. The use of the passive voice here raises the question of the interests of an invisible subject in dividing this originary unity from without. We are reminded that the isolation of spiritual from material life served an ideological function: it justified the maintenance of spiritual, confessional, and moral authenticity discrete from the profane realm of physical life "among the nations." [52] It is in this context that Bergmann's project to reassemble the dualistic structure in a way that caused it to consume itself must be read.

THE PROPHET AMONG SLAVES

While Buber may have exerted the most direct influence on Bar Kochba Zionism before the war, Ahad Ha'am always stood as a towering figure in the minds of its members. Judging from Bergmann's allusions to him—he was the subject of very early Bergmann lectures—it is unlikely that his influence came to Bar Kochba only through the mediation of Buber or Berthold Feiwel. Perhaps because of the preoccupation of many of his essays with specific and even arcane issues of Zionist debate, special attention has been given to the apparently less polemic piece from 1904 entitled "Moses." [53] It was very likely this essay that inspired Bergmann to undertake the editing of the volume *Worte Mosis* (Words of Moses) in the Bruns' Verlag series Die Weisheit der Völker.[54] Among Bergmann's prewar writings on Jewish subjects, this work is largely overlooked, for it too seems to diverge from his programmatic Zionist essays. It was through the vehicle of the figure of Moses, then, that both

Ahad Ha'am and Hugo Bergmann were able to cloak their deeply polemical projects in the garments of quasi-biblical scholarship.[55]

Both Ahad Ha'am and, citing him, Bergmann begin their pieces by reminding the reader that the attribution of any work to Moses has been called into question, indeed that his actual existence cannot be proven. There is a discordance between historical "facts" (set by the authors inside disdainful quotation marks) and the "historical reality of the ideal Moses [. . .] this ideal figure is a creation of the Jewish spirit; and the creator creates in his own image." Constructed in the form of a defense against positivist historical criticism, these introductory paragraphs do two things: they call into question pedestrian notions of immutable "reality" and unreal myth, and they equate the figure of Moses with the essence of Judaism. The latter move serves to privilege the Moses commentator in the broad field of Jewish debate. In a recent monograph on Ahad Ha'am, Stephen Zipperstein points to this special status of the Moses figure, often a symbol of "decency, righteousness, justice and self-sacrifice."[56]

Thus Ahad Ha'am's first question, posed as an inquiry into "what type of man" Moses was imagined to be, contains the seeds of a political program. Answering in the negative the possibilities of judging Moses' seminal role to have been as warrior, statesman, or lawgiver, he finds in scripture the answer that he was in fact a *prophet,* and more than that, the master of prophets, the symbol of Hebrew prophecy. The prophet in the Jewish tradition is first of all a speaker of truth, second an uncompromising "extremist," wholly fixated on his ideal, and finally the figure incarnating the idea of justice, the realization of truth. These characteristics set the prophet apart from the world; his word can reach the masses only through priestly intermediaries. It is by this process that the spiritual can give impulse to the material.

The essay makes the claim of constituting a representation of Judaism in its deepest and most immutable essence. At its most creative and sincere moments, the People of the Prophets sees the truth and *acts* upon it, accepting sacrifice, rejecting compromise, without hesitation. And even when Judaism has seemed furthest from these ideals, the Mosaic spark has reappeared to endow it with new life. In the course of the "Moses" text Ahad Ha'am self-consciously casts himself as the prophet of a slavish generation of world Jewry. Following him, Bergmann not only works from Ahad Ha'am's basic premises, but identifies himself in the role of the prophet as well.

This focus on prophecy underscores the element of *future,* which Ahad Ha'am as well as Buber saw as central to the eternal mission of Judaism. The prophet is not so much a seer of the future as he is its agent, in a present that is to him unbearable and unreal. The dwellers of the present are the masses, for whom the prophetic future and the inspirational past are equally remote. Of course, the future that takes form in the space cleared by Buber's *Addresses* is above all qualified by wholeness and unity.

The issue of unity is present even in Bergmann's reiteration of Ahad Ha'am's discussion of the authorship of the Pentateuch and existence of Moses. In Bergmann's formulation:

> Whether or not painfully meticulous philological research has the Pentateuch of Moses shattered into so many layers: that book, which was in truth, since it had true effects, since it reared the human race—this book is a unity.[57]

Taking off from Buber, it is "unity" itself that is the theme of the Pentateuch and the heart of the Jewish religion. At issue in the Exodus is first of all the unity of the community. Bergmann's retelling of the story is the struggle between the faith of the prophet and the indecisiveness of the masses, who demand miracle after miracle, who doubt his word and his God, and who repeatedly come to the idea of returning to Egyptian slavery. The struggle of the prophet in the desert between the Egypt of servitude and the promised land of freedom is an internal struggle. The future is blocked by the slavish elements of the community; the community is divided into two hostile camps:

> "May he who stands with God come to me!" This war cry, which was called—and is—to split the whole world for all time into two camps, resounds first from [Moses'] mouth. And those that come together about him are sent out by the prophet: "Gird your swords and go through the camp from gate to gate and slay all, brothers, friends, and relatives . . . "[58]

The internal struggle against slavishness, indecisiveness, incompleteness [*Halbe*] is repeatedly brought into the present by such qualifiers as the "—and is—" above. The trek from slavery to freedom is a violent one; the negative elements must be rooted out (*ausrotten*), if slavish nature is not to overcome those on the side of God. And did not even Moses waver, "as many more prophets after him wavered and as we all waver, when the divine speaks to us . . . "?[59] For the struggle in the desert is not just within the community, but within each individual. The spiritual mission of Moses and Judaism aims to make whole on the levels of humanity, the community, and the disunified or undecided subject.

In this way, the potential role of the prophet taken on by Bergmann becomes projected onto the reader, who must also decide between "choosing" and "letting happen." While the correct decision seems clear, Bergmann continuously returns to the wavering of Moses himself, to the repeated crises of the "liberated" people in the desert, the impossibility of the purity and permanency of the choice to liberate oneself. Bergmann's text presents the messianic hope of freedom always coupled with a certain pessimism—as if, despite the gesture of the will to freedom, one may not be sure of emerging from the desert in one's own generation. Franz Kafka, upon hearing his old schoolmate's lecture "Moses and the Present," was impressed, and yet concluded:

> In any case, I have nothing to do with it. The truly horrible paths between freedom and slavery cross each other without a guide for the way ahead and with the immediate dissolution of the paths behind. There are innumerable such paths, or only one, it cannot be determined, for there is nowhere to see them from. There am I. I cannot get away. I have nothing to complain about. I do not suffer excessively, since I do not suffer constantly, it doesn't pile up—at least I do not feel it all of the time, and the degree of my suffering is far less than it perhaps ought to be.[60]

With Bergmann, Kafka does recognize the crucial and tortured inner process of wandering to be linked to a communal dilemma, but it is nonetheless *definitionally* a solitary journey of one's own. This is no less paradoxical than the relationship to German culture that Kafka had described to Oskar Pollak in their discussion of the "national museum" represented by Goethe's house.[61] The only recuperable "traces" of the great figure would be his solitary "footsteps through the land," and yet one can never possess this legacy. One is entitled only to the traces of one's own, companionless journey (which, as we see above, are instantly swept away). Bergmann's presentation of a choice between slavery and freedom seems not as hopeless, but it does have this pain behind it: the modern self, for Bergmann as much as for Kafka, finds itself neither in Egypt nor in the promised land, but in the uncharted desert between the two. In the last analysis, Bergmann's assumption that one forges a path to freedom not alone, but as part of the community, does not make the trek any easier—since the internal struggle against slavishness and the pain of self-liberation, the "despair" over territory left behind and not yet found, is located within the self.

"I HAVE CAUSED THEE TO SEE IT WITH THINE EYES, BUT THOU SHALT NOT GO THITHER . . . "

Bergmann's project in his edition of *Worte Mosis* and in the Passover essay and lecture, all in 1913, provide an explication of the kinship of the European spiritual crisis of the present to the Jewish historical past, and, with it, to the Zionist vision of the future. Zionism belongs to

> the spiritual movement of our time. [. . .] If one were to try to represent the movement called Jewish Zionism in its universal [*allmenschlichen*] significance, perhaps one would do best to describe it as a striving *for the renewal of humanity through the spirit.* It is clear in this definition what the signature of these times is, of the times in which we live and against which we fight: the antispirit [*der Ungeist*], materialism in the broadest sense of the word.[62]

I will risk overstating this point because it is the kind of point that one tends to overlook, or to incorporate into a compromised form that is more familiar and seems more consistent. The Zionism here described, taken from Ahad Ha'am and Martin Buber and fired in the crucible of Prague identity, is not "also" spiritual, nor "primarily" spiritual, but *spiritual in its definition*—defined as the movement established to struggle against matter, to expulse the concept of territory from its midst. The revolution of Moses, the revolution of the "liberating deed," is above all an internal struggle to leave slavish materiality behind in the land of slavery.

The striking ambivalence of these texts foregrounds the painful confrontation of the most radical and creative forms of cultural Zionism with Zionism's basic tenets, which cannot do without a stress on the issue of physical territory in some sense. Bergmann did hold on to the idea of territory in Palestine as Ahad Ha'ams "spiritual center" of the circle of Jewry, "in some way or another." [63] But throughout his essays, and in the policy of *Gegenwartsarbeit* and its justification, Bergmann stressed the dangers of ignoring the periphery, of assuming the importance of the center to be greater, of assuming that the existence of a center would even (necessarily or automatically) affect Judaism in exile. To the pessimist Brenner's claim that "*Galut* [exile] is everywhere," even in Palestine, Bergmann merely adds the corollary, "*Everywhere can Galut be overcome.*" [64] It is in this context that we must understand the goals of the Zionist cultural program Bergmann insisted on implementing in the West: "We want to get out of the *Galut,* even while we remain in it physically." [65] In the ritually repeated inscription of a spiritual territory in

Bergmann's texts, there is an implicit flight from the concept of "territory" itself.

The discussion by Deleuze and Guattari of the operation of a minority discourse, which forges a subversive line of escape from within the major language ("deterritorialization"),[66] applies then not only to Kafka, but to the Zionism of his classmate Bergmann. At first glance, Zionism seems to represent a strategy for what Deleuze and Guattari call "re-territorialization": an attempt to overcome an essential alienation through the construction of an artificial bridge to a majority culture or territory. But, in fact, it is rather the deterritorializing gesture that qualifies Bergmann's discourse. Neither does "spirit" here effect a deliberate mystification to evade the issue of territory; "territory" is the ever-present subtext of a discourse that seeks to dismantle it.

So was Jerusalem in the hearts of the slaves in Egypt, was freedom to be found without setting foot in the promised land?

It is in the last chapter of the Pentateuch that the Lord shows the prophet the whole land, saying, "I have let you see it with your own eyes, but you shall not cross over into it." The citation lends itself well to the dichotomy set up in cultural Zionism, with the division of sight or understanding from far off in the primary clause, and the physical step onto territory in the second. From Odessa, Ahad Ha'am explains that there is no place for Moses in the Holy Land; the purely spiritual prophet can have no role in the necessarily profane confrontation with the physical territory. From Prague, Bergmann's complementary interpretation is that the physical conquest of the land is not what is decisive, but rather the victory or defeat of the spirit; the prophet has succeeded in creating a spiritual territory to home the people of religion, the bearers of the religious idea.

Nearly eighty years after Ahad Ha'am's prophetic essay on prophecy, Amos Oz rides through the Israeli-occupied West Bank, studying "the elusive cunning of the Biblical charm of this landscape."[67] He, too, finds it fitting to recall Moses on Mount Nebo, and to wonder what becomes of holy territory when it is set foot upon, if it is no longer yearned for by the Jewish spirit, but possessed. Ahad Ha'am left Russia not for Palestine, but for London, where he remained until moving to Tel Aviv in his sixties. Hugo Bergmann also made his way to London, where he served as secretary of the Department of Culture of the Zionist Organization before arriving in Jerusalem in May 1920.

Indeed, the view of the Holy Land from "far off" in Prague was a completely separate and contradictory experience from that of "crossing over" into it. In the short course of years from the outbreak of war until the journey to Palestine, that vision dissipated; even memory of the sense of it seemed to dissolve. It was in the first decade of his residence in Jerusalem that Bergmann wrote on the occasion of the fiftieth semester anniversary of the old rival organization Barissia, with the ideological barriers between the groups already forgotten:

> On this day in which Barissia celebrates its fiftieth semester, we alumni of Bar Kochba and Barissia should recognize the great *error* we committed as students: we thought that we could create a Jewish content in our lives through lectures, discussions, and activities. So we splashed around in the shallowness of the so-called Jewish Renaissance and grew into Jews without substance: *Am Ha'aretzim*.[68]

Barissia and Bar Kochba are on the same side of the duality now, on the side of useless chat in exile, with no real relationship to Judaism. On the other side stands heavy substance, depth, "reality," reachable only in the center of Zionism. As if to put a final nail in the coffin of the innovative alternative discourse he did so much to develop as a youth, or else as an unknowing landmark of how far he had strayed, Bergmann describes himself and his youthful cohorts as foolish and out of touch, ironically deploying the Hebrew term *Am Ha'aretzim*: country folk, or "people of the land." In a 1923 letter to Robert Weltsch, Bergmann openly doubts the value of all of the activities of Bar Kochba and calls the Central European Zionism of Buber "senseless."[69] Finally, in an apologetic preface to a late reprint of his famous essay on the Kiddush Hashem, Bergmann explains: "I was young then, did not know real [*das wirkliche*] life yet and did not know how difficult it is to sanctify God, particularly in political life." But he penned these words in his eighty-fourth year, in 1967, when he had probably forgotten whether or not the young Bergmann knew how impossible that was.

CHAPTER 6

New Orientations

Judaism, Desire, and the Gaze Eastward

Heute Geschichte des Judentums von Grätz gierig und
glücklich zu lesen angefangen. Weil mein Verlangen danach
das Lesen weit überholt hatte, war es mir zuerst fremder als
ich dachte und ich mußte hie und da einhalten, um durch
Ruhe mein Judentum sich sammeln zu lassen.

Today began eagerly and happily to read Grätz's history of
the Jews. Because my anticipation had far outrun the reading,
it was at first more foreign than I thought and I had to stop
here and there in order by resting to allow my Jewishness to
collect itself.

diary, 1 November 1911

As the first Zionist in the Prague circle, Bergmann began to think about
his Jewishness earlier and in different ways from others in his cohort, but
the issue would have a powerful impact on the lives and work of each
one of them in the second decade of the century. It is possible to identify
a "turn to Jewishness" in this period among German-speaking Jews more
generally, in the Reich as well as in Austria, and the turn also coincided
with discussions of German and Eastern Jewry in the German press at
large. What was the function of this figure of Jewishness, often conflated
with the exotic figure of Eastern European Judaism, and why did it suddenly become so salient? For the German-speaking Jews of Prague, there
were complicated effects associated with the appropriation of the vessel
of the exoticized Eastern Jew, at once fascinating and repugnant, both
radical other and an image of a lost authentic self. The ascription of authentic identity to this strange and desired figure marked an important
shift in the history of Prague German-Jewish identity, for it opened not
only a new space, but a new kind of space.

DEFENDING SELF

The first issue of what would become Bohemia's largest Jewish-national journal appeared in Prague on March 1, 1907. The journal was titled *Selbstwehr: Unabhängige jüdische Wochenschrift* (Self-defense: Independent Jewish weekly). By "independent" the creators of the journal meant that it would remain aloof from party affiliations in the name of bringing together Jews of differing political persuasions—even if, at the same time, it openly sought to undermine Jewish support for the secular parties in favor of a specific ideological program. A "Jewish" weekly, the journal was intended for a public that considered itself Jewish, without agreeing on what that actually meant. But above all—as the title announced in bold gothic lettering—this was an organ of Jewish "self-defense."

Selbstwehr was founded by Bar Kochba's more "earthly" and combative rival Barissia, and its program in the years between the first number in 1907 and the end of the First World War may be seen as an attempt to forge a national identity for Bohemian German-speaking Jewry. The debates carried on within its pages record the confessions of a nation in the process of inventing itself. The self-invention process was represented as a struggle—an internal struggle, to paraphrase Buber, not a reaction to outside forces. The opening lines of the first article announce this struggle:

> A proud title, and more than a title: a protest and a program. A protest, a declaration of war against everything rotten, unwhole, decaying within Judaism and a forceful, resolute affirmation of the young, self-conscious, budding strengths and efforts of the Jewish *Volk*.[1]

This was an aggressive project, for the word "*Selbstwehr*" implies a more active form of resistance than self-protection, or "*Selbstverteidigung*." But it was not directed against the antisemitic enemy without, as one might imagine in the context of growing hostility from both Czech and German camps in Bohemia.[2] The "declaration of war" announced in the first number of the journal was a civil war, much like what we found in Bergmann's interpretation of the Moses story or Werfel's spiritualist expressionist revolution. The construction of a new national identity depended first on this destructive gesture, on cutting away the decadent and impure elements of Judaism, so that a more integral Jewish communal self could be carved out.

The new Jewish nationality shared its grammar with German and Young Czech national movements. The passage quoted above seems today as antisemitic as it is antiliberal. But beyond this *völkisch* coloration, the language was just as typical of contemporary Czech nationalism, which styled itself as a youthful and vital alternative to a decaying and corrupt German patrimony. Closely echoing Czech-national rhetorical tones, the introductory article goes on to describe the Zionist movement as a good example of the "young Jewish Renaissance initiatives" (*jungjüdischen Renaissancebestrebungen*) that were worthy of attention. This deliberate double reference to the Young Czech movement forced readers to attend to the comparability of the Jewish condition with that of another "minor nation," one that also suffered culturally and spiritually from a lack of national independence, and one that had been enjoying increasing political success. The comparison fed naturally into one of the Bohemian Jewish nationalists' primary goals: official recognition of Judaism as a nationality within the Habsburg state.

Unlike the Czechs, the Jewish-national Bohemians could entertain no ambitions about national independence or quasi independence within the monarchy. Rather, they continued the respectful imperial allegiance of their liberal parents.[3] Nevertheless, while the journal could maintain a studied neutrality toward the language and nationality conflict,[4] the representation of the journal's authors and audience as an independent nation detached from the Czech-German struggle was difficult to achieve in a German-language newspaper. If language had been the focus of national identification and of the national conflict in Prague and Bohemia, what was to be done without a common Jewish language? What was to be the ground of Jewish nationality?

In an article straightforwardly titled "Religious Community or Nation?" Jacob Chill began the list of qualities making up Jewish nationhood, with the key notion being descent or *Stamm* (literally "stem" or "trunk," though in this context closer to "tribe").[5] Even when betraying its closest affinity with other contemporary discourses, Jewish-national rhetoric favored this botanical metaphor over the preferred *völkisch* figure of "blood," and explicitly shunned what was identified as "contemporary racial thinking."[6] Chill found another powerful notion in *Kultur,* exactly the element in which German liberals of Jewish confession had held the most stock. But Chill was concerned with Jewish culture, as reflected in biblical literature, a canon comparable to the great German literary tradition.

A closer look reveals that the concept of *Stamm* was generally used to

identify the Jews as non-Germans—in other words, as a negative signifier that was in and of itself not powerful enough to serve as cornerstone
of an independent Jewish nationality. Beyond descent (whereby the notion of the Jews of the world as in fact of common descent must have
been a questionable proposition) and beyond culture (precisely when the
astonishing plurality of Jewish cultures was becoming increasingly evident), some other commonality was required. That quality was to be
found in the more abstract concept of spirit (*Geist*).

As in *völkisch* discourse, the element of spirit in Jewish-national ideology served as an oppositional figure to the bourgeois-liberal value system of the contemporary era. *Selbstwehr* identified the youthful movement of Zionism as spiritual, idealist, and focused on the general good;
the liberal-assimilationist way of life, in contrast, was clearly materialis-
tic and self-serving.[7] The road of assimilation and liberal progress, in
this image, was leading the Jews away from the essential spirit that made
them Jews, and hence away from their authentic identities.

In the lead article of the first issue of *Selbstwehr,* the editors expressed
their hopes of winning the "respect of our opponents," offering their respect in return. In practice, though, the actual enemy, German liberalism, was treated with no respect whatsoever. The antiliberal and even
openly antisemitic German Bohemians shared many of the premises of
the Jewish nationalists. Not so the liberal "also-Germans" (*Auchdeut-
schen*), as they were often called in the journal.[8] Those "Germans of
Mosaic persuasion" were handled particularly sharply in this 1907 article published under the pseudonym Niels:

> Like martyrs they bear all sorts of humiliations for their beloved Germanness,
> in which sadly no one believes but themselves. These queer daydreamers still
> hold fast to the fiction that it is only confession—the invisible, unstressed,
> and often enough completely unfamiliar element of their religion—that sep-
> arates the Jews from the Germans. But fictions can only defer the truth, it will
> never let itself be sent away [. . .][9]

Note the appeal to the "truth." The issue was never posed as a matter of political expediency or historical contingency, but rather as one of
essential truth. It was important to the author to stress that assimilation
was based on a fiction. Here, and elsewhere in the pages of *Selbstwehr,*
Jewish nationality was represented as an essence, as something eternal and originary. Jewish national consciousness is no product of antisemitism, but appears rather as an inevitable historical necessity. In this
moment in 1907, *Selbstwehr* identified the turn from an inauthentic,

assimilated Bohemian Judaism to a true Jewish national identity. With revolutionary decisiveness the article continues:

> And even if there are thousands of them, the *Volk* lives and shakes the half- and quarter-Jews off like foul fruit. Yes, plenty of rotten fruit still hangs from the Jewish tree of life and some unhealthy juices live off it. But a new wind blows. It shivers and shakes the tree until the foul fruit falls. And the Zionists help with all their bodies' strength to cleanse the old stubborn trunk [*Stamm*] of all the bad juices and blossoms and fruits, for it is still healthy within. Then they shudder, and call the Jewish-nationals antisemites. And they are: against those Jews who harm and deny the Jewish people and who wish to hinder the work toward purification and liberation.[10]

"Niels" was right when he forecast that the assimilated liberal Jews were about to reach the end of their rope. In the years between 1907 and 1910, as many young Jewish German liberals like Felix Weltsch and Max Brod were moving toward some sort of Jewish national identification, German liberalism in Bohemia was also changing form. By 1910 the possibility of counting oneself a Bohemian Jewish German liberal had become more difficult than ever; in March the Liberal Party transformed itself into the *judenrein* German National Union, upon which the *Selbst-wehr* announced gleefully that the Jews,

> naturally not the German-liberal Jews but—pardon the expression—the Jew- ish Jews, are overjoyed over the death of an unwhole, unjust, unsalvageable system that can finally be discarded. No one weeps a tear over the passing of this German liberalism except for the German-liberal Jews, whose hope to be accepted as real Germans has been robbed forever.[11]

In reporting that a racist exclusionary policy had now made its way even into the German-liberal camp, the reporter reserved his contempt for those Jews who would not wish to be excluded, whereas the sponsors of the antisemitic policy come forth as honest men who recognize that "cultural consciousness" does not a German make—that it is a question of German nationality, *Stamm.*

Jewish-Czech assimilation was not treated any more sympathetically in *Selbstwehr* than German-Jewish liberalism. While the concern with Czech assimilationist Jews was certainly secondary to the offensive on German-liberal Jews, the powerful paternalism of the German-liberal periodical tradition in Bohemia survives in force in these descriptions.[12] The pages of *Selbstwehr* contained a volatile tension between this per-sisting German chauvinism toward the Czechs and an increasing and ro-mantic admiration for the Jews of Slavic Europe.

Selbstwehr stands as a network of conflicting rhetorical currents emanating from diverse sources. The "self-defense" the weekly claimed as necessary was clearly less directed at an external enemy than it was at the internal one, the bourgeois-liberal status quo. The contributors' attack on the modern Western Jew—on themselves—constituted a defense of a self that had already been lost to late nineteenth- and early twentieth-century Prague. To recover this mythical self, the Jewish nationalists were obliged to move on from their attack on liberalism, to reach for sources beyond the immediate models of German- and Czech-national rhetoric. They looked eastward for an image of their essential selves, and for the secret to their place in a hostile modern world.

AMONG THE NATIONS

The feuilletons of *Selbstwehr* testify to the writers' attempts to recapture the lost unity of Judaism. Depictions of the Jewish past alternate with sketches of exotic contemporary Jewish communities, with the favored setting of the latter the underdeveloped and insulated communities of the distant East. In the first weeks of 1910, for instance, there appeared reports titled "The Jews of Kurdistan," "News on the Jews in China," and "The Caucasian Mountain Jews." [13] At issue here was not the plurality of Jewish cultures, but instead a certain identification on the part of the writers with the East, with the communities untainted by modern Western life, as if the roots or even the essence of the Jewish self had been preserved there.

In the piece on the mountain Jews of the Caucasus, the complexity of this far-flung sense of identification comes into view. The narrator, who in the course of a battle is forced to kill one of the "primitive and warlike" Circassian people, asks the name of his dying victim:

"Ahmet the Jew," he gasped . . . I felt as though I had murdered my father, my own father . . . [14]

The author's choice of the paternal metaphor, rather than the more common description of compatriots as brothers, is significant. The further eastward of Prague, the further from modern Western influences, the nearer a Jew stood to the imagined originary Jew. With a literary gesture the essayist replaced his own German-liberal father with a figure that was anathema to the cultivated and assimilated Prague Jews of the previous generation.

The power of this image of familial relation to the Eastern Jew was so strong in this period that it burst the bounds of the ideological realm of Jewish nationalism. The archetype of Jew against Jew in a battle between states of course became particularly salient after the outbreak of World War I, and it reappeared in a story by none other than Franz Werfel.[15] The narrator in Werfel's tale first becomes aware that his victim is a Jew and therefore his "brother" as the opponent dies with the words "Sh'ma Yisroel" on his lips. This experience lifts Werfel's soldier to a higher level of consciousness, and eventually drives him into madness. For Werfel, who was certainly far from a Jewish nationalist, the image was useful as a model of a brotherhood of humanity, and as an antidote to the myth of the *Kriegserlebnis* (or redemptive "war experience").

The universalistic possibilities inherent in this nationality located in a spiritual space between East and West were far from alien to Jewish nationalists. It was during the war that most Prague Jews had their first substantive contact with Eastern (primarily Galician) Jews, and that the issue of the Jewish spiritual position "between" East and West took on territorial implications. In 1916, the liberal Jewish nationalist H. Kadisch expressed one revealing view in the pages of *Selbstwehr:*

> The world war has shown more clearly than ever how the Jewish people has *its own national interests* and a *historical mission* that is related to these interests. Just as it is for the *Habsburg monarchy itself, it is the task of the Jewish people to be a mediator between Orient and Occident,* in current areas of residence as well as in *Palestine.*[16]

The same author who had earlier declared that Jewish nationalism was compatible with Austrian patriotism now shifted ground to enter the realm of a people's historical missions: a loftier plane with more earthly effects. Certainly Central European Jews were frequently patriots of the empires that protected them, whether as liberals in the emancipated West or in the pre-emancipated villages and towns; conversely, people caught up in nationalist rebellions against imperial power predictably turned their wrath on the Jews, who seemed as allied with imperial authority as they were vulnerable. But here Kadisch suggested a deeper affinity. The Habsburg Empire and its Jews were allied, not on account of mutual interest, but rather because of a shared world mission. The previous, symbiotic relation in which the Jewish parasite performed a Germanizing imperial function was supplanted within Kadisch's text by a prophesy of a *central* role for the Jewish translator within the Habsburg monarchy, which in turn was promised a central role in Europe and the world.

Kadisch's text resisted the *völkisch* tones of Niels's denunciation of Judaism's "foul fruit," instead turning the language of German liberalism to the service of Jewish-national ends; another Kadisch essay, cited previously, discusses at length what the author calls the "new liberalism" (a term that did not seem to attract many adherents). While classical Prague German liberalism hotly resisted the notion of Judaism as a nationality, Kadisch's vision of the blossoming of the mosaic of minor nations under the protection of the Danube monarchy retained an overpowering flavor of the German-liberal worldview. The imperialist implications of this liberal project were completely exposed in the essay, which went on to describe the imminent "*Confederation of Peoples from Hamburg to the Persian Gulf.*" The accomplishment of this attractive and progressive end depended upon the monarchy's key to *Mitteleuropa*, the means [*Mittel*] to unite East and West, the mediators [*Vermittler*]: the Jews, newly conscious of their own nationality and newly oriented toward their Oriental roots: "[. . .] for this reason the maxim on which the future of Austria *and* the Jewish *Volk* depend must be: *Eastward and forward.*" [17]

The peculiar configuration of identifications for the German-speaking Jew in Bohemia at this moment tended to push the Jewish nationalists' conceptions beyond the ordinary bounds of the "national." In this context of an extended and revised Habsburg-liberal discourse, the nationally conscious Jews become the vanguard of a postnational Europe. Perhaps the paradox, reminiscent of Bergmann's gesture discussed in the previous chapter, was implicit in the unusual circumstance of this particular nationalist moment: a moment of discovery and intensive exploration of the national spirit, where at the same time the corporeal aspects of the nation—a language and a territory—were conspicuously lacking. The image of this national spirit without a territorial vessel led in a number of Bohemian constructions to ideas even less predictable than Kadisch's reformulation of the rationale for Habsburg domination in Central Europe. Even the term "Zionism" seemed in this context to refer less to the reunification of Jewish national spirit and territory than to a more general project; as Max Brod obliquely explained in *Selbstwehr,*

> For me there can be no doubt that the "Jewish nationalist" may not be a "nationalist" in the sense of the word commonly in use today. *It is the mission of the Jewish-national movement, of Zionism, to give the word "nation" a new meaning.*[18]

A national struggle to overcome national strife? A material battle for the soul? Such contradictions were the typical, often creative and idealistic products of a thing that even in its name seemed to harbor a certain tension: Jewish nationalism. But the tension itself, the space between the spiritual enclosure of world Jewry and its territorial dispersion, seemed to Max Brod by the end of the war to make this "nationalism" particularly useful to the resolution of the crisis confronting twentieth-century Europe:

> Zionism is for me the intensification and activation of the Jewish national characteristic of universal humanistic feeling, and with it an essential hope for the idea of peace.[19]

This sort of translation of the ancient Jewish self-image as a light among the nations, as I have been arguing, is closely bound up with the gaze eastward, the dispossession of the emancipated and assimilated Western Jewish mask and the embrace of the originary self/other of the East.

THE VOYAGE EAST

It makes sense that an interest in the East came earlier to Hugo Bergmann than to his classmates, just as his conviction that his personal identity was entangled in the state of Jewish communal identity long preceded a comparable awareness on the part of Brod, Kafka, and Felix Weltsch.[20] After attending the 1903 Austrian Zionist Party convention in Bielitz, Bergmann set out on a trip to the eastern reaches of the Habsburg state, to Galicia.[21] "It has long been my passionate wish one day to see Jews with caftans, side locks, and real, right Jewish blood. Finally I am there."[22]

The unfortunate metaphor of blood, which the more mature Buber would invoke even after the outbreak of war, was the "layer" (Buber) of internality, the essential self. Young Bergmann sought the Jew of true Jewish essence, "blood" (*mit . . . echtem, rechtem Judenblut*). As he began his voyage out to the periphery and inward to the Jewish self, he reflected that it was "remarkable how even way out here the ring of Zionism encircles us." The word "Zionism" in Bergmann's diary is even more ambiguous than usual: its referent is Jewish politics, to be sure, and also Jewish religion and the fabric of Jewish life. Bergmann spots Zionism in the *heder* and in the market, he hears it in Jewish prayer and in the tones of Yiddish. The imperial periphery is the Jewish core; as Western civilization loses its grip on the Prague student, a natural Jew emerges in his diary. A score of anecdotes, with no excess of subtlety, express the antagonistic relation between the Western ideal of cultivation and a knowledge of the self:

> A quite little tot pushes himself through the door. He looks in longingly, says with great pride how he already "meets" the Alef-Bet [Hebrew alphabet]. I know a lot of bigger fellows who still do not meet it.[23]

Bergmann's descriptions of the full-grown Jews of Galicia are by and large as patronizing as this reference to a small boy. Yiddish diction is recorded as naive error, marked in Bergmann's text with condescending quotation marks; superstitions and customs are described as the habits of children. In a meeting with the miracle rabbi in the village of Stanislau, mystical Jewish knowledge persists in Bergmann's mind as the converse of Western learning:

> We discuss Jewish poverty. The dear man has no idea about anything that happens outside of Stanislau. Besides Galicia he knows but one country: Hungary, and in Hungary but one town: Pressburg [Bratislava]. When I bring up East Africa he asks, is that in Hungary? [. . .] Beyond Galicia and Hungary, Eretz Israel is the only geographical name familiar to him. He certainly does not know where it is, simply somewhere out in Fairy-Land.[24]

A German's prejudices about Eastern Europe go undisguised in Bergmann's descriptions, which often enough find romance in the region's backwardness. The result is a combined disgust and delight in the filth of the market and the *mikveh*, the coarseness of the people and wild gesticulations, the overcrowding, the nursing of an infant in public. The narrator may distance himself from the objects of his writing through thinly veiled mockery and disdain, but he never confesses any feeling of alienation; rather, he speaks of how he is drawn to Cracow as to home [*mich . . . angeheimelt*].

It is of little use to focus merely on the banality of Prague German disdain for East European culture, as much as that strikes the reader today. The fascinating aspect of the diary is the persistent desire for union with an existence that seemed uncivilized, unhygenic, and uncultivated. The attraction of the clamor of Talmudic argument, drowning out the sober tones of Western political discussion, is its "powerful resonance of millennia." The mystical resonance was for Bergmann contained within the Yiddish-Hebrew vehicle of political discourse and biblical exegesis, as it was in Hassidic melodies and in the wooden synagogues and homes. Remorsefully he recalls debates over the appropriateness of choirs and or-gans in Reform synagogues in the West, the sterilized observance these Eastern Jews condemn as "an impurity."

Bergmann's Galician diary ends with just such an alternation of purity and impurity: a visit to the ritual bath in a Jewish village, where he is overcome with an "unpleasant vapor odor." Pressing further into the building toward the bath, he discovers: "A filthy pool, that is the place of purification." This reaction to the primitive bath is less of a surprise than the impulse to press farther into the dark building, and to immerse oneself in the filthy pool.

Bergmann's diary is a very articulate and early example of an impulse toward East European Jewry that will possess each of the Prague circle writers in one form or another. It is no less marked in "universalists" such as the socialist Kisch, the Christian-spiritualist Werfel, or the expressionists Kornfeld, Fuchs, and Pick than it is in those more explicitly associated with Zionist or other Jewish ideological identities. Even these writers who stood opposed to the readers of *Selbstwehr* resisted the attraction of the East no better than did the journal's more avid readers, such as Franz Kafka.[25]

According to Werfel's own report, his reaction to the "discovery" of Oriental Jewry was one of alienation sooner than identification: "What did I have to do with these people, with this foreign world? My world consisted of the great European artists with all their antagonisms from Dostoyevsky to Verdi."[26] But this retrospective confession may be less revealing than the following passage from Werfel's notebook from the front in 1917; it was written to be included in the author's public dispute with Kurt Hiller over the issue of "activism":

> Our debate is the fruit of a distinct life-feeling [. . .] Allow me to point out a geo-ethnographic truth that seems to me to be important. You were brought up in Prussia and are a son of the center of Europe. I was born in a city which, since it was inhabited by Slavs and Jews, was always a gateway to the East.[27]

Certainly this quotation in its own way represents a retrospective distortion on Werfel's part, perhaps even a deliberate and manipulative one. For it is hard to imagine how in 1917 the Prague of 1907 could have seemed Oriental, how its Jews could have formed a link to the East, with the Germans altogether invisible. But it is also clear that Werfel is identifying the more mystical strain of his work, and the work of the Prague expressionists more generally, with an Eastern influence of which they had perhaps not been fully conscious, and which was absent in Berlin. In contrast, "Germany, land of millions of organizations, has quite a lot of 'activity.' " Felix Weltsch attributes what he takes to have been the political moderation of his circle to this position "between East and West, and indeed between Eastern and Western Jewry, at the same time as the most easterly extended part of Western Jewry, whose position 'in the middle' had considerable qualities of the 'middle.' " [28]

Egon Erwin Kisch's preoccupation with Oriental Jewry is demonstrated in a volume appearing well after the war, *Stories from Seven Ghettos*. Even more relevant is his long preoccupation with the Golem myth, which touched upon his Prague identity at the same moment that it bound him and his city to a mystical Jewish tradition. Seeking to reach further into the Golem myth, Kisch traveled to a village on the Galician-Hungarian border, an experience in some ways reminiscent of Bergmann's excursion.[29] There he interviewed a local "mystagogue," a cabalist and expert in all things relating to the Golem, who believed unflinchingly in its continued existence. The encounter is interesting in the sense that the local man, never having left Eastern Europe, was intimately familiar with the Golem tale and with it the life and even the streets of old Prague, which he had memorized from a German travel guide. Kisch traveled east to discover the essence of his own Western city; the interview with a stranger was for Kisch an insight into the self. This narrative structure, where the search for one's origins coincides with the desire for the exotic other, is repeated in a wide range of Prague circle texts. At its most radical, this gesture exceeded paternalism and sympathy, and offered an empathic model of the relationship between self and other that was at odds with the logic of identity. Not only did this model promise an alternative object of identification to the assimilationist model of identification with German culture; the model, as will become clear, was a *dissimulative* one that allowed a radical departure from the terms of national identity inherited from German liberal discourse.

Rudolf Fuchs, in his 1913 collection of expressionist poems, *Der Meteor,* betrays the eroticism inscribed in the desire toward the Jewish past/essence and the East.[30] In the first segment of the triptych "Juden" (Jews), Fuchs takes the reader into a "darker world," where one's steps echo "through eternities." Indeed, references to darkness appear no less than five times in the course of the poem. The collective and mystical experience described throughout is at odds with a modern individuated and rational (Western) existence. The frenzied night dance around the golden calf (ill chosen as a primordial Jewish experience) is one of a series of mystical images that leads into the desire for the embrace of the Jewess. In this darkened, mystified Hebraic landscape, the "Jewess" becomes an exotic and erotic figure, whose relation to the urban bourgeois Jewish women of Prague, or Vienna and Berlin, must have been difficult to retrace.

The poem "Nach Osten gesungen" (Sung to the East) also creates a frenzied, dark, and erotic space in which expressionist experience coincides with a mystical vision of the East and of Jewishness. Storms and clouds invade a confused landscape; redemption is sought in the Bible, but found in an encounter with the feminine interlocutor: "and from now on am I no longer a stranger in Canaan!" The irresistible and seamless shift between images of mysticism, the Orient, Jewishness, and finally the erotic feminine object is a recurring tendency, and these figures remain in play through various ideological incarnations of Prague circle authors.

EMPIRE AND "OSTFRAGE"

The Habsburg East, as Hannah Arendt would point out in *The Origins of Totalitarianism,* in several ways served for German Austria the function of empire that more modern European powers satisfied on other continents. The dream of the *Selbstwehr* essayist, that the Habsburg Jews could play a role in the expansion of the Habsburg middle realm "from Hamburg to the Persian Gulf," is evidence of the imperial ambition embedded in the notion of Central Europe. The lack of any overseas colonies, nonetheless, was an indicator of the difference between the sort of "empire" comprised by the Danube monarchy and those empires at the forefront of European and world power. Austria-Hungary seemed to be an empire in an antique sense, along the lines of its eastern and southern neighbors, the Russian and Ottoman empires; indeed, these were the three weakest of the recognized world powers. The Habsburg realm was like the empire of Borges's story, where an aging map frays at the edges, exactly representing the relative weakness of imperial hold. These ways of imagining this empire as ancient and decaying correspond somehow to the self-image of the Habsburg state, its attempts to modernize notwithstanding; the aging emperor Franz Josef put his reticence to accept change on display, as though this quality were, as he himself was, a symbol of the realm.

These ways in which the monarchy was unlike the colonial empires have impeded modern scholars from including it in discussions of the European imperial experience. Conversely, and more significantly, the burgeoning theoretical work on empire has hardly been brought to bear on Central Europe.[31] Needless to say, from a number of perspectives, the exertion of imperial control over the eastern reaches of Cisleithania was hardly comparable to the colonization of Africa or Asia. The ways in which the colonial experience was formative for the identity formation of the European metropoles, however, may be much more applicable to the Central European relationship to Eastern Europe than has been recognized.[32] One telling example is the role of the gendering of the Orient as feminine and the eroticization of the relationship between center and periphery. This construction—suggested by the Fuchs poems above, and a central feature we will explore more intensively in the remainder of this chapter and in the next—is completely consistent with the rhetorics of the colonial powers, where territorial and sexual conquest were perennially conflated.

In all events, it is indisputable that there was in this period an increasing preoccupation with the identity of Eastern Europe and the question of its place in the Habsburg Empire, and this preoccupation was signaled by the vague term in wide use in the early twentieth century, "the eastern question" (*Die Ostfrage*). The state that was an empire in an antique sense began in the early twentieth century to think and talk about its East in terms closer to two enviable models: the ultramodern "empires" of the new German Reich on the one hand, and the Western powers with their overseas colonies. In this sense, this case conforms to Edward Said's argument in *Orientalism* that the metropole's investment in Orientalist discourse is twofold: first of all, the discourse supports and is also in dialogue with a network of interests tied to territorial control, and second, the shaping of an identity of the Orient is a practice that cannot be separated from the construction of metropolitan identities.[33]

How does the work of the Prague circle authors fit into this complex picture of culture, power, and identity? One can identify, on the one hand, a collusion with imperial interests implicit in the representation (taking possession, in a way) of Czech Prague by Kisch, of the modern Czech arts by the translators Brod, Pick, and Fuchs, and of the Yiddish East, for example, by Bergmann and Brod. Yet in each case, even in the most Kiplingesque moments of Max Brod's work, the elements of "extremes of self-consciousness, discontinuity, self-referentiality, and corrosive irony"[34] were necessarily present at a far more literal level than was ever possible in the cultures of imperialism Said discusses. The radical move from representing the East as a double for the self to the identification of the self *as* other turned an already circular structure back onto itself a second time. The position of the Prague Jewish writers was one in which their "centered" identities as cultural spokesmen coincided with their powerfully felt marginalization. The result was the oddly twin tendencies toward complicity with colonization and sensibility as colonized, both increasing as the stability of the empire visibly diminished.

Obviously, this peculiar reflexive identity worked against notions of essential and fixed identities, notions that were reaching new levels of orthodoxy as world war approached. The relation between the two most naturalized of these identities, nation (or "race") and gender, is an intriguing aspect of this period, and a key to the ways in which retrenchments of gendered and raced identities by Prague Jews slipped into unconventional refigurations of these. The play between collusion and subversion of dominant paradigms of territorial power is compellingly parallel to the shifting ways in which Praguers imagined their own Jewishness and its relationship to "Eastern" figures, whether Czech Slav or Galician Jew. The Praguers' part-desiring, part-disdaining gaze toward the Eastern other was never separate from their search for themselves.

CZECH GIRLS, SHEPHERDS, AND JEWESSES

Before the main character of Brod's novel, the boarder Wilhelm Schurhaft, had ever seen the household's Czech serving girl Pepi, something in him was awakened by the overwhelming scent of pine needles in the places where she had been.

Reading passages from Brod's 1909 novel *A Czech Servant Girl* today, the Czech critical objections to German condescension seem easier to comprehend than those of German nationalists, who saw the work as a treasonous and unnecessarily flattering gesture of conciliation toward the Slavs. While the novel may be even less a work of political innovation than of artistic achievement, it does remain an extraordinarily articulate example of the entanglement of discourses of gender and nationality in Prague. It is the first source to look to for a clue to the morass of issues of desire and patronization, longing and disdain, in the German-Jewish gaze to the East.

Pepi (or "Pepička") is the name of the servant who simultaneously embodies the qualities of both woman and Slav. The term "primitive" is used to describe her several times in the text, including a reference to her "dumb, primitive soul"; the closeness of the Slav to nature—represented, for instance, by the pine-needle scent—is contrasted to the odor of wet towels emanating from her German patroness; Pepi is a "frightened soul," member of a people with a "childish soul"; the lady of the house, then Wilhelm, and finally Pepi herself refer to her with the term *Luder*—"tramp," with an animalistic connotation.[35] The promiscuous sexuality of the female is mirrored in the Czech language, the narrator notes, which even in its inflections of verbs cannot resist marking them by gender.[36] Brod's Slav/Woman is mysterious and irresistible, capricious and deceitful; she is simple and tied to physical, material needs. Drawn to her, the protagonist is shaken from his masculine loftiness:

> Earlier, in my scholastic period, I had absolutely no capacity for the concrete. Now in contrast I was in touch with the naked facts, and my capacity for the abstract seemed to be burst . . . [37]

This association of woman with the physical, the material, or the purely sexual is replicated in Central European texts of all sorts in this period, and was elevated to the status of a system in the emblematic tractate of the Moravian-born Otto Weininger, *Sex and Character*. In Weininger's text as well is the notion that nations, like individuals, are composed of particular balances of the masculine and feminine principles.

The association of the Czech language and culture as the masculine Aryan's feminine other is the subject of a clever book by the brilliant German-Czech "hermaphrodite" Paul/Pavel Eisner.[38] In another book, an essay on the importance of the Prague context to the content of Kafka's work, Eisner devotes a great deal of attention to issues of eroticism and nationality in Prague. He associates the "high erotic tension" of Prague with the "exotic charm of the Slavic girl," for instance. Eisner further points out not only that Czech women served as housekeepers, cooks, and nursemaids in bourgeois Prague German homes, but that "the young German Jew received his erotic initiation usually from Czech women." [39] This formulation itself very clearly contains within it the latent identification of the German (Jew) as male and the Czech as female; similarly, Eisner (himself a Prague Jew only somewhat younger than Brod and Kafka) continues with this sort of assumption in his analysis of Prague literature: in his identification as Czech of a promiscuous female servant in *Description of a Struggle;* in his conclusion that the girls at Wenceslaus Square Kafka described must have been Czech "according to all statistical probability"; the evidence of a character of Brod's "who is the daughter of a laborer and must be thought of as Czech"; and, finally, the assertion that "the woman figures in Kafka's stories and novels, though some of them are furnished with the masks of German first or even last names, point unmistakably to the Prague environment, and thus almost exclusively to Czech models." [40]

These presumptions in Eisner's text more likely affirm than question his thesis, since they are grounded in the same earth as the works they describe. Young men as sympathetic to the Czech people as Brod, Kafka, and even Paul/Pavel Eisner seemed not to be capable of resisting the identification of Slavs with their physical nature, and in particular to focus on the fairer of their number. Such, at any rate, was the complaint of a certain Ružena Jesenská, journalist and aunt of Kafka's later lover.[41] While Brod later shrugged off the complaint, calling Milena's aunt a "reactionary," there were predictably other Czech voices to object to the representation of their nation in Brod's novel.

Even if Brod's novel offended some Bohemian German-national newspapers as deeply as Brod later claimed, so that Brod's name was banned forever from their pages, the German-liberal Heinrich Teweles and the Bar Kochba Zionist Hugo Herrmann seemed for once to agree with each other, and probably with many in the public: if the book had been intended to be a "conciliatory work," it was as unlikely to be successful as the copulation of a bourgeois German with a proletarian Czech was to halt national strife.[42] The review of the novel in *Bohemia* had so great an investment in asserting that the work "had nothing in the least to do with politics" that it devoted most of its space to the point.[43] Brod's friend Otto Pick reported it as an unheeded gesture for conciliation, but Brod himself denied any such intention, stating flatly in his own "defense" that he had not written a political novel.[44] A year and a half earlier, however, after a segment had been printed in Franz Blei's journal *Die Opale*, Brod mentioned to an important Czech editor the novella "in which I give expression to my sympathy for the Slavs."[45]

Ein tschechisches Dienstmädchen, written at a moment straddling the fin de siècle and the expressionist decade, grew out of Brod's desire to move past indifferentist-aestheticism and to touch on a spiritual-humanist message.[46] The critical uproar is evidence that, while sexual relations between the nationalities may well have been commonplace, the type of representation the novel offered was original. As in our previous discussion of Kisch's work, it should be recalled that the Concordia poets' Prague sooner resembled classical Weimar or Athens than a city of national conflict. Brod chose to set a novel in Prague in which a young man's indifferentism would be overcome by a spiritual-humanist redemption, and that simple formula led inevitably down one path: that of the "erotic symbiosis."

It was of little comfort to the Czech reader that a new generation of Prague Germans such as Brod, Kisch, and Gustav Meyrink was exploring paths to what Kisch had called the true Prague novel, taking nourishment from the Slavic atmosphere and the national conflict rather than ignoring these. The action in Brod's novel takes place within the German-masculine subject, moved or inspired by a Czech-feminine object. As the leading Czech critic Arne Novák articulated in 1917, after the publication of the Czech translation of Meyrink's *Golem,* the healthy organism of Czech Prague life independent of the shrinking German island was beyond these writers' sight:

> [T]his is a matter of a systematic and premeditated attack by German writers who are imposing a fully refined conception of the world of our Prague: they look at life here through a dualistic curtain. Two races live on the Moldau, of differing languages, customs, and blood: one born to spiritual and physical pleasure, noble manners and enterprise; today extending a greedy hand after every woman, tomorrow possessed by mystical dreams—and the second servile and uneducated, cowering at the wall and waiting there for alms or a slap in the face, reserved for supplying Aryans or Semites with servants or barmen, "sweet girls" and prostitutes.[47]

Implicated in the "systematic and premeditated attack" were not only Meyrink and Brod, but also the German writer most occupied with the Czech "real life" of the city, Egon Erwin Kisch. Kisch was outraged by Novák's comments, which also condemned his only novel, the 1914 naturalist *Der Mädchenhirt,* for depicting the underworld of Czech prostitution.

Kisch's novel, the title of which (literally *The shepherd of girls*) is a German translation of a Czech phrase, is set in a working-class Czech neighborhood on the bank of the Moldau that was commonly called the Kampa "island." The protagonist is the boy Jarda, the illegitimate son of a neurasthenic German nobleman named Karl Duschnitz; the boy's mother sends him to German schools in hopes of providing him the opportunity to break out of the confines of his nation-class. Thus the character is a synthesis of Czech and German elements, from the perspective of "nature" as well as of nurture. "Czech" and "German" are never represented by Kisch in terms of distinct forms of what was called "national life," nor even of culture, but only and quite specifically in terms of power relations, social structures in an almost purely economic sense. The national conflict itself is represented in the novel as a new form of an ancient class struggle:

> It was no new hatred that was ignited in the people of the Kampa ghetto. But now for the first time it got its name, its direction, its liberation. Before this, the hatred was directed vaguely and inarticulately against everyone better off,

everyone rich, enviously, against anyone upon whom one was economically dependent. Now it is: against the Germans! It was conceived as though these things were the same [. . .] The Germans, yes, that's who the rich are—we are the poor. The banks, the officials, the institutions, the nobles on the Klein-seite—all Germans, while the poor raftsmen, the carpenters, the factory workers, the drivers, the servants, the beggars—all Czechs [. . .] The concepts "German" and "rich" were compounded in Czech Prague: national hatred was class hatred.[48]

This conflation of class and nation ultimately offered Kisch the opportunity to redeem his own position in the nationality conflict; as a class struggle, one had the freedom to position oneself ideologically, rather than being frozen in an essential identity over which one had no control. On the other hand it might be said that Kisch's insight was due to a closer understanding of the Czech position: the identification of the social with the national movements, or of the national opponent as class enemy, was precisely the gesture made by Slavic radicals such as Petr Bezruč.[49]

Jarda's extraordinary exposure to a dominant nation-class to which he does not belong does not have the effect his mother had wished. The youngster is hyperconscious of the structure of domination and would challenge it in an instant or even destroy it with violence. This revolutionary element in the character is evident in the father's terror of him in the only scenes in which they meet. But the primary way in which the character empowers himself is through his mediation of women.

At the very moment that Jarda becomes aware of his provenance, his career as a pimp begins. Sitting in the bordello with his fellow waiters, he puts the pieces of the puzzle together: "Jaroslav Chrapot is no rafter's son, he is the son of a noble gentleman." In the same scene he conspires to profit from the negotiation of sex. This association of national power with sexual power becomes further entrenched as Jarda mediates the prostitution of the girl he loves. His domination over women, the fantasy that all women are his slaves, is actually born as a defense against being a cuckold: he wishes to own, rather than to love, a woman who must be a slave to German and bourgeois clients. Seeing the girlfriend of an acquaintance prostitute herself without her boyfriend's knowledge, Jarda concludes: "he could play the lord, but this way he plays the fool." Through this conscious, intervening act of mediation, Jarda appropriates all the power in the three-way relationship, and the client is transformed from exploiter to exploited.[50]

Insight into the inner life of Jarda's father, the German Duschnitz, adds further complexity to these structural relations. The meek, nearly

impotent noble aesthete has harbored secret fantasies of sexual domination, which become reified only in the life of the son. Duschnitz
contemplates:

> It had to happen this way: in the son, the desire of the father toward woman
> had found fulfillment, and to such a degree that women were even his slaves,
> whom he could sell [. . .] It was the father's wish within him enriched by deed.
> An inheritance of that hour in which once, long ago, a deed and a woman fell
> to Karl Duschnitz.[51]

As a literary device, the erotic metaphor allows Kisch to complete a
circle from the economically potent but sexually powerless Duschnitz to
his mirror-image son. While the same structural dualism is in operation
here as in Brod's work, there are important differences. In *Ein tschechisches Dienstmädchen* the erotic symbiosis and redemptive moment occur entirely within the male-German subject; Pepi shakes Wilhelm out of
his aestheticist indifference, but she remains throughout an impenetrable
riddle, and is not herself altered by the affair. The novel was adventurous
in depicting German-Czech contact in a positive light, but all action still
revolved around the German protagonist; even the servant girl's ultimate
suicide was presented only insofar as it affected Wilhelm Schurhaft.

Der Mädchenhirt is from the start primarily played out in Czech
Prague, but the difference from Brod's novel goes further than that. The
action of the novel, internal as well as external, all turns on the symbiosis of German and Czech, male and female principles within the subject Jarda. The abstracted, neurotic German-masculine idea finds firm
ground in which to root in the Czech womb; as above, it is reified within
the Czech-German progeny. Behind each of the conflicts of the novel
stands the imposing edifice of social power relations, and the threat of a
collapse of that order is implicit, even though the "corrupted" central
figure is doomed to a tragic end.

As Kisch's notes and correspondence suggest, various alternative end-
ings were considered by the author, all of which involved a final inter-
face of father and son. The resolution of the Prague novel, as of the text
of events unfolding in the city around the author, necessarily turned on
the negotiation between these oppositional factions of nation and political and social power. In the final version of the text, Jarda's life ends
tragically, with the promise of redemption through the father's magnanimous intervention barely missed. The paternalist pity toward a tragic
Czech lower class notwithstanding, Kisch's novel is supported by a network of complex and overlapping relations of power and dependency,

and all gestures toward redemptive resolution rest upon the promise of their harmonious interaction. As such, the novel points to a far more sophisticated and sensitive treatment of the Prague setting as theater for a symbiosis of East and West than that offered by Max Brod.

Yet by the time Kisch had written *Der Mädchenhirt* Max Brod was by far the most successful Prague Germanophone writer of his generation, having published a dozen varied volumes of prose and poetry, literary criticism, translations, and a philosophical treatise, not to mention a long list of newspaper essays and reviews. Once Kisch had completed a draft of the manuscript for his first (and only) novel, what better critical reader could he find than the venerable peer Brod? The latter's comments and suggested revisions illuminate differences between the two writers' standpoints, but more than that they illustrate the dynamic relations of nation or "race," gender identifications, and social stratification in Prague at the moment before the outbreak of the First World War.

Brod recognized and saw value in principle in a naturalist project—that is, what he recognized as a study of social degradation in the Prague context. The leftish impulse of Kisch's work, though, seemed to him necessarily inferior to the ideological artistic justification Brod had recently discovered. Thus he finds in the most Zolaesque scenes of the novel, those played out in the Czech Prague underworld, and especially the inner narration of the protagonist as he suffers in a syphilitic delirium, some of Kisch's best writing yet:

> Here there is true social sensitivity, forcefulness, greatness, it stands far above anything you have written before. And that already brings me to my reservation: why is not the whole novel of this quality?
>
> And I know the answer, too. I could express it in a very precise way: because you are not a Zionist (whereby of course I do not refer to the party, but rather the conviction).
>
> But I want to try to be exact: In essence your novel is lacking pathos, the great passion for an idea [. . .] the great love. [. . .] The book becomes for the reader something like an interesting nature story, rather than an inner experience.[52]

For Brod, Kisch's minute observations of the life of the destitute classes is too detached, too much like the utterly informed but purely "external" notes of a birdwatcher. The problem with naturalism for Brod, therefore, is not its commitment to depict the unattractive elements of modern urban life, but rather its documentary position with respect to this representation: "naturalism" becomes "nature story."

From our contemporary perspective, the final draft of Kisch's novel is not lacking in pathos, and certainly not in sensitive and empathetic portrayal of the characters; compared with Brod's work it seems hardly less passionate, merely considerably less purple. But Brod's extension of the exaggerated German Prague prose style (especially apparent in the half generation previous—in Paul Leppin and Viktor Hadwiger, for instance) is integral to his new ideological aesthetic. With deep and sentimental coloration, Brod projects outward the "inner experience" of the characters.

The relationship of this expressionist project to Zionism is perhaps the most jarring shift in the above passage from Brod's critical letter. Brod makes the shift with neither explanation nor ellipsis, as if it stands to reason how the inconsistency of the novel, the lack of passion throughout, and Kisch's refusal to embrace Zionism are bound together. The secret of these skips is found in the Brod essay we have discussed earlier, "The Jewish Poet of German Tongue," which was published a few months before Brod wrote these comments.[53] Brod's suggestion that the Jewish writer had no true access to the foreign territory of German language without his analogous territorialization to Jewish nationalism has its parallel in the critique of Kisch: neither naturalist representation nor proto-socialist sympathy seemed to Brod to be enough to allow the author to enter his characters' inner life. Kisch needed Zionism (not the external party apparatus, but the inner experience of Zionist conviction) in order to discover the "great love" that a work on the destitution of Czech Prague would require.

Brod goes on in the letter to specify more explicitly that Kisch does not feel enough love for his own characters. He recommends changes in the plot that would allow the sort of dynamic redemptive moments that occur in Brod's own overdramatic texts. In this case, he recommends that Jarda go to his first girlfriend, now a prostitute in his charge, for a night of lovemaking, only to meet love in her arms for the first time:

> Here we must see the triumph of the common [das Volkstümliche], the Czech, the touching. Here the bitterness toward society must be intensified once more.

Thinking back on Brod's essay, we can understand how Kisch's distance from the Jewish (ergo any) Volk in Brod's view necessarily blocked access to the common, popular, or national (volkstümlich) essences of his objects of study. The discovery of the Jewish Volk within the self is not only a vehicle allowing access to German poetic language, but uniquely suited for entry into the Oriental essences of simplicity and sentiment.

This location would shed a new and more meaningful light on the social conflict that Kisch had amply illustrated.

Where is the Jew in these two tales of Prague? In both cases the issues of nationality are always described as a dialogue of Czechs and Germans. The Zionist response to Brod's novel, however, indicated that Wilhelm Schurhaft was rather transparently a product of a Viennese German-liberal Jewish family. Brod in turn took for granted that Kisch's German aesthete Duschnitz was an assimilated German Jew, and suggested that Kisch make this more explicit (a recommendation the author ignored). The conspicuous absence of the Jews from the authors' exposed diagrams of Prague nationality does not indicate merely an oversimplified view of the issue in the pre-Zionist Brod and Kisch. Rather I would suggest that these gestures toward prose representations of national mediation in themselves spring from a growing vision of a special Jewish role between the two nations, East and West, Slavic nature and German culture.

There is a remarkable convergence of competing discourses at this pivotal moment, as a postliberal Brod is in the process of formulating new visions of nationality, ideology, and culture. The German-liberal paternalism is preserved in Brod's image of the childishly amoral Czech; Brod suggests that perhaps Jarda "does not even know what a pimp is, ever since childhood he has heard that a girl gets 100 crowns, and so forth." This moment of Czech-national amorality/immorality could be lifted directly from Otto Weininger's diatribe against W, the female principle. Like W, the Czech responds to raw physical impulses, and can never be anything beyond that pure sensuality.

The conflict in the person of Jarda, for Brod, is inherited from his unnatural hybrid origins. From the Czech/female mother he inherits sensuality and the sexual impulse, from Duschnitz the "skepticism in the midst of pleasure, the inability to have pleasure!" The cerebral Duschnitz is utterly detached from physicality, unable to act, while the Czech is a victim of pure sensuality. In each lies the hope of the other. For this reason, Brod felt that a more conclusive scene between aesthetic father and revolutionary son was needed as a climax to Kisch's novel. His suggestions here are revealing:

> Entrance at Duschnitz's home. The old man is occupied with some passionate hobby, for instance the solution of chess problems, boundlessly lonesome.—Scene between the two. Overwhelming love, emotion, at the same time though a horrible dread of one another. (Here it would be to my taste,

although probably not to yours, to show the source of the "corrupted" man to be in the damnable offense of racial mixing).

The passage discloses the dependence upon the Weiningerian bifurcation and even, in the final line, an undiscussed racialist strand of Brod's thinking. The fear of the Prague German privileged class toward the Czech rings liberal again (while *völkisch*-national German Bohemians may also have feared the Czech political advance, they expressed it as hatred rather than dread). Yet, the main point Brod is trying to make is after all at odds with both German-liberal and *völkisch* views of Prague politics: resolution is completely dependent upon an intensive interaction between the opposing principles of East and West, not an assimilation of these into a single whole, but a reconfiguration.

To identify what sort of configuration Brod was imagining, one might look back briefly to the first novel he published after *Ein tschechisches Dienstmädchen,* the novel *Jüdinnen* (Jewesses), where ideology as such is represented to be at odds with being.[54] In that book, Brod plays the ideological positions of the male characters against one another, from the stubborn and outmoded liberalism of Nußbaum, to the younger tendency of Weiningerian self-hating "Aryan-liberal" Jewishness Alfred, to the young Brod himself, appearing in the indifferentist Hugo. Each of these positions is defined in the course of the novel as an ultimately aesthetic-intellectual position, grounded in each case in vague feelings of attraction and taste on the part of their adherents. Rather than representing Zionist arguments through another character in particular, Brod's real effort lies in representing Jewish essence in the figure of the Jewess. Closer to nature, further from society, the Jewish country girl does not deliberately choose a system of thought to suit her; she simply is the essence of her *Volk:*

> A real Jewish country girl [. . .] healthy, hips like a plump little calf, eats for three, plain heavy stuff, spreads her butter two fingers thick on the bread if she can, works for four, fixes homemade liqueurs, prays every morning and evening, hollers around the house . . . [55]

This was not exactly the image of the young Jewish lady known in Brod's Prague. It was, on the contrary, a romantic construct of simplicity, strength, wholesomeness, and rootedness that did not remotely resemble the life of deterritorialized Western Jewry. This construct comes forth in the novel to oppose the frenzy of aestheticized ideologies in the last decade of the Habsburg monarchy.

It is useful to take a very short detour to the remarks of Willy Haas in the famous Prague circle project *Herder-Blätter* of 1911, the year *Jüdinnen* was published. In Haas's lecture "Rationalist and Transcendental Ethics," as the title implies, a familiar bifurcation is reproduced by calling on the oppositional pairs of reason and intuition, impression and action, aesthetics and ethics, externality and internality, and at the base of it all, rootlessness and rootedness. The essay focuses on the decadence of contemporary Jewry: modern Jews embody an "overdeveloped rationalism" that is related to their "rootlessness." This apparent spiritual rootlessness is a reflection of their "external social rootlessness, social isolation." [56] In the novel contemporary with this essay, Brod mocked the exaggerated aesthetic rationalization of his assimilated male Jewish characters; as an antidote to the problem Haas identified, Brod sought to recover Jewish rootedness, simple being.

Thus Jewish essence is represented in a rural, Eastern figure quite consciously opposed to Western Jewish conditions, and above all in woman. It is no coincidence, then, that the liberal Nußbaum, when asked why he so detests Zionism, can only compare it to the women's movement: one must be against both of them, he blurts out, with an expression of distaste which indicates that he finds them both "inelegant, even plebeian *(pöbelhaft)*." [57] This, too, evokes the Weiningerian dualism, which associated the mass political movements of the modern age with the encroachment of the female principle.

If Western Jewry is to find safe haven in the modern world, Brod implies, it will need to regenerate its decayed roots; as elsewhere in this chapter, the search for something "that was both noble and Jewish at the same time" [58] implied a turn to the sexual and territorial other, to woman and to the East. If the attention to the Orient and to woman as keys to redemptive resolution appeared as themes in these Prague circle works of the half century preceding World War I, it was to be during that war that contact with the East would first take place on a grand scale, and where sympathy would give way to actual identification with these exotic creatures.

ANIMAL STORIES

The war solidified German-Jewish interest in Eastern Judaism, prompting a series of debates on Eastern questions and on what became known very generally as "the Eastern question." Beyond the special attention these debates received in the Prague Jewish organ *Selbstwehr,* they effortlessly occupied most of the space in Martin Buber's innovative German-language journal devoted to Jewish life, *Der Jude*. First appearing in April of 1916, when German-speaking Jews were practically unable to think about Judaism without immediately invoking the life of East European Jewry, it was fitting that the publication was directed by the man who had turned his attention to the favorable reception of that life so early, and with such wide reception.[59]

The attention to Eastern Jewish life as an alternative to West European assimilationism coincided with the search for a new, unified, and territorialized Jewry. In Buber's opening article of April 1916, he referred to modern West European Judaism in the past tense; invoking the same metaphor as Willy Haas, who in turn was quoting Otto Weininger, Buber spoke of a Judaism that was "no longer rooted [*wurzelhaft*]"; in place of a deep grounding on native earth it had assimilationist "roots" in the air (*Luftwurzeln*) that could have no nourishing function.[60] Of course we now can see the relationship of these recurring images of rootedness to the metaphor of *Stamm* that was preferred by Jewish nationalists. The title page of the *Der Jude,* an attractive *Jugendstil* design, featured large lettering and the single image, just below the center of the page, of a blossoming tree.

From the start, Buber engaged the Prague writers he had known since the *Drei Reden* seven years earlier: Hugo Bergmann and Max Brod, in particular, but also Oskar Baum, Felix and Robert Weltsch, and others. Brod, remember, attributed his turn to Zionism to Buber's Prague visit. In the first years of his new Jewish consciousness, the years of *Jüdinnen* and the critical letters to E. E. Kisch on the latter's *Mädchenhirt,* Brod was allured to the Eastern Jew—for example, the Yiddish actor Djak Levi—as to an exotic animal:

> I remember my agitation when, in one of his conversations with me, Max Brod spoke of the beauty of the fur hat and silken, long coat, truly Rembrandt-like. I answered him heatedly: "The fanatic Eastern Jewry can impress you modern, cultivated Jews, but we are happy that we pulled ourselves from that world." Max Brod only smiled good-naturedly.[61]

This sort of admiration for the Eastern Jew, the fascination with the extravagant other coupled with an undisguised paternalism, predictably consisted of the same elements as the German-liberal disdain for the East European Jew—who would come to be known as the *Ostjude*—developed in the nineteenth century.[62] This moment seems in retrospect to have been a midstation to the position of identification with the Ostjude during the war. Yet none of the Prague circle went as far as Brod's distant relative and Kafka's friend Jiří Langer (1894–1943), author of popularizations of Jewish mysticism, who went through a kind of "conversion" from Western Jew to Ostjude.[63] Still, by the time *Der Jude* was first published, Brod and his fellow Prague Jews had experienced Eastern Jewry in a more substantial and direct way, through the presence of Jewish refugees in their city, and Brod was ready to declare their spiritual superiority.

He did so in an article in the first issue of *Der Jude,* in which he looked back on the past year of teaching young Jewish girls, East European refugees of the war. This volunteer activity had unexpectedly turned out to be Brod's "only solace in this spiritless time." The confrontation with the East, then, came not only as a result of the contact of Western soldiers with Eastern life at the front and of Prague Jews at home with a new influx of refugees; Brod implies that the spiritlessness of the period, with its culmination in the war, was the vacuum that the image of the East waited readily to fill. This point is reinforced by comparing the Prague experience with that of Vienna or Berlin, where the presence of Eastern Jews long preceded the war, and where such generous views of the essence of the Ostjude were indeed difficult to locate.[64] For Brod at this moment, the Eastern Jews filled a spiritual space he had located before meeting them:

> [. . .] that there are hearts that long for poetry and religion! True, I had believed that there were even before. But now I have experienced it with immediacy and with the true force of nature. I thank my pupils.[65]

In the first line we see that the contrast to the soullessness of the period is found in the desire "for poetry and religion," an interesting coupling that in one stroke moves toward the poeticization of religion as toward the sanctification of literature (one is forced to recall the same double gesture, more forcefully and self-consciously formulated, in Kafka's famous definition of writing as a form of prayer). The vacuum, according to this passage, would appear to lie in an ascetic aestheticism, where the longing for either literature or religion is repressed, and where the fusion of the two is out of the question. Brod admits a previous suspicion, actually the "faith," that such hearts existed. Had not Brod himself, if not perhaps one or two of his friends as well, been such a heart? The answer follows in the next line: Brod himself was not capable of the "immediate" (*unmittelbar*) experience he found in the East Europeans, nor could his own experience be invested with "the true force of nature" (*mit wahrer Naturkraft*). His contact with this spiritual union of art and faith is the contact with the Eastern pupils themselves, for which he thanks them.

The reference to the "immediacy" (*Unmittelbarkeit*) of the other turns on the assumption of the mediate and mediary position (*Mittelbarkeit*) of Brod and his associates, the Central European (*mitteleuropäisch*) Jews standing between West and East, matter and spirit, culture and nature.[66] The last pairing is implicit throughout Brod's article, as it is in his direct reference to the "natural force" of the experience with his pupils.

Our English word "pupils" erases the omnipresent mark of gender in Brod's references to his *Schülerinnen,* and that mark is apparent in sentences where the declined noun does not appear. Indeed, Brod's whole description of the Ostjude is inflected in this manner; just as he found the Jewish country girl to be the image of *völkisch* essence to contrast with urban, rationalist and spiritless ideology in the novel *Jewesses,* femininity coincides with the mystical characteristics of the Ostjude. "An enchanting freshness and naivety emanates from the girls," Brod declares. They are "spiritual through and through"; the dualism of internality and externality is evoked in his description of these "true Jewesses to their innermost selves [. . .] pulsing with Jewish essence and the ancient, undisturbed desire toward spiritualization sown by religion."[67] The passion of the girls' "desire toward spiritualization" (*Sehnsucht nach Vergeistigung*), as their hearts' desire (*Sehnen*) for religion and poetry, is parallel to the rationalist male Prague Jew's impulse toward the Czech servant, or the country Jewess. The gaze eastward and inward was charged with longing.

The figure of the Ostjude is a construct of the spiritualized, natural, feminine essence contrasting the masculine existence within European culture. Brod blatantly excludes the Ostjude from his continent as he commends her "much more immediate relationship to the spirit than is common in Europe [. . .]"[68] It is interesting that all of this discovery of true spiritual desire and understanding has been demonstrated to Brod through his hours of tutoring the Galician girls in what today would be described as a Western civilization or great books curriculum. He envies the students' innocence, as well as their integrity as part of a Jewish *Volk;* consistent with his thesis in "The Jewish Poet of German Tongue," he associates this *Volkstum* with the accessibility of other national literatures to the students. The innocent (ignorant) Galician girls had more access to the essence of great German culture, claims Brod, then he had had in the context of his deterritorialized German-Jewish *Gymnasium*.

The self-critique of the West European Jew implied in this last comment still does not efface the construct that privileges the West as more advanced, civilized, mature, further from barbarism and from an animalistic state than the East. To the contrary, the structure is maintained, while the innate characteristics of instinct, childish intuition, and peasantlike groundedness are lauded over the deterritorialized decadence of the Prague Jew. In an article of the following month, Brod derides Prague German-Jewish girls of the same age as his Galician students, deploying a rhetoric of insular decadence very close to the Czech critic Arne Novák's description of the Prague circle writers. Brod writes:

> Our Western Jewesses are either shallow and superficial or else [. . .] they fall into nervousness, testiness, conceit, despair, isolation. [. . .] [T]he Galician girls as a whole are so much fresher, more spiritually substantial, and healthier than our girls.[69]

The contrast of Galician to Prague Jewish girls seems precisely analogous to Novák's comparison of Czechs and Prague Germans. Yet, Brod does not challenge the German-liberal myth of the rural, simple, and uncultivated Slav/Czech/Ostjude, as Novák had. Brod preserves the image of Eastern primitiveness and animality, and exalts it. The self-conscious Western Jewish decision to identify with the East and to return to one's roots through the rediscovery represented the will to retreat from civilization, as in Kafka's wish to be a red Indian; it was the adult's wish to recover the lost innocence of childhood, and the willingness to surrender cultivated humanity for a more authentic and animal nature.

Franz Kafka, too, found a powerful attraction in this discourse of the Eastern other, as immediately comes to mind when we think of his fascination with the Yiddish theater and his friendship with the Yiddish actor Yitzhak Löwy, or perhaps the progression of his romantic relationships from the assimilated Berlin Felice to the Czech Milena to his final relationship with the East European Dora, with whom he dreamed of Palestine. Kafka's texts do not escape from the association of the East with animality, but rather inscribe it with a literalism approaching absurdity, a gesture that has at the very least the effect of denaturalizing the discourse. In the following passage from the undelivered letter to his father, it is revealed that the image of the Ostjude is both unwillingly and irresistibly inherited from the German-liberal generation:

Innocent, childlike people, such as, for instance, the Yiddish actor Löwy, had to pay for that. Without knowing him you compared him, in some dreadful way that I have now forgotten, to vermin [*Ungeziefer*] and, as was so often the case with people I was fond of, you were automatically ready with the proverb of the dog and its fleas.[70]

The discourse is no less apparent in Kafka's defense of the Yiddish actor as "innocent, childlike" than it is in his father's references to vermin and fleas. It is notable that both images, vermin and fleas, are parasitic references. It seems to me that there is some ring of truth in the Marxist interpretation of Kafka's animals as beings of bourgeois unusefulness—a thesis that would be confirmed by this passage.[71] How curious it is, too, that the model for this analogy within Kafka's writings is located in the invectives of the father Heřman/Hermann Kafka, in whom the Bohemian-Jewish transformation from "animal" Eastern origins to Western Germanophile civility took more literal form than it did for most Praguers. Hermann Kafka immigrated to Prague from southern Bohemia, where he spoke Czech and Yiddish before German, and where he had led the life of a Jewish peddler.[72]

Thus the rediscovery of the essence of the Western Jewish self in the Ostjude had the effect of reversing the Central European Jewish metamorphosis since the eighteenth-century Josephine patent of toleration through emancipation; Franz Kafka awoke one morning to find himself transformed into just such vermin (*Ungeziefer*) as the Polish actor Julius Löwy and his own father had been. Gregor Samsa awakens to this condition "from restless dreams," and the depiction of emancipation and assimilation as absurd liberal illusions, which had after all been punctuated with pogromlike flashbacks, was familiar to all Central European Jews of Kafka's generation through Zionist as well as *völkisch* representations. The description of Samsa's metamorphosis into a gigantic insect (*zu einem ungeheuren Ungeziefer*) contains the resonance of a primal past in the repetition *unge . . . unge;* within this transition to an animal state is the recovery of a primitive collective past as well as of childhood.[73] Mark Anderson's description of the relation of Samsa's animalistic conversion to childhood, the animal's "innocence," the kinship of the horrifying metamorphosis to a purifying "rebirth" and "childlike awakening," takes on new meaning within this context of the rediscovery of and identification with the Ostjude.[74]

Certainly the reversion of the adult to the child, or the conversion of human to animal, is never a total process in Kafka, and the simultaneous coexistence of and dialogue between these opposing selves are objects of irony and ambiguity—and also of pain. The hyperconsciousness of these tensions seems to separate Kafka's representations from Brod's, and as such the Kafka texts point to creative moments in which the Ostjude topos may become a vehicle for innovation rather than chiefly a reflection of an antisemitic image. Demonstrating this are Kafka's contributions to the journal *Der Jude:* two short fictions appearing in consecutive issues in 1917 for which Kafka chose the common title *Two Animal Stories.*

The background to the publication is not insignificant. At Brod's suggestion, Buber had solicited a contribution from Kafka as the former was organizing material for the first issue of *Der Jude.* To the invitation Kafka responded cryptically:

> I am (some hope or other naturally adds "still") much too depressed and insecure to be permitted to have any say in this community, even in the softest voice.[75]

If Kafka indeed hoped to feel grounded and find a voice within "this community," that would (claims of Kafka's later Zionism notwithstanding, as I argued above) not come to pass. A decade later, Brod would suggest that Kafka consider taking over the editorship of *Der Jude,* to which Kafka replied: "How could I think of such a thing, with my boundless ignorance of things, my total disengagement to people, with the lack of any firm Jewish ground under my feet? No, no."[76] Kafka's insecurity about his place in the "community" may be illuminated by a diary entry from two months before his hesitant letter to Buber. The entry reports on the visit accompanied by Jiří Langer to a Hasidic "miracle rabbi" residing in a Prague suburb. Kafka's impressionistic account begins with an image of his groping about in this milieu, with his entrance into the house, images of women and of children, "Above perfectly dark, a few blind steps forward with hands outstretched."[77] In this context it should also be mentioned that what stands out in the longish paragraph that is Kafka's description of this contact with Hasidic mysticism are the repeating oppositional images of darkness and lightness: "perfectly dark"; "pale twilight"; "white-gray walls"; "white head scarves"; "pallid faces"; "impression of bloodlessness"; "all black"; "the whiteness of skin." As the younger Hugo Bergmann, Kafka identifies these Ostjuden with a curious mixture of filth and purity, and ends with a focus on the whiteness of a hand, such a whiteness as one remembers from the dreams of childhood.

By 1917 Kafka was enough at ease with these cohabiting contrasts to submit stories for publication in *Der Jude*. The first to appear was "Jackals and Arabs," which would later be published in the collection *A Country Doctor*.[78] It is the tale of the entreaty of the jackals to a European visitor, camping in a desert oasis in the accompaniment of the Arabs. The conflict between jackals and Arabs is the crux of the story; the jackals fear and despise the Arabs, and cherish a myth of a future savior from the north who will smite their enemies with a pair of rusty scissors the jackals take with them everywhere. Perhaps because of these elements, or because of the Arabs' love of the animals they whip into submission with robust mockery, the story was at once, already by the reader Buber, taken to be an analogical parable. Early interpreters read the conflict as corresponding to that of the European Jews (jackals) and the powerful Gentiles they lived among (Arabs).[79] This sort of reading is anything but unusual; in fact, my point is that it is a normative practice in Kafka interpretation that defaces the multivalent power of the parables. It is more surprising to find that, in the endless search for an appropriate decoding key, it was first in 1967 that it was noted that there were three and not two parties in the story, and no less than quaint that even then the critic could posit as "his interpretation" that there was something messianic to the figure of the narrator. In this adventurous reading, as well, the jackals represent the Jews, and the Arabs the Gentile world.[80]

Certainly the resemblance of the jackals to Jews is well taken, as is the suggestion by Politzer that there is something Hasidic and prayerlike in their movements, "lithe bodies moving nimbly and rhythmically, as if at the crack of a whip," and their ritually repeated plea for "cleanliness, nothing but cleanliness," employing the word *Reinigkeit,* the term commonly used relating to kashruth. Yet, even this observation contributes to an opening of the issue of correspondences: the Eastern other, as I have been stressing, was not only a distinct but an *oppositional* figure to the assimilated European Jew. The figuration of the Easterner as animalistic, ergo feminine (in the story, the matriarchal society of jackals counts generations of mothers), closer to nature and subservient to a cultured master, is consistent with Brod's discourse on his Galician pupils. But that figure has taken form not only in images of the Ostjude, but also in German images of the Slav, or specifically of Prague German images of the Czech. In fact, if we were to match the three nations of Prague with the three groups in the story, we might just as easily identify the underling but frightening jackals as the Czech masses, the potent and proud Arabs as the Germans, and the mysterious mediary figure of the narrator as Kafka himself—as the German-speaking Prague Jew. The mediary figure is the hope of the jackals, who honor him threateningly with train bearers who lock their jaws through his clothing.

To try to determine which of the myriad possible analogical assignments is the most plausible one is a misdirected exercise. Walter Benjamin's identification of all Kafka's short pieces as acts in *Amerika*'s "Nature Theater of Oklahoma," and therefore "a code of gestures which surely had no definite symbolic meaning for the author from the outset," already provided an early (and unheeded) alternative to the setting of the stories into a grid of fixed correspondences.[81] Benjamin's insightful link of the power of the pieces to the "ever-changing contexts and experimental groupings" engineered by the author takes on fuller meaning within the theater of Prague identity. In a tale like "Jackals and Arabs," the web of relations of power, fear, need, tradition, and circumstance is an elastic structure that sustains varied projections—flexible identifications possible from the position of an author poised between identities. Even the German Bohemian can be seen threatened by the encroaching inferior but powerful other, a projection that lends a different tone to the jackals' wish to destroy the Arabs to obtain final purity *(Reinigkeit)*. Each of these various possibilities puts the triangle in a different light, and each is sabotaged at a different point: the need for a savior to exterminate the enemy; the desert exile of the jackals based in the contempt for the territorialized Arabs; the jackals' disdain of the Arabs as carnivores or their eerie inability to resist carrion.

The second contribution to *Der Jude* was "A Report to an Academy," in which the articulate once-ape Red Peter recounts his conversion to humanity.[82] We will not dwell on this story, although there is much interesting material in it; the story was already seen by its first readers (again we include Buber) as a parody of West European Jewish acculturation. The English translation of the first lines does not reproduce the original references to *"mein äffisches Vorleben"* ("my former life as an ape") and *"Affentum"* ("apedom," translated as "since I was an ape"), and therefore no longer implies from the very opening the parallel terms "Jewish" (*"mein jüdisches Vorleben"*) and "Judaism" (*"Judentum"*).

Again we may briefly remind ourselves of the metaphorical power of the animal, and again we may replace what is commonly seen as "Jewish" with "Eastern." The confrontation of Eastern Judaism with Western society was taking place before the eyes of Prague German-speaking Jews in the year this tale was published; indeed this fact reminds us that the sort of "training" described here was presided over primarily by well-meaning assimilated Jews, such as Max Brod with his Western civilization instruction for Galician schoolchildren, and Felice Bauer, whose work with East European refugees at the Berlin Jewish Home was orchestrated by Kafka himself, as we have seen. Again there is a multivalence present that is generally overlooked in interpretive literature, and it is a multivalence that corresponds to the specificity of the situation of the German-speaking Jew in Prague.

The brutal training Red Peter recounts in sterilized academic discourse foregrounds the pain of the confrontation between animal nature and the requirements of society, and, no less or more than is the case in "Jackals and Arabs," yields effects far more general than a representation of a single specific and historically contained case.[83] Red Peter himself alludes to the former apedom of the members of the academy he is addressing, a primitive state that "cannot be further removed from you than mine is from me." The apish condition itself corresponds to a universal condition, and again the potential alternation between identities is the strength of the parable.

There is a true correspondence, I think, between the tendency to search for fixed analogical correspondences to the figures in Kafka's short fictions and an uncritical engagement in the discourse of the Ostjude. That is, German culture between the Enlightenment and the Holocaust repeatedly returned to the Ostjude topos, a metaphorical figure that more than occasionally began to be taken literally. Rather than divesting himself of that topos, Kafka was absorbed by it completely; it saturated his animal stories to the point where it became impossible to trace the distinctions between the natural animal and the cultivated citizen, the borders between East and West were transgressed, and the compass lost its bearings.

Through these reorientations, Kafka was able to find himself in some form among the Jews, as he wrote to Buber after his stories were accepted for publication and two years after voicing his cryptic skepticism:

> So komme ich also doch in den "Juden" und habe es immer für unmöglich gehalten.

Kafka reflects to Buber, "and so I get into *The Jew* after all, and I thought it was impossible," with a sentence in which Kafka finds himself, to his own surprise, in the midst of the Jewish circle. Kafka's contribution to Buber's journal represented, at least, a resolution of the issues prohibiting him from coming to terms with the community of Jewry, as he indicated in the previous letter to Buber and in his diary comment

discussed in the previous chapter. Buber read the two stories and was ea-
ger to publish them under the collective title *Gleichnisse,* "Parables,"
with the additional meaning of "Likenesses." [84] In Kafka's return letter
one feels his cringe upon this reduction of the mechanics of the stories
to crude analogical correspondences. He replied:

> I ask that the pieces not be called "Parables," they are not really parables. If
> they should have a common title, then best perhaps "Two Animal Stories." [85]

The reader's desire to place Kafka and oneself at a fixed point in a
text that then becomes a moral map uncannily resembles the investment
of late nineteenth- and early twentieth-century German-speaking Jews in
the reification of the image of *Ostjudentum.* The "desire" of the Prague
Jews toward the East and their perception of their own special relationship to it put them at the "center" of a larger Central European initiative to reassess the constellation of metaphors of East and West. Some
held a mirror up to the discourse of Orient and Occident, reversing the
valences, or a lens that exchanged down for up, or, as Franz Kafka,
jumbled the identifications to a degree that rendered them mutually inseparable and cryptically insoluble.

In these respects, the new orientations entailed in the turn to Jewishness had the reverse effect from what would have been supposed in the
previous generation: rather than shrinking the terrain of Prague German-
speaking Jewry, it opened frontiers to spiritual authenticity, recovery of
national life, the healing of bonds with the Czechs as well as with the
Jews of the East: Judaism, rather than German culture, as the German-
liberal parents had imagined, was the stuff with which to begin to put
together bridges.

CHAPTER 7

Middle Ground

Translation, Mediation, Correspondence

Die feste Abgegrenztheit der menschlichen Körper ist
schauerlich

The sturdy boundedness of the human body is ghastly

diary, 30 October 1921

MIDDLE NATION

As we survey the landscape of culture produced by German-speaking
Prague Jews, the keen interest in translations from Czech to German
stands out. This interest—virtually nonexistent if not taboo in Prague
German-liberal life, as well as in the burgeoning culture of *völkisch* Bohemian Germandom—seems at first glance to have transcended the
ideological objectives of its dedicated agents: it figures powerfully on the
agendas of the socialists Kisch and Rudolf Fuchs, the Zionist Brod, and
the Christian (or expressionist) revolutionary Werfel, while in the case
of the poet-translator Otto Pick it seems to be an end in itself. The
obsession with the act of mediation and all it entailed in fact served a
common ideological function for these writers, divergent as their stated
programs claimed to be. The structural conditions of "translation," of
"mediation," and of the question of "correspondences" between texts as
between text and world are each grounded in an ideological complex of
"identity" that anchored Prague German-speaking Jewish writers to untenable territory. Yet, working through the laws of translation, mediation, and correspondence also had the potential effect of denaturalizing discourses of identity and territory, of providing an opening through
means of the very laws of closure. Individual translators were literally
denounced as traitors by Germans of Bohemia and Prague, but their allegiances were not to the Czechs but rather to this "middle ground" of

mediation inhabitable only by themselves. Together they constituted a strange sort of "nation" between the hostile Czech and German fronts; they produced a body of work that became the national literature of that people, and that inscribed a territory for them apart but not isolated from German and Czech Bohemia.

In spite of the fact that the translation project was not as purely altruistic as concurrent and retrospective observers might depict it, and even taking into consideration the remnants of paternalistic chauvinism toward the Czechs that accompanied their efforts, the role of these translators in the integration of Czech cultural modernism into the general European arena can hardly be exaggerated. Not only in the fields of poetry and prose, but in the visual arts and especially in music, a handful of German-speaking Jews from Prague introduced this vital culture to "the world." To measure the importance of this gesture to the individual artists, one has only to consider the limitations of the bourgeois Czech-speaking culture market, situated primarily in Prague, as against the massive audiences of a network of cultural centers across two Central European empires, providing entry into Western Europe. By the end of the World War, witnessing the death of the Habsburg Empire and the birth of Czechoslovakia, the Czech arts had become vogue across the continent, and such household names as Hašek and Janáček had found a place in Paris that they had hardly been able to secure in Prague.

The engagement with Czech culture on the part of these German-speaking Praguers represented a manifest transgression of the German-liberal tradition. German-speaking Prague had turned its back on the blossoming and vital Czech renaissance, ignoring the activities of the National Theater and the Czech literary and artistic initiatives taking place around them.[1] The political implications of those initiatives—their implicit challenge to the cultural foundation of German hegemony in Prague and Bohemia—was never glossed over or misread. German-liberal journals such as *Bohemia* were littered with diminutions of Czech culture, in academic analyses of Czech culture's inferiority, insignificance, or derivation from German culture, or in open and insulting attacks on Czech cultural heroes.[2]

A more subtle and particularly revealing example is offered in a culture-critical article in a 1912 issue of *Bohemia*. In "Talent and Genius," Oskar Ewald constructed a dichotomy that he presented as central to the crisis of the age, in which the nationality conflicts of Bohemia in particular were an ever-present if unspoken subtext.[3] The essayist posited that the present age suffered from an overproduction of talents, without a corresponding proliferation of true genius. "Talent" in the essay was associated with a number of other terms: "technique," "specificity," "civilization," and "ability," which Ewald opposed to "genius" and its associated terms: "art," "universality," "culture," and "being." Elements of the former might be carried over—*translated* [*übertragen*]— from people to people. True "genius," "culture," true "art" could not cross such borders—"they are not separable from their roots." Most peoples are capable of talent and of developing the external means of developing a "civilization," but no genius will spring from their soil. For genius and culture could be products only of those few "culture-nations" that the German liberals saw no need to identify.

Ewald's essay is interesting on a number of levels, not least for its enlistment of a familiar Germanic dichotomy in a very different way from that deployed by Franz Werfel, for instance. But it also sheds light on the valence of "translation" in this context: it enlisted the notion of (un)translatability to offer on the one hand an explanation for the undeniable surge of Czech culture and a defense against the attack on the rationale for German-liberal hegemony in Central Europe; at the same time, it justified the resistance to translate Czech culture, which it reduced to a simple and even belated improvement from a state of nature to the trappings of civilization. Such development, which as Ewald explained could not include cultural work of any universal artistic merit, may be important to the civilization in question, but why would anyone want to translate these products into a *Kultursprache* like German?

The anatomy of translation markets can be said to reflect relations of cultural hegemony in and of themselves; a "trade imbalance" of translation exports from (over imports to) hegemonic cultures is in this sense predictable, belonging to a structure of cultural power and exchange rather than proceeding from a program of censorship.[4] This text, however, exposes a sharp and uneasy awareness of the threat a recognition of Czech cultural production would represent, and demonstrates the way the German-liberal humanist construction of universal culture was commandeered to refortify national chauvinism. The vitality of the young Czech arts was a thorn in the German-liberal side that was tended by constant discursive reinscription of borders closing them off from the realm of "the universal," and even the realm of "culture." By contrast, the translators each sought to bridge cultures as a means to universalism, although their personal images of "universality" differed sharply from one another. Werfel and his earliest and most important promoter, Max Brod, had an irreconcilable falling out over this very issue.[5] But

Brod was not alone in identifying his Jewishness with his mediary role. There were Czechs, as well, who identified the Jews—particularly those Czech-speaking Jews counted among their number—as "mediators between the Czech people and humanity." [6] Alluding to the solidarity of Jews as a people coupled with their cosmopolitanism, one Czech essayist found in the Jews a model as well as a means to achieving a more universalist Czech culture. Significantly, the author supplied Zamenhof's invention of Esperanto as his example of the Jewish contribution to humanity.

Translation—the act of carrying over, setting over, or taking over, even taking possession of [*übertragen, übersetzen, übernehmen*]—did not serve merely to open markets for Czech culture. The diverse and broad-ranging initiatives of Brod, Pick, and Fuchs, along with others of their circle, seemed to bridge the abyss between peoples in Prague into which they themselves had fallen, and at the same time seemed to promise to carve out a space that they could safely occupy as its national poets. But what sort of space did they occupy, what paths did the bridges open, what national poetry was this?

OTTO PICK'S CIRCLE

Otto Pick (1887–1940) was closely associated with the writers already introduced through friendships, through literary relations, and especially through his untiring efforts to promote the work of German Bohemian writers of universalist tendency. He was born in the Prague suburb Königliche Weinberge (now the Prague quarter Vinohrady), and therefore attended the suburban grade school rather than the Prague Piarist school. Neither did he attend the Prague humanistic *Gymnasium* with Brod and most of the others, opting instead for the more technical education of the *Staatsrealschule* and then for a career in banking. He had nonetheless been instrumental in organizing the Prague circle's major collaborative project, the *Herder-Blätter,* and gone on to publish translations, reviews, and his own poetry in Bohemian and German journals until finally taking over the editorship of the *Prager Presse* in the new Czechoslovak state. This was certainly due in part to his demonstrated commitment to a new relationship between Germans and Czechs in Bohemia—a complex vision that has yet to be examined closely.

Pick's own career as a poet was placed second to his role as translator and mediator—not only by his audience and publishers, but, most important, by himself. The bulk of his work testifies to this, as does the majority of his correspondence with potential publishers and others in the literary world. His efforts toward bringing the work of Czech writers to the German public led to the introduction of the now well-known Karel Čapek to Western Europe, as well as the important figures Otokar Březina and Fraňa Šrámek. While Pick is most remembered for his mediation of Czech work to German audiences, he was no less active in securing a place for German (particularly Prague German) literature in Czech cultural life.

The result was that Pick's work—his translations as well as his poetry—was retrospectively judged to have been a futile attempt to defer the crisis in which Central Europe was to find itself before the end of Pick's life.[7] Indeed, it would be cynical to depreciate the humanistic contribution that this life and work represent. Yet, the way that contribution was designed and actually operated is lost in the romantic reconstructions of his supporters. Those reconstructions often employ territorial metaphor. Brod counts Pick among the first to "ram the Chinese wall between the German and Czech cultural domains."[8] A less aggressive and perhaps slightly subtler image is offered by Oskar Baum, who wrote of Pick's offbeat "fantasy of a United States of the World."[9] Perhaps most telling is Willy Haas's identification of Pick as the spiritual heir of Adalbert Stifter, a reincarnation of a type long-since extinct, who could claim "he knew no 'Germans' and 'Czechs,' but only 'Bohemians' and 'the [Bohemian] Fatherland.'"[10]

Haas's construction is fascinating in the sense that it displaces Pick from the milieu of national conflict that was exactly and unambiguously the impetus of his work; it finds Pick at home instead in the myth of a pre-1848 "Bohemism" that rejected national identification altogether. There is certainly some flavor of Bohemian "local patriotism" or *Landespatriotismus* to be found in Pick's life and work, as in the life and work of Egon Kisch. But in Pick's concentration on strongly nationalist Czech poets, as well as on German Bohemians who were utterly cosmopolitan and primarily Jewish, it cannot be accurate to represent the territory inscribed in his work as a multinational and nationless "Bohemia."

This very fact irked Egon Erwin Kisch's tenaciously German-national brother Paul in his perusal of Pick's collection *Deutsche Erzähler aus der Tschechoslowakei* (German writers from Czechoslovakia).[11] Kisch saw Stifter as the exception in a long tradition of German Bohemian literature under the Romantic literary influence of East Elbian writers. With this construct of literary geography and history, Paul Kisch projected a cultural image of his country that coincided with his political ideal, the

Anschluß of German Bohemia with Germany. Within Paul Kisch's mental map of Bohemia, Pick's selection of authors predictably left much to be desired: the "derailed journalist" Max Brod was for Kisch emblematic of the type of writer promoted by Pick, indeed of the sort of Bohemian German that Pick himself represented. Kisch could only conclude "that Otto Pick and those around him are the last ones that have any right to put themselves up as the chosen administrators and organizers of German writing in Bohemia [. . .]" They lacked the prime virtue necessary "for anyone who wants to do honest work in this country [*Boden*]": a sense of "national honor." [12]

The danger for Paul Kisch was not that Pick was creating a movement of Bohemian "nationalism" that transcended nation; as Haas himself stressed in paying Pick this compliment, such an alternative was not only out of step but completely nonexistent. Kisch scorned what might be called the Bohemian *kleindeutsch* solution of claiming an identity for the circle of "Otto Pick *and those around him*"—that is, of grounding a center for the marginalized Prague circle. It is ironic that the critical Paul Kisch himself was a member of the "nation" he accused Pick of representing—an identity that was to exclude him from participation upon the realization of his pan-German dream in 1938. The power of ideological topography as World War I approached was, however, not merely in the consciousness of German nationalists like Paul Kisch; it was the property of Praguers of all persuasions, and Otto Pick set out to take control of it.

IN THE PRAGUE WOOD

In an obscure 1912 feuilleton, Pick mapped out his version of a Central European sociocultural topography, consciously restructuring the more pedestrian nationalist model represented in Paul Kisch's attack. [13] The text, "Man in the Woods," was a review article of contemporary German writing relating to nature and landscape, and an attempt to identify a more modern and appropriate literary form to replace the sort of "*Heimatkunst*" ("homeland art") or "*bodenständige*" ("native" or "soil-rooted") literature preferred by Paul Kisch. The fault of that sort of literature according to Pick was its isolation from the sensibilities of modern, urban humanity. The simple depiction of landscape—indeed the word "meadow"—instantly evoked the experience and sensation of a reality in the rural person, whereas the city dweller must resort to fantasy. The meanings of these words, the languages spoken by peasants, were therefore different from the words and language of Pick's readers. Although the essay appeared in a Prague German-liberal newspaper, he evaded any reference to national difference; he replaced this and other distinctions with the single and irrevocable divide between people grounded in the land and the landless urban dwellers:

> Because of this inborn schism of concepts, the popularization of a "native" literature has become impossible.

Pick identified the need for a new kind of landscape literature, a glimpse of which he found in a few recent books. Pick was looking for representations of the relationship of modern man to nature—a necessarily indirect relation. The adjective deployed here for "indirect" [*mittelbar*] is literally "mediate," a relation that can be and must be mediated. The task of the new *Heimatkünstler* is essentially, therefore, a kind of translation.

The first book Pick reviewed moved toward this revised depiction of nature. It was a novel (*Insect Stories,* by Robert Michel) about an officer injured as he fell from his horse, who must remain still until help would come. Forced to look hour after hour upon an insect near his head, he became fascinated with the life of the creature, and a new world was opened to him. The landscape, for Pick, was something modern man knew only as a nonplace between places, and its discovery could be a revelation.

"Landscape," then, which represented the simple and immediate experience of the territorialized farmer, was the locale of the urban reader's desire and the source of spiritual transcendence. If Paul Kisch's attack on Pick's circle was essentially the familiar diagnosis of the deterritorialized nonnation of intellectual German-Jewish Prague, Pick departed from his attacker only in the solution he prescribed to the dilemma. For Pick, the Romantic "East Elbian" solution (corresponding to the territory of *völkisch* German Bohemia) was out of touch with modernity; the busy insect world that caught his eye, the hinterland he himself chose to mediate to the denaturalized German cultural world, was a Czech landscape.

The assumption that the Slavs were closer to nature than the Germans, as we have seen, belonged to the common language of Germans on both sides of the "eastern question." Pick's own proclivities toward spiritualism—it should be remembered that his poetry is and was considered expressionist—led him to concentrate on the Czech mystic Otokar Březina. The dichotomy of nature and culture was the spine of Pick's review "Man in the Woods." It did not merely set up the distinction of

rural peasants from urban literati, but implied a catalogue of oppositions; the way one placed oneself on this map had ideological implications that Pick did not shy away from indicating.

The second book he reviewed was not a novel at all, but a survey of the
kind popular around that time, in which around eight thousand workers responded to a number of broad questions, and the more interesting
answers were printed. The book was called *Die Arbeiterfrage*, and the
question of interest to Pick was "Do you often walk in the woods? What
do you think when you are lying on the forest ground, with no one anywhere around?"[14] Referring back to his earlier discussion of rural and
urban man, Pick wrote:

> All at once it occurs to one that workers actually constitute a race of men
> unto themselves—neither urban nor rural. Rather they are bound by virtue
> of their birth to nature, but through their work to the cities.
>   It becomes clear from their responses how powerfully and how often the
> two oppositions fight for the soul of these men.

Pick represented that struggle with the selection and careful order-
ing of a few of the workmen's responses. The ideological content of that
struggle becomes apparent as the representation unfolds. The first set of
responses were those closest to the sensibilities of Pick's urban, bourgeois, German-speaking readers: miners and factory workers describing
how they go to the forest to think, bringing along a novel or an academic
work, to watch ant colonies or to be at one with nature. As if a German
expressionist cohort of Pick himself, one laborer answered: "Then I
could embrace the whole world as my brothers."

Tension builds in Pick's selection of citations, beginning with apa-
thetic comments and building to increasing feelings of resentment, the
wish to be elsewhere, or cynicism: "Trespassing in the woods is prohibited and violators will be prosecuted"; "it makes me wonder how it happened that the count could claim this wood as his own"; "peace and
quiet, truth and no poetry." Thus the struggle between the poles of nature and culture begins to sound ever more like the struggles of classes
and of nations, the battle for territory. A *völkisch* tone creeps into the
descriptions, and the text becomes suddenly threatening:

> A forceful cry drowns out the rest: "In the wood I feel a great blood relation-
> ship to living nature and such a triumphant feeling as can only come from the
> clear and starry sky. The universal thought that overcomes me in the wood
> is: 'To the devil with this culture. Away with the stinking mines, the smutty
> cities, filthy streets and apartments, selfish men and modern barbarians!'"

> Others dream of a future state. One bold one writes: "Then I think, this is
> the wood that I will conquer for my descendants!"

Such was Otto Pick's observation of the meaning of territory, its relationship to ideology, and the role of culture in the complex. He was no
less sensitive to these issues than the pan-German nationalist Paul Kisch,
who resented Pick's rejection of a Germanic Bohemian *Heimatkunst*.
Pick, like Paul's younger brother Egon (Erwin), had a different model in
mind, sensing that the immediate relation of territory, nation, and culture enjoyed in the German Bohemian hinterland would serve neither
himself nor his ideals. With that option unavailable, the relationship between his world and a territorialized culture would have to be mediated
in some way; and so he sought to provide that passage between Prague
and the woods.

SWEET WORK(S)

In 1912, the same year that "Man in the Woods" appeared, Pick published his first two books: the first, *Freundliches Erleben,* was a volume
of his own expressionist poetry; the second, *Flammen,* was a translation
of novellas by Fraňa Šrámek. Pick was twenty-five years old, and although he had been a bank clerk for eight years, with a year out for military service, he had been engaged in journalism for at least half of that
time.[15] With a technical education and no university background, his
command of Czech was central to his entry in the literary world. The
role he had created for himself was twofold: his contributions to journals in German-speaking Austria and the German Empire often focused
on Czech literature, while he was also able to publish in Czech journals
on German-language literary manifestations, mostly by Prague Jews.

The layers of Pick's journalistic activities and his own ambitions are
densely intertwined. Pick attracted the attention of his future publisher,
Axel Juncker, with his reviews in Czech journals of Brod's *Jüdinnen* and
other works published by the Juncker house.[16] Juncker was instrumental in the early publication of Prague circle writers; Pick had an interest
not only in having his own poetry published by Juncker, but also in
promoting the young Jewish writers in Prague through these reviews,
and he encouraged Juncker to consider other works by yet unpublished
Prague circle writers.[17] Around the same time, Pick attempted to have
Oskar Baum's first novel (*Das Leben im Dunkeln* [Life in the dark], a
novel about the life of the blind that had mediation as a central theme)

published in the Czech-nationalist journal *Národní listy*.[18] Pick sometimes made such suggestions in the same letter in which he offered to translate *and* critique Czech work for German publications.[19] The recommendation of Baum's book in fact had the support of a positive review in the Czech journal *Přeled*, composed by none other than Pick. Baum in turn was sending Otto Pick's translations of the Czech-speaking Prague Jew František Langer to Martin Buber for consideration for publication.[20] The expressionist poet Pick used his influence at Central Europe's most cutting-edge journals to publish translations of Czech work, culminating in a special *Saturn* issue of his translations of Šrámek.[21]

The correspondence between Pick and his Czech and German publishers, the Czech writers he translated, and his German-Jewish friends is dominated by this network of mutual promotion, in a manner that goes beyond the everyday politics of German literati in this period. Through this intense mediation of Czech literature to Germans, Prague German-Jewish literature to Czechs, and the latter to a broader German public, Pick was creating and expanding a domain that had not been recognized before. Prague German literature was no longer a peripheral branch of German culture, and neither was Czech literature a marginal European manifestation of mainly anthropological interest.[22] Pick's activities played a meaningful role in a rising awareness in Berlin as well as Paris: something was going on in Prague.

As the decade continued, Pick's activities centered ever more on translations from Czech into German and the mediation of their publication. In 1917 Pick's translation of Šrámek's play *Léto* (Summer) was accepted for production in Vienna, and he pushed tirelessly to have a modern Czech drama taken on by Max Reinhardt in Berlin.[23] He laid particular hopes on the work of Stanislav Lom (a pen name for Stanislav Mojžíš), with whom he was in steady correspondence from his field post in 1917. He translated the play *Vůdce* (Leader), and when Reinhardt showed no interest, he approached less important theaters, and even magazines and book publishers.[24]

Pick was away from Prague, and so details of this particular moment of his ongoing activity are preserved in a correspondence between translator Pick and artist Lom. The documents reveal not only to what extent Pick championed the work of little-known Czech writers, but also the eagerness with which he took on new projects—in each letter requesting another prose piece or poem that he might translate and send to a German magazine. For a writer like Lom, Pick's interest was of course a windfall. The resulting relationship is one in which the "artist," flattered for his brilliance by the "translator," is completely at the latter's mercy. He waited for Pick to express interest in some piece or other, and then promptly sent it off. Pick then turned out the product immediately and sent it where he chose; Lom was never consulted, nor asked permission, nor did he review translations as a rule, despite his excellent German. It is also curious (and consistent among the Prague translators) that Pick wrote to the Czech writers and even Czech publishers in German. From our vantage, this fact seems a silent concession to the assumption that German was the *Kultursprache* of the Bohemian lands, a prejudice that the translation project as a whole was doing much to overcome.[25]

Thus a paternalistic tone is apparent in Pick's correspondence, and it is a tone one recognizes as well in the letters between Fuchs or Brod and "their" artists. One is reminded of Werfel's anger at the audacity of a Czech renaissance that sought to exclude German culture (whose "child" it could only be).[26] And so a series of German-liberal assumptions remained in the consciousnesses of those who sought to break from them. Yet, there is in the letters also the sense of the inferior position of the translator before the greater genius of the artist. One senses that the "sweet work" of translation is for Pick ultimately secondary to (less immediate than?) the creation of "works."[27]

Pick's own "work," however—that is, his original poetry—is itself a sort of translation. The mysticism behind his expressionist work becomes more familiar when seen alongside the Czech mystic Otokar Březina, translated and revered by Pick. Searching for a native root of that provocative mysticism within himself, Pick turned to the obscure Judaism of previous generations in the poem "Wenn der Vater betet" (When father prays).[28] But this experience, too, is a foreign and mediated one; with the father's manner of loving "marvelously transformed" on "certain days of the year," he seems possessed by some distant historical and religious moment. This produces a stunning complexity of figures of translation: Březina's mysticism is the medium through which Pick seeks his own poetic voice, but to make it his own he must raise from the dead an ancestral language far more remote to him than Březina's. Translation or *Übernehmen* may go even further than an appropriative operation (to *take on* culture) to an "expropriative" one in moments of cultural revival or "renaissance": national literary and linguistic spaces can be poached from past or foreign landscapes.[29] Pick's resuscitation of his own Jewish mystic origins fails, though, to reiterate Březina's national-religious mysticism. Pick speaks of Březina's nationalism as Brod speaks of Judaism, but the former is more authentic in Pick's eyes, the one closer to him:

> Fruitful, creative nationalism, as the poet conceives it, has nothing in common with that other sort, which builds barracks and exists to uniform humanity. True nationalism builds and binds peoples.[30]

Franz Werfel, too, implies that this "great mystic of our time" is both universalist (Březina's "mystic humanism," each of his poems a "congregation" or "brotherhood") and nationalist (the humanism "of the Taborite Republic," the "heartfelt melody of Smetana's music").[31] The poet represents "the pure manifestation of the creative substance of the Czech people." Werfel himself collaborated on a translation of two of his works (which, considering Werfel's modest command of Czech, were probably mainly poetic revisions of the translation of Emil Saudek). Werfel's description of the spirituality of the poetry and its gesture toward mystical communion sounds self-referential; Pick on the other hand knew no direct source for that experience. He had only indirect [*mittelbar*] access to it, and so he let it pass through his hands, to mediate [*vermitteln*] it to others.

The example of Otto Pick begins to show the performativity of an act of translation which, through a cycle of inversions of subject–object and original text–translated text relations, muddies rather than clarifies formal identity relations. It is a commonplace of contemporary translation theory to stress the diacritical function of translation, or to foreground the impossibility of linguistic equivalence. Yet, there is a danger, in focusing on "difference in translation," of reifying the category of identity through the back door more powerfully than more naive approaches to translation could ever do. George Steiner's classic study of translation resorts to this reification in a revealing way when he concludes that semantic contrast or difference "defines conversely": "To experience difference, to feel the characteristic resistance and 'materiality' of that which differs, is to reexperience identity. One's own space is mapped by what lies outside . . . "[32] Of course the "reexperience" lends greater authenticity to identity than the primary and necessarily subjective experience—just as the translation or copy supremely "authorizes" the original it has not "authored." The territory searched for in Pick's translations and translation activities is precisely not a linguistic ground defined by its difference to a defined other, a "space mapped by what lies outside," but an only vaguely defined space not even between, but beyond, identity and difference. The troubled moment of each of his activities, within the creation of "original" works and within the "work" of mediation, was a turbulence experienced by other Prague translators as well—a nostalgia for a kind of rest that was supposed to be natural. The tension between the territorial binary of national particularity and universalism is paradoxically worked through in translation activity that takes literally translation's promise of cultural ventriloquism and the identity of texts. The success and the failure of Pick's efforts both emerged from his acceptance of the premise of his own voicelessness.

UNTIMELY MEDIATIONS

Rudolf Fuchs (1890–1942) was unique among the translators in that he was born in Czech Bohemia rather than Prague, and learned German as a second language. He was fond of remembering that his hometown of Poděbrady was the town of the Bohemian King Jiří (1420–1471), the "Hussite King," the last of Czech language and the "utraquistic" faith. But although that language and the religion of Hus were the ones native to Bohemia, King Jiří was to remain an anomaly of Bohemian history, just as Fuchs seemed everywhere to be an outsider, even if he could only have been a product of Bohemia and of Prague.

Fuchs first entered the circle of young German-speaking Praguers at the age of seven, when his parents sent him to the *Nikolanderschule*. According to his own retrospective reconstruction, it was there that he learned German and that, almost as early, he committed himself to his future role as translator and propagandist for Czech culture, visual art as well as literature.[33] As his early alienation at the *Nikolanderschule* implies, Fuchs was poised to become an extreme case of the homeless condition inscribed in the young Franz Werfel's poetry. This condition was not alleviated through Fuchs's devoted and even fanatical embrace of differing group-based ideologies: his close identification with the spiritual and historical base of Judaism, his tireless attachment to Czech culture and a Bohemian culture that included the Germans, and his ultimate commitment to socialism. The complementarity of these fervent attachments seems to have remained Fuchs's personal secret—just as the failure of others to perceive and accept that personal vision as a political solution was his tragedy.

Like Otto Pick, Fuchs was not only a translator but a poet in his own right. There is record of his poetic ambitions as early as 1909, when the teenager sent his work to be critiqued by none other than the Concordia hero Hugo Salus.[34] In the following year, Fuchs appeared in the text that has come to define the Prague circle, the *Herder-Blätter.* By the time his poetry was published in a substantial way, Fuchs stood squarely in the expressionist camp, as shown by his two anthologies no less than by his ongoing contributions to such journals as *Saturn, Aktion,* and *Weiße Blätter.*[35] But Fuchs also published in the Zionist journal *Selbstwehr;*[36] he contributed "Feuerfugen vor dem Volke Israel" to the Prague Zionist collection *Das jüdische Prag,* and Judaism was often the focus of his poetry.[37] Clearly, as for Paul Kornfeld, Jewish history and symbolism were Fuchs's personal keys to a more universalist spiritualism. The tensions among Fuchs's manifold identifications were to become more problematic during the war, as he began to see them as bases for a politically revolutionary program.

The most important of Fuchs's works, the one to receive the most attention in its own time and in remembrances of his career, was the controversial translation of Petr Bezruč, *Schlesische Lieder* (Silesian songs).[38] The poet sang of the oppression of the Czech rural poor in the Austrian part of Silesia—a native *Volk* suffering under the national hierarchy of the Habsburg crown. The first of these translations had already appeared in the *Herder-Blätter,* but the volume *Silesian Songs* was ready to appear in the middle of World War I, when Bezruč was declared a traitor and his work banned in the monarchy. After Fuchs's arrest, military investigation, seizure of translation manuscripts, and conscription in the military, he continued to work on the publication of the translations, which had to be slipped by the censors on their way to Kurt Wolff in Leipzig. Wolff published them in 1916.

The songs made clear the spectrum of nationalities involved in the oppression of the mountain people: Bezruč directed his attack less against an imperial government than against German-speaking landowners and teachers, Polish clergy, and (perhaps inevitable in populist attacks) Jewish merchants.[39] Coming from a Czech country town most certainly did not qualify Fuchs as an insider in any sense; his correspondence with Bezruč and other Czech writers was in German, as was the case for the other translators.[40] It is not enough to heroize Fuchs for his efforts in spite of Bezruč's "open antisemitism and chauvinism;"[41] such a judgment overlooks the fact of frank identification, and not mere sympathy, with the project that put Fuchs's career and person at greatest risk. Fuchs saw his activity as expressly political; the "knowing soldier" was fighting, however, for an army that did not understand how he belonged.[42]

Franz Werfel introduced the Fuchs translations of *Silesian Songs* with the quotable phrase "Our heart feels co-national with all the oppressed of all peoples." The songs do not protest a nationalist oppression of the people with any universalist resistance, but with a populist nationalism of the most powerful mark—a "self-willed being," in Fuchs's words; a latent, territorialized power living beneath the visible surface of Central Europe.[43] It is difficult to reconstruct the way that subterranean *völkisch* power merged in Fuchs's mind with rabbinic Judaism and expressionist revolt, and finally spilled out into a unique sort of Marxism. Jürgen Serke strikes an interesting chord in his book, at any rate, when he introduces Ernst Bloch into his text beside Rudolf Fuchs. In both men, a deeply religious and Jewish spirit lay at the heart of a different socialism.[44]

It was a socialism with which Fuchs's fellow socialists were not quite comfortable, nor certainly were the Stalinists who were later to have the task of placing him, or some version of him, delicately into the canon. Yet his position was socialist and certainly revolutionary enough to alienate others after the war. One should not be surprised to read Max Brod's version of the story, which presents a case of political conversion from an "Israel-orientation" to communism.[45] Fuchs's view of political polemics must have been completely foreign to the author of *Streitbares Leben*—so that the fact that the first translations of the social revolutionary Bezruč appeared in Brod's own *Herder-Blätter* was as easy for Brod to overlook as was Fuchs's poem "Moses," published in the *Prague Jewish Almanac* decades after his entrance into the Communist Party.

Whatever consistency Fuchs perceived within his varied and highly personal ideological and national identity, he could find neither comrades nor compatriots to publish his substantive work after the war. Neither in Kurt Wolff, the friend of Prague expressionists, nor in the fellow rabbinic revolutionary Paul Kornfeld, nor in the Vienna contact Stefan Zweig did he find a colleague to support publication of his work.[46] A prose collection, two volumes of poetry, and two plays were circulated over the two decades after the war without finding a publisher, until finally another play, historical and more orthodox socialist in bent (subtitled *Ein Massendrama*), was printed by a small leftist press.[47]

The future career of Rudolf Fuchs had its ups and downs, but it seems safe to say that he was never appreciated for his total vision, but rather segments of his aesthetic identity were selectively accepted: Fuchs the translator would publish another anthology of Czech verse, Fuchs the art critic would contribute to the *Prager Presse* under Otto Pick, a Jewish Fuchs would be published in a Jewish almanac, a German Bohemian Fuchs would be represented in a collection of writing from the region, a socialist Fuchs would be recovered by East German scholarship. It is one of those cases that exceed irony by such a distance that it suddenly seems logical that the first and only readers to see a relation between Fuchs's Jewishness, cultural Czechophilism, and Marxism were the Nazis. Giving Fuchs's work more attention than did his supporters, they campaigned against him before 1938 and thereafter drove him to death in exile.

Fuchs forged and fanatically defended a territory that no other shared, or that those who could have shared did not grasp. He was a man without a country in the only country that could have borne him, just as he was an anachronism in the precise and only moment in which such a person could exist. He entitled a poem from the 1932 collection, which no publisher would find appropriate, "Unzeit"—"out of season"—but the word resonates with an otherworldly sense of being outside of time. This sense of the word is stressed in his opening line, where he declares *Unzeit* as his hometown. Who could say what Fuchs was thinking—if he dwelt upon his Jewish, Czech, or Prague German identity, or his special ideology, or upon the world war he had survived or the one well on the way—when he wrote these lines?

> Zur Unzeit ward ich geboren.
> Mich gebar das Volk
> Und verlor mich auf der Wanderung . . . [48]

> I was born out of season.
> The people bore me
> And lost me on the journey . . .

OF GOOD SOLDIERS AND BRIDGES

The commitment to translating, mediating production of, or simply calling attention to new Czech works of art, music, and literature was widespread among Prague German-speaking Jewish writers, and at the same time practically unique to them, so that this aspect of their activity seems inseparable from their own work. Beyond the activities of Werfel, Pick, and Fuchs, Egon Erwin Kisch was interested in the project, translating a bit and coming very close to taking on the first translation of Hašek's *Good Soldier Švejk*.[49] He turned down requests from Czech poets to translate short pieces and have them published, ostensibly because his connections were to newspapers rather than journals. He did offer to pass on such work to his friend Rudolf Fuchs, who could get his translations published in Pfemfert's *Aktion*.[50] The letter containing the offer was written shortly after that journal's pivotal "Bohemia" issue of May 1916, including not only the notorious Bezruč work in Fuchs's translation, but also Pick's translation of prose by Březina and a glowing review of Josef Suk's music by Max Brod.[51] Brod's flattering treatment of Suk was to have far-reaching consequences, for Suk would soon drop Brod a line encouraging him to visit the Czech National Theater to hear an unknown work by an obscure Moravian composer—Leoš Janáček's opera *Její Pastorkyňa*, which after Brod's translation would be known to the world as *Jenůfa*.

Brod is credited with the "discovery" not only of Janáček, but also of Hašek, since both Czech masters were little regarded by the Czechs themselves until they received German and general European attention. It was Brod who declared Hašek a comic master along the lines of Rabelais and Cervantes, and whose later dramatization of *Švejk* turned the protagonist into a sort of national hero. The problems of translation in Prague were highlighted when the novel was actually published in translation: the rendering of Czech slang with *Prager Deutsch* was the point of focus of criticism as well as praise for the translated work.[52]

The relationship between the "act of border crossing" effected by Brod's mediation activities and the "erotic symbiosis" of early works such as *Ein tschechisches Dienstmädchen* has been noted by Peter Demetz.[53] Indeed, the connection between these activities was made by Brod's contemporaries. More idiosyncratic is the judgment by Zdeněk Landes that the Jews of Brod's generation lived "in the medium of the Czech-German symbiosis."[54] Surely the word "symbiosis" would have been foreign to Czechs and Germans alike in this context. Landes strikes the mark more convincingly, and also creatively, with the assertion that "Max Brod vaults the Jewish bridge from the German word to Czech creativity."[55] The Jew in this representation is himself the bridge between two apparently unbridgeable cultures; furthermore, this image dovetails with Brod's own notion of "*Distanzliebe*," placing the Prague German-speaking Jewish writer in a position separate from German language (and, here, Czech culture as well), while at the same time privileging him in relation to both. It is inexplicable how Landes, after establishing the real "symbiosis"—or the condition of mutual necessity of these entities—could conclude that Brod's life work represents the "purely non-self-interested love of a Jewish writer of German tongue for the great creative products of the Czech people."[56] Even if Brod's voluminous correspondence with cultural figures of the Czech and German worlds were not everywhere marked with undisguised self-interest, which it unmistakably is—even then, how unfathomable could the Prague German-Jewish writer's need to build bridges in this context be?

In Brod's early meditations on the concept of translation, we can detect a Prague stamp in two senses: first of all, the sensitivity to the difficulty of translation, if not its impossibility; and second, the ontology behind his vision of translation, which is saturated with the recurring themes of his context. In the philosophical tract on which he and Felix Weltsch collaborated, a derivative and often stilted text with the pretentious title *Anschauung und Begriff: Grundzüge eines Systems der Begriffsbildung*, a clear distinction is made between "scientific" and "aesthetic" text translations. Scientific concepts can be "carried over" into another language, whereas the poetic text can only be "recomposed" (*"nachgedichtet"*).[57] "One must openly accept the fact that only particles of the original of such works of art can pass over into the other language. Everything else is lost."[58] What Brod calls the polarity of language, the dualism between form and content, reveals the persistence of themes that represented themselves in so many aspects of the nationality conflict and contemporary cultural manifestations. The section of Brod and Weltsch's text on the translation of aesthetic moments is not headed "untranslatability" (*"Unübersetzbarkeit"*) but rather "*Unmittelbarkeit.*" The "immediacy" of the aesthetic text, or its untranslatability, is posed in precisely the same terms as Brod's central aesthetic problem—the immediacy of experience and the problem of its transposition to the written page.[59] In this sense Brod's fairly pedestrian philosophical theory of translation is doubly self-reflexive, and points to identical problems of correspondence between art and experience and between translation and original; the hope of the aesthetic moment for Brod is the momentary recovery of such immediacy, rather than mediation.

In Brod's forward to his 1914 translation of Catullus as well, the translator projects the contemporary Prague politico-cultural problematic onto the Roman poet:

> Catullus's language is often folksy [*volkstümlich*] (words from everyday language, from comedy, from the provinces), which he puts into harmony with lofty Greek learned speech with eloquent grace.[60]

The language of Catullus seems to the Praguer Brod to map out a sociocultural and linguistic landscape that the poet is able to harmonize masterfully in the page. As true art, it is grounded in the *Volk,* in popular speech, even in provincial language (we compare the interest in *Prager Deutsch* to the sterling High German of the Concordia poets). The folk-based language is artfully harmonized with the "elite parties" (*"erhabene Parteien"*) of the text, the nonnative but powerful minority of Greek words. Continuing with his description of Catullus, who sounds more and more like a Prague German writer of Brod's generation, Brod declares him the master of "contradictions" and "crossings": "His poems are primarily a movement between two [oppositional] poles." [61] After carving out this specific image of Catullus, Brod's project in (re)producing these themes in the translated text (actually more of a reworking of an earlier translation, since Brod was no classical scholar) becomes somewhat easier.

Brod's expropriative gesture of translation seems at first to illustrate the slippage between Schleiermacher's famous dictum on translation—that it should "move the author toward the reader"—and Nietzsche's translation as "conquest" or "in-corporation," where the great moments of translation are precisely those where a sense of historical difference is eclipsed by nationalist narcissism. [62] And yet, as with the question of aestheticism itself in Brod's evolving oeuvre, there is in this a circularity of difference and identity, of historicity and ahistoricity. This circularity is effected in the Catullus translation by means of the double movement that figures Catullus as a proto-Brod, mediating between oppositional poles, generating a moment of aesthetic immediacy through an occupation of difference. Thus as the distance between Catullus's and Brod's positions/texts is violated rather than "mediated," similarly unavoidable difference is posited as the center of their shared position/text. The identity of translator and poet is made possible by the figuration of the poet as translator.

This elaborate identification with the material continued throughout Brod's translation activities, which took on particular importance—as with Pick and Fuchs—during the war. In Janáček, too, Brod discovered bridges between folksiness and high art, contradictions and crossings. The focus on these elements repeated the effect of transforming the artists themselves into translators; in a comic reversal, art was created in the image of translation, struggling within a space between oppositional poles. Mediation, generally defined as a secondary activity, became the primary aesthetic act in Brod's texts as they "selflessly" brought foreign works to a German public.

LAYERS OF TRANSLATION

On Josef Suk's suggestion, Brod attended the 1916 Prague premiere of the major opera by the sixty-two-year-old Moravian composer, whose work had appeared in Brno more than a decade before. He reviewed the work in an article called "Tschechisches Opernglück"; the good fortune of the Czech opera, however, was more than anything the appearance of this glowing review in what was arguably the major Central European journal of the performing arts, the Berlin *Schaubühne*.[63] Brod's review was translated into Czech and reprinted in Prague and Brno. Janáček and Brod exchanged letters, and the former set off at once for Prague, convinced that the latter was the man who would be the perfect mediator for the work, translating the libretto, having it published, and finding a German company to produce it.[64]

Brod's reluctance to take on the project at first is documented, but we know that the decision process was rapid, with Janáček reporting Brod's commitment to the future publisher less than a month after the appearance of the original review.[65] Brod claimed he was won over by the formidable personage of Janáček himself. The idea of translation informed even Brod's memory of this encounter, with the composer himself appearing to be a Slavic "translation" of German genius:

> This head with its high, beautifully arched brow, the flashing, urgent wide-open eyes, the mouth: it is Goethe's head, as Stieler painted it, but here transposed into Slavic softness . . . [66]

From this description, in conjunction with the *Schaubühne* review, it is clear that Brod was seduced by a certain image of the composer and his work. The project unified an image of a truly grounded folk culture (not merely Czech, but even more provincial—Moravian) with the ultimate high art form, opera. This is a starting point for an understanding of Brod's stake in the project.

The preface to Brod's translation, published two years later, focused on the music theory presumably at work in Janáček's opera. "Word-melody" is what Janáček spoke of as the "composition of prose," the development of melodies based in the speech rhythms of the text he was working from, Gabriele Preissová's drama.[67] Janáček is quoted in the preface:

> How many variations of the speech motif of one and the same word did I encounter! Here it sparkled and was supple, there it was hard and piercing. But I sensed in the speech motif something much deeper still; something that was

not out in the open. Within the melody I felt traces of more internal, private processes.[68]

How appealing this description of the artistic process must have been to Max Brod. Here were his oppositional poles, here his art grounded in *Volk* and transformed into universal music, here was the aesthetic space of translation itself. "The motifs of every single word in '*Její Pastorkyňa*' are formed in the image of life."[69] Janáček's work was itself a transposition of Preissová's prose, which reproduced in text form the folk life of Moravia. These layers of reproduction turn the writing of opera into a technical translation of life, unite life and art, and ground the highest and most abstract of art forms in a territorialized folk culture. It was fully consistent of Brod to reject the way most critics read the preface, which turned the word-melody theory into a direct transcription of Slavic speech rhythms to music: rather than that aestheticist gesture, Janáček used the word melody as a vehicle for access to the true *Volk*.[70] Janáček's use of folk themes follows a similar pattern. The folk melodies are not reproduced within the opera so much as they appear in translation from folk song to high art—"transformed through his genius into the highest art," as one critic has called it—rather than being quoted "in unalloyed form."[71]

The union of this music and the German word into a still rarer and more precious alloy held a promise that Brod could not resist. For that, though, it was not enough to fuse an authentic folk-grounded music with German; Brod's main concern was the sort of language that would be appropriate for the alloy. *Operndeutsch*—"opera German"—would rend the life from the work: "One thing saved me: the joy of creating an opera text that had nothing to do with 'opera German.'" "*Opernhaftig-keit*" ("opera-ishness") for Brod was antonymical to "humanism."[72] In a letter to Janáček, Brod made his objection even clearer:

> The translation, according to my artistic convictions, must be an artwork in and of itself; no "opera German," then, but rather a healthy, ordinary [*volks-tümlich*] language.[73]

No better a solution, however, was the other pole: to select a German dialect into which to translate the entire text. This solution was even more painful to Janáček than to Brod, since it would butcher the work to have it sung throughout in, for example, a German Tyrolean dialect, as Hugo Reichenberger suggested for the Vienna production.[74] Brod's translation, in contrast, was in standard German, slightly idiomatic, with a few "colorations" of dialect, and above all without the stilted constructions of stage German.

Brod worked with utmost cordiality with the composer, but was poised from the first for power struggles with the editor and, above all, Reichenberger. The latter was given Brod's text for suggestions, and returned it full of them, mostly in the direction of *Operndeutsch*. While Brod won that battle (by threatening to withdraw the translation altogether), he was hardly more tolerant of the few changes decided upon by editor Emil Hertzka. Of course ego was more at stake than art, but in particular Brod was not willing to accept the "opera-ish" displacement of a single verb.[75]

The Vienna production ran into serious controversy, sparked by the attack of three German-national parliamentary representatives. They objected to the increasing number of non-German operas taken on by the house, and in particular to the Czech nationalism manifest in *Jenůfa*.[76] *Bohemia* supported the action, and criticized Brod in a prominent article. Accustomed to controversy, Brod reacted little to the incident, virtually laughing it off to the distressed composer.[77] Even well after the conflict, it is interesting that Brod did not look back on his translation as a political act, as Fuchs self-consciously had. Rather, he continued to insist that the opera was not a "national" one:

> "Jenůfa" is not a Czech national opera, it has nothing to do with national-historical dreams [. . .] "Jenůfa" is a human opera that takes place among Moravian peasants. [. . .] This artwork does not have the least to do with national politics in Austria.[78]

Yet, another passage explains better how the work could seem profoundly national, even *völkisch*, without being partisan; one in which nationality is elevated into human identity, or perhaps merely confused with it. Brod is describing the final scene of the opera:

> The music, which throughout has been of sharply national character (I like to call Janáček a Moravian Smetana [. . .]), the music suddenly becomes really universal, purely musical music—the mediary level of ethnography has been drowned in the great ocean of humanity. [. . .]
>
> How much this closing scene, more than philosophical essays, can place us in the center of that loving idea [. . .] how much more than all the theory in the world does this divine music say to me about the essence of the nation and true nationalism . . . [79]

In this passage and elsewhere, Brod betrays the German-liberal assumption that music with Slavic folk themes is less universal than German classical music. The latter is "purely musical music," not music along with something else. More important perhaps to an understanding of what Brod thought he was doing in the translation project is in the second half of the citation. It is the reference to a moment when, through a true folk-grounded gesture, the universal is achieved, as with his *übernational* notion of Jewish nationalism. Brod found a work in which the "genius of the *Volk*" was made to sing, and he wanted to make it speak.

CORRESPONDING WITH "MILENA," TRANSLATING "KAFKA"

While Franz Kafka was more fluent in Czech than Max Brod, Franz Werfel, and other Prague Jews who translated Czech works into German, he did not produce translations. Just as his sensibility regarding the territorial status of language seems, when set against the most creative play of his circle of friends, to be purer and less compromising, or more direct (*unmittelbar*), so the tension between the fascination with the passage between linguistic/cultural spaces and the consciousness of the necessary failure of such attempts at passage is more salient in Kafka's writing than the act of translation itself. Ironically but significantly, Kafka's encounter with the notion of translation does not take place in an expropriation of Czech literature, but is clearest (or in its most naked form) in the correspondence with Milena Jesenská, which begins with the Czech journalist's attempts to consult the author of the text she wishes to translate into her native tongue, "The Stoker." Translation is thus struck as an inaugural trope in what will become one of modernity's most impressive love correspondences. The problem of "translation" as well as of "correspondence"—of moving over, of (cor)responding—is at the core of a set of questions about lovers/beloveds and sexuality as well as about writing/s and textuality in eight intensive months of letter writing to Milena. The difficult logic of the ideology of mediation I have been trying to outline is pressured to the extremes in these letters, so that it is not in spite of but rather through the very laws of difference and mediation that the status of identity and the possibility of immediacy or authentic experience are put to the test. That this radical articulation of these themes emerges in such condensed form after the war, from the new and different ground of the first Czechoslovak state, cannot be overlooked. In this sense the correspondence stands as a sort of coda of the Prague circle moment, where an almost schematic recapitulation is possible only in self-conscious retrospect.

While translation was the occasion for the initiation of the Kafka–
Jesenská correspondence, Kafka was at once jealous of it, pointing out
the paradox of the mediator, who establishes distance in order to bridge
it, or who opens dialogue even while standing in the way. In a few weeks
in April 1920, Jesenská's initial inquiry regarding her translation of "The
Stoker" had already become a deeply personal exchange. Receiving the
draft manuscript at the end of the month at a spa in Merano, Kafka
replied:

> When I pulled your translation out of the large envelope, I was almost dis-
> appointed. I wanted to hear from you and not the voice from the old grave,
> the voice I know all too well. Why did it have to come between us? Then I re-
> alized that this same voice had also come between us as a mediator.[80]

The figure of translation/mediation is already carefully manipulated
in this early letter, where instead of the translator mediating between an
original and translated text, the voice of the text stands between Kafka
and Milena. Another important transgression in this brief passage is the
subtle identification of the voice of the Czech text as the voice of the literary text "The Stoker" itself—not as a copy or as the mediated voice of
the author, who stands apart from it and writes of it as an object without personal pronoun, but as the voice of the text, familiar and past,
raised from the dead rather than lost in translation. The resentment in
the passage is thus never directed at the translator's meddling with the
authorial voice, but to the contrary, at that haunting voice itself, unexpectedly and without invitation returning in its original form from
the netherworld. The mark of "jealousy" in this resentful response is directed at the fact that the caressing hands of the translator have veered
away from the living body of Kafka's epistolary text to the corpse of his
old story. The hidden arousal of the passage emanates nonetheless from
the promise that Kafka's bodies/texts could appeal to those hands. The
rest of this passage points in this direction:

> But apart from that it is inconceivable to me that you would take on such a
> troublesome task, and I am moved by your faithfulness toward every little sen-
> tence, a faithfulness I would not have thought possible to achieve in Czech, let
> alone with the beautiful natural authority you attain. German and Czech so
> close to each other?[81]

What Kafka will not let pass is the intimacy effected by the act of
translation, the real and physical closeness that has been created in the
translated text. Returning to the translations themselves, contemporary
readers find them to be unprofessional and long on errors;[82] "accuracy"

was not at issue in Kafka's reading, even if "fidelity," in some sense or other, was. The attention and care, the costly effort (*Mühe*) spent by Milena, is "felt" by the author as her touch (*tief rührend*); these very terms appeared in an even earlier letter regarding the forthcoming translation: "You are toiling [*Sie mühn sich*] over the translation in the middle of the dreary Vienna world. Somehow I am both touched and ashamed [*rührend und beschämend für mich*]" (5). He feels and is shamed by this intimate touch of his text, up and down every little sentence ("*tief rührend . . . Sätzchen auf und ab*"). And the touching element is no less the virtue of the translation, its fidelity (*Treue*). Thus if we attend to this letter as a literary construction it becomes clear that Kafka has transformed the business of this translation into an intimate intercourse that Milena has initiated. Further, by pointing up the correspondence between body and text, Kafka has invited Milena into an affair that can take place in writing, in letters, and attributed the invitation or seduction to her.

   "Fidelity" in translation is never an innocent term, and in all translation contexts belongs to an overdetermined set of gender relations aligning creative originality with male artists and mimesis with the feminine.[83] Lori Chamberlain has traced these gendered "metaphorics of translation" and pointed out the dual double standard of the translation and marriage relations: while the translation is subject to the test of fidelity, faithfulness remains a noncategory for the original.[84] In Kafka's letters, as we will see, translation does not serve to authorize the original, but rather it is the process that brings to light the inauthenticity of the original text; Milena's "fidelity" demonstrates Kafka's, or Kafka's text's, infidelity to himself/itself. "Fidelity" was a heavily charged term in this correspondence with Milena, who had already confessed to Kafka the travails of her open marriage with Ernst Pollak (another German-speaking Prague Jew), saying of this arrangement "I am the one who pays." Kafka warns Milena, too, that he fears the Czechs will not forgive this literary fidelity of her translation of "The Stoker," the betrayal of the Czech language to which she "belongs" by the faithful attachment to the German (-Jewish) text—or, in an antisemitic image Kafka plants later in the letters, the abduction of the Czech maiden by the German-Jewish rake.

   The projection of this voice from the old grave into the Czech body, which revivifies it, is a black magic Kafka had not thought possible. But the magic that Kafka wishes to sustain is not the product, the resurrected voice of the text, but rather the act of translation—the moment where difference still exists, and yet where the German text is absorbed into the body of Czech language. The closeness of German and Czech — a proximateness beyond his dreams — depends upon this retained difference. In the context of the correspondence, Kafka is resisting the closure that the completed text sealed in the large envelope threatens to represent. The erotics of translation seems at this point easily — too easily — to map itself onto the Prague milieu of Brod's *Ein tschechisches Dienstmädchen*: the creative power of the German text faces the feminine Czech translation, reproductive and at the same time seductive, sexy in its exoticism and as a result of the exaggerated imbalance of power. It is thus at this moment that Kafka seeks to sustain the creative and erotic tension of translation by asking Milena to write in Czech, not because she does not command (*beherrschen*) German, for she commands it astonishingly, or when she does not it voluntarily yields to her, or bows to her (*beugt es sich vor Ihnen freiwillig*), thus remaining at her command. But this erotic tension is not the genuine encounter Kafka desires: Milena herself is lost in German translation, adapted to the dreary world of Vienna. He wants to read her in Czech because she "belongs" to it and not to German, "because the whole Milena can only be there." And so he asks that she write in her native tongue.

Hence the meeting with Milena will take place in letters, in Czech texts where "the whole Milena is," and in German writing, of which Kafka is made. The transposition or translation of Milena's body (in)to the text of the letter is explicit in Kafka's responses to the Czech letters: "I see you more clearly, the movements of your body, your hands, so quick, so resolute, it is almost a meeting." Milena's textual presence supersedes Kafka's bodily presence in the spa in Merano, so that consummation is still deferred: "And still I would be lying if I said I missed you: it is the most perfect, most painful magic, you are here, just as I am and even more so [. . .] I occasionally imagine that you, who really are here, are missing *me* here and asking: 'Where can he be? Didn't he write that he's in Merano?'" (34). Within the framework of the correspondence exchange, bodies pass into texts and become more corporeal there than they are on the earth. At least that is the case for Kafka's ephemeral body, consumed by tuberculosis, unable to sleep and barely alive until it is grounded in the earth of the letters:

> It is so wonderful to have received your letter, to have to answer it with my sleepless brain. I can't think of anything to write, I'm just walking around here between the lines, beneath the light of your eyes, in the breath of your

mouth as in some beautiful and happy day that stays beautiful and happy even when the head is ill, tired and one departs Monday via Munich. (26) [85]

So if the form and movements of Milena's body can be touched only on the page of her Czech letters, Kafka sets himself onto the page of his own letters in anticipation of her reading. If (as he wrote in a previous love correspondence) he is not inclined toward but rather made of literature, his daylight radiates from her reading eyes, his air is her breath on the page. The image produced by writing and the sight evoked by reading are easier to arrange than the stopover in Vienna: "And so *auf Wiedersehn* (but it doesn't have to be in Vienna, it can also be in letters)" (58). All this contact stands in for the physical encounter that is constantly deferred—here by returning from Merano to Prague by way of Munich rather than Vienna. In fact Kafka would not be ready to return from his cure in Merano on Monday, and three more weeks of diligent letter writing would precede the revived conflict of whether and how to stop to see Milena.

Naturally, a love affair of letters can be enabled only by the deferral of physical meeting or distance from Vienna; the space between writer and reader is the prerequisite for writing to be produced. [86] The love affair was thus concentrated in letters, with Kafka's work and illness and Milena's marriage serving the useful function of keeping the lovers apart. In the course of the correspondence, Kafka and Milena met only twice: once for four days in Vienna, and once for a single day at the Czech-Austrian border. Even here, the meetings retained a secondary function to letter writing, rather than the letters having served as instruments to facilitate meeting. On June 25, 1920, a Friday, Kafka was still not sure whether he would travel via Vienna the following Tuesday; in a second letter that day he was ready to commit, but not to a rendezvous point, for "I would suffocate by then if I were to name a place right now and then have to see this place for three days and three nights, empty, waiting for me to arrive Tuesday at a certain hour" (60). Naming in the context of the letters brings into immediate and tangible existence: naming a future meeting place creates a physical space apart from the correspondence itself that is painfully empty and impossible to bear. The next line has a confusing syntax and frugal punctuation: "*Gibt es überhaupt Milena auf der Welt soviel Geduld, wie für mich nötig ist?*" ("Is there Milena anywhere in the world as much patience as I need?") It seems at first to ask whether Milena is in the world at all (is she not really bound to the territory of letters?), and then reveals that the direct object is "patience." And yet even this more pedestrian meaning of the sentence is strange, depending as it does upon the assumption that corresponding with Milena in letters over three months has not required the patience demanded by making an arrangement to see her on Tuesday. He did take the train to Vienna on Tuesday. Upon arriving at the South Station, he sat down with a cup of chocolate and . . . wrote Milena a letter. The question of the arrival of this letter is more his concern than his own presence in Vienna:

> This letter probably won't arrive before 12:00, or rather I'm sure it won't, since it's already 10. So not until tomorrow morning—perhaps it's just as well, for I am indeed in Vienna [. . .] but I am not entirely here [. . .]

It is almost as though, instead of this correspondence mediating their meeting, Kafka's presence in Vienna is another excuse to write a letter. At least in this case it is clear that the letter does not facilitate their physical contact as much as it defers it another day. In this day a ghostly Kafka will pass through Vienna, "as invisible as possible," until Milena receives his letter and finds his hotel. It is certainly not insignificant that they did meet, that there is reference to a successful copulation, and that they did write endlessly about the possibility of meeting again. But even then it is arguable that, just as letters are assumed to reflect upon and anticipate experience, in this case the reverse seemed to be true. Our record of what transpired during the brief Vienna tryst includes Milena's description of a lengthy visit to the post office as well as Kafka's note on July 27: "You see, you need a new pen nib, why didn't we make better use of our time in Vienna? Why didn't we spend the whole time in the stationer's shop, for example; it really was so beautiful inside and we were so close to one another"(113).[87] Life is about letters.

The tension between life and writing as well as the deferral of physical trysts in order to write letters have long been recognized in Kafka's earlier letters to Felice Bauer in Berlin (1912–1916), where "life" or "happiness," being with Felice, was explicitly identified as a cancellation of the possibility of writing.[88] In the correspondence with Milena, though, the dichotomy of life/writing is intensely refracted by the element of (un)translatability: Milena is physically present in the letters in a way that Felice could not be, and Kafka then surrenders himself to the textual Milena in a manner neither ascetic nor renouncing. Yet even Milena needed to be educated in this art of correspondence, where letters do not mediate experiences and identities but rather take their places. She may have been flattered by the volume of correspondence coming from Prague, but was doubtless puzzled at the currency of letters within this dialogue. Kafka's obsessive accounting of the number of letters he had received and sent, his recurring anxiety about the possibility of letters being lost in the postal system, his descriptions of how her letters and his to her ruled over his daily life were noted by Milena, who could not understand:

> [Y]ou once asked how it happened that I made my stay here dependent on one letter, and then you immediately answered your own question: *nechápu* [I don't understand]. A strange word in Czech and even in your mouth it is so severe, so callous, cold eyed, stingy, and most of all like a nutcracker, pronouncing it requires three consecutive cracks of the jaw or, more exactly, the first syllable makes an attempt at holding the nut, in vain, the second syllable then tears the mouth wide open, the nut now fits inside, where it is finally cracked by the third syllable, can you hear the teeth? Particularly this final, absolute closing of the lips at the end prohibits the other person from expressing anything to the contrary, which is actually quite good at times, for instance when the other person is babbling as much as I am now. (21)[89]

It is not for nothing that these complex effects are attached to the brittle word expressing the lapse of mutual comprehension, a closing off or cracking of the hope of translatability. It is a foreign word in Czech, Kafka claims, and so even in/on Milena's tongue does not seem to belong to her, or her to it: callous, cold eyed, stingy. While excusing himself for babbling, Kafka is also warning Milena to defend the letters against foreign interventions that will destroy the delicate mechanisms that make these letters a mutual territory of the two languages and two genders. Chief among these mechanisms is precisely the primacy of letters that is challenged by Milena's reply: *nechápu*.

The interesting focus on the physical effects of words, the effects performed not by their referentiality but by their "wordliness," belongs to the cabalistic science, as Kafka knew. Interestingly, the phenomenological magic of this word and others is inaccessible to the Czech native speaker; Kafka speaks of these performances as side effects the Czech language has for German ears. The examples he offers of such effects are violent. In the same letter he responds to Milena's question "[A]re you a Jew?"

> And on top of that Milena is still going on about anxiety, striking my chest or asking: *jste žid* [are you a Jew]? Which in Czech has the same movement and sound. Don't you see how the fist is pulled back in the word "*jste,*" so as to gain muscle power? And then in the word "*žid*" the happy blow, flying unerringly forward? (21)[90]

From this point forward, "Jew" and "Jewishness" remain important textual figures in the letters, and the dynamics aligning them from within with the figures of "Ängstlichkeit" and "Angst," fear and anxiety, and from without with rejection and violence never subsides. A reading of the valence of "fear" in the letters would alone take up the full space of an analytic essay on this correspondence. In shorthand I would suggest that it serves a function parallel to the complex operation of the trope of size and inferiority in the letter to the father that I have already discussed: he writes Milena that his fear represents a "retreating from the world."[91] In fact, at several points where Kafka discussed this fear in the correspondence he promised to send her the letter to his father, which he finally did. This gesture reinforces the primacy of letters, since it identifies referents for the letter, a space outside the letter text, chiefly in another letter. Similarly, the play with presence and absence in the letters to Milena are covert workings through of the set of concerns established in the letters to Felice. Even the "real-life" relations of Kafka and Milena in this period are compelled within the boundaries of the correspondence: leaving Julie Wohryzek for Milena is a process enacted by showing her Milena's letters, writing her letters, and, most important, mediating an exchange of letters between Milena and Julie. Julie in turn sent Milena's letter to her back to Kafka, full of angry underlinings and notations, which he in turn sent on to Milena with his own commentary. At Kafka's suggestion, Milena also began a correspondence with Max Brod that continued as a subtext to the primary text of the correspondence with Kafka; she asked Brod to keep to himself her questions about Kafka's true state of mind and of body, which she felt he represented deceptively in his letters to her.

This traffic of letters seems in retrospect to have been implicated in the drive within the correspondence to subvert the hierarchy that privileges unmediated experience in the world over the allegedly mediate function of writing, the authentic over the copy, the original over the translation. While Kafka's letters were gravely engaged in a confrontation with the problems of mediation, communication, and the meeting of souls, they also work toward hermetically sealing the world of the letter texts from the pollution of outside air, even as they exist only to be opened, to be read. Correspondence, of course, like translation, like mediation, is not supposed to close itself off, but rather to make connections of various kinds. *Korrespondenz,* from the Latin *correspondentia,* has connection as its first connotation, as in social connection, the traffic of letters—reportage, such as that in letters or reported to a public by a journalistic "correspondent." The "correspondence" that is an exchange of letters aspires to one of its homonyms as an ideal: "correspondence" is the perfect agreement of two voices, to respond in unison with another. And then there is the moment of correspondence connecting a word or image, a historical moment or a spatial coordinate, with an/other, a co-incident. The task of translation, to borrow from Walter Benjamin's famous essay (roughly contemporary to Kafka's exchange with Milena), is to resist the trap of this sort of correspondence, for the aura of the work does not rest in its apparent referents, but in the moment that is free from such correspondences, where it is closest to a perhaps unattainable "true language." And yet this linguistic purity can be pointed to first with the true translation, transparent, a specular arcade or passage instead of an opaque linguistic wall.[92]

By delivering himself as object of translation, by surrendering to his own absorption into the Czech and feminine body of Milena's text, the Kafka that was "made of literature" broke free from the tenuous mooring that was left even to him: that of German literary territory. Benjamin sheds light on this territorial displacement, too, when he writes:

> Unlike a work of literature, translation does not find itself in the center of the language forest but on the outside facing the wooded ridge; it calls into it without entering, aiming at that single spot where the echo is able to give, in its own language, the reverberation of the work in the alien one.[93]

Hence this "reverberation" is an echo of what Benjamin names "pure language," prehistorical or a-territorial precisely because of the irretractable historicity and territoriality of the literary text. The translation points the way to a momentary and inconsummable promise of antiterritorial purity: "the text rises into a higher and purer linguistic air" (75) ("*In ihr wächst das Original in einen gleichsam höheren und reineren Luftkreis der Sprache hinauf*" [14]). It is not that the original is technically untranslatable into another language, but even on its native ground it immediately begins to grow distant from itself and irrecoverable. Thus through an orthodox concentration on the laws of linguistic territoriality one finds oneself pushed from the centered discourse of author–language–territory to the extremity, where the text is not even identical to itself, but where an echo of the voice of the text, the gesture toward the moment of "true language," can be listened for in the translation.

Mark Anderson has written an excellent essay on Kafka's "unsigned" letters to Milena in which he convincingly demonstrates the disaggregation of the authorial subject that is thematized in the letters. The usefulness of the correspondence to the disavowal of identity—for instance, the assimilation of Kafka's name or signature into the figure of Milena— is eloquently established in that essay, and its relevance to this discussion of figures of territory and translation is manifest. In the postwar period, in this correspondence with a Czech woman in Vienna (Milena) rather than a German Jew in Berlin (Felice), the boundaries between art and life, writing and happiness, subjectivity or identity and mediation are subject to thoroughly radical critique: the original is secondary to translation, Kafka defines himself through Milena, but "Milena," too, is an ungrounded and mediated figure. The name into which he is absorbed, "Milena," so full it is hard to lift (*"vor Fülle kaum zu heben"*), seems to him itself a Greek or Roman translated or moved over to Bohemia, "violated" by Czech, "betrayed" by the unfaithful Czech stress on the first syllable—and this unbearable object is yet "in color and form a woman to be carried out of the world in one's arms . . . and she presses herself into your arms willingly and full of trust, except the strong accent on the "i" is bad, doesn't the name jump right back away from you? Or might that just be a leap for joy, which you yourself perform with your burden?" (44–45)[94] This tragicomic image of Milena's name is to be given serious weight, since it is to become the vehicle for the disappearance of Kafka's own signature from the letters. Its gravity should become clear in another passage from the letters that I would like to read closely: a paragraph on a single sheet of paper of July 14, 1920, responding to a single line of a previous letter from Milena:

> You write: "Ano máš pravdu, mám ho ráda. Ale F., i tebe mám ráda ["Yes you are right, I am fond of him. But F., I am also fond of you"]—I am reading this sentence very precisely, pausing in particular at the i [also]—it is all correct. You would not be Milena if it were not correct and what would I be if you weren't, and it is also better that you write it from Vienna than say it in Prague. All this I perfectly understand, maybe better than you and yet out of some weakness I cannot get over the sentence, it reads endlessly, and finally I am transcribing it here for you to see as well and for us to read together, temple to temple.[95]

In a single line of Milena's, Kafka finds a diagram for the circular relations of territorial translation, and he offers it as a primer. The condition of their correspondence is not only their emotional attachment to one another, as I have mentioned, but also their physical detachment: this tension between Vienna and Prague, between Milena's physical presence with Ernst Pollak and the distance from Kafka/Prague that calls for letters. Milena's dual affirmation ("yes, I love him,"—as one translation

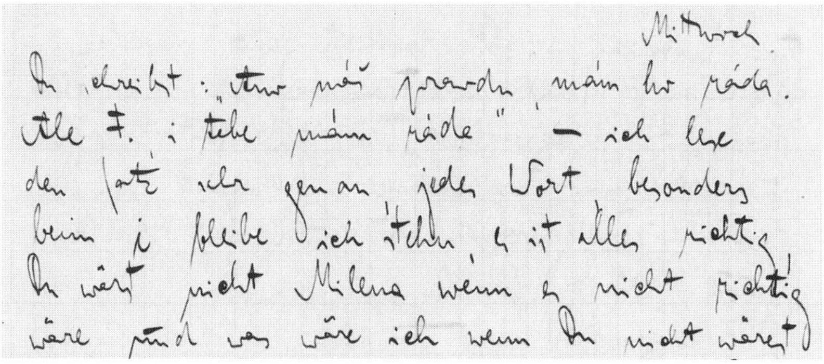
Mittwoch
Du schreibst: „ano mám pravdu, mám ho ráda.
Ale F., i tebe mám ráda" — ich lese
den Satz sehr genau, jedes Wort besonders
beim i bleibe ich stehn, es ist alles richtig,
Du wärst nicht Milena wenn es nicht richtig
wäre und was wäre ich wenn Du nicht wärest

Fig. 3. Detail from manuscript page of a letter to Milena Jesenská dated 14 July 1920. Courtesy of DLSN.

goes—"but F., I also love you") guarantees both conditions. Kafka here, as throughout the letters, does not translate Milena's Czech but transcribes it directly, inserted within his German text; he then takes her through a reading of it in order to create reciprocal conditions of writing and reading (as he tells her at the end of the passage—so they can read together, temple to temple). Reading this simple, fairly musical sentence requires the ruthless precision he has offered glimpses of before: instead of speaking of contents and referents, the active function of reading reverberates around the sound of the words, the rhythm of clauses, the shape and relation of letters. To return to the terms of Benjamin's discussion of translation, rather than gleaning meanings (*Bedeutungen*) that can be transmitted (*vermittelt*) by German correspondents to the Czech words, the sense (*Sinn*) of the sentence comes to Kafka by standing in its middle—pausing at the "i" of the phoneme "i-tebe," pronounced in Czech as a single word.

The perfect symmetry of the sentence is first exposed by Kafka's reiteration of it, even as its "rightness" proceeds from its attachment to "Milena," paralleling "i-tebe," "you-too," performing (as Kafka wrote before) simultaneous yielding and resistance, or a leap with a burden. We see that this double movement of yielding and resistance is severalfold: it is in the "you, too" of "i-tebe," it is in the name "Milena," and it is in the melodic sentence as a whole, teetering from Pollak to Kafka, weighted on each end by the repeated "mám ráda-mám ráda." The sentence is Milena's because it is *Milena,* as Kafka writes: "es ist alles richtig, Du wärst nicht *Milena* wenn es nicht richtig wäre . . . ," reiterating that the double movement is contained in the name that covers the passage. Thus the parallel musical counterpoint of Milena's name and her sentence allows Kafka to read one as the other, so that when he comes to a standstill at the "i" he finds himself again in the midst of "Milena," and as he reveals this correspondence we find the tall thin figure "l" "remaining standing" at her center (*"beim i bleibe ich stehn"*).

And what would he be if she were not, he asks? Kafka lays a trap here, too—indeed, throughout the correspondence—for the reader is tempted to see in this repeated gesture the neat assimilation of the authorial subject into Milena. Mark Anderson, who has done the most to point to this question of absorption in the letters to Milena, productively brings his essay on the correspondence back to his own exemplary readings of "Josephine, the Mouse Singer" and "The Hunger Artist," suggesting that the erasure of the authorial name was more at stake than its "merging" into the name/body of Milena. Indeed, the double movement I have been describing asserts the impossibility of such a closure. For Kafka does not "remain standing" at rest in this passage, but (as the latest translation would have it) "pauses" for a moment in the midst of "Milena," while the tension effected by his reading puts it into motion again. The power of deterritorialization, as I have suggested in my reading of Kafka's lecture on Yiddish, lies in its highly charged motility as against the complacent figure of "rest" represented by "assimilation," or territorialized language. Or, to look back to the letter to his father, territorialized strength, size, and weight are resisted by a weakness, lightness, and flight (in this correspondence, "fear") represented by and representing writing. It is out of this particular "weakness" (appearing as "some weakness or other" in the above passage) that the machine is put back into motion: "I cannot finish the sentence, it is an endless reading" (*"kann ich mit dem Satz nicht fertig werden, es ist ein endloses Lesen"*), and so, as his own sentence is beginning to seem endless, he offers it back to Milena, " . . . mám ho ráda . . . i tebe mám ráda. . . . . mám ho ráda . . . i tebe mám ráda . . . "—the endless circle of translation/correspondence that points to a utopian moment of identity and union only as it utters its necessary impossibility. *Volvitur in rota*[96]— turned upon the wheel, torture on the wheel (German: *Foltern auf dem Rad*).

Kafka does offer Milena an image of a torture machine a couple of months later (see reproduction below). But September 1920 was worlds apart from July 14, according to Kafka's own periodization of the correspondence: "The person writing to you now [27 October 1920] is the person you know from Merano. After that we were one, there was no more talk of knowing one another, and then once again we were split"

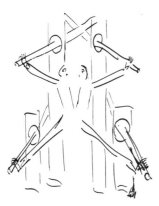

Fig. 4. Kafka, sketch from a letter to Milena Jesenská dated 20 September 1920. Courtesy of DLSN.

(210–11) ("*Dann waren wir eines, da war vom Sichkennen keine Rede mehr und dann sind wir wieder gespalten worden*"). The brief period of "correspondence" (in the sense of overlaid voices) in the correspondence, or the moment of unison of the echo of the text and of the translation, falls between the consummation of the affair in Vienna and the failed connection in Gmünd. But by this I would not want to suggest that the above rhetorical figures of union ("*waren wir eines*") and disunion ("*sind wir wieder gespalten worden*") in the letters reflected respective successful consummation and impotence in the hotel rooms; it is clearly the reverse that is the case, with this letter constructing sexual performance as a metaphor for the dynamics of the correspondence. In the latter period of division or "*Spaltung,*" Kafka drew the above sketch and sent it to Milena (see figure 4).

The "delinquent's" hands and feet are fastened to poles running through four posts; the poles are "slowly pushed outward until the man is torn apart in the middle," according to Kafka's explication of the drawing. But there are two figures in the illustration: the "delinquent"; and the "inventor" of the machine, leaning against a column on the right, arms and legs crossed. The inventor is inflected as masculine in the written description, but the figure in the drawing is of ambiguous gender, with a wide rectangle ending at the pelvis that could be either a long, wide shirt or a short skirt or dress, with dandyishly delicate crossed legs and hooflike pointed toes, and with the doubled V-shape of the unnaturally high crossed arms suggesting a woman's bust. This feminine posture is associated with "putting on airs," "as if the whole thing were his original invention, whereas all he really did was watch the butcher in front of his shop, drawing out a disemboweled pig" (201). Thus the torture machine is not an expression of creative originality, but a copy claiming the status of an original; what's more, it is not the translation of a great work, but rather of the commonest brutality. The ambiguity of the inventor figure suggests a fluidity of roles and identities in the drawing: s/he is clearly a spectator, not in immediate control of the spectacle (the person or mechanism driving the poles is invisible, just as the empowered subjects in *The Trial* and *The Castle* are unseen and somehow beside the point). Inasmuch as the inventor is revealed to be the translator, the figure must remain open for Milena; and yet we know that it is Kafka who has "invented" this torture, who has conjured up both figures, and that both must also be open to stand in for him. This busy-ness (the illustration is sent as evidence of how he has been keeping himself busy, his "occupation," "*Damit Du etwas von meinen 'Beschäftigungen' siehst*") is a dark reflection on the possibility of writing that comes after the hope offered earlier by the translation relationship has passed. Responding to Milena's translation of a torture scene from Upton Sinclair's *Jimmy Higgins*, Kafka comments on their shared tastes: "Yes, torture is extremely important to me—I occupy myself solely [*ich beschäftige mich*] with torturing and being tortured." Both subject and object positions, torturing and being tortured, are pathetic (*kläglich*), illusory, opposed to real action, and both are identified with this occupation of writing. Kafka is occupied by torture for the reasons other torturers are: "to get the damned word out of the damned mouth" (214–15) ("*um aus dem verdammten Mund das verdammte Wort zu erfahren*" [290]). The dark letter in which the torture illustration was enclosed contains two paragraphs beyond the picture and its explication. The first assesses the remnants of the territorial bond between translator and writer: "you possess property [*Besitz*] here in Prague, no one is challenging that except the night, which is fighting for it, but it fights for everything. But what property! I'm not making it smaller than it really is—it's something so big, in fact, it could even eclipse a full moon up in your room. And you won't be afraid of so much dark? Dark without the warmth of darkness" (200–201). This dark picture of their common territory, "the narrow ground we share," is symptomatic of the September letters, indeed of the letters through the autumn of 1920 until the interruption of the correspondence in November. Just as Milena wrote of their future life together, of the promise of being together sooner than Kafka expected, the tangibility of their relationship seemed to evaporate in the correspondence. Losing her will mean losing even every illusion of territoriality, as Kafka writes; he will be Robinson Crusoe, even more so than Robinson himself, who at least had an island, where Kafka had surrendered even his name (September 5); his relative independence from Milena is established by the "boundlessness" of his dependency on her (*"eben weil die Abhängigkeit so über alle Grenzen geht"*); he is resigned to the "insurmountably high waves" of the "sea" between Prague and Vienna"; he is an animal she had drawn out into the open where it did not belong; with her he wasn't standing on solid ground (*"hatte keinen eigentlichen Boden unter mir"*), he had no idea how high he had been floating above the earth then. By November she had come to describe this darkness as an illness—all such illnesses, he replied, are "matters of faith (*"Glaubenstatsachen,"*), "anchorages" of needy humanity in "some maternal ground or other" (*"Verankerungen des in Not befindlichen Menschen in irgenwelchem mütterlichen Boden"*). Thus the narrow, shared ground of mediation is lost in the letters to this illness—a grounding he compares to what used to be religious communities, while such community was possible. The suffering subject is described here with an image of concentric circles, but they are no longer communal or shared territories. Milena sees but does not want to accept that his circle is humanly uninhabitable (*"im Umkreis um mich ist es unmöglich menschlich zu leben"*).

It is thus with no small degree of violence (even if "the tongue that wants to speak must be bitten through") that the correspondence must be cut off: letters are torn up, are sent back unopened, or lie about in their envelopes. The "decisive thing," Kafka concludes, has been "my increasing (letter by letter) inability to go beyond the letters," and "the *irresistibly strong voice, literally your voice* calling on me to be silent," followed by words stricken beyond recognition. In the final diagnosis, the letters are only symptoms of an incurable illness opposed to life but inseparable from Kafka's circle of living; they leave no space for rest or peace but "are pure anguish, *they are caused by incurable anguish and they cause incurable anguish.*" Moreover, Kafka says of this illness, the condition is worsening—and the descent of the letters from September through November would seem to confirm this—and how could it survive winter? In fact Milena would hear from Kafka no more that season, and Kafka clearly considered the correspondence ended. "You will speak with M.," he wrote Max Brod in May 1921, "I will never have that pleasure again. When you speak to her about me, speak as you would of the dead. I mean as far as my 'externality,' my 'extraterritoriality' is concerned."[97] This direct reference to extraterritoriality (*Exterritorialität*) was drawn from the Vienna writer Albert Ehrenstein, one of the few to recognize Kafka's importance in his own lifetime, who had first published the short piece "Ansichten eines Exterritorialen" ("Perspectives of an extraterritorial") years before.[98] "When I was with Ehrenstein recently," Kafka continues, "he said in effect that in M. life was reaching out a hand to me, and that I had the choice between life and death . . . " The mapping of territoriality onto life and its ascription to Milena struck Kafka as deeply true, but how, he pondered, could anyone think Kafka had any choice?

Indeed, Kafka's November letter to Milena was nearly the last, but at the end of March two years later there is another letter to Milena, this time using the formal *Sie* as he had early in Merano. He does not feel the need to apologize for his silence, since

> after all, you know how much I hate letters. All my misfortune in life [. . .] derives, one might say, from letters or from the possibility of writing letters. People have hardly ever deceived me, but letters always have, and as a matter of fact not those of other people, but my own. [. . .] The easy possibility of writing letters—from a purely theoretical point of view—must have brought wrack and ruin to the souls of the world. Writing letters is actually an intercourse with ghosts and by no means just with the ghost of the addressee but also with one's own ghost, which secretly evolves inside the letter one is writing or even in a whole series of letters, where one letter corroborates another and can refer to it as witness. How did people ever get the idea they could communicate with one another by letter! (223)[99]

And so, finally, the writing that is Kafka's affair with Milena and is "Milena," that is Kafka's existence, his prayer and his friendship, his gait and his faith—all these circular figures circle again around to "Prague," the city of ghosts. As the young Kisch uncannily mapped a Moldau wrapped around the city instead of feeding into and cleansing it, Kafka's letter circles in upon itself and surrenders even the intention to communicate, to mediate, to move forward. This circularity has a history, even as it can be found embodied in the figures of friendship and walking in the very first known Kafka correspondence, that with Oskar Pollak. Similarly, while the tension between writing and living was melodramatized in order to be collapsed in the letters to Felice Bauer, the correspondence with Milena works through this issue of correspondence with even more pained intensity; in the former he articulated the correspondence of writing and his life, living and prayer—but in the latter the prayer of writing was clearly now the "pure anguish" of "an incurable disease" that can only end in death.

There is no correspondence, in the sense of perfect resonance or unison, among the varied encounters with the question of translation of Prague Jewish authors in the early twentieth century. It does not even seem as though Otto Pick, Rudolf Fuchs, Max Brod, and Franz Kafka set out with anything like a common goal or interest as they engaged with the figure of translation, and yet, in striking contrast to the Czechs and the Bohemian Germans, they were irresistibly drawn to such an engagement. The translation project was certainly significant in European cultural history for its effects, but its impetus was never an ideology of "pluralism." Pluralism, it has been noted, has a liberal face but remains a hegemonic device to absorb and control difference. Rather than attempting to trace the humanistic impact of the Prague Jews' encounter with translation, I have chosen to see it and them as symptoms—recall that the symptom is always the failed repression, as psychoanalysis teaches—as strange, uncomfortable, or unwelcome embodiments of unresolved issues below the surface of Central European life. While all around them ranks were closing to demarcate territory and to seal boundaries that seemed too porous, these works and these writers represented themselves as the impossibility of such territorialization: as the mobile, ungraspable tension between identity and otherness, as the nonspace between self and other. As mediation.

Conclusion

Middle Europe

Das Glück begreifen, daß der Boden auf dem Du stehst,
nicht größer sein kann, als die zwei Füße ihn bedecken.

Grasp the joy that the ground on which you stand
cannot be any greater than your two feet cover.

Octavo Heft G, mid-November, 1917

This study began with the paradoxical claim that its subjects were at
once atypical and symptomatic of their period, and therefore of a special kind of interest. This tension between a radically idiosyncratic position and a more general, grounded or "healthy" condition is not trivial,
and more should be said about it. The question here remains how the
Prague circle's particularity and relevance—or, to pursue a metaphor,
its simultaneous peripherality and centrality—were of a piece. To begin
to answer that question, I would like to return to Hannah Arendt's reading of Kafka, which I mentioned in the preface. Arendt attends to the
way history is represented "territorially" in this passage from Kafka's
notebooks:

> He has two antagonists: the first presses him from behind, from the origin.
> The second blocks the road ahead. He gives battle to both. To be sure, the first
> supports him in his fight with the second, for he wants to push him forward,
> and in the same way the second supports him in his fight with the first, since
> he drives him back. But it is only theoretically so. For it is not only the two
> antagonists who are there, but he himself as well, and who really knows his
> intentions? His dream, though, is that some time in an unguarded moment—
> and this would require a night darker than any night has ever been yet—he
> will jump out of the fighting line and be promoted, on account of his experi-
> ence in fighting, to the position of umpire over his antagonists in their fight
> with each other.[1]

The passage promises to inform an inquiry into questions of placement and of history in its fusion of spatial and temporal imagery: past

and future are mapped onto threatening physical presences behind and ahead. But Kafka warns the reader not to neglect the inscrutable motives of the subject himself, for he is not merely an object of antagonistic forces, however hopeless his position appears. Hannah Arendt uses this passage to illustrate the exceptional moment in a dialectic between reflection and action, which, as she describes it,

> sometimes inserts itself into historical time when not only the later historians but the actors and witnesses, the living themselves, become aware of an interval in time which is altogether determined by things that are no longer and by things that are not yet.[2]

This "odd in-between period" ("[t]his small non-time-space in the very heart of time") is obviously for Arendt the most deeply philosophical moment, which simultaneously contains within it the revolutionary potential for political innovation. In Kafka she sees the bridge from the "abstract" to the "real," the "most advanced position," even where he seems to her to be out of season: he is useful in her text as a key to understanding the moment of potential rebirth after the catastrophe of two world wars.

If Arendt's assessment that such time-spaces contained "a moment of truth" seems from our contemporary perspective a bit sentimental, her analysis dovetails brilliantly with the recent privileging of "in-between spaces" constituted out of marginality. Just as the language of minority culture studies—the central critical importance of noncentered groups— is immediately resonant with the rhetoric of Prague circle self-images, Arendt's insights link this critical power to historical reflection and revolutionary change. The crisis of the subject in Kafka's notebook, the "he" oppressed by past and future, appeared to Arendt to have been so remarkably out of step because of "his" preoccupation with his own historicity; the self-consciousness of the subject's own out-of-placeness is precisely what places him as a symptom of the historical moment in which he so uncomfortably appears.

The German-speaking Jewish writers born in Prague between 1882 and 1892 stood apart from the generations before them, as well as from contemporary writers outside of their milieu. Signs of this difference were detectable in the earliest writings of the teenage Franz Kafka, Egon Kisch, and Felix Weltsch. These texts already betrayed the prescience of a nascent dilemma that these young Praguers identified as intensely personal, and at the same time analogous to a more general crisis, aesthetic as well as sociopolitical. By the pure force of unusual circumstance, the writers

were highly self-conscious of a discourse they were in the midst of, one
that posited the separation but mutual necessity of the figures of author,
text, and nation. It is clear by now why that constellation offered no
space to the German-speaking Jewish writers of Prague. Nevertheless,
their cultural innovations worked to enter that system and to carve out
a unique space for themselves via a radical reconfiguration of its terms.
For example, the aspect of mutual necessity of author, text, and nation
was clearly inherited from the Prague German-liberal rationale of self-
empowerment, and was shared with concurrent competing ideologies.
German nationalists like Philipp Knoll identified the unique status of
German culture in Prague and Bohemia as evidence of the disastrous effects of the inorganic constitution of a Czech nation. Oskar Ewald differentiated Slavic "talent" and "civilization" from the true "genius" of
German *Kultur* for the same reason: to argue that Central European culture could not survive if severed from its German roots. Precisely the
same metaphor was applied in 1916 by the Czech critic F. X. Šalda to
express the notion that there "is no Prague German literature," in spite
of the existence of Prague German writers: the blossom of true literature
cannot exist without the tree (of a nation); the tree cannot live without
roots in the soil (of a homeland).[3]

While Czech and German nationalists were engaged in hostile and yet
compatible rhetorical projects, Prague circle literature entered the rhetorical edifice and carried its terms to the limits of their logical consequences. In Kisch's reportage, in Bergmann's Zionist program, in the
translations of Pick and Fuchs, in the expressionist poetry of Werfel, and
in Kafka's letters, there is not a rejection of the laws of modern territoriality, but an acceptance of them in the extreme.[4] At the same time, the
radicalized rootlessness yielded by the most original of these cultural
products is the source of their power; the degree of that rootlessness is
what Deleuze and Guattari quantify as the coefficient of deterritorialization: what the Zionist Bergmann describes as a will to flight that is nested
within the longing for roots.

So much for the mutual necessity of culture, *Volk,* and self (or of text,
context, and authorial subject). These terms were further qualified by
their mutual discretion from one another. It is well known that the fin
de siècle was the most comfortable home of the assertions of the segregation of art known under the general heading "aestheticism." Where
Prague circle writers seemed to engage in aestheticist cultural practice,
they undermined it without mercy. The irresistible direction toward culture of all action within the circle of Prague German-Jewish life, the con-

sumption of the whole by this construct of "culture," causes us to rethink the formula suggested by Carl Schorske's representation of fin-de-siècle Vienna that I have called the "aestheticist hypothesis." Instead of the "retreat into culture" Schorske has made famous, the unselfconscious and absolute nature of the Prague circle's relationship to art demonstrates the will to unity within a new definition of art, rather than to segregation, and encourages the observer to take dead seriously Kafka's claim to be "made of literature." The fusion of spheres that are supposed to be separate resulted in a situation in which cultural activity necessarily and unpurposively contained within it all political expression: neither ascetic aestheticism nor politicized art, but instead, aestheticized life. A real understanding of this condition is obscured by a certain aestheticism of our own age—a coarser and more cynical variety that seems incapable of questioning the unqualified, eternal irrelevance of art to a radically materialized life. In this respect the state of things today surely exceeds the most pessimistic projections of Prague circle contemporaries Max Steiner, Karl Kraus, and Otto Weininger. The challenge in exploring the significance of Prague circle cultural production has been to find a linguistic strategy to destabilize the position inherited by both writer and reader, and, to paraphrase the comment by Rainer Nägele quoted in the introductory chapter, to bridge the gap between an irretractable present and an irrecoverable past. The particular difficulty arises because the specific past to be recovered, what can be called the Prague circle moment, is not only different from but violently opposed to present reality. It is not random chance that leads Homi Bhabha to describe the critic of nationalist narratives in this familiar language: Bhabha speaks of the "turning of boundaries and limits into the *in-between* spaces through which the meanings of cultural and political authority are negotiated." [5] Both the Prague circle project and this study of that project have represented attempts to occupy Bhabha's "narrative positions between cultures and nations, theories and texts, the political, the poetic and the painterly, the past and the present [. . .]" [6]

   While Jewish identity has been at issue in each of the preceding chapters, the compelling connection between that identity and what is going on in the life and work of the Prague circle is difficult to pin down. [7] Framed narrowly, one particular function of Jewish identity recurs in the diverse works explored in this book, and that function frequently appears to coincide with the authors' relationship to their Prague origins. For this generation, being Jewish and being Praguers were both associated with being "in the middle," with the function of mediation, and with either being between conflicting elements or hovering above them. This took most obvious form in the mediation between German and Czech cultures, but it also took form in more abstract oppositions that seemed to be of broader, even universal, consequence: East and West, antiquity and future, or ideality and materiality (in Werfel's terms, heaven and earth). The gendering of the dichotomy (it was gendered from the start, actually) was a central element in this process. The messianic synthesis of the indelible dichotomy was in different ways perceived to be Judaism itself, at least by the Zionists Bergmann (to whom Judaism was "the spiritual movement of our age,") and Brod (to whom Jewish nationalism was synonymous with the overcoming of nationalism).

Jewishness was inseparable from the aesthetic identities of the translation project. Interesting in this regard was the identification on the part of translators like Pick and Fuchs with the work they were translating, so that the translation role itself placed them between "German" and "Czech" identifications. The significance of this sort of alternation for Kafka is articulated, among other places, in the 1916 letter to Felice, in which he faces the contradiction of one review describing the *Metamorphosis* as "fundamentally German" with a Brod article lauding Kafka's "typically Jewish" stories. Again enlisting territorial metaphor, while at the same time exposing the peril of territory for the writer between identities, Kafka puzzles: "A difficult case. Am I a circus rider on 2 horses? Alas, I am no rider, but lie prostrate on the ground."[8]

Kafka was alone, on the ground or in the corner ("I have hardly anything in common with myself and should sit quietly in the corner . . . "), but he was not the only one to find himself between identities, without territory, and in need of radical alternatives. Such alternatives manifest themselves in Kisch's grounding of a genre between high and low art to synthesize German writer and Czech homeland; the alternatives take different form in Paul Kornfeld's expressionist manifesto, Hugo Bergmann's Zionism, and the innovative roles of translation probed by Fuchs, Pick, and Brod. The assertion of the commonality of a single Prague circle project forces an assessment of the success of the diverse initiatives of this generation of writers, or of what can be referred to more broadly as the Prague circle project. How would "success" be defined in this context? If these cultural products are not to be seen as lonesome voices of liberal reason destined to be drowned out, then how are they to be judged? Did they achieve redemptive moments of escape from territoriality as such; did they create radical alternatives, however untenable?

To revise a Marxian maxim somewhat ironically, the Prague circle could not get around nationality, and so it went straight through to come out the other side.[9] Its innovations did not combat German or Czech nationalisms per se, but rather sought escape from the encompassing system of terms within which they were slated for extinction. When I write that this escape route was not charted *around,* but rather *straight through,* a system of identity, ideology, and culture, I am already pointing toward the troubled status of this project, where collusion is found as often as subversion. If, in place of this entanglement, the Prague circle project is thought of in terms of a specific political program—for example, a self-conscious liberal ideological alternative vainly responding to a period of crisis—then there is not much to be gained from its study. I have argued against this position throughout. A parallel argument is suggested by Benedict Anderson, whose 1983 analysis of the phenomenon of nationalism has enjoyed revived attention with the enthusiastic revival of the phenomenon itself.[10] Anderson notes that the persistence and stubborn resiliency of nationalism imply that it may be less effectively understood alongside competing "self-consciously held political ideologies" than in terms of the "large cultural systems that preceded it, out of which—as well as against which—it came into being."

This locution, like the claim that one needed to set a course "straight through" territorial identity, suggests a dialectical structure that I have identified in many Prague circle cultural products ranging over Kornfeld's discourse on enclosure and exclusion, the play of art and politics in Werfel's essays, Bergmann's notion of Zionist "rooted flight," and the juxtaposition in Kafka's letters to Felice Bauer of writing and happiness, Zionism and the "much more important" thing that lies beyond it. In each of these cases and in others discussed in these chapters, such as the play of selves-and-others/bodies-and-texts in Kafka's correspondence with Milena Jesenská, the laws of territorial identity were meticulously engaged in ways that creatively opened a horizon beyond themselves. The constellations provided by these examples are provocatively comparable to what Benjamin obliquely and controversially described in his Arcades project (*Passagenwerk*) notes as "dialectical image," except that in these examples they are posited in spatial terms (territorialization and flight, self and other, here and there) rather than, as in Benjamin, in temporal or historical terms (the "been" and the "now"). The oppositions do not operate in a narrative sequence that moves dialogically forward, but offer a moment where difference and identity are more than mediated: they coincide in a momentary flash (*"blitzhaft zu einer Konstellation zusammentritt"*): what Benjamin has called "dialectics at a standstill."[11]

Benjamin's apparent paradoxes of the dialectical image and dialectics at a standstill—motion standing fast, or static history—resonate with the conflation that David Harvey has identified in *The Condition of Postmodernity* as "time-space compression."[12] Even as Harvey introduces this term to define what had in 1988 come to be called "postmodernity," in specific opposition to the modernity that preceded it, he recognizes the "affinity" of the postmodern with the Central European turn of the century on the one hand, and with the crisis leading up to the First World War on the other.[13] Harvey in turn is indebted to Henri Lefebvre, who was clear about the source of the crisis he was describing in *The Production of Space:*

> The fact is that around 1910 a certain space was shattered. It was the space of common sense, of knowledge (*savoir*), of social practice, of political power, a space thitherto enshrined in everyday discourse, just as in abstract thought, as the environment of and channel for communications [. . .] Such were the shocks and onslaughts suffered by this space that today it retains but a feeble pedagogical reality [. . .] This was truly a crucial moment.[14]

Another thinker identifying the fin de siècle as such a critical moment, closer to our temporal and geographical mark, was Robert Musil. In a stunning and unfinished essay called "The German as Symptom," Musil focused on the Central European crisis of this period to define the modern state of ideology.[15] Musil urged his would-be reader to look beyond the "veneer of decadence" surrounding the Central European fin de siècle and to "recall one fact above all": that this was a moment of futurity, of the will to make the world anew; it was "the last spiritual and intellectual movement of great vital force" in German-speaking Europe. The thing of real "significance" to be found there, he wrote in his unfinished notes for the essay, was "not an ideology but doubtless the beginnings of one."

Out of and simultaneously against the cultural system of territory emerged the Prague circle, for a moment. This is not to say that this generation was an important site of resistance to a territorial ideology that was yet to do its most horrific damage. More modest, and more consistent with the themes of the above chapters, would be to say that the creative works of the Prague circle constituted islands in the rift of a modern crisis, or projected bridges intended to span a declining world and a new one, which never materialized. If it had, those works would not seem to be speaking in a language of islands, bridges, and circles, but with other terms, which cannot be discerned, and which could not be deciphered from our vantage. There isn't any map.

Notes

CHAPTER 1. PRAGUE CIRCLES

1. Kafka to Oskar Pollak, 24 August 1902, *Briefe, 1902–1924,* ed. Max Brod (New York, 1958), 11; cf. the translation by Richard and Clara Winston in Franz Kafka, *Letters to Friends, Family, and Editors* (New York, 1977), 3. All translations in this manuscript are mine, except where an English edition is specifically cited.

2. J. P. Stern has coyly attributed this tendency to Kafka in one sentence, and in the next declared this to disqualify popular contextual explanations: "Kafka is one of those writers who cause us to revise our notions of the borders between the literary, the documentary and the autobiographical aspects of a work of literature, and by so doing creates his own context. His achievement owes little to the ambience of the German-speaking and largely Jewish writers of Prague." J. P. Stern, *The Heart of Europe: Essays on Literature and Ideology* (Oxford, 1992), 5. But it is precisely the movement toward the collapse of these borders that characterizes Prague German-language Jewish literature in Kafka's period.

3. The central texts in this regard are Gary B. Cohen, *The Politics of Ethnic Survival: Germans in Prague, 1861–1914* (Princeton, N.J., 1981), and Christoph Stölzl, *Kafkas böses Böhmen: Zur Sozialgeschichte eines Prager Juden* (Munich, 1975). Another very thorough work that has been useful despite its focus on different directions of Bohemian Jewry is Hillel J. Kieval, *The Making of Czech Jewry: National Conflict and Jewish Society in Bohemia, 1870–1918* (New York, 1988). Additional articles by these historians are listed in the bibliography and cited in chapters as appropriate. A comprehensive study of Czech-German interaction by Jan Křen, *Die Konfliktgemeinschaft: Tschechen und Deutsche, 1780–1918* (Munich, 1996), first published in *samizdat* in 1988 and recently translated into German, provides a thorough political-diplomatic background. Czech historian Jiří Kořalka has offered succinct insights into the nationality conflict

in this period in articles such as "Das Nationalitätenproblem in den böhmischen Ländern, 1848–1918," *Österreichische Osthefte* 5 (1963): 1–12. Before these works, the cultural historian of Prague in this period would have had to depend upon earlier studies such as Hermann Münch, *Böhmische Tragödie* (Braunschweig, 1949), Elizabeth Wiskemann, *Czechs and Germans* (New York, 1938), and R. W. Seton-Watson, *A History of the Czechs and Slovaks* (London, 1943), each of which is competent in its own way, and yet none of which, nor all taken together, suitably represent the overlap of social, economic, linguistic, religious, and cultural identities that make up the Prague "national" landscape in our period.

4. Cited in Pavel Eisner, *Franz Kafka and Prague* (New York, 1950), 92.

5. A brief burst of interest in Prague German-Jewish cultural history began with a rather simplified representation of the demographic breakdown and ethnic identity in Prague in the very early study by Pavel Eisner, *Franz Kafka and Prague,* and somewhat later in Hans Tramer, "Prague—City of Three Peoples," *Leo Baeck Institute Yearbook* [hereafter *LBI Yearbook*] 9 (1964): 305. These informal inquiries raised questions that remain at work here, but they also planted seeds of simplification and generalization that continue to bear fruit. The extraordinary complexity of issues of interpretation of available statistics has been fleshed out in more recent work such as Gary B. Cohen, "Jews in German Society: Prague, 1860–1914," *Central European History* 10 (March 1977): 28–54, as well as the books by Cohen and Kieval already cited.

6. Emancipation had begun in the 1840s, and by 1852 the Jewish ghetto was dismantled and the Prague Jews were equal under law—although practical emancipation and actual integration began some years later. See Ruth Kestenberg-Gladstein, *Neuere Geschichte der Juden in den böhmischen Ländern* (Tübingen, 1969). Cf. Michael Riff, "Jüdische Assimilation im böhmischen Vormärz," in *Juden im Vormärz und in der Revolution von 1848,* ed. Walter Grab and Julius Schoeps (Stuttgart, 1983), 58–82.

7. One should be careful not to hypostatize and oversimplify the positions of the "antiliberal" Bohemian Germans. The Association of the Bohemian Wood took by and large considerably more moderate positions than the free associations of industrialized western (centered at Eger) and northern (centered at Reichenberg) Bohemia; a political spectrum and ideological contest characterized the public sphere in each of these regions. Antisemitism was central to their programs and rhetoric in varying degrees, and elements of liberal policy (e.g., free education, anticlericalism, free market) were sometimes sustained even within the most radical programs. Nonetheless, even where nationalist programs in the periphery arguably emerge from liberal sources, as is most apparent in an organization like the Deutscher Schulverein, as Pieter Judson has shown, this evolution of liberalism was out of the view of Prague's "old-fashioned" German liberalism. A political culture in the broad sense, and an ideology in a still broader sense (i.e., a common language that went beyond partisan sympathies and specificities of program), set these regions against the German liberals of Prague, as was attested to in their rejections of Prague German leadership, as well as in the need for a separate student organ in Prague to accommodate

the influx of students from these regions (the *völkisch*-oriented student union Germania).

8. This artificially sustained image of German-liberal hegemony was even out of step with contemporary Bohemian German-liberal politics, whose leaders were not Jews, and who were constantly revising their platform and rhetoric so as not to alienate their support outside of Prague.

9. These conflicting layers of identity and their relation to issues of minority literature in another context are described with the image of the babushka doll by Arab Israeli author Anton Shammas. See "Ahmat Ha-Babushka" [The guilt of the babushka], *Politika* 5–6 (February-March 1986): 44–45, and "Al Galut V-Sifrut" [On exile and literature], *Igra* 2 (1989): 67–70. These works and the issues they raise are cited in a review article by Hannan Hever, "Hebrew in an Israeli Arab Hand: Six Miniatures on Anton Shammas's *Arabesques*," *Cultural Critique* 7 (fall 1987): 49. For an antidote to the tendency to oversimplify the structure of minority discourses, see the "methodological postscript" of Jeffrey Peck, *New German Critique*, no. 46 (winter 1989): 203–8.

10. James Clifford, *The Predicament of Culture: Twentieth-Century Ethnography, Literature, and Art* (Cambridge, 1988), 11, cited in Utz Riese, "Postmodern Culture: Symptom, Critique, or Solution to the Crisis of Modernity? An East German Perspective," *New German Critique*, no. 57 (fall 1992): 161.

11. Ibid.

12. While similar stories have been reported in various memoirs, these come from Otto Rosenfeld, "Prag, eine literarische Stadt," *Deutsche Zeitung Bohemia*, vol. 90, no. 320 (21 November 1917), morning edition, 3.

13. The question of the huge cultural contribution of such a small social group opened the decisive (if all too brief) exploration of the Prague context by Czech and East German scholars in the late 1960s: see Eduard Goldstücker, "Die Prager deutsche Literatur als historisches Phänomen," in *Weltfreunde: Konferenz über die Prager deutsche Literatur,* ed. Eduard Goldstücker (Prague, 1967), 26–27.

14. Rosenfeld, "Prag, eine literarische Stadt," 4.

15. This image of Prague, albeit without a critical exploration of its social meanings and origins, is eloquently presented in Angelo Maria Ripellino, *Praga magica* (Turin, 1973).

16. The very clear articulation of this position by literary critic Arne Novák in *Venkov* 12, no. 86, will be discussed at length in chapter 6.

17. Oskar Wiener, ed., *Deutsche Dichter aus Prag* (Leipzig, 1919), 6.

18. Carl E. Schorske, *Fin-de-Siècle Vienna: Politics and Culture* (New York, 1980).

19. Gustav Meyrink, "Prag: Eine optimistische Schilderung in vier Bildern von Gustav Meyrink," *März* 1, no. 4 (February 1907): 350–55.

20. Egon Erwin Kisch, Notizbuch II (1.1.1904–30.8.1904), uncatalogued material in E. E. Kisch papers, Památník Národního Písemnictví, Literární Archiv (Memorial for National Literature, Literary Archives), Prague-Strahov [hereafter PNP]. The original reads: "'Vergebliches Mittel' / Es fließt das Moldauwasser / In einem Kreise um Prag / Erscheint mir wie ein nasser, / Ein kalter

Kopfschmerzumschlag / Alle die Prager Geschöpfe / Ge[ge]n deren Krankheit
Symptom. / Doch fürcht ich den Schmerz ihrer Köpfe / Den heilt nicht der stol-
zeste Strom / Den heilt gewisslich kein nasser / Kein kalter Kopfschmerzumschlag. / Es fließt das Moldauwasser / Vergebens also um Prag."

21. Most explicit in Pieter M. Judson, "'Whether Race or Conviction Should
Be the Standard': National Identity and Liberal Politics in Nineteenth-Century
Austria," *Austrian History Yearbook* 22 (1991): 76–95; for the Jewish case see
esp. Wilma A. Iggers, "The Flexible National Identities of Bohemian Jewry,"
East Central Europe 7, no. 1 (1980): 39–48.

22. The tendency begins immediately with the intensification of the nationality conflict. An 1881 account, for instance, points to the 1409 coalition of Hus-
sites and feudal lords as the beginning of a Czech attack on Germans in Bohemia
leading directly to the contemporary crisis of the Charles University. Philipp
Knoll, *Vortrag über die Prager Universitätsfrage* (Vienna, 1881), 3 ff.

23. The manifesto of "Bohemism" may be Bernard Bolzano's *Über das Ver-
hältnis der beiden Volksstämme in Böhmen* (Vienna, 1849); the need for explication dispels the promise that this was an era of near nationlessness in Bohemia.
The ideology of Bohemism was one alternative among others, and seems to have
been limited to privileged layers of society; it had a distinctly aristocratic and religious character. Historians generally acknowledge the ideology of local patriotism along with the likelihood of national components to class and religious
struggles before 1848. See Wiskemann, *Czechs and Germans*, chap. 1; Gary B.
Cohen, "From Bohemians to Czechs and Germans," in Cohen, *Politics of Ethnic Survival*, 19–51; Hellmut Diwald, *Lebendiger Geist: Hans Joachim Schoeps
zum 50. Geburtstag* (Leiden, 1959), 91–115.

24. Gary Cohen points out that the call to relocate German-Bohemian educational and social welfare institutions out of Prague began in the 1880s but that
the movement took on this name in 1897, aiming to recenter to the northern city
of Reichenberg (Liberec). See Cohen, *Politics of Ethnic Survival*, 245.

25. E.g., Peter Horwath, "The Erosion of 'Gemeinschaft': German Writers
of Prague, 1890–1924," *German Studies Review* 4, no. 1 (February 1981). The
Bohemist utopia he imagines is taken from William M. Johnston, *The Austrian
Mind* (Berkeley, 1972), 276–79. Horwath has uncritically lifted many of his
anti-Czech platitudes directly from chauvinist German sources of the period,
and in doing so revealed the instrumentality of "local patriotism" for German
national power.

26. J. Kořalka, "Nationale und regionale Identität der Tschechen und der
Deutschen in den böhmischen Ländern," *brücken: Germanistisches Jahrbuch*
(1991/1992), Neue Folge 1:9–17.

27. In Meißner's 1848 autobiography, cited in Philipp Knoll, *Das Deutschthum in Böhmen* (Dresden, 1885), 3.

28. The most revisionist (and convincing) exposition of the conceptions of
nationality of the 1848 revolutionaries is in Pieter Judson, *Exclusive Revolutionaries: German-Liberal Politics and Rhetoric in the Austrian Empire* (Ann
Arbor, 1996), 49–68.

29. Ibid.

30. See Paul Samassa, *Der Völkerstreit im Habsburgerstaat* (Leipzig, 1910),

2–3; J. J. Boehm, "Wann ist Böhmisch eigentlich Tschechisch?" *Sudetenland* 26, no. 3 (1984): 195–201; see also the response of Adolf Fritsche, *Sudentenland* 27, no. 2 (1985): 126–27. Another strategy is offered by a German nationalist after the dissolution of Austria, who suggests that the etymology of the term (from the original name "Böheim") is yet another proof of the German place in the Czech lands. See Friedrich Bodenreuth, *Alle Wasser Böhmens fließen nach Deutschland* (Berlin, [c. 1938]), 9.

31. Fritz Mauthner, *Muttersprache und Vaterland* (Leipzig, 1920), 6–7.

32. Belonging to the hereditary lands of the Habsburg crown, Bohemia and Moravia, with upper and lower Austria, were considered the heart of the monarchy. The German areas of western and northern Bohemia in particular were the most heavily industrialized areas of the entire empire.

33. "Deutsche Fragen und das Deutsche Reich," *Prager Tagblatt* 33, no. 3 (3 January 1909), morning edition, 1–2.

34. The historiography of the Habsburg monarchy in this period appears somewhat schizophrenic with regard to liberalism. On the one hand, a special brand of the *Sonderweg* thesis argues that reactionary Austria-Hungary did not allow for the development of economic and social conditions that would put a bourgeoisie at the helm of a democratic political culture. On the other hand, there is the recognition of a permeating German-liberal culture against which emerging forces such as the "nationalities," the Christian socials, or the von Schönerer movement reacted. One can identify a master narrative of Austro-German liberalism's tragic history as beginning in the aftermath of the Josephine reforms, an early liberalism sometimes identified as courtly and bureaucratic, with a small bourgeois-democratic component that spearheads the 1848 initiative. After the failure of the 1848 revolution, liberalism is resuscitated with the rise of the *Verfassungspartei* in the 1860s, but is soon undermined by fractious interests and deprived of political power from the victory of Taaffe's conservative "iron ring" in 1879. Politically impotent from then on, "late liberalism" fades from the scene altogether by the second decade of the twentieth century. Clearly, this deceptive narrative is possible only by limiting one's view of liberal influence to electoral success. The landmark argument for taking German liberalism in Austria much more seriously is Harry Ritter, "Austro-German Liberalism and the Modern Liberal Tradition," *German Studies Review* 7, no. 2 (May 1984): 227–48. Ritter's important intervention remarkably situates this blind spot in the historiography within an analysis of contemporary ideological perspectives. The classic works attempting to cover the liberal tradition in the monarchy were Karl Eder, *Der Liberalismus in Altösterreich: Geisteshaltung, Politik und Kultur* (Vienna, 1955), and Georg Franz, *Liberalismus: Die deutschliberale Bewegung in der Habsburgischen Monarchie* (Munich, 1955). A more recent history of the liberal political history is Lothar Höbelt, *Kornblume und Kaiseradler: Die deutschfreiheitlichen Parteien Altösterreichs, 1882–1918* (Vienna, 1993). Höbelt captures the liberal cast of nineteenth-century nationalism, but focuses largely on political history. John Boyer's account of the political decline of the liberals in Vienna and its larger Habsburg context is relevant here; see John W. Boyer, *Political Radicalism in Late Imperial Vienna: Origins of the Christian Social Movement, 1848–1897* (Chicago, 1981), esp. 316–410. Pieter Judson's *Exclu-*

sive Revolutionaries has done the most to take on Ritter's challenge to think through a history of liberalism in sociocultural terms. For an expansion of these themes focused on the period of the 1848 revolution, along with the question of a liberal legacy of 1848, see also Pieter M. Judson, *Wien brennt! Die Revolution von 1848 und ihr liberales Erbe* (Vienna, 1998).

35. See, e.g., Judson, "Whether Race or Conviction"; Cohen, *Politics of Ethnic Survival;* Dan Segal, "Nationalism, Comparatively Speaking," *Journal of Historical Sociology* 1, no. 3 (September 1988): 301–21. The Judson article even suggests, provocatively, that late nineteenth-century Austrian conceptions of German ethnicity were inseparable from associations of middle-class liberal ideologies.

36. Thus one representative describes the avoidance of the erection of a Czecho-Slovak state in central Europe as the "life work" of his generation of German-liberal Bohemian politicians. This example illustrates the way in which the fiction of Habsburg supranational interest yielded to a defensive German national position in German-liberal discourse. See Ernst Freiherr von Plener, *Reden, 1873–1911* (Stuttgart, 1911), x.

37. Philipp Knoll, "Das Deutschthum in Prag und seine augenblickliche Lage" (lecture delivered to the German Club in Prague on 20 March 1883), *Beiträge zur heimischen Zeitgeschichte* (Prague), 1900, 169–70.

38. Knoll, *Das Deutschthum in Böhmen*, 7.

39. See, e.g., Hermann Bachmann, ed., *Deutsche Arbeit in Böhmen: Kulturbilder* (Berlin, 1900), and August Sauer, *Kulturpolitische Reden und Schriften* (Reichenberg, 1928). Sauer was the most influential professor of Germanics at the Charles University; Kafka's revulsion for the discipline of *Germanistik* ("may it fry in Hell," Kafka to Oskar Pollak, stamped 24 August 1902) is bound up at least in part with Sauer's predominance in German literary criticism in Prague, as Kafka's editors have noted.

40. The term "literary popes" is Brod's; see Max Brod, *Streitbares Leben: Autobiographie* (Munich, 1960), 200.

41. Prager Schulerhaltungs-Verein, *Prager Deutsche Worte: Individuelle Meinungsäußerungen deutschen* [sic] *Bewohner Prags über lokale Verhältnisse am Ende des 19. Jahrhunderts* (Prague, 1900).

42. An excellent memoir of the life of the German Theater in this period is Otto Pick, *Um das Deutsche Theater in Prag* (Prague, 1931). The author, himself an important Prague circle poet and translator, will be discussed at length in chapter 7.

43. Ottokar Stauf von der March, *Zum Kampf um die Erhaltung des Deutschtums* (Berlin, 1920). The essay quoted here was written in 1914.

44. One good source for the range and character of German student organizations in Prague in this period is a propaganda volume, Ortsrat Prag des Deutschen Volksrates für Böhmen, *Prag als Deutsche Hochschulstadt* (Prague, 1911). A rich (if incomplete) archive of Halle material is housed at the Charles University Archive, Prague. The contents of the archive and the Halle history have been summarized by the archivist Antonín Slavíček in a thesis for the Charles University, "Dějiny a archiv spolku Lese- und Redehalle der deutschen Studenten in Prag" (1973), partially published in the university archive's journal.

45. Kieval, *Making of Czech Jewry*, 77.

46. Carton B611, IIB28, Archiv Univerzity Karlovy (Charles University Archive), Prague [hereafter AUK]. See also plate 8: a postcard of a *völkisch* image of a man-in-the-mountain overlooking a bucolic landscape was pasted into the *Rapportbuch* with references to the battling ethnic presences in Prague and, indeed, in the Halle.

47. E.g., entries 25 November 1910—2 December 1910, Protokollbuch der Sektion für Literatur und Kunst (1910–1912), carton B605, AUK. The section records from the years of Brod and Kafka's direct activity are lost; however, Brod was involved in this particular conflict.

48. Brod, *Streitbares Leben*, 228.

49. The annual reports of the Halle demonstrate the participation in the Literary Section of Kafka and Brod along with Willy Haas, Emil Utitz, Hugo Bergmann, Franz Werfel, Oskar Pollak, and others, although these figures are not at all the founders, nor do they ever make up a majority of the participants in the section membership, as Brod in his memoir implies. See *54. Bericht der Lese- und Redehalle der deutschen Studenten in Prag über das Jahr 1902* (Prague, 1903) and the reports for the years following. The reports are collected in "Jahresberichte," carton B641, AUK.

50. Max Brod, *Der Prager Kreis* (Stuttgart, 1966), 9 ff.; Brod claims to be offering a more relaxed conception of what he claimed had been referred to as a "Prague School" ("Prager Schule"). Yet, the reference on which Brod bases this revision is certainly Kurt Krolop's seminal article "Ein Manifest der 'Prager Schule,'" *Philologica Pragensia* 7, no. 4 (1964). Krolop placed the term in quotation marks precisely to stress the lack of any prescriptive school or cohesive group and to lay the focus on generational cultural and social questions. The quotation marks around the term are significantly omitted from Brod's bibliographic reference to the article.

51. See, e.g., Paul Reimann, *Von Herder bis Kisch: Studien zur Geschichte der deutsch-österreich-tschechischen Literaturbeziehungen* (Berlin, 1961), 157, where a "loose circle of writers" led by Kisch and Fuchs opposes itself to German Bohemian chauvinism and the Habsburg state; references to the Fanta circle are in Felix Welsch, ed., *Dichter-Denker-Helfer: Max Brod zum 50. Geburtstag* (Mährisch-Ostrau, 1934), 103; see also the unpublished 1918 memoir on the Fanta circle by Felix Weltsch et al., "Nachrufe am Sarge von Frau Berta Fanta," M.E. 430, typescript in Leo Baeck Institute, New York [hereafter LBI]; Gertrude Urzidil, "Zur Quadratur des Prager Kreises," *Literatur und Kritik* 99 (October 1975): 528–36; H. G. Adler, "Die Dichtung der Prager Schule," in *Im Brennpunkt: Ein Österreich*, ed. Manfred Wagner (Vienna, 1976): 67–98; Hans Demetz, "Meine persönlichen Beziehungen und Erinnerungen an den Prager deutschen Dichterkreis," in Goldstücker, *Weltfreunde*, 141; the generational criterion is applied in Elemír Terray, "Einige Bemerkungen zu den 'Herder-Blättern' und der Prager Avantgarde," in Goldstücker, *Weltfreunde*, 147; the replication of Brod's definition of the membership of the Prague circle is apparent in Margarita Pazi, *Fünf Autoren des Prager Kreises* (Frankfurt am Main, 1978). The reification of the circle reaches its most absurd extreme in F. W. Carter, "Kafka's Prague," in *The World of Franz Kafka*, ed. J. P. Stern (New

York, 1980), 35: "In the 1880s a group of Prague German-Jewish authors founded a club known as the 'Prague circle' ('Der Prager Kreis'), which was later to achieve international recognition and included Kafka, Max Brod, Franz Werfel, Oskar Baum, Ludwig Winder, Leo Perutz, Egon Erwin Kisch, Otto Klepetár and Vilém Haas."

52. See chapter 6. On the dearth of literary activity by women among this very active generation of male writers, see Wilma Iggers's contribution to *Yale Companion to Jewish Writing and Thought in German Culture, 1096–1996,* ed. Sander Gilman and Jack Zipes (New Haven, 1997), 306–12. Czech and Czech-Jewish women, in contrast, had a considerable presence in the same period; cf. idem, *Women of Prague: Ethnic Diversity and Social Change from the Eighteenth Century to the Present* (Providence and Oxford, 1995).

53. Josef Körner, "Dichter und Dichtung aus dem deutschen Prag," *Donauland* 1, no. 7 (September 1917): 777–88.

54. Rudolf Illový in *Veřejné mínění* (16 November 1913), cited in Reimann, "Die Prager deutsche Literatur im Kampf um einen neuen Humanismus," in Goldstücker, *Weltfreunde,* 9. The writer had been a classmate of Kafka's.

55. Max Brod, "Prager Dichterschule?" *Der Friede* 2, no. 33 (6 September 1918): 160.

56. Norbert Frýd, "Die deutschen Dichter Prags: Vom Ende einer Insel," *Im Herzen Europas* 2, no. 3 (March 1959): 4–6.

57. Kafka, *Briefe,* 9: "Als ich Samstag mit Dir ging, da ist es mir klar geworden, was wir brauchen. Doch schreibe ich Dir erst heute, denn solche Dinge müssen liegen und sich ausstrecken." Cf. the translation of Richard and Clara Winston in Kafka, *Letters to Friends, Family, and Editors,* 1–7.

58. Kafka, *Briefe,* 9: "Wenn wir miteinander reden: die Worte sind hart, man geht über sie wie über schlechtes Pflaster. Die feinsten Dinge bekommen plumpe Füße und wir können nicht dafür. Wir sind einander fast im Wege, ich stoße mich an Dir und Du—ich wage nicht, und Du—. Wenn wir zu Dingen kommen, die nicht gerade Straßensteine oder 'Kunstwart' sind [. . .] werden wir plötzlich traurig und müde. Warst Du schon mit jemandem so müde wie mit mir?"

59. Most of the literature on Kafka and homosexuality tends to be psychologizing and not generally useful to my discussion. The exception, where the structure and effects of the homoerotics of Kafka's writing are elegantly explored within the fin-de-siècle cultural context, is Mark Anderson's article "Kafka, Homosexuality, and the Aesthetics of 'Male Culture,'" in *Gender and Politics in Austrian Fiction,* Austrian Studies, no. 7, ed. Ritchie Robertson and Edward Timms (Edinburgh, 1996), 79–99. Anderson's discussion of Kafka's fragment "Die Brücke" is particularly relevant.

60. Ibid., 10–11: "Wir reden drei Jahre miteinander, da unterscheidet man bei manchen Dingen nicht mehr das Mein und Dein. Ich könnte oft nicht sagen, was aus mir oder aus Dir ist, und Dir wird es vielleicht auch so gehn. Nun bin ich wunderbar froh, daß Du mit dem Mädchen umgehst.[. . .] Aber Du sprichst oft mit ihr, nicht nur des Sprechens wegen. Du gehst mit ihr irgendwo da oder dort oder in Rostok und ich sitze am Schreibtisch zu Hause. [. . .] Ich sitze am Schreibtisch zu Hause und gähne. Mir ist es schon so gegangen. Kämen wir

da nicht von einander los? Ist das nicht seltsam? Sind wir Feinde? Ich habe Dich sehr lieb."

61. It goes without saying that all of these dynamics are steeped in their contemporary sexist and heterosexist discourses (what are now called essentialist assumptions of gender, such as the association of woman with earthliness or her opposition to lofty art and thinking; the identification of homosexuality as pathology and its ellision with masturbation). The narrow path between scrupulous attention to the complicity of Kafka's texts with these discursive contexts and his self-conscious deployment of them has been forged in the latest wave of American Kafka research. See Mark M. Anderson, *Kafka's Clothes: Ornament and Aestheticism in the Habsburg* Fin-de-Siècle (Oxford, 1992), and Sander Gilman, *Franz Kafka: The Jewish Patient* (New York, 1995).

62. Kafka, *Briefe,* 13: "Warum schreibe ich Dir eigentlich das alles. Ich wußte ja vielleicht, daß das hoffnungslos war, wozu hätte man seine eigenen Füße. Warum schrieb ich Dirs? Damit Du weißt, wie ich zu dem Leben stehe, das da draußen über die Steine stolpert, wie die arme Postkutsche, die von Liboch nach Dauba humpelt. Du mußt eben Mitleid und Geduld haben mit Deinem Franz."

63. Postmarked 20 December 1902; ibid., 14–16.

64. Franz Kafka to Oskar Pollak, 21 December 1903, *Briefe,* 23: "Aber außerdem kann ich in der Fremde gar nicht schreiben. Alle Worte sind mir dann wild zerstreut und ich kann sie nicht in Sätze einfangen [...]"

65. Peter Sloterdijk, *Weltfremdheit* (Frankfurt am Main, 1993), 25.

66. Ibid., 25–26.

67. Kafka, *Briefe,* 16: "Sein Herz schmerzte ihn und er konnte es niemandem sagen. Aber kranke Fragen krochen ihm von den Beinen zur Seele hinauf.

Warum ist er zu mir gekommen? Weil ich lang bin? Nein, weil ich ... ?
Weine ich aus Mitleid mit mir oder mit ihm?
Hab ich ihn am Ende lieb oder haß ich ihn?
Schickt ihn mein Gott oder mein Teufel?
So drosselten den schamhaften Langen die Fragezeichen.
Wieder nahm er die Strümpfe vor. Fast bohrte er sich die Stricknadeln in die Augen.
Denn es war noch dunkler.

Also überleg es Dir bis zum Karneval.

Dein Franz

68. The intellectual historical work reflecting this absorption of textual analysis from the literary disciplines in the 1980s was sweepingly reviewed in the landmark article by John E. Toews, "Intellectual History after the Linguistic Turn: The Autonomy of Meaning and the Irreducibility of Experience," *American Historical Review* 92 (October 1987): 879–907. The revitalized and often sophisticated emphasis on historical, social, and political contexts within literary studies in the late 1980s and through the 1990s can be located in the range of work identified under the broad rubrics of the "new historicism" and "cultural studies."

69. Scott Spector, "Beyond the Aesthetic Garden: Politics and Culture on the Margins of *Fin-de-Siècle Vienna,*" *Journal of the History of Ideas* 34, no. 1 (October 1998): 691–710.

70. See Schorske, *Fin-de-Siècle Vienna*, xvii–xxix. Cf. Peter Novick, *That Noble Dream: The "Objectivity Question" and the American Historical Profession* (Cambridge, 1988); see also Carl E. Schorske, *Thinking with History: Explorations in the Passage to Modernism* (Princeton, N.J., 1998), 3–34. Even more significantly, one might add the extensive interpolation of subject positions and self-conscious reflection on authorial positionality in critical work in the fields of cultural studies, anthropology, and social theory.

71. See Michael S. Roth, "Performing History: Modernist Contextualism in Carl E. Schorske's *Fin-de-Siècle Vienna*," *American Historical Review*, 99 (June 1994), 729–45, reprinted in idem, *The Ironist's Cage: Memory, Trauma, and the Construction of History* (New York, 1995), 47–68.

72. Gilles Deleuze and Félix Guattari, *Kafka: Toward a Minor Literature*, trans. Dana Polan (Minneapolis, 1986).

73. Cf. "The Nature and Context of Minority Discourse," *Cultural Critique*, nos. 6 and 7 (spring/fall 1987), and *New German Critique*, no. 46 (winter 1989).

74. Stanley Corngold, "Kafka and the Dialect of Minor Literature," *College Literature* 21, no. 1 (February 1994): 89 and 93–94.

75. Kafka to Pollak, postmarked 24 August 1902, *Briefe*, 12.

76. Ibid.: "Weißt Du aber, was das Allerheiligste ist, das wir überhaupt von Goethe haben können, als Andenken . . . die Fußspuren seiner einsamen Gänge durch das Land . . . die wären es. Un nun kommt ein Witz, ein ganz vortrefflicher, bei dem der liebe Herrgott bitterlich weint und die Hölle ganz höllische Lachkrämpfe bekommt—das Allerheiligste eines Fremden können wir niemals haben, nur das eigene—das ist ein Witz, ein ganz vortrefflicher."

77. Křen, in a condensed and yet remarkably sensitive statement, argues that the isolation or territorial crisis (the word used in the German version of his book is "Aussonderung") of the Jews in the battle between Czechs and Germans resulted in their various forms of *flight:* to socialist internationalism, to supranational Habsburg Austrianism, to Zionism, or (he includes) to the "world" of Kafkaesque fantasy. See Křen, *Die Konfliktgemeinschaft*. Of course, the hypostatized image of flight provided here represents what I have just called artificial reterritorialization, rather than deterritorialization. But just as the very work Deleuze and Guattari examine can be packaged as reterritorialization, much of the work they dismiss could be brought into their analysis.

78. For some useful overviews of the impact of spatial analysis on social theory see Patricia Yaeger, "Introduction: Narrating Space," in *The Geography of Identity*, ed. Patricia Yaeger (Ann Arbor, 1996), 1–39; Doreen Massey, *Space, Place, and Gender* (Minneapolis, 1994), 1–16; Neil Smith and Cindi Katz, "Grounding Metaphor: Towards a Spatialized Politics," in *Place and the Politics of Identity*, ed. Michael Keith and Steve Pile (London, 1993), 67–83.

79. While Lefebvre's work on space was published in French in the 1970s, the 1991 English translation coincided with the massive turn to geography in social theory described here. See Henri Lefebvre, *The Production of Space*, trans. Donald Nicholson-Smith (Oxford, 1991). Neil Smith and Cindi Katz trace the spatial turn in theory back to Althusser and Foucault; see Smith and Katz, "Grounding Metaphor," 71–74.

80. See David Harvey, *The Condition of Postmodernity* (Oxford, 1990); also

Fredric Jameson, "Postmodernism, or the Cultural Logic of Late Capitalism," *New Left Review* 146 (1984): 53–92, and idem, *The Geopolitical Aesthetic: Cinema and Space in the World System* (Bloomington, Ind., 1992); Edward W. Soja, *Postmodern Geographies: The Reassertion of Space in Critical Social Theory* (London, 1989); Massey, *Space, Place, and Gender;* Neil Smith, *Uneven Development: Nature, Capital, and the Production of Space* (Oxford, 1984); J. Nicholas Entrikin, *The Betweenness of Place: Towards a Geography of Modernity* (Baltimore, 1991).

81. See esp. Jameson, "Space: Utopianism after the End of Utopia," in *Postmodernism; or, The Cultural Logic of Late Capitalism* (Durham, N.C., 1984).

82. Arjun Appadurai, "Sovereignty without Territoriality," in Yaeger, ed., *Geography of Identity,* 40–58.

83. The editors of the special number of *Cultural Anthropology* devoted to the theme "Space, Identity, and the Politics of Difference" are more cautious about identifying the ways in which the stasis and fixity implied by classical anthropology were always fictive; they do agree with Appadurai—with reason—that mobility, displacement, and a sense of deterritorialization mark the present age in particular. See Akhil Gupta and James Ferguson, "Beyond 'Culture': Space, Identity, and the Politics of Difference," *Cultural Anthropology* 7, no. 1 (February 1992): 6–22.

84. Walter Benn Michaels, "Race into Culture: A Critical Genealogy of Cultural Identity," in *Identities,* ed. Kwame Anthony Appiah and Henry Louis Gates, Jr. (Chicago, 1995), 32–62.

85. See Smith and Katz, "Grounding Metaphor"; Dick Hebdige, "Metaphors out of Control" in *Mapping the Futures: Local Cultures, Global Change,* ed. J. Bird (London, 1993); Massey, *Space, Place, and Gender,* 1–14; and Liz Bondi, "Locating Identity Politics," in *Place and the Politics of Identity,* 84–101. Gupta and Ferguson warn that the study of "culture" itself is complicit with dangerously hypostatized notions of identity; see Gupta and Ferguson, "Beyond 'Culture,'" 11–12.

86. Sara Suleri, *The Rhetoric of English India* (Chicago, 1992), 11, cited in Yaeger, "Narrating Space," 15.

87. The tendency is apparent in virtually all of the sources mentioned thus far; it approaches the status of major theme in popular works such as Jürgen Serke, *Böhmische Dörfer: Wanderungen durch eine verlassene literarische Landschaft* (Vienna, 1987). Most unexpected, however, is the clear articulation of a version of this liberal interpretation in the socialist historiography already mentioned, the work of the mid- to late 1960s by Reimann, Goldstücker, and Krolop.

88. See F. Jameson, *The Political Unconscious: Narrative as a Socially Symbolic Act* (Ithaca, N.Y., 1981), 35, and R. Nägele, introduction to *Benjamin's Ground: New Readings of Walter Benjamin* (Detroit, 1988), esp. 9.

CHAPTER 2. WHERE'S THE DIFFERENCE?

1. This self-perception of the Prague German-Jewish bourgeoisie is apparent in Felix Weltsch, "The Rise and Fall of the Jewish-German Symbiosis: The Case of Franz Kafka," *LBI Yearbook* 1 (1956): 257: "The leading lights [of Prague

German culture] were mainly Jews; the public was mainly Jewish and material support came to a decisive extent from Jewish manufacturers, merchants and bankers."

2. Ibid.

3. Stefan Zweig, *Die Welt von Gestern* (Stockholm, 1947).

4. See, for example, Christoph Stölzl, "Aus dem jüdischen Mittelstand der antisemitischen Epoche 1883–1924," in *Kafkas böses Böhmen* (Munich, 1975), 44–107.

5. Schorske, *Fin-de-Siècle Vienna,* 304. Cf. my discussion of Schorske in chapter 1 and in Spector, "Beyond the Aesthetic Garden."

6. See Edward W. Said, *Culture and Imperialism* (New York, 1993), xiii : "In time, culture comes to be associated, often aggressively, with the nation or the state; this differentiates 'us' from 'them,' almost always with some degree of xenophobia. Culture in this sense is a source of identity, and a rather combative one at that [. . .] culture is a sort of theater where various political and ideological causes engage one another."

7. The German Liberal Party (*Verfassungspartei*) recognized its symbiotic relation with the Jewish population, even as sociopolitical realities began to inhibit its abilities to speak out openly against antisemitism. See Ernst Plener, *Erinnerungen,* vol. 2 (Stuttgart, 1921); Cohen, *Politics of Ethnic Survival,* 82.

8. Brod, *Der Prager Kreis,* 40.

9. Fritz Mauthner, *Erinnerungen,* vol. 1, *Prager Jugendjahre* (Munich, 1918), esp. 49–53; see also my discussion in chapter 3.

10. Heinrich Weltsch's personal notebook, with the title page "Bunte Blätter: Gedichte von Heinrich Weltsch," as well as his collected birthday greetings and Merano travel diary, demonstrate the ease with which the German-speaking Jews of his generation could meld Jewish content into the lifestyle of the cultivated Prague German bourgeois. See esp. "Meiner lieben Großmutter zum 80. Geburtstage," 28 March 1877, 10. Of particular interest is "An die Liberalen," in "Aus meinem Meranoer Liederbuche" (Merano, February 1893), which closely identifies liberalism with Judaism, Judaism with its own long history, and their common enemy, antisemitism, as a fleeting phenomenon. Carton 1, Felix Weltsch Archives (Ms. Var. 418), Jewish National and University Library, Jerusalem [hereafter JNUL].

11. Emil Utitz, *Egon Erwin Kisch: Der klassische Journalist* (Berlin, 1956), 31.

12. Knoll, *Das Deutschthum in Böhmen,* 7–8. See also "Über das Deutschthum in Prag und seine augenblickliche Lage" and *Vortrag über die Prager Universitätsfrage.* The language of instruction at the Charles University was of course Latin, until 1784.

13. Or, in Pieter Judson's formulation, German cultural "quality" was pitted against sheer "quantity" of members of competing language groups. Judson, *Exclusive Revolutionaries,* 269.

14. Knoll, *Das Deutschthum in Böhmen,* 8.

15. Knoll, *Vortrag über die Prager Universitätsfrage,* 16.

16. See esp. Pieter Judson, "Inventing Germans: Class, Nationality, and Co-

lonial Fantasy at the Margins of the Hapsburg Monarchy," *Social Analysis* 33 (1993).

17. See Dr. Richard Batka, "Zum Geleite," *Deutsche Arbeit* 1, no. 1 (October 1901): 1: "Perhaps an organ for the cultural life of the Germans in Bohemia will have to explain why it is so late in coming [. . .]"

18. Advertisement appearing in various issues of *Bohemia;* see, e.g., 18 September 1912, morning edition, 11.

19. See Paul Reimann, "Die Prager deutsche Literatur im Kampf um einen neuen Humanismus," in Goldstücker, *Weltfreunde,* 10. The term *"welthistorisch"* is of course Hegelian. Reimann points out that certain German thinkers work against this notion, notably Herder and Goethe.

20. See Christoph Stölzl, "Zur Geschichte der böhmischen Juden in der Epoche des modernen Nationalismus," part 2, *Bohemia* 15 (Munich, 1974): 138–40; and Derek Sayer, *The Coasts of Bohemia* (Princeton, N.J., 1998), 141–47; cf. "Der Prozess Hanka gegen Kuh," and "Zwei Begräbnisse: Der Streit um die Königenhofer Handschrift," in E. E. Kisch, *Gesammelte Werke in Einzelausgaben* [hereafter *GW*], ed. Bodo Uhse and Gisela Kisch (Berlin, 1960–1993), 2:542–51, 9:114–18; and Paul Kisch, "Hanka fecit!," *Bohemia* 18 and 19 (September 1917); compare the novel of Fritz Mauthner, *Die böhmische Handschrift* (Constance, 1897).

21. The considerable complexity of Masaryk's role in the case is indicated in a document cited by Roman Szporluk. Masaryk's letter to Edward Albert of 29 September 1888 identifies in the conflict a battle over Czech national academic authority, with the modern, philosophical-scientific culture represented in Masaryk's position challenging the traditional authority of transparently ideological humanistic disciplines. The letter serves as an antidote to the generally accepted liberal reading of Masaryk's intervention, but also sheds light on the density of complexes of power and culture in Czech Prague. See Roman Szporluk, *The Political Thought of Tomáš G. Masaryk* (New York, 1981), 61.

22. See Oskar Ewald, "Talent und Genie," *Bohemia,* 20 September 1912, morning edition, 1–3.

23. "Deutsche Redeübung," Notizbuch 7. Klasse (1900), carton 1, Felix Weltsch Archives (Ms. Var. 418), JNUL.

24. Professor Heinrich Rietsch, in a lecture entitled "Musik und Volkstum," proposed the thesis that there are three stages in the development of a national music: first "naive folk singing," then "the use of folk themes in artistic music," and finally "artistic music standing on its own feet." The professor then explained that the Slavic peoples were currently in the second stage, the Germans, Italians, and French in the third. The Germans were supposed to have reached the second stage in the sixteenth century. See *Prager Tagblatt* 33 (1909), "Vorträge."

25. For this and below quotations, refer to "Das deutsche Volkslied," 1–22, Felix Weltsch Archives (Ms. Var. 418), JNUL.

26. "Unterschiede in der Bearbeitung eines Stoffes als Epos und als Drama, nachgewiesen am 'Nibelungenlied' und an Friedr. Hebbels Drama 'Die Nibelungen,'" "Deutsche Redeübung II," Notizbuch Klasse 8 (1901), carton 1, Felix Weltsch Archives (Ms. Var. 418), JNUL.

27. In chapters 5 and 6 I will discuss Zionism and other manifestations of Jewish nationalism among the Prague circle generation. Weltsch himself made his greatest contributions in the 1920s and after, exploring the reconciliation of Zionist and democratic ideals.

28. Felix Weltsch, "The German Folk Song," Felix Weltsch Archives: "*Ich revociere alles 1907*". Roger Chickering reminds me that the use of the Latin-root "revocieren" is not only awkward, but resists well-established German-national linguistic-political norms. See R. Chickering, "Language and the Social Foundations of Radical Nationalism in the Wilhelmine Era," in *1870/71– 1898/90: German Unifications and the Change of Literary Discourse*, ed. Walter Pape (Berlin, 1993), 61–78.

29. Richard Hamann and Jost Hermand, "Heimatkunst," in *Stilkunst um 1900* (Munich, 1973), 326–47.

30. E. E. Kisch, *Vom Blütenzweig der Jugend: Gedichte* (Dresden, 1904).

31. Notizbuch 1, dated 2 December 1903–1 January 1904, 26–28. Uncatalogued material in PNP, Prague-Strahov. For access to these notebooks, Kisch's student newspapers, and all other uncatalogued material from the Strahov archive cited in this chapter I express my gratitude to Dr. Josef Poláček. Cf. the text as printed in E. E. Kisch, *Vom Blütenzweig der Jugend: Gedichte* (Dresden, 1904), reprinted in *GW*, 12:17–18. Discussion and excerpts of various versions of the poem cited here have been printed by Dr. Poláček in *Philologica Pragensia* 8, no. 2 (1965): 243–44; Fritz Hofmann, *Egon Erwin Kisch: Der rasende Reporter: Biographie* (Berlin, 1988), 39; and J. Haasová-Nečasová, "Aus frühen Notizbüchern," in *Aufbau und Frieden* (Prague, 1958). The text from the notebooks follows, with textual modifications included in brackets:

> Aber wir? Wir haben Sänger
> Und wir haben eine Heimat;
> Aber fremd stehn diese beiden
> sich als Gegner schroff genüber.
> Uns're Dichter singen Lieder
> Von der Spanier Stiergefechte,
> Von Toreros, Matadoren,
> Von Italiens Glutenhimmel
> Und vergessen *ihres* Landes.
> Oder spotten sie der Heimat [des Volkes]
> Und des harten Böhmenvolkes [der Tschechen]
> statt zu sinnen ob dem Volke,
> Das in gleicher, steter Sphäre
> Auf genau demselben Kampfplatz
> Mit dem deutschen Volk hier wohnet
> Und trotz allem sich die Sitten,
> Sich die Laster und die Fehler
> Und die Schönheit ihrer Liebe
> Zu dem Vaterlande Böhmen
> Durch manch Säculum erhalten.
> Uns're Dichter sprechen feige:
> "Wir sind keine Chauvinisten
> Doch der Rassenkampf gebietet
> Daß wir von dem Volke [Heimat] schweigen,
> [Von der Heimat jenes Volkes]
> Das als Gegner wir betrachten."

> Und weil sie dies Volk nicht kennen,
> Kennen sie nicht seine Lieder,
> Seine Sagen, seine Mären
> Kurz: sie kennen nicht die Heimat.
> Arme Dichter! Das Gefühl des Mitleids
> Mischt sich eng in das, des Neides
> Mit den anderen Nationen,
> Die von der Heimat liebend singen.
> Ach könnt *ich* es! Könnt ich singen
> Von der hunderttürm'gen Heimat
> Von der Stammburg, den Palästen,
> Von den Schlössern, von den Sagen
> Von den Wällen und Basteien
> Tausendfachen Nachhall wecken
> [Wollt] Würd' ich mit den Heimatliedern
> Aber [ach!] aus jedem Verse
> Starrt der Ohnmacht grelle Fratze
> Schadenfreudig mir entgegen
> Das Gefühl des Neids, des Mitleids
> Und der Ohnmacht
> Läßt mich nur die Frage knirrchen [stammeln]:
> Land, wann wird dein Retter kommen?
> Und die Antwort kann ich stammeln:
> Wenn dein erster Sänger kommt!

32. In *Der freche Franz und andere Geschichten* (Berlin, 1906); reprinted in *Prager Kinder;* see *GW,* 2:260–67.

33. *Der freche Franz,* 118–19.

34. Robert Fantl, in the Prague monthly *Das Echo,* cited in Josef Poláček, "Der junge Kisch," part 2, *Philologica Pragensia* 9, no. 3 (1966): 247–48.

35. That this is not an isolated case is testified to by the comparable responses of German reviewers to Kisch's later novel *Der Mädchenhirt* and Brod's *Ein tschechisches Dienstmädchen* (see my discussion in chapter 6).

36. Cf. Poláček, "Der junge Kisch," part 2, 251.

37. Kisch Notizbuch 2 (1 January 1904–30 August 1904), uncatalogued material, Egon Erwin Kisch papers:

> *"Ich bin ein Ritter"*
> Ich bin ein Ritter stolz und hehr
> Mein Herz führ ich im Wappen
> Die Feder, die ist meine Wehr
> Die Verse meine Knappen.

38. Ibid.

39. Kisch is no less committed to the role of cultural savior in an essay on Lessing's *Laokoon,* when he imagines a future for himself "known as a literary, critical herald, famous . . . " See E. E. Kisch, "Zu Lessing's Laokoon," fourth notebook (1905–1906), uncatalogued material, E. E. Kisch papers, PNP. Published in part in Josef Poláček, *Literarní Archiv* 7 (1972).

40. In Brod's construction of a Prague circle, Kisch is peripheral at best, while in discussions of the Prague circle in secondary literature of the socialist countries he is predictably at its center. He was clearly in close association with Brod, the translators, and other figures at various times, and is included in the

first discussions of a new Prague German literary movement in the period under discussion.

41. Willy Haas compares the Prague circle agenda to the position of Stifter, "daß er nicht 'Deutsche' und 'Tschechen' kenne sondern nur 'Böhmen' und 'das Vaterland.'" See Haas, "Otto Pick: Ein Blatt des Gedenkens," *Stifter-Jahrbuch* 3 (1953): 67.

42. *GW*, 2:176.

43. In a letter to Mrs. Knopf, 24 March 1939, no. 926, Egon Erwin Kisch papers, Museum for Czech Literature, Prague. This letter is cited along with Kisch's Prague-set works as evidence of Kisch's "Heimatsbewußtsein" in Dieter Schlenstedt, *Egon Erwin Kisch: Leben und Werk* (Berlin, 1985), 17.

44. "Das prager Erbe," in *F. C. Weiskopf: Gesammelte Werke*, ed. Grete Weiskopf and Stephan Hermlin (Berlin, 1960), 8:304. The essay was written in 1945.

45. See Poláček, "Der junge Kisch," part 2. Egon's association with this sort of fraternity can be attributed in large part to the influence of his older brother Paul, the nationalist *Bohemia* editor who favored the inclusion of Bohemia in a *großdeutsch* empire. The elder Kisch studied in Vienna, and his own fraternity environment, useful for a contextualization of these issues, is described in an unpublished memoir essay by Walter Shostal, "Die Wiener Burschenherrlichkeit der Republik Österreich und A. H. Paul Kisch: Erinnerungen." The text was edited and distributed at the GDR Cultural Center in Prague's 1990 conference on Bohemian journals and newspapers by Josef Poláček; a copy is held in PNP.

46. The correspondence is found in the Kisch papers at PNP, and has been published in part in Josef Poláček, ed., *Briefe an den Bruder Paul und an die Mutter, 1905–1936* (Berlin, 1978). As early as 9 October 1907 we find Egon making light of Paul's "burschenschaftliche Ehre." By 6 May 1918, he teases Paul by collecting "for him" the most vulgar anti-Czech propaganda brochures.

47. Beyond the enthusiasm for Strobl in Kisch's correspondence, a review article in response to Strobl's later novel *Das Wirtshaus "Zum König Przemysl"* (Leipzig, 1913) articulates Kisch's position more clearly. There he claims that "the" Prague novel has yet to be written, but that Strobl has written "a" Prague novel, and a very good one. The centrality for Kisch of the fraternity life, "coleur" politics, national conflict among students, and the like is well represented in this essay. See "Ein Prager Roman," *Bohemia* 86, no. 64 (6 March 1913), morning edition, 1–2; reprinted in *GW*, 8:127–31.

48. Egon Erwin Kisch to Paul Kisch, 29 December 1910, papers of Friedrich Kisch, PNP. Printed in Josef Poláček, *Briefe,* 37–38. For a brief and complete survey of the discussions of the *Deutsche Hochschule* in the correspondence, see Poláček, *Briefe,* 427, n. 35.

49. Egon Erwin Kisch to Paul Kisch, 1 November 1910, papers of Friedrich Kisch, PNP, and cited in Poláček, *Briefe,* 35.

50. The attraction of the duel as subject matter is demonstrated by the contribution "Alt-Prager Mensurlokale" in *Deutsche Hochschule* 1, no. 8 (May 1911): 87–88. The piece was reprinted from an earlier *Bohemia* feuilleton and collected in *Aus Prager Gassen und Nächten;* see *GW,* 2:185–89; see also "Geographie der Mensuren," in *Die Abenteuer in Prag, GW,* 2:420–26. It is also the subject of one of Kisch's most well-known stories, "Niklas Kleisers Mensur"; see

Prager Kinder, in *GW,* 2:250–54. Both pieces stress the traditional, even ritual aspects of the *Mensur* (student duel). This aspect, and the necessarily underground nature of the activity, held particular appeal for Kisch.

51. Egon Erwin Kisch to Paul Kisch, 12 April 1911, papers of Friedrich Kisch, PNP; also in Poláček, *Briefe,* 45–46. The revisions were published both in the *Deutsche Hochschule* and *Aus Prager Gassen und Nächten* versions (see note above).

52. O. Scheuer, *Deutsche Hochschule* 2, no. 3 (December 1911): 33–34.

53. Egon Erwin Kisch to Paul Kisch, 12 April 1911, Friedrich Kisch papers, PNP. Printed in part in Poláček, *Briefe,* 45–46. The blurb was never published in *Deutsche Hochschule.*

54. F. C. Weiskopf feels that much of Kisch's work can be explained by his "literary relation with the group of international authors led by Émile Zola and Theodore Dreiser, who in contrast to their romantic and metaphysical colleagues sought to make a new art form out of the narration of facts: the reportage." F. C. Weiskopf, *Gesammelte Werke,* 303.

55. "Von den Balladen des blinden Methodius," in *Marktplatz der Sensationen* (Berlin, 1956), 8–9.

56. See *GW,* 2:529–41, 542–51; and *Marktplatz der Sensationen,* in *GW,* 8:7–18.

57. Kisch, *Marktplatz der Sensationen,* in *GW,* 8:29–30. I took some license with the verses, which read: "Hilsner, du arger Mann / Was hast im Brezinawald getan," and "Kaufet nicht beim Juden ein / Kaffee, Zucker, Möbel / Die Juden, sie erschlugen uns / Ein sehr junges Mädel."

58. See "Debut beim Mühlenfeuer," in *Nichts ist erregender als die Wahrheit: Reportagen aus vier Jahrzehnten,* ed. Walther Schmieding (Cologne, 1979), 1:19–20.

59. Kisch, *Die Abenteuer in Prag,* 34.

60. One critic defines the reporter's modes of representation according to a four-stage model, ascending from the invisibility of the reporter behind the factual report, through various degrees of presence as observer and narrator, to the final stage: "The reporter becomes the actual object of the reportage. He is the hero of the report, his research is the central theme." Jutta Jacobi, *Journalisten im literarischen Text* (Frankfurt am Main, 1989), 114.

61. See "Bären als Türhüter," *Bohemia,* 19 August 1917, morning edition, 3, and "Zu den zwei goldenen Bären," *Bohemia,* 2 September 1917, morning edition, 3–4.

62. In the first decade of the century, Brod was the object of admiration as well as envy on the part of Kisch and others, as in this response to an editor's insistence on shortening a Kisch feuilleton: "Do you think they would allow themselves to inflict such a barbarism on Max Brod [. . .]?" E. E. Kisch to Paul Kisch, Berlin, 25 January 1906, papers of E. E. Kisch.

63. The phrase was actually applied to Brod's work *Heidentum, Christentum, Judentum: Ein Bekenntnisbuch;* see Franz Rosenzweig, "Apologetisches Denken," *Der Jude* (1923), cited in Robert Weltsch, *Max Brod and His Age,* Leo Baeck Memorial Lecture no. 13 (New York, 1970), 3.

64. See esp. *Streitbares Leben* and *Der Prager Kreis.*

65. Robert Weltsch, *Max Brod and His Age*, 5.

66. See *Max Brod and His Age, Streitbares Leben, Der Prager Kreis,* and in particular the work of Margarita Pazi, including *Max Brod: Leben und Persönlichkeit* (Bonn, 1970).

67. Even in its most typical forms, it seems to me a distortion to think of aestheticism in terms of a true or even an intended disengagement from social and political life, or as Jonathan Loesberg defines this misrepresentation, "a vague synonym for imagining a realm of art entirely separate from social or historical effect and then advocating an escape into that 'unreal,' aesthetic universe," *Aestheticism and Deconstruction: Pater, Derrida, and De Man* (Princeton, N.J., 1991), 3–4. In this section it should become clear that the relationship of Brod's indifferentism to the Prague context is much more deliberate and *specific* than in any work that calls itself "aestheticist."

68. Cf. chapter 6.

69. Felix Weltsch, "Philosophie eines Dichters," in idem, *Dichter-Denker-Helfer.*

70. One case is William M. Johnston's leap from the Prague literati over the philosopher Bolzano and his German precursor Johann Friedrich Herbart to Leibniz; Leibnizian philosophy, therefore, is described as a "dominant tradition" in the Prague of our period, and the source of literary gnosticism in the Prague circle. Johnston's "Marcionist" thesis can be useful, as long as we recognize a gnostic tendency in philosophy and expressionist literature as parallel, contemporary symptoms of the Prague disease, rather than tracing the journey of a stable unit-idea. See William M. Johnston, "Prague as a Center of Austrian Expressionism versus Vienna as a Center of Impressionism," *Modern Austrian Literature* 6, no. 3/4 (1973): 178, and idem, "Marcionists at Prague," in *The Austrian Mind,* 265–73.

71. Schopenhauer was vogue among Prague circle youth (and further afield in this period), which did not mean he was read seriously. Some egregious emulations of Schopenhauer can be found in Prague circle ephemera, such as this aphorism from Kisch's notebooks: "Was wir wollen? Das wissen wir Menschen nicht. Aber das brauchen wir gar nicht zu wissen. Die Hauptsache ist, daß wir überhaupt wollen und der Wille zum Wollen ist allein für sich schon willenswert." Egon Erwin Kisch, Notizbuch 4 (begun 10 September 1905), uncatalogued material in Egon Erwin Kisch papers, PNP.

72. Max Brod, *Tod den Toten!* (Stuttgart, 1907), 173.

73. Thus I originally described indifferentism as "ethico-aesthetic." In sending a copy of *Tod den Toten!* to be reviewed in *Künstler und Kritiker,* Brod immodestly but characteristically asserts that he has tried in the work to "call attention to some problems of aesthetics and ethics that are unfolded there for the first time." Max Brod to Carl Busse, 9 August 1906, in Busse II, Staatsbibliothek preußischer Kulturbesitz, Berlin [hereafter STABI].

74. See *Schloß Nornepygge* (Berlin, 1908).

75. As in this notebook passage: "[S]o können wir es nicht verneinen, daß es eine Poesie geben soll—und vielleicht *nur* diese Poesie—eine Poesie die keines Mittel ist, eine Poesie die keine Verwendung kennt, eine Poesie die kein Zweck ist, eine Poesie die nur an und für sich besteht, eine Poesie die nichts weiter will

als einen schönen Augenblick, eine schöne Stimmung, eine schöne Scene, einen schönen Traum [...]" Notizbuch 3 (30 August 1904–8 September 1905), uncatalogued material, papers of E. E. Kisch, PNP.

76. Max Brod to Herwarth Walden, 18 December 1908; see Brod Bl. 5, Sturm-Archiv, STABI.

77. For example, the review of Felix Braun's poetry, "simple poems" capitalizing on nature imagery, whose "young aroma" leaves Brod "entzückt." *Prager Tagblatt* 33 (1909), Sunday supplement, 29. See also "Zufällige Konzerte," *Die neue Rundschau* 19, no. 3 (1908): 1086–88.

78. "Es wird gut sein, wenn man statt in biographischen und weltanschauungs-Zusammenhängen die Bedeutung Flauberts in dieser fünffachen Originalität erlernt [...]"; see "Flaubert," *Der Sturm* 1, no. 32 (1910): 253. The review is a concrete example of what Brod elsewhere more abstractly described as "technical criticism"; see Brod, "Technische Kritik," *Saturn* 2, no. 11 (November 1912): 239–41.

79. See the two letters from Alfred Kerr to Max Brod of 30 September 1911 and 1 November 1911, Alfred Kerr, Akademie der Künste, Berlin [hereafter AdK]; and Max Brod to Herwarth Walden, 1 March [1910], "Brod" in Sturm-Archiv, STABI.

80. Leppin: "Unser einziges Programm ist die Wahrung der Unabhängigkeit von Allem und Jedermann, von jeder Institution, jeder Richtung, jeder Person und jedem Vorurteile," *Wir: Deutsche Blätter für Künste* 1 (1906); Brod: "So wie wir nämlich überzeugt davon sind, daß die auf das überirdische hindeutende hymnische Kraft der Dichtkunst keines Nebenwerks und keines Parteiinteresses bedarf, um mit der ihr einwohnenden lauteren Hoheit für die Menschheit wirksam zu sein [...]," *Arkadia: Ein Jahrbuch für Dichtkunst* 1 (1913).

81. In 1907, at the peak of Brod's indifferentist period, he fashioned himself in this way in an autobiographical statement: "Ich bin am 27. Mai 1884 in Prag geboren. Ich habe bisher äußerlich nichts Bemerkenswertes erlebt. Es geht mir nicht schlecht. Ich habe einige gute Freunde. Heuer habe ich in Prag meine juristischen Studien beendet und gedenke jetzt, bei Gericht anzutreten." In "Brod," Brümmer 2, STABI.

82. Otto Zoff, "Indifferentismus in der Literatur (Max Brod)," *Die Grenzboten* 72, no. 22 (28 May 1913): 412.

83. Ibid., 413.

84. *Tod den Toten!*, 164–65.

85. Max Brod, *Ein tschechisches Dienstmädchen* (Berlin, 1909), 11. The allusion to the "shattering of windowpanes" is autobiographical: the windows of the German-Jewish quarter in the old city, where Kafka, Brod, and Kisch all lived, were those that were broken in the anti-German rioting of the late nineteenth century.

86. Max Brod, "Panorama," *Die neue Rundschau* 23, no. 2 (1912): 1342–44.

87. "Der Ordnungsliebende," *Die neue Rundschau* 19, no. 2 (1908): 782–83.

88. Else Lasker-Schüler, "Max Brod," *Der Sturm* 1, no. 40 (1911): 319.

89. Ibid., 320.

90. Max Brod, *Der Bräutigam* (Berlin, [1912]), 41.

91. Peter Demetz in Max Brod, *Der Prager Kreis* [Nachwort] (Frankfurt am Main, 1979), 246.

92. The term "erotic symbiosis" is Demetz's. For the mediating function of Prague circle literature and a discussion of the translation project, see chapter 7.

93. Heinz Politzer, "Der Lyriker," in Robert Weltsch, *Max Brod and His Age*, 35.

94. Mark M. Anderson, *Kafka's Clothes: Ornament and Aestheticism in the Habsburg* Fin de Siècle (New York, 1992).

95. F. Kafka, *Betrachtung*, cited in ibid., 37. Anderson's translation retains the strangeness of the original German.

96. An exception to this can be found in the collection *Der junge Kafka*, ed. G. Kurz (Frankfurt am Main, 1984). For Anderson's reading of the early work, including both *Betrachtung* and *Beschreibung eines Kampfes,* see "The Traffic of Clothes," in *Kafka's Clothes*, 19–49.

97. "In this sense the German-language literature of Prague was a model in vitro for contemporary literature *tout court:* as a voice of a threatened [. . .] minority [. . .] it was violently confronted with that problematic consciousness of language and its artificiality that lies at the base of the drama and the truth of modern writing." Claudio Magris, *Der unauffindbare Sinn* (Klagenfurt, 1978), 13.

CHAPTER 3. THE TERRITORY OF LANGUAGE

1. Kafka, *NSF,* 8: "Wie viel Worte in dem Buche stehn! Erinnern sollen sie! Als ob Worte erinnern könnten! Denn Worte sind schlechte Bergsteiger und schlechte Bergmänner. Sie holen nicht die Schätze von den Bergeshöhn und nicht die von den Bergestiefen."

2. The classic text exploring the relationship of Wittgenstein's thought to the Habsburg cultural and intellectual context is Allan Janik and Stephen Toulmin, *Wittgenstein's Vienna* (New York, 1973); see esp. 120–66 for the discussion of Habsburg philosophies of language.

3. Joseph Peter Stern, "Karl Kraus: Sprache und Moralität," in *Ornament und Askese im Zeitgeist des Wien der Jahrhundertwende,* ed. Alfred Pfabigan (Vienna, 1985), 168–77; see esp. 171.

4. "Dieses Interesse [für eine Psychologie der Sprache] war bei mir von frühester Jugend an sehr stark, ja, ich verstehe es gar nicht, wenn ein Jude, der in einer slawischen Gegend Österreichs geboren ist, zur Sprachforschung *nicht* gedrängt wird," and "[. . .] daß ich als Jude im zweisprachigen Böhmen wie 'prädestiniert' war [. . .] der Sprache meine Aufmerksamkeit zuzuwenden [. . .]" Mauthner, *Erinnerungen,* 32 and 50.

5. F. Kafka, *Tagebücher* [hereafter *TB*] (New York, 1990), 622. This passage and Kafka's relationship to Judaism will be discussed in more detail in later chapters. For a sampling of the identification in Kafka with Jewishness see, e.g., Ritchie Robertson, *Kafka: Judaism, Politics, and Literature* (New York, 1985); Giulano Baioni, *Kafka: Letteratura ed ebraismo* (Turin, 1984); Karl Erich Grö-

zinger, Stéphane Mosès, and Hans Dieter Zimmermann, eds., *Franz Kafka und das Judentum* (Frankfurt am Main, 1987); André Németh, *Kafka ou le mystère juif* (Paris, 1947); Evelyn Torton Beck, *Kafka and the Yiddish Theater: Its Impact on His Work* (Madison, 1971); Max Brod and Hans-Joachim Schoeps, *Im Streit um Kafka und das Judentum: Der Briefwechsel zwischen Max Brod und Hans-Joachim Schoeps,* ed. Julius H. Schoeps (Königstein, 1985).

6. This was at least technically the case, according to Alfred Fischel, ed., *Das Österreichische Sprachenrecht: Eine Quellensammlung* (Brünn, 1910), xciii–xcv.

7. See Cohen, *Politics of Ethnic Survival,* 48–49.

8. See Ernst Plener, *Erinnerungen* (Stuttgart, 1921), 2:191–211. The texts of the various language ordinances in the monarchy, beginning as early as 1527 and with a particular focus on Bohemia and Moravia, are collected in Fischel, *Das österreichische Sprachenrecht.* The volume also contains a lengthy introduction and index.

9. "Utraquismus: gemäßigte Richtung der Hussiten, die das Abendmahl in beiderlei Gestalt (Brot u. Wein) forderten [zu lat. *utraque* 'jede von beiden'],″ *Wahrig Deutsches Wörterbuch* (Gütersloh and Munich, 1991), 1347.

10. Plener, *Erinnerungen,* 2:186; and idem, *Eine Kreisordnung für Böhmen* (Vienna, 1900), 32.

11. See Plener's speech "Sprachenverordnung und nationale Abgrenzung" (15 December 1885), in Dr. Ernst Freiherr von Plener, *Reden, 1873–1911* (Stuttgart, 1911), 325–53, esp. 353; see also 303 and 365, and idem, *Erinnerungen,* 1:215.

12. Ernst Plener, "Antrag Wurmbrand über die Sprachenfrage" (28 August 1884), in *Reden,* 277.

13. See Cohen, *Politics of Ethnic Survival,* 88 (see nn. 4 and 5). Cohen also succinctly describes the ways in which, despite the government's attempts, the census figures immediately became identified with nationalist aims (89). For the Czech perspective on issues around the census category, see Jan Srb, *Obcovací řeč jako prostředek sesilující národní državu německou v zemích koruny české zvlášť a v Rakousku vůbec* [Everyday language as a means of strengthening the national position of Germans in Czech lands in particular and in Austria generally] (Prague, 1909). On the census issue see also Kieval, *Making of Czech Jewry,* 60–62.

14. "*in das wildfremde, fremdsprachige Reich. . . .* " Egon Erwin Kisch, *Der Mädchenhirt* (1914), in *GW,* 1:48.

15. See Plener, *Kreisordnung,* passim.

16. See, e.g., "Eine neue Sprachgrenzschule," *Bohemia,* 18 September 1912, morning edition, 5; cf. "Ein tschechischer Gewaltakt: Sperrung der deutschen Schule in Türnau," *Bohemia,* 24 September 1912, morning edition, 4–5.

17. In the above-cited article on the closing of a German school due to persecution by the populace, for example, the word "barbaric" is deployed, and the Czech protesters' actions ironically set against a reference to law and order in the Austrian "Kulturstaat."

18. See, e.g., *Bohemia,* 14 September 1912, morning edition, 4.

19. See esp. Pieter Judson, "'Not Another Square Foot!' German Liberalism and the Rhetoric of National Ownership in Nineteenth-Century Austria," *Austrian History Yearbook* 22 (1991): 83–88, 91–95; and idem, *Exclusive Revolutionaries*, 204, 215–17, 219. An excellent source for this discourse is the demographic analysis by Heinrich Rauchberg, *Der nationale Besitzstand in Böhmen* (Leipzig, 1905). In his preface, Rauchberg, a professor at the German university in Prague, explains the many uses of "nationaler Besitzstand," including the state of national representation within elected bodies, public offices, in schools, held property and business interests, and so on. Rauchberg's narrower definition is: "*als Besitz der Deutschen und der Tschechen in Böhmen an Land und Leuten,*" adding, "*Alles andere ergibt sich daraus*" (v–xi). Cf. idem, *Das Zahlenverhältnis der Deutschen und der Tschechen in Böhmen* (Munich, 1902 [?]).

20. *Bohemia,* 23 September 1912, midday edition, 1–2.

21. See, e.g., the appeal to combat the "Czech threat to the centuries-old" German community of Littau to the Lese- und Redehalle from the Moravian town's *Deutsches Haus*. Box 826, III C38 (7 February 1906), AUK.

22. Gary Cohen significantly chooses the street sign issue to set the stage for his study. See Cohen, *Politics of Ethnic Survival,* 3; also see 148–49, and 168. In the previously cited 1900 survey *Prager Deutsche Worte,* one pithy response to the question of what events or efforts had most effectively advanced the fortification of the Germans in Prague was: "Czech street signs."

23. See "Die Städtische Verwaltung geht im Kampfe gegen das Deutschtum voran," *Prager Tagblatt,* 9 January 1909, morning edition, 1. Cohen points out that concrete action such as withholding of administrative services to the German community or interference with the educational system would have been appealed and struck down by higher authorities. Cohen, *Politics of Ethnic Survival,* 148.

24. See, e.g., "Die Anarchie bei der Post" and "Der Postskandal und die Sprachenaktion," *Prager Tagblatt,* 17 January 1909, morning edition, 1–2, and this series of concerns: "Die Tschechisierung der Post," "Die Tschechisierung der Berghauptmannschaft," "Die Tschechisierung bei der Statthalterei," all in *Prager Tagblatt,* 15 January 1909, morning edition, 1–3.

25. "Sorgen der Prager Stadtväter," *Bohemia,* 21 September 1912, morning edition, 1.

26. Egon Erwin Kisch, who collected such things, noted this eighteenth-century description from *Auxilia Historica* (1724): "Es wird aber besser teutsch hierinnen als in vil andern teutschen Landen gesprochen: welches hob sonderlich dem Frauen-Zimmer auf der kleinen Seithen zu Prag zugelegt wird." Egon Erwin Kisch Notizbuch 5, uncatalogued material in PNP. Kisch cited the material in "Vom Kleinseitner Deutsch und vom Prager Schmock," in *GW,* 2:469.

27. Augustin Ritschel, "Das Prager Deutsch," *Phonetische Studien* 6, no. 2 (1893): 130.

28. Pavel Trost has offered a compelling parallel case in discussions of Baltic German, which in the early nineteenth century had been praised as free of "*bäuerliche Mundart*" and then described by Treitschke as "*eine verkümmerte Sprache ohne Lebenskraft*"; discussions of the 1920s and 1930s alluded to con-

tamination from Latvian and Estonian languages and an artificial appropriation of literary German. See Trost, "Prager Deutsch und Baltendeutsch," *Germanistica Pragensia* 5 [= *Acta Universitatis Carolinae, Philologica* 5], (1968): 17–20.

29. Ibid., 130.

30. Ibid., 129.

31. See, e.g., Jaromír Povejšil, "Ein Kennzeichen des Prager Deutsch," *Philologica Pragensia* 5, no. 4 (1962): 207–10. Much of what German phoneticists described as "Prager Deutsch" was no more than pronunciation typical of much of Austria or southern Germany. The term is also often conflated with the term *Kucheldeutsch*, the German spoken by native Czech speakers in their intercourse with Germans. The broad range of potential referents available to a critic of "Prager Deutsch" provides marking posts of the turf of interest to him, thereby leaving clear traces of his own agenda. This is as apparent in the above example of the linguist Ritschel as it is in the example of Kisch below.

32. Kisch, "Prager Deutsch," *Bohemia*, 14 October 1917, 3–4. The later version of the piece, entitled "Vom Kleinseitner Deutsch und vom Prager Schmock," was published in *Die Abenteuer in Prag;* see *GW*, 2:469–477.

33. Professor Reiniger, "Prager Deutsch," *Bohemia*, 16 October 1917, morning edition, 3.

34. Heinrich Teweles, "Prager Deutsch," *Bohemia*, 21 October 1917, morning edition, 3–4.

35. See esp. Peter Demetz, "Noch einmal: Prager Deutsch," *Literatur und Kritik* 1, no. 6 (September 1966): 58–59; Klaus Wagenbach, *Franz Kafka: Eine Biographie seiner Jugend* (Berne, 1958), 81–96; Hartmut Binder, *Kafka-Handbuch* (Stuttgart, 1979), 1:83–85; Rudolf Fischer, "August Schleicher und das Prager Deutsch," *Forschungen und Fortschritte* 36, no. 3 (1962): 87–90; Emil Skála, "Das Prager Deutsch," *Zeitschrift für deutsche Sprache* 22, no. 1/2 (1966): 84–91, and idem, in Goldstücker, *Weltfreunde,* 119–25; Viliam Schwanzer, "Störungen in der deutschen Sprachstruktur durch Isolation und Einwirkungen des Slawischen," *Zeitschrift für deutsche Philologie* 87 (1968): 86–96.

36. Mauthner, *Erinnerungen,* 51–52.

37. Ibid., 52–53.

38. Max Brod, *Der Prager Kreis* (Frankfurt am Main, 1966), 44. See also 45–47.

39. Bath-Hillel, "Mauthner der Jude," *Neue Jüdische Monatshefte* 3, no. 6 (25 December 1918): 136.

40. The title of Brod's contribution to Verein jüdischer Hochschüler Bar Kochba in Prag, *Vom Judentum: Ein Sammelbuch* (Leipzig, 1913), 261–63.

41. The terms are: "Die Fähigkeit zu großer dichterischer Gestaltung und zu naivem Gefühl [. . .]"; "heroische Kräfte," "volkstümliche Naivität"; "biblische Größe und ostjüdische Einfachheit." Ibid., 261.

42. "[. . .] da es nicht das Erbe seiner Ahnen ist, das er verwaltet, sondern fremder Besitz [. . .]"; ibid., 262.

43. Ibid.

44. See Max Brod, *Die Frau, die nicht enttäuscht* (Amsterdam, 1933), and idem, *Der Prager Kreis,* 67.

45. See Brod's review of Wolfenstein's *Die Freundschaft: Neue Gedichte* (Frankfurt am Main, 1917), *Selbstwehr* 12, no. 6 (8 February 1918).

46. This process, along with a deeper analysis of Bergmann's "cultural Zionism," is described in detail in chapter 5.

47. Quoted in "Zur Geschichte des Bar-Kochba" (third installment), ed. R. G. Pacovsky, *Zirkular* [newsletter of the *Iggud Vatikei Bar Kochva* (Association of Former Members of Bar Kochba), Tel Aviv], April 1967, 3.

48. In addition to the article in *Unsere Hoffnung,* cited at length below, see *Die Judenfrage und ihre Lösungsversuche* (Prague, 1903); "Jüdische Schulfragen," *Revue der israelitischen Kultusgemeinden in Böhmen* (October 1903); "Eine Bücherei für die jüdische Jugend," *Selbstwehr* 2, no. 2 (1908); and the reviews of Jewish literature in *Jüdische Volksstimme* 10, no. 9 (1907); *Die Welt* 11, no. 30, and 14, no. 49; and *Selbstwehr* 2, no. 2.

49. Hugo Bergmann, "Über die Bedeutung des Hebräischen für die jüdischen Studenten," *Unsere Hoffnung* 1, no. 3 (June 1904): 86.

50. Ibid., 87.

51. Hugo Bergmann, "Bialiks neue Lieder," *Die Welt* 14, no. 49 (9 December 1910): 1296–97.

52. For further detail see Baioni, *Kafka: Letteratura ed ebraismo,* 37–44.

53. See Hugo Bergmann, "Einiges über das Jüdische ('Jargon')," *Unsere Hoffnung* 1, no. 3 (1904): 85–88; "Reise nach Galizien," in *Tagebücher und Briefe von Schmuel Hugo Bergman,* ed. Miriam Sambursky (Königstein/Ts., 1985), 9–15; Beck, *Kafka and the Yiddish Theater*; Baioni, *Kafka: Letteratura ed ebraismo,* 37–62.

54. Abraham Kohane, "Wie haben die Juden des Prager Ghetto vor 150 Jahren jüdisch gesprochen?" *Selbstwehr* 11, no. 1 (5 January 1917): 4–5.

55. Ibid., 5.

56. *TB,* 57–59.

57. Mark M. Anderson, *Reading Kafka: Prague, Politics, and the* Fin de Siècle (New York, 1989), 11.

58. Franz Kafka, *Nachgelassene Schriften und Fragmente in der Fassung der Handschrift* [hereafter *NSF*], ed. Hans-Gerd Koch, Michael Müller, and Malcolm Paisley, vol. 2 (New York, 1992), 126.

59. The address was delivered on 18 February 1912. See "Einleitungsvortrag über Jargon," *NSF* 1:188–93. All English citations below are from Kaiser and Wilkins's translation, *Dearest Father: Stories and Other Writing* (New York, 1954), 381–86.

60. "Einleitungsvortrag," *NSF,* 1:188–189.

61. Sander L. Gilman, *Jewish Self-Hatred: Anti-Semitism and the Hidden Language of the Jews* (Baltimore, 1986), 138–48.

62. Heinrich Teweles, *Der Kampf um die Sprache: Linguistische Plaudereien* (Leipzig, 1884), 16.

63. Ibid., 54.

64. Mauthner, *Beiträge zur Kritik der Sprache,* 492, cited in Gilman, *Jewish Self-Hatred,* 232.

65. Kafka, *Briefe,* 336.

66. "Das Deutsch der Prager Literatur ist ein rissiges und verfolgtes Ausdrucksmittel [. . .]"; Claudio Magris, *Das unauffindbare Sinn,* 13.

67. Kafka, *Briefe,* 337–38.

68. Deleuze and Guattari, *Kafka,* 21.

69. Kafka, *Briefe,* 337.

70. Ibid.

CHAPTER 4. ENCIRCLING HUMANITY

1. Certainly the influence of the movement touched Pick, Fuchs, Baum, and Brod, and some of their work self-consciously aligns itself with the trend, despite the "Brodian maxim" that reads: "the less talented [one is], the more expressionist" (see *Der Prager Kreis,* 207). In any event, the broadening of the definition of a literary movement to include work of very different styles because of common "themes" such as "epistemological insecurity and the loss of metaphysical consolation" would render the category completely useless. Cf. Silvio Vietta, "Franz Kafka, Expressionism, and Reification," in *Passion and Rebellion: The Expressionist Heritage,* ed. Stephen Eric Bronner and Douglas Kellner (South Hadley, Mass., 1983), 201–16.

2. See Dieter Sudhoff, "Der Dichter des Tages oder Die Last der Welt: Über Leben und Werk von Franz Janowitz," in Klaus Amann and Armin A. Wallas, eds., *Expressionismus in Österreich: Die Literatur und die Künste* (Vienna, 1994): 253–74.

3. See, e.g., Adolf D. Klarmann, "Wesenszüge des österreichischen Früh-Expressionismus," *Modern Austrian Literature* 6, no. 3/4 (1973): 161–69; and William M. Johnston, "Prague as a Center of Austrian Expressionism versus Vienna as a Center of Impressionism," *Modern Austrian Literature* 6, no. 3/4 (1973): 176–81.

4. The authority was Kurt Pinthus, and the remark was reported by Walter H. Sokel in *The Writer in Extremis: Expressionism in Twentieth-Century German Literature* (Stanford, Calif., 1959). Kurt Krolop has located the moment of the reading in 1911, not 1910, as Pinthus was reported to have said.

5. Published in *Der Weltfreund: Gedichte* (Munich, 1911), 108–09; in *Herder-Blätter;* and in *Menschheitsdämmerung: Ein Dokument des Expressionismus,* ed. Kurt Pinthus (Berlin, 1920; reprint, 1959), 279.

6. Brod, *Streitbares Leben,* 12–65, and idem, *Der Prager Kreis,* 169–72.

7. The German text reads: "Ich weiß / [. . .] Das Gefühl von schüchternen Gouvernanten im fremden Familienkreis [. . .] So gehöre ich Dir und allen! / Wolle mir, bitte, nicht widerstehn! / O, könnte es einmal geschehn, / Daß wir uns, Bruder, in die Arme fallen!"

8. Werfel, *Der Weltfreund: Gedichte* (Munich, 1911), 20:

> Wo ist . . .
>
> Ich trage viel in mir.
> Vergangenheit früherer Leben,
> Verschüttete Gegenden,
> Mit leichten Spuren von Sternenstrahlen.

Oft bin ich nicht an der Oberfläche,
Hinabgetaucht in die fremdeigenen Gegenden bin ich.
Ich habe Heimweh.
O Reste, Überbleibsel! o vergangene Vergangenheit!
Wie nach der Kindheit Heimweh,
Wie nach dem hohen Kindersessel Heimweh.
Wie nach vergessenen Personen Heimweh.
Heimweh,
Wie nach verlorener Zärtlichkeit von Menschen,
Die mich kalt ansehn
Und nicht mehr in die Wangen kneifen.

9. Dr. Goldstücker is also the critic who considers most thoroughly the presence of Prague in these and later works, and who discusses (if briefly) the complexity of the feelings of the words "Heimweh" and "Fremdsein" in this context. See Goldstücker, "Franz Werfel, Prag, und Böhmen," in *Bild und Gedanke: Festschrift für Gerhart Baumann zum 60. Geburtstag,* ed. Gunter Schnitzler (Munich, 1980), 402–3.

10. The communal implication of the title was apparently also conceived to contrast to a title of the previous generation of Young Prague aestheticists, Hadwiger's *Ich bin* of 1903. See Kurt Krolop, "Ein Manifest der 'Prager Schule,'" *Philologica Pragensia* 7, no. 4 (1964).

11. *Einander: Oden-Lieder-Gestalten,* 3d unabridged ed. (Leipzig, 1917), 53.

12. Ibid., 60.

13. "Das Fremdsein ist mein Handwerk," according to Adolf Klarmann, *Franz Werfel: Das lyrische Werk* (Munich, 1975), and cited in Goldstücker, "Franz Werfel, Prag, und Böhmen," 402.

14. Werfel, "Nachwort zur ersten Auflage" (written 1913), in *Wir sind: Neue Gedichte,* 3d ed. (Leipzig, 1917), 125.

15. Ibid.: "Das Buch 'Wir Sind' ist das erste in der Steigerung von Büchern, die einmal, als ein Werk, den Titel 'Das Paradies' tragen sollen."

16. Cf. the dichotomy of "Erde" and "Welt" in Martin Heidegger, *Der Ursprung des Kunstwerks* (reprint, Stuttgart, 1967).

17. Julius Bab, "Franz Werfel," *März* 3 (1916): 164–70; emphasis added.

18. Franz Werfel, "Wenn die Russen tanzen, wenn Battistini singt," first published in Adolf D. Klarmann, ed., *Zwischen Oben und Unten: Prosa—Tagebücher—Aphorismen—Literarische Nachträge* (Munich, 1975), 199–200.

19. One attempt to revive the study of Kornfeld's dramas in light of his theoretical essays is represented by Karl Ludwig Schneider, "La théorie du drame expressioniste et sa mise en oeuvre chez Paul Kornfeld," in *L'expressionnisme dans le théâtre européen,* ed. Denis Bablet and Jean Jacquot (Paris, 1971), 111–18. The essay unfortunately focuses rather superficially on thematic similarities, rather than relating the structure of Kornfeld's dramatic theory and expressionist vision to his plays.

20. "Gerechtigkeit: Ein Fragment," *Die Erhebung: Jahrbuch für neue Dichtung und Wertung* 2 (1920), 313. The fragment continues to p. 319. Reprinted in Paul Kornfeld, *Revolution mit Flötenmusik und andere kritische Prosa, 1916–1932* (Heidelberg, 1977), 60–64.

21. Paul Kornfeld, "Gedichte in Prosa: I. Gebet, II. Gebet um Wunder," *Berliner Börsen-Courier*, no. 603 (25 December 1920). Located in Paul Kornfeld Collection, AdK, sig. Pz.

22. Paul Kornfeld, *Legende* (Berlin, 1917), see esp. 23, 66–7, 96 ff.

23. Paul Kornfeld, "Gespräch am Abend," in *Das jüdische Prag: Eine Sammelschrift* (Prague, 1917), 33–34.

24. Indeed, the place of that metaphor in a collective political unconscious of revolt has been the object of a well-known recent study of the French Revolution. See Lynn Hunt, *The Family Romance of the French Revolution* (Berkeley, 1992).

25. A symptomatic problem is inherent in Adolf Klarmann's comment comparing the father-son conflict in Austria to Germany, concluding that the former was "not nearly as crude as in the empire; patricides occur [. . .] sooner in desirous dreams than in deeds." Klarmann, "Wesenszüge des österreichischen Früh-Expressionismus," 164. Again, the distinction between (internal) dream and (external) deed is what the Prague sons sought to "kill"; the primacy of the spiritual (dream) over the material (deed) is at the center of the revolutionary process.

26. "Kornfeld. Verschiedenes. Autobiographisches. Tagebuch 11.12.1905—24.10.1906," Sig. 73.416, Deutsches Literaturarchiv—Schiller-Nationalmuseum, Marbach am Neckar [hereafter DLSN]. See esp. the entries dated 16.12.05, 10.2.06, 15.2.06, 8.8.06, and 26.9.06.

27. Ibid.; see esp. 4.12.06 and 20.7.07.

28. See, e.g., Peter Gay, "The Revolt of the Son: Expressionist Years," in *Weimar Culture: The Outsider as Insider* (New York, 1968), and Mary Gluck, "Liberal Fathers, Postliberal Children," in *Georg Lukács and His Generation, 1900–1918* (Cambridge, Mass., 1985), 76–105.

29. Ibid., p. 76.

30. Max Brod, *Franz Kafka: A Biography*, trans. G. Humphreys Roberts (New York, 1947); see p. 78 n.

31. Ibid., 92.

32. The Prague expressionist poet and translator Otto Pick wrote a four-page recommendation of the novel to a publisher, introducing the author as "a Viennese friend." See Nachlaß A. Juncker, Nr. 153, dated 21 November 1911, STABI.

33. Ernst Weiß to Martin Buber, 5 July 1912, Martin Buber Archives, JNUL, cited in Margarita Pazi, "Franz Werfel und Ernst Weiß," *Modern Austrian Literature* 6, no. 3/4 (1973): 55.

34. "Wie wir einst in grenzenlosem Lieben / Späße der Unendlichkeit getrieben [. . .]. "Vater und Sohn," in *Wir sind* (Leipzig, 1914), 31; *Herder-Blätter*, February 1912, 8–9; and *Menschheitsdämmerung*, 281–82.

35. See Gilman, *Franz Kafka: The Jewish Patient*, 32, 159, and 182.

36. Deleuze and Guattari, *Kafka*, 17.

37. All quotations from the text are my translations and are taken from the critical edition edited by Jost Schillemeit (= *NSF* 2:143–217).

38. "Elf Söhne," in *Das Franz Kafka Buch* (Frankfurt am Main, 1983), 243.

39. Jürgen Serke, *Böhmische Dörfer: Wanderungen durch eine verlassene literarische Landschaft* (Vienna, 1987).

40. Kornfeld, *Die Verführung* (Berlin, 1918), reprinted in *Zeit und Theater, 1913–1925,* ed. Günther Rühle, vol. 1, *Vom Kaiserreich zur Republik* (Frankfurt am Main, 1980), 247.

41. Ibid., 256.

42. Ibid., 268.

43. Paul Kornfeld, "Theater in Frankfurt," *Das junge Deutschland* 1, no. 6 (1918): 202. Reprinted in *Revolution mit Flötenmusik,* 56.

44. *Die Flöte: Dramaturgische Blätter des Herzoglich Sächsisches Hoftheaters Colburg-Gotha* 1, no. 3 (June 1918): 44–45. The essay had first been printed as an afterword to the publication of *Die Verführung.*

45. Paul Kornfeld, "Der beseelte und der psychologische Mensch: Kunst, Theater, und Anderes," *Das junge Deutschland* 1, no. 1 (January 1918): 1–13. Segments of the essay, besides the already-noted *Verführung* afterword of 1916, appeared in *Der Anbruch* (1918) and *Die Dichtung* (1920). References below are to the pagination of the abridged but most accessible version in *Revolution mit Flötenmusik,* 31–45.

46. *Revolution mit Flötenmusik,* 31.

47. Ibid., 32.

48. Ibid., 32.

49. Ibid., 37.

50. Margarita Pazi, " 'Smither kauft Europa': Über eine unbekannte Komödie Paul Kornfelds," *Orbis Litterarum* (Copenhagen) 29 (1974): 133–59.

51. Hermann Grab, "Die Schönheit häßlicher Bilder," in *Dichter-Denker-Helfer: Max Brod zum 50. Geburtstag,* 28–31. The younger Grab is described by Brod in turn as the last of the Prague circle; see *Der Prager Kreis,* 233–40.

52. Brod, "Die Wallfahrt zu Orazio," *Der Sturm* 2, no. 42 (1911): 333–34.

53. As in the essay "Technische Kritik," *Saturn* 2, no. 11 (November 1912): 239–41, cited in chapter 2.

54. Indeed, the document can be seen as an emblem of that movement. See Manon Maren-Grisebach, "Kornfelds Manifest als Programmschrift des Expressionismus," in Kornfeld, *Revolution mit Flötenmusik,* 45. Maren-Grisebach, the most prominent Kornfeld scholar, also identifies the text as proceeding from Kierkegaardian thought, similarly manifest. Relating the dualism further back to Pietism, the Christian tradition, and eventually to Platonic-idealist thinking, while comprehensible, certainly does little to enhance the essay, while decontextualizing it completely.

55. Sokel, *The Writer in Extremis,* 52 and 53.

56. Ibid., 52.

57. See Martin Heidegger, *Sein und Zeit* (Tübingen, 1967); trans. John Macquarrie and Edward Robinson, *Being and Time* (New York, 1962).

58. "The Origin of the Work of Art" (1934), in translation in Martin Heidegger, *Poetry, Language, Thought* (New York, 1971). Cf. Paul Kornfeld, "Letzter Sinn der Kunst," *Zimmertheater Heidelberg Programmheft* 3 (1980–1981), in Paul Kornfeld Collection, AdK.

59. *Prager Tagblatt* 39, no. 105 (18 April 1914): 6. The article, with its important implications for Prague expressionist studies, was forgotten until its re-

printing in Kurt Krolop, "Ein Manifest der 'Prager Schule,'" *Philologica Pragensia* 4 (1964): 329–36.

60. In the lecture "L'ordre du discours," printed in German in Wolfgang Lepenies and Henning Ritter, eds., *Die Ordnung des Diskurses* (Munich, 1974), 8; emphasis added.

61. Steiner is mentioned in passing in Brod, *Der Prager Kreis*, 39, and given more importance in an equally fleeting way in Hans Demetz, "Meine persönliche Beziehungen und Erinnerungen an den Prager Kreis," in Goldstücker, *Weltfreunde*.

62. Max Steiner, *Die Rückständigkeit des modernen Freidenkertums: Eine kritische Untersuchung* (Berlin, 1905), 6.

63. Ibid., 122–23.

64. Ibid., 124.

65. See Tagebuch 11.12.1905—24.10.1906, Sig. 73.416, in "Kornfeld. Verschiedenes. Autobiographisches," entry for 19 August 1907, DLSN: "There are few women [*Weiber*] left today; they all complain about feelings and in a way they do not even have any, either as a result of decadence or because they have quasi-weaned themselves from them. Since they are not women, they want to be men. They want to study [. . .], and so on. That would be fine, if it did not take place at the cost of femininity. The more industrious the girls are in their studies, the less they are women and the more like feminine men. In other words, a girl that [. . .] does not have feminine feelings is something horrible, is something unnatural, is something lifeless—."

66. Brod, "Die Wallfahrt zu Orazio," 334.

67. Ibid., 333–34.

68. See the analysis of Gunter E. Grimm, "Ein hartnäckiger Wanderer: Zur Rolle des Judentums im Werk Franz Werfels," in *Im Zeichen Hiobs: Jüdische Schriftsteller und deutsche Literatur im 20. Jahrhundert*, ed. Gunter E. Grimm and Hans-Peter Bayerdörfer Königstein/Ts., 1985), 261. Grimm's references are to Werfel's writings in Klarmann, *Zwischen Oben und Unten*, 674–76.

69. "Fragment gegen das Männer Geschlecht," *Der Friede* 2, no. 48–49 (23 December 1918), reprinted in Klarmann, *Zwischen Oben und Unten*, 205–10.

70. Slavoj Žižek, *Metastases of Enjoyment: Six Essays on Woman and Causality* (London, 1994).

71. Diary entry from 28 July 1918, ibid., 637, translated and cited in Lionel B. Steiman, *Franz Werfel: The Faith of an Exile: From Prague to Beverly Hills* (Waterloo, Ontario, 1985), 40–41.

72. See chapter 2.

73. Franz Werfel, "Der Besuch aus dem Elysium," *Herder-Blätter* 1, no. 3 (May 1912; facsimile reprint, Hamburg, 1962): 6.

74. *Die Verführung;* see esp. p. 284.

75. See Rudolf Fuchs, *Der Meteor: Gedichte* (Heidelberg, 1913); see, e.g., "Bahnfahrt."

76. Franz Janowitz, "Weltverwandtschaft," *Herder-Blätter* 1, no. 1 (April 1911; facsimile reprint, Hamburg, 1962): 30.

77. See chapters 6 and 7.

78. There is by now an impressive bibliography on the twin phenomena of destabilization and powerful entrenchment of gender paradigms in central Europe around World War I, but the single work that must be mentioned is Klaus Theweleit's classic study of the Freikorps, *Männerphantasien* (2 vols. [Reinbek bei Hamburg, 1980]).

79. Franz Werfel, "Aphorismus zu diesem Jahr," *Die Aktion* 4 (1914): 902–5. Citations are from the longer manuscript reprinted in Klarmann, *Zwischen Oben und Unten*, 792–96.

80. Franz Werfel, "Warum haben Sie Prag verlassen?" *Prager Tagblatt* (4 June 1922), reprinted in Klarmann, *Zwischen Oben und Unten*, 592, and in Kurt Krolop, "Hinweis aus eine verschollene Rundfrage, 'Warum haben Sie Prag verlassen?'" *Germanistica Pragensis* 4 (1966): 47–62.

81. See Oskar Baum, Ms. Var. 350, Martin Buber Archives, item 80.34, JNUL. Cf. Thomas Mann, *Betrachtungen eines Unpolitischen* (Frankfurt am Main, 1983).

82. Werfel-Spirk Correspondence, no. 59, DLSN.

83. Ibid., letter dated 30 June [1916].

84. Ibid., letter dated 21 October 1916.

85. Franz Werfel, "Brief an einen Staatsman," in *Das Ziel: Aufrufe zum tätigen Geist*, ed. Kurt Hiller (Munich, 1916), 91–98; reprinted in Klarmann, *Zwischen Oben und Unten*, 210–15.

86. Franz Werfel, "Ex abrupto," *Die Aktion* 6, no. 43/44 (28 October 1916), reprinted in Klarmann, *Zwischen Oben und Unten*, 796–97. Here once again we can identify a metaphysics that claims status as a model for a general crisis of humanity, and yet also maps onto the particular condition of the writer (the negotiation of being and expression through the medium of language), as well as the even more particular, and language-bound, misery of Prague. Thus in 1916, having left Prague two years before the war began, Werfel reflects on the problem of mediation and the fissure between being and expression as "the origin [*Urgrund*] of a terrible and enduring condition: that of mistrust."

87. "Der Staat und das andere," Werfel-Spirk Correspondence no. 18, DLSN. Cf. Werfel's contribution to *Die Zukunft der deutschen Bühne: Fünf Vorträge und eine Umfrage* (Berlin, 1917), reprinted in Klarmann, *Zwischen Oben und Unten*, 590–91.

88. The survey comment to which this essay responded focused in fact on this issue of artistic autonomy, in various ways: "Die Zukunft der deutschen Bühne darf und kann nicht abhängig gemacht werden von obrigkeitlicher Bevormundung, noch von Stimmung und Willensäußerung einzelner Gruppen oder organisierter Massen [. . .] Diese Freiheit verlangt, daß die deutschen Bühnen [. . .] den deutschen dramatischen Eigenbau nicht zu Gunsten der ausländischen Bühnenschriftsteller zurückdrängen [. . .] Klarmann, *Zwischen Oben und Unten*, 590–91.

89. Franz Werfel, "Substantiv und Verbum: Notiz zu einer Poetik," *Die Aktion*, nos. 1–2 (1917); reprinted in Klarmann, *Zwischen Oben und Unten*, 216–21.

90. Klarmann, *Zwischen Oben und Unten*, 220–21.

91. Franz Werfel, "Die Zukunft der Schule: Eine Entgegnung an Fritz Mauthner," *Berliner Tageblatt,* October 27, 1915; reprinted in Klarmann, *Zwischen Oben und Unten,* 557–59.

92. Franz Werfel, "Die christliche Sendung: Ein offener Brief an Kurt Hiller," *Die neue Rundschau* 28 (1917): 92–105; reprinted in Klarmann, *Zwischen Oben und Unten,* 560–75.

93. Activist responses to this open letter appeared in Hiller's *Das Ziel,* as well as in an article by Max Brod in the first issue of Martin Buber's *Der Jude.*

94. "Rede an die Arbeiter von Davos," in Klarmann, *Zwischen Oben und Unten,* 531–34.

95. Franz Werfel, "Blasphemie eines Irren," in *Die neue Dichtung,* ed. Kurt Wolff (Leipzig, 1918); reprinted in Karl Otten, *Ahnung und Aufbruch: Expressionistische Prosa* (Darmstadt, 1977), 285–91, see p. 287.

96. Werfel-Spirk Correspondence, dated November 1918, DLSN.

97. Ibid., unnumbered letter dated [?.] [?.] 1918.

98. Egon Erwin Kisch, *Soldat im Prager Korps* (Leipzig, 1922), 74; reprinted as *Schreib das auf, Kisch! Ein Kriegstagebuch,* in *GW,* 1:218.

99. Kisch, *Soldat im Prager Korps,* 196, *Schreib das auf,* 307–8: "Gegen die Juden sei die Stimmung in der Bevölkerung erbittert, weil viele Lokalanstellungen mit ihnen besetzt seien."

100. Werfel-Spirk Correspondence, letter of 31 July 1916, DLSN.

101. I will take a more detailed look at Buber's philosophy and his influence in Prague in the following chapter.

102. Werfel-Spirk Correspondence, letter of 17 April [1917], DLSN.

103. Martin Buber, "Ekstase und Bekenntnis," in *Ekstatische Konfessionen* (Jena, 1909), 16–18; reprinted in idem, *Theorie des Expressionismus,* ed. Otto F. Best (Stuttgart, 1976), 94–96.

104. In the polemic with Kraus, Werfel writes: "And in the last analysis you are the son of your people. Show me the Jew who was not dualistic, divided! And perhaps this I and Thou is this duplicity, this dialogue between essence and conscience is perhaps the most precious possession and the reason that Nietzsche called Judaism the "ethical genius among the peoples." The Jew recognizes the dualism in man as the last inexorability, and therefore reserves exclusively for God the attribute: the One and Only." Franz Werfel, "Die Metaphysik des Drehs: Ein offener Brief an Karl Kraus," *Die Aktion* 7, no. 9/10 (3 March 1917); also in Klarmann, *Zwischen Oben und Unten,* 581–90, see p. 584.

105. One could speak both of the substantial expressionist interest in Judaism as a theme on the one hand, and, on the other, of the expressionist influence on Jewish identities to be discussed in the next two chapters. Cf. Armin A. Wallas, "Zeitschriften des Expressionismus und Aktivismus in Österreich," *Expressionismus in Österreich:* 49–90; see esp. 83–90.

CHAPTER 5. CIRCUMSCRIBING SPIRITUAL TERRITORY

1. Bergmann (or Shmuel Hugo Bergmann, as he would be known after his residence in Palestine/Israel) is not forgotten in the history of Zionism generally, particularly for his role in founding the Jewish National and University Library

in Jerusalem, where he also served on the Faculty of Philosophy. Much of his later Zionist work can certainly be thought of in relation to his Prague experience, particularly his minority view on coexistence with the Arabs in Palestine. His role in the B'rith Shalom ("Covenant of Peace") Zionist group, which advocated a single, binational state, is interesting in this regard if only because Bergmann's Prague had been a shared space laden with ethnic conflict, in a multiethnic state that proved untenable. Nonetheless, Bergmann's thinking before 1918 is of a different mark from his post-Prague work, and it is this idiosyncratic thinking that I would like to examine here.

2. Hugo Bergmann to Franz Kafka, 1902. Reprinted in part in *Tagebücher und Briefe von Schmuel Hugo Bergman,* ed. Miriam Sambursky (Königstein/ Ts., 1985), 1:9.

3. Diary entry, 8 January 1914, *TB,* 622.

4. Founded in 1893 under the name Maccabäa, the organization went through several changes of name and charter before adopting the name Bar Kochba and an openly Zionist line in 1899. For more detail on the origins and development of the association, see Stuart Borman, "The Prague Student Zionist Movement, 1896–1914" (Ph.D. diss., University of Chicago, 1972).

5. The date of the founding of Maccabäa corresponds to the year that German *völkisch*-minded students broke off from the Halle to form the antiliberal and antisemitic competitor Germania. It is interesting to note that at the turn of the century, both Germania and Bar Kochba memberships consisted by and large of students from outside of Prague. This supports the thesis that the Prague "island" was out of step with ideology in the Bohemian and Moravian periphery. The Jewish-national association was founded by Russians studying in Prague, and the students responsible for the adoption of a Zionist line were Czechspeaking Prague "transplants." See Kieval, *Making of Czech Jewry,* 93–98.

6. Ibid., 99.

7. Felix Weltsch speaks significantly of their "distinctive—though perhaps not a leading—role in the Zionist movement." See "Realism and Romanticism: Observations on the Jewish Intelligentsia of Bohemia and Moravia," in *The Jews of Czechoslovakia. Historical Studies and Surveys* (Philadelphia, 1971), 2:440. George Mosse calls the Prague Bar Kochba "a germinal group in the intellectual history of modern Judaism," implicitly recognizing that their somewhat idiosyncratic position was in another way paradigmatic. See George L. Mosse, "The Influence of the Volkish Idea on German Jewry," in *Germans and Jews: The Right, the Left, and the Search for a "Third Force" in Pre-Nazi Germany* (New York, 1970), 82.

8. *Zirkular* [newsletter of the Iggud Vatikei Bar Kochba (Association of Former Members of Bar Kochba), Tel Aviv], April 1967, 4.

9. The term is most often associated with Martin Buber. Giuliano Baioni puts this "cultural Zionism" at the center of his description of Kafka's context; see Baioni, *Kafka: Letteratura ed ebraismo,* 3–36. The now less common term "spiritual Zionism" was at the time used interchangeably with "cultural Zionism." Several important references have been made to the Bar Kochba association as exemplary of a certain spiritualist tendency among central European

Zionist youth at the turn of the century, focusing especially on the influence of Martin Buber. Most important is Mosse, "The Influence of the Volkish Idea," 77–115. Cf. idem, *German Jews beyond Judaism* (Cincinnati, 1985), 37–41. In this later volume Mosse mentions in passing the unique Zionism of Prague Jews Hugo Bergmann, Hans Kohn, and others as "a part of Zionist history which demands to be written" (77). See also Paul Mendes-Flohr, *Divided Passions: Jewish Intellectuals and the Experience of Modernity* (Detroit, 1991), 83–85.

10. "[T]he efforts of the Zionists to achieve here what is already reality in the East—the creation of Jewish cultural circles [*Kulturkreise*]—are still in their beginnings [. . .] Iwri [Hugo Bergmann], "Das Babel der Kleinvölker: Prager Brief," *Jüdische Zeitung* (Vienna), 13 December 1907.

11. "The immediate significance of Zionism was that it inspired the Jewish youth for the Jewish cause for the first time. Until then [Judaism] had been an object of love and passion, but not of striving action. Now for the first time that which informed the basis of their life was demanded of young people: they were to put Judaism to the test in reality, this was to be the realization [*Verwirklichung*] of Judaism. The drive to realize Judaism in life has been the foundational force of Bar Kochba in all times." *Zirkular*, January 1967, 3.

12. "Über die Bedeutung des Hebräischen für die jüdischen Studenten," *Unsere Hoffnung* (Vienna) 1, no. 3 (June 1904): 85.

13. Hugo Bergmann, "Religiöser Zionismus," *Europäische Revue* 1, no. 12: 370–373.

14. Ibid.

15. Theodor Herzl, "Die Jagd in Böhmen," *Die Welt*, 5 November 1897.

16. "Word and weapon to defend Judah's honor" might be a good rendering. Cf. Borman, *Prague Student Zionist Movement*, 55–75. Of course, the second-century historical figure Bar Kochba, a revolutionary military hero, would have suited members of Barissia better as a model than those of the Bar Kochba Association. After a Prague performance of Goldfaden's play *Bar Kochba*, Kafka noted: "The members of the Bar Kochba Association had come on account of the name of the play, and must have been disappointed. From what I know of Bar Kochba from this play, I would not have named any association after him." See diary entry of 5 November 1911, *TB*, 229.

17. According to Hugo Brauner, "Zur Geschichte der Verbindung," in *Fünfzig Semester "Barissia"* (Prague, 1928), cited in Kieval, *Making of Czech Jewry*, chap. 4, n. 95.

18. Viktor Kellner, quoted in *Zirkular*, January 1967, 3.

19. The program was introduced at the Conference of Austrian Zionists in 1901 by Berthold Feiwel. See Kieval, *Making of Czech Jewry*, 102. Kieval claims that Feiwel "may have had the most direct role in Bar Kochba's formulation of Zionism as a 'spiritual revolution,'" and cites Barbara Kestenberg-Gladstein's agreement in "Athalot Bar Kochba," in *Prag v'Yerushalayim*, ed. Felix Weltsch (Jerusalem, 1954), 94. Jonathan Frankel identifies *Gegenwartsarbeit* as "revolution in the diaspora"; see Jonathan Frankel, *Prophecy and Politics: Socialism, Nationalism, and the Russian Jews, 1862–1917* (Cambridge, 1981), 281; see also 319–21.

20. Bergmann, "Größerer Zionismus," in *Jawne und Jerusalem: Gesammelte Aufsätze* [hereafter *JJ*] (Berlin: Jüdischer Verlag, 1919; reprint, Königstein/Ts., 1981), 7.

21. "If Palestine is going to mean anything to us, if it is to be our cultural center and if we want to be the periphery unto which its light radiates, than we must prepare ourselves to take on that light." Ibid., 8.

22. One example of the revolt of the periphery can be identified in the previously mentioned "*Los von Prag*" ("Free from Prague") movement, where Germans from northern and western Bohemia, resenting Prague's anachronistic liberalism, attempted to move the cultural and ideological center of German Bohemia to Reichenberg (Liberec).

23. The secondary literature on Zionism often refers to the "cultural controversy" of the early twentieth century as an early theater of the conflict between secular Zionism and orthodoxy. Beyond the practical question of Zionist educational policy lay the core ideological question of how Jewish culture—indeed, Judaism—was to be defined. Bergmann and the Bar Kochba membership were atypical of German-speaking Jews in their attachment to the cultural question. Herzl's attempts to defer the discussion certainly had a tactical side to them, but he was perhaps not entirely disingenuous (if simultaneously strategic) when he confessed to an assembly of delegates that he hadn't the foggiest notion of what the "cultural question" meant. For the best summary see Ehud Luz, *Parallels Meet: Religion and Nationalism in the Early Zionist Movement (1882–1904)*, trans. Lenn J. Schramm (Philadelphia, 1988), 137–58.

24. The speech is reprinted as "Die zionistische Kulturarbeit im Westen," in *JJ*; see p. 14.

25. Ibid., 13.

26. See Max Brod, "Franz Kafkas Glauben und Lehre," in *Über Franz Kafka* (Frankfurt am Main, 1966), esp. p. 270; "Franz Kafka und der Zionismus," *Emuna* 10, no. 1/2 (1975): 33–36; and "Humanistischer Zionismus im Werk Kafkas," in *Auf gespaltenem Pfad: Zum 90. Geburtstag von Margarete Susman*, ed. Manfred Schlosser (Darmstadt, 1964), 278–81; see also Felix Weltsch, *Religion und Humor im Leben und Werk Franz Kafkas* (Berlin, 1957), 38; cf. Schmuel Hugo Bergman [Hugo Bergmann], "Erinnerungen an Franz Kafka," *Universitas* 27 (1972): 739–50. Klara Carmely reinforces the image of a Zionist Kafka in *Das Identitätsproblem jüdischer Autoren im deutschen Sprachraum* (Königstein/Ts., 1981), 162–66. Nonetheless, the strong impression of a trajectory, if a troubled one, to a Zionist identification is the clear conclusion of more detailed revised accounts; see Binder, *Kafka-Handbuch*, 1:370–76, 435–37, 491–510; idem, "Franz Kafka and the Zionist Weekly *Selbstwehr*," *LBI Yearbook* 12 (1967): 135–48; Ritchie Robertson, "'Antizionismus, Zionismus': Kafka's Responses to Jewish Nationalism," in *Paths and Labyrinths: Nine Papers Read at the Kafka Symposium Held at the Institute of Germanic Studies on 20 and 21 October 1983* (London, 1985), 25–42; and idem, *Kafka: Judaism, Politics, and Literature*.

27. Kafka to Bauer, 11 November 1912, *Letters to Felice* [hereafter, *LF*], ed. Erich Heller and Jürgen Born, trans. James Stern and Elisabeth Duckworth (New York, 1973), 37.

28. The notion of Zionism and the Zionist figure of the "muscle Jew" (after Nordau) as an inverse image of the antisemitic stereotype was already in currency in this period. Recent literature rethinking this aspect of Jewish identity in interesting ways includes Paul Breines, *Tough Jews: Political Fantasies and the Moral Dilemma of American Jewry* (New York, 1990); George L. Mosse, *The Image of Man: The Creation of Modern Masculinity* (New York and Oxford, 1996); and most specifically (and provocatively) of all, Daniel Boyarin, *Unheroic Conduct: The Rise of Heterosexuality and the Invention of the Jewish Man* (Berkeley, 1997).

29. "Diese ganze Litteratur ist Ansturm gegen die Grenze und sie hätte sich, wenn nicht der Zionismus dazwischen gekommen wäre, leicht zu einer neuen Geheimlehre, einer Kabbala entwickeln können." *TB*, 16 January 1922, 878.

30. *LF*, 500.

31. Ibid.; emphasis added.

32. Ibid., 482.

33. See Brod, *Streitbares Leben*, 67.

34. Hillel Kieval argues convincingly that an "elective affinity" may have had its roots in Buber's childhood in the multinational and polyglot Austrian Galician Lwów (Lemberg): "Buber offered in his own person the mirror image of the Prague Zionist. From a corner of the Habsburg monarchy that was nationally ambivalent, yet Jewishly traditional, he had emerged to reaffirm, redefine, and recreate his Jewish national personality." See Kieval, *Making of Czech Jewry*, 129.

35. See *Martin Buber: Briefwechsel aus sieben Jahrzehnten*, ed. Grete Schaeder (Heidelberg, 1972). The complete Buber correspondence is found in the Martin Buber Archives (Ms. Var. 350), JNUL.

36. Martin Buber, *Drei Reden über das Judentum* (Frankfurt am Main, 1916), 7. The first edition was printed in 1911. In spite of the impact that contemporaries insisted the addresses had on this generation of central European Jews, Buber scholars and others have given them much less attentive readings than, for instance, his later philosophical work, his retelling of Hasidic narratives, or his Bible work. See, e.g., Maurice Friedman, *Martin Buber: The Life of Dialogue* (Chicago, 1955), 31–33; cf. idem, *Martin Buber and the Eternal* (New York, 1986); Paul Mendes-Flohr and Steven Kepnes, *The Text as Thou: Martin Buber's Dialogical Hermeneutics and Narrative Theology* (Bloomington, Ind., 1992).

37. Buber was only five years older than Bergmann, and no more than ten years older than the university students active in Bar Kochba. In the rhetoric of expressionism as well as that of the *völkisch* nationalist movement, "youth" takes its place alongside "renewal" in the battle against a "decadent" and even "senile" liberalism.

38. Buber was originally invited to be a guest speaker at a Bar Kochba *Festabend*, open to the public, in January 1909. The stunning reception of the first lecture led to subsequent invitations for return lectures by Buber, which took place in April and December 1910.

39. Buber, *Drei Reden*, 15.

40. Ibid., 26. Buber's disturbing and frequent use of the term "blood"—"the deepest layer" of the self—is not easily overlooked, even if it is always deployed

as metaphor. What is interesting about the way the metaphor operates in the text is that it is always associated with "choice" in a way its *völkisch* counterpart of course could never be. This is not unrelated to Michael Löwy's observation that Buber's radicalism lies in its refusal of a desire for a premodern or presocial (Tönnies) community of blood (*Blutverwandschaft*) in favor of a postsocial community based in free choice, connected to what Löwy calls "elective affinities" (*Wahlverwantschaften*), after Goethe and Weber. See M. Löwy, *Rédemption et utopie: Le Judaïsme libertaire en Europe centrale: Une étude d'affinité élective* (Paris, 1988), 64–65. Notwithstanding, the more sinister "elective affinity" George Mosse pointed out in his article on *völkisch* thought and this generation of central European Jewish rhetoric is at least as salient.

41. Buber, *Drei Reden*, 29.

42. Ibid., 27: "This is what I call the personal Jewish question, the root of all Jewish questions, the question that we find in ourselves, and which we must decide within ourselves."

43. Ibid., 44.

44. Degeneration in the sense expanded upon by Max Nordau is directly called upon and identified as the mark of contemporary Judaism, from which the coming Jewish generations must be liberated. Ibid., 29–30.

45. Ibid., 56.

46. Ibid., 74.

47. Hugo Bergmann, "Die Heiligung des Namens," in *Vom Judentum: Ein Sammelbuch,* ed. Verein Jüdischer Hochschüler Bar Kochba in Prag (Leipzig, 1913), 33.

48. Strange by Bergmann's own account; see "Die Heiligung des Namens," 33. Ordinarily the term refers to martyrdom for Jewish faith, a meaning that is not referred to in the essay.

49. Leviticus 22:32.

50. Bergmann to Buber, 2 May 1913, Buber, *Briefwechsel,* 329–30.

51. Buber to Bergmann, 7 May 1913, Buber, *Briefwechsel,* 331.

52. This strategy of the Jewish bourgeois is analogous to the segregation strategy that Georg Lukács identified in fin-de-siècle aestheticism: he related the strict, narrow, "ascetic" life of the bourgeois to the program *"l'art pour l'art"* and the attempt to create an unpolluted aesthetic sphere. See the 1909 essay on Theodor Storm in Lukács, *Die Seele und die Formen,* 82–116.

53. The original Hebrew essay that Bergmann used appeared in *Hashiloach* 13 (1904). The German translation in the same year appearing in *Ost und West* suffers unfortunately from abridgement. An unabridged translation into English appears in Leon Simon, ed., *Ahad Ha-am: Essays—Letters—Memoirs* (Oxford, 1946), in the East and West Library's Philosophia Judaica series edited by Hugo Bergmann. Another complete translation was published in Leon Simon, ed., *Selected Essays by Ahad Ha-am* (Philadelphia, 1936).

54. Hugo Bergmann, *Worte Mosis* (Minden, Westphalia, 1913).

55. Bergmann was more explicit about the contemporary analogy in the essay "Pessach und die Menschen unserer Zeit," in *JJ,* 75–80. The essay is dated 1913 and probably derives from his lecture "Moses und die Gegenwart." While it is tempting to compare Martin Buber's study of Moses with these by Ahad

Ha'am and Bermann, Buber's *Moses* is much later, completed in 1944, and self-consciously genealogizes itself within a tradition of biblical scholarship rather than these polemic pieces he knew well. See Buber, *Moses* (Heidelberg, 1952). A popular survey of the changing representations of the figure of Moses is offered in Daniel Jeremy Silver, *Images of Moses* (New York, 1982).

56. Joshua Eisenstadt Barzilai cited in Steven J. Zipperstein, *Elusive Prophet: Ahad Ha'am and the Origins of Zionism* (Berkeley and Los Angeles, 1993), 42. Thus the Zionist "fraternal society" formed with Ahad Ha'am in 1889 was named Benei Moshe.

57. Bergmann, *Worte Mosis*, 3.

58. Ibid., 27.

59. Ibid., 11.

60. *TB*, 17 December 1913, 616.

61. See Kafka, *Briefe*, 12, and my discussion in chapter 1.

62. "Pessach und die Menschen unserer Zeit," in *JJ*, 75.

63. See "Ein Schwarzseher," in *JJ*, 66.

64. Ibid.

65. "Die zionistische Kulturarbeit im Westen," in *JJ*, 15.

66. Deleuze and Guattari, *Kafka*.

67. Amos Oz, *In the Land of Israel*, trans. Maurie Goldberg-Bartura (London, 1983), 121–22.

68. From an article of unknown origin, dated May 1928, clipping in file 10a, Shmuel Hugo Bergman Archives (Arc. 4° 1502), JNUL.

69. See the manuscript "Robert Weltsch and Hugo Bergman: Eine Freundschaft aus der Zeit des jungen Zionismus," by Escha Bergmann, file 136b, Shmuel Hugo Bergman Archives (Arc. 4° 1502), JNUL. The Bergmann–Robert Weltsch correspondence is found in the same archive, file 1334, folders 1–11.

CHAPTER 6. NEW ORIENTATIONS

1. "Selbstwehr!" *Selbstwehr*, 1 March 1907, 1.

2. See Stölzl, *Kafkas böses Böhmen*.

3. See *Selbstwehr*, 12 April 1907, 1, as well as the article by Dr. H. Kadisch of 30 August 1907, where it is declared: "Unser jüdischer Nationalismus schließt nicht aus, sondern ein unsere großösterreichische Gesinnung [. . .]" (2).

4. *Selbstwehr*, 1 March 1907, 1.

5. *Selbstwehr*, 27 September 1907, 1.

6. See, e.g., the article by Kadisch cited above.

7. Simon Stern, in *Selbstwehr*, 23 August 1907, 2.

8. Conversely, it is interesting to note that a new journal "for German-national liberal fraternity students in Austria," written by and for German-speaking Jewish liberals, attacked Zionist ideology more forcefully and seriously than it did racialist German thought. See Dr. O[skar] Sch[euer], "Zum Kapitel: 'Deutschtum und Judentum,'" *Deutsche Hochschule* 3, no. 8 (May 1913): 90–91.

9. Niels, "Faule Frucht," *Selbstwehr*, 28 June 1907, 3.

10. Ibid., 4.

11. *Selbstwehr,* 4 March 1910, 1.

12. See, e.g., *Selbstwehr,* 18 September 1910, 6.

13. *Selbstwehr,* 21 January 1910, 6; 4 February 1910, 2; 14 January 1910, 1.

14. *Selbstwehr,* 14 January 1910, 1.

15. Franz Werfel, "Ein Ulan," *Das Zeit-Echo,* Heft 3 (1914): 26–27.

16. Dr. H. Kadisch, "Die Juden und das neue Europa," *Selbstwehr,* 7 January 1916, 3.

17. Ibid., 4.

18. Max Brod, "Der Zionismus," *Selbstwehr,* 13 September 1918, 2–4.

19. Ibid.

20. See my discussion of Bergmann's 1902 letter to Kafka in the previous chapter.

21. See "Zur Geschichte des Bar-Kochba (dritte Fortsetzung)," *Zirkular,* April 1967, 4: "[. . .] in an attempt to get to know the Jewish people in its mass centers as well as its ways of life and spiritual form, he undertook a trip to Galicia [. . .]"

22. Hugo Bergmann's diary of the trip to Galicia is in the Shmuel Hugo Bergman Archives (Arc. 4° 1502), JNUL, Jerusalem; printed in full in Bergman, *Tagebücher und Briefe,* 9–15. See pp. 9–10.

23. Ibid., 10.

24. Ibid., 13.

25. See Binder, "Franz Kafka and the Zionist Weekly Selbstwehr."

26. See Klarmann, *Zwischen Oben und Unten,* 696.

27. Ibid., 576.

28. Felix Weltsch, "Charakterologie der böhmisch-mährischen Juden," German typescript in Felix Weltsch Archive (Ms. Var. 418), carton 5, JNUL. An English version of the essay may be found in Weltsch, *Jews of Czechoslovakia,* vol. 1.

29. Egon Erwin Kisch, "Dem Golem auf der Spur," in *Nichts ist erregender als die Wahrheit,* 1:41–55.

30. Fuchs, *Der Meteor.*

31. The attempts to apply what is being called postcolonial theory or criticism to the central European case have hence focused on the German Empire's overseas colonies, despite the fact that these were few and late, and arguably less central in German (and certainly German Austrian) national fantasies than the drive to the East. Nonetheless, fascinating research is emerging out of the study of the German overseas colonies and the fantasies associated with them. Relating to the issue of gender fantasies that we will be discussing, for instance, see Susanne Zantop, *Colonial Fantasies: Conquest, Family, and Nation in Precolonial Germany, 1770–1870* (Durham, N.C., 1997); Lora Joyce Wildenthal, "Colonizers and Citizens: Bourgeois Women and the Woman Question in the German Colonial Movement, 1886–1914" (Ph.D. diss., University of Michigan, 1994), and Marcia Klotz, "White Women and the Dark Continent: Gender and Sexuality in German Colonial Discourse from the Sentimental Novel to the Fascist Film" (Ph.D. diss., Stanford University, 1995).

32. I am thinking of a spate of research emerging in the wake of Said's, in-

cluding (selectively) Anne McClintock, *Imperial Leather: Race, Gender, and Sexuality in the Colonial Conquest* (New York, 1995); Mary Louise Pratt, *Imperial Eyes: Travel Writing and Transculturation* (London, 1992); Ann Laura Stoler, *Race and the Education of Desire: Foucault's History of Sexuality and the Colonial Order of Things* (Durham, N.C., 1995); and Sara Suleri, *The Rhetoric of English India* (Chicago, 1992).

33. See Edward W. Said, *Orientalism* (New York, 1978), and the new edition with afterword, New York, 1994), esp. pp. 1–28. The triad of identity, power relationships, and culture is rich ground for a wide range of inquiries, and has been extended in an interesting way in Said's more recent *Culture and Imperialism* (New York, 1993).

34. Said, *Culture and Imperialism*, 188.

35. Max Brod, *Ein tschechisches Dienstmädchen* (Berlin, 1909); see, e.g., pp. 41, 101–2, 106, 107, 119–20. The same patronizing admiration of the simplicity of the Slav/woman is found in a poem by Rudolf Fuchs, "An ein tschechisches Mädchen" (To a Czech girl):

> und ihre Blicke fragten: "Traun,
> Wo soll ich mir den Stamm behaun?
> Wo werd ich meine Hütle baun?
> Wo jag ich mir ein feistes Stück?
> Wo ist das Glück? Wo ist das Glück?"

The poem was first published in Rudolf Fuchs, *Die Prager Aposteluhr: Gedichte, Prosa, Briefe*, ed. Ilse Seehase (Halle, 1985), 28.

36. Brod, *Ein tschechisches Dienstmädchen*, 116.

37. Ibid., 123.

38. Pavel Eisner, *Mílenky:. Německý básník a česká žena* [Beloveds: German writers and the Czech woman] (Prague, 1930).

39. Eisner, *Franz Kafka and Prague;* see pp. 23–24 and 58–65.

40. Ibid., 61, 63, and 64.

41. Described in Brod, *Streitbares Leben*, 343.

42. Heinrich Teweles in *Prager Tagblatt* of 31 March 1909, cited by Manfred Jähnichen in Goldstücker, *Weltfreunde*, 159; Hugo Herrmann in *Jüdische Volksstimme* of 20 April 1909, cited in Kieval, *Making of Czech Jewry*, 139.

43. *Bohemia Sonntags-Beilage* 107 (18 April 1909): 33–34.

44. Otto Pick in *März* 3, no. 3 (March 1909): 155, and Brod in *Prager Tagblatt*, 1 April 1909, cited by Manfred Jähnichen in Goldstücker, *Weltfreunde*, 159.

45. Brod to Procházka, 12 December 1907, Fond Arnošt Procházka, PNP. Procházka was editor of the *Moderní Revue*.

46. He wanted to show "daß ein Mensch in Prag leben kann, den mehr als nationale Kämpfe das gemeinsame Menschliche der zwei Nationen interessiert." See the above-cited article in *Prager Tagblatt*, 1 April 1909.

47. Arne Novák, "Pražský román?" *Venkov* 12, no. 86 (12 April 1917): 3.

48. *Der Mädchenhirt* (1914), in *GW*, 1:46–7.

49. As F. C. Weiskopf pointed out in a 1926 essay: "[. . .]in den schlesischen Liedern des Petr Bezruč [. . .] ist dann diese Verknüpfung bis zur völligen Ver-

schmelzung gediehen." See F. C. Weiskopf, *Gesammelte Werke,* 8:26. A discussion of Bezruč appears in the following chapter.

50. *Der Mädchenhirt,* 55, 60, 78.

51. Ibid., 138.

52. Brod to Egon Erwin Kisch, 21 January [1914], Inv. 223–29, Fond Friedrich Kisch, PNP.

53. Brod, "Der jüdische Dichter deutscher Zunge," in *Vom Judentum: Ein Sammelbuch* (Leipzig, 1913), 261–63.

54. Max Brod, *Jüdinnen* (Berlin-Charlottenburg, 1911).

55. Ibid., 69.

56. Willy Haas, *Herder-Blätter,* no. 1 (April 1911; facsimile reprint, Hamburg, 1962): 10–12.

57. Brod, *Jüdinnen,* 105.

58. Ibid., 326.

59. Martin Buber, at the invitation of Bar Kochba under the leadership of Hugo Bergmann, had lectured in Prague in 1903 on the "Jewish Renaissance," having already recognized the privileged role of Eastern European Judaism in relation to a contemporary Jewish agenda (see Kieval, *Making of Czech Jewry,* 103). After an extended retreat from public life, in which he immersed himself in Hassidic study, Buber had decisive influence on the turn to the East of Prague Jews and German-speaking Jews at large via his publication of *Tales of Rabbi Nachmann* (1907) and *Legend of the Baal-Shem* (1910) and through the previously discussed Prague *Reden* of 1909–1910. See also Martin Buber, "Der Geist des Orients und das Judentum," in *Vom Geist des Judentums* (Leipzig, 1911).

60. Martin Buber, "Die Losung," *Der Jude* 1, no. 1 (April 1916): 2.

61. Djak Levi, "Tsvey Prager Dikhter" (1934), cited in Beck, *Kafka and the Yiddish Theater,* 222.

62. This fascinating field, which I have been taking for granted throughout this chapter, has only relatively recently begun to be explored, and rather exclusively (at least with any degree of specificity) in American scholarship. See Sander Gilman, "The Rediscovery of Eastern Jews: German Jews in the East, 1890–1918," in *Jews and Germans from 1860 to 1933: The Problematic Symbiosis,* ed. David Bronsen (Heidelberg, 1979); and idem, "The Invention of the Eastern Jew," in *Jewish Self-Hatred,* 270–86; cf. Steven E. Aschheim, *Brothers and Strangers: The East European Jew in German and German Jewish Consciousness, 1800–1923* (Madison, Wisc., 1982). An excellent introductory treatment may be Paul Mendes-Flohr's essay on fin-de-siècle Orientalism in *Divided Passions.*

63. The best-known works are *Die Erotik der Kabbala* (Prague, 1923) and, translated from the Czech by Stephen Jolly, *Nine Gates to the Chassidic Mysteries* (New York, 1976). A much-quoted preface to the latter edition by the author's brother describes the family's horror upon seeing a Hasidic Jiří return to Prague after his visit and "conversion" in Galicia.

64. See Aschheim, *Brothers and Strangers.*

65. Brod, "Erfahrungen im ostjüdischen Schulwerk," *Der Jude* 1, no. 1 (April 1916): 34.

66. A more detailed discussion of the issue of mediation follows in the next chapter, "Middle Ground."

67. Brod, "Erfahrungen im ostjüdischen Schulwerk," 34.

68. Ibid. Sander Gilman has shown very concisely and definitively that "Ostjude" was not a word defined by geographical boundaries, as demonstrated by Karl Emil Franzos's descriptions of "enlightened" Jews living in the same countries as "Ostjuden," and as we see in the opposition in Arthur Eloesser's title "From the Ghetto to Europe." See "The Rediscovery of Eastern Jews," 338–39.

69. Max Brod, "Brief an eine Schülerin nach Galizien," *Der Jude* 1, no. 2 (May 1916): 124.

70. Franz Kafka, *Brief an den Vater/Letter to His Father,* trans. Ernst Kaiser and Eithne Wilkins (New York, 1953), 24–25.

71. See Friedrich Tomberg, "Kafkas Tiere," *Das Argument* 6, no. 1 (1964).

72. Although Kafka's family history has often been recounted, and not always consistently, the most exhaustively detailed version appears to be found in Hartmut Binder, *Franz Kafka: Leben und Persönlichkeit* (Stuttgart, 1983), 16–30.

73. The figure of the *"Ungeziefer"* appears in this period in Kafka's notebooks, again in comical contrast to bourgeois life as Kafka refers to the *"für mich nötigen Ceremonien unter denen ich ja nur weiterkriechen kann nicht besser wie ein Ungeziefer."* See *TB,* 117.

74. Anderson, *Kafka's Clothes,* 138.

75. Kafka to Martin Buber, 29 November 1915, Buber, *Briefwechsel,* 1:409.

76. Kafka to Max Brod, 31 July 1922, *Briefe,* 403–4.

77. *TB,* 14 September 1914, 751.

78. Franz Kafka, "Schakale und Araber," *Der Jude* 2 (1917–1918): 488–90. Citations from the story that follow make use of the translation of Willa and Edwin Muir in *The Penal Colony: Stories and Short Pieces* (New York, 1976), 150–54.

79. See, e.g., the very early contribution of André Németh, *Kafka ou le mystère juif* (Paris, 1947), 36–37.

80. William C. Rubinstein, "Kafka's 'Jackals and Arabs,'" *Monatshefte* 59 (1967): 13–18. Rubinstein reviews the various critical readings of the story up until 1967 in his article.

81. Walter Benjamin, "Franz Kafka: On the Tenth Anniversary of His Death," in *Illuminations:. Essays and Reflections,* ed. Hannah Arendt, trans. Harry Zohn (New York, 1968), 120.

82. Franz Kafka, "Ein Bericht für eine Akademie," *Der Jude* 2 (1917–1918): 559–65.

83. Cf. Patrick Bridgwater, "Rotpeters Ahnherren, oder: Der gelehrte Affe in der deutschen Dichtung," *Deutsche Vierteljahrsschrift für Literaturwissenschaft und Geistesgeschichte* 56, no. 3 (September 1982), 447–62.

84. Adding density to this complex of crisscrossing meanings is Kafka's 1922–1923 text "On Parables," in Kafka, *Parables and Paradoxes* (New York, 1961), 10–11. As Charles Bernheimer has skillfully shown, Kafka sees in the *Gleichnis* the potential of *gleich-werden,* the dissolution of the barriers between

language and referent, author and text, parable and life. See Charles Bernheimer, "Crossing Over: Kafka's Metatextual Parable," in *Flaubert and Kafka: Studies in Psychopoetic Structure* (New Haven, 1982), 45–55.

85. Kafka to Buber, 12 May 1917, Buber, *Briefwechsel*, 494.

CHAPTER 7. MIDDLE GROUND

1. A typical representation of this situation can be found in Egon Erwin Kisch, "Deutsche und Tschechen," in *Marktplatz der Sensationen: Entdeckungen in Mexiko* (Berlin, 1947), 72–81. Gary Cohen notes a certain tension between these claims of total separateness—a claim of ideological importance both to the nationalist press of the period and to Kisch and others dedicated to combat cultural segregation—and actual practice, where music lovers in particular more than occasionally visited "adversary" national theaters. Yet, that these visits were the exception rather than the rule is the dominant impression left by even those memoirs where such activity is mentioned, such as in Richard Kukula, *Erinnerungen eines Bibliothekars* (Weimar, 1925), 37–38; and Egon Basch, "Wirken und Wandern: Lebenserinnerungen" (photocopied typscript, n.d., LBI), 16–20. Cf. Cohen, *Politics of Ethnic Survival*, 131 and n. 96.

2. Beyond the numerous examples cited in chapter 2, cf. the degrading and fallacious report of the death of the exiled Czech nationalist writer Horálek in *Bohemia* 254 (14 September 1912), morning edition, 4.

3. Oskar Ewald, "Talent und Genie," *Bohemia* 260 (20 September 1912), morning edition, 1–3.

4. See esp. Richard Jacquemond, "Translation and Cultural Hegemony: The Case of French-Arabic Translation," in *Rethinking Translation: Discourse, Subjectivity, Ideology,* ed. Lawrence Venuti (London, 1992), 139–58. Beyond the mirrored imbalances of political-economic relations and the record of translation publication Jacquemond points out in his first pages, certain questions of content (e.g., exoticization/Orientalizing) suggest parallels between the Czech-German case and postcolonial translation paradigms. In this regard see also Samia Mehrez, "Translation and the Postcolonial Experience: The Francophone North African Text," in Venuti, *Rethinking Translation,* 120–38; and Mahasweta Sengupta, "Translation, Colonialism, and Poetics: Rabindranath Tagore in Two Worlds," in *Translation, History, and Culture,* ed. Susan Bassnet and André Lefevere (London, 1990), 56–63.

5. While Brod is self-aggrandizing in suggesting that Werfel's brilliant "Die Christliche Sendung" (with the subtitle "An Open Letter to Kurt Hiller" somehow ignored by Brod) is a response to Brod's "Unsere Literaten und die Gemeinschaft," these essays, and the Brod essay in *Der Jude* following the publication of Werfel's article, are excellent representations of the authors' differing notions of universality. See Brod, *Streitbares Leben,* 82; "Unsere Literaten und die Gemeinschaft" and "Franz Werfels christliche Sendung" in *Der Jude* (1916 and 1917); and Franz Werfel, "Die Christliche Sendung."

6. See Batět, *Rozvoj,* no. 44, 2, reported in *Selbstwehr* 4, no. 46 (18 November 1910).

7. See, e.g., Franz Werfel, *Die Brücke-Most* 4 (21 May 1937), 21. Werfel fol-

lowed Pick's career closely and often lauded him. The two served together at the front during World War I and remained in contact with one another.

8. See Brod, in *Otto Pick zum 50. Geburtstag* (Prague, 1937), 11.

9. Baum, in *Otto Pick zum 50. Geburtstag,* 10.

10. Willy Haas, "Otto Pick: Ein Blatt des Gedenkens," *Stifter-Jahrbuch* 3 (1953): 67.

11. See Paul Kisch, "Deutsche Erzähler aus der Tschechoslowakei: Abschnitte deutscher Literaturgeschichte," *Deutsche Zeitung Bohemia* 96, no. 31: 3–4.

12. Ibid., 4.

13. Otto Pick, "Der Mensch im Walde," *Bohemia* 243 (3 September 1912), morning edition, 1–2. Quotations below are taken from this text.

14. Adolf Levenstein, ed., *Die Arbeiterfrage* (Munich, 1912).

15. See Nachlaß Brümmer, Biographien, 2. Reihe (autobiographical description dated 9 June 1912), STABI.

16. See Nachlaß A. Juncker, nos. 152 (20 June 1911), 153 (21 November 1911), and 154 (24 January 1912), STABI.

17. As in his recommendation to publish *Die Galeere* by Ernst Weiss, which has been cited in chapter 4 (see Nachlaß A. Juncker, 153 [21 November 1911], STABI). In this direction, Oskar Wiener gives special acknowledgment to Pick for his role in obtaining contributions from the "younger" generation of Prague poets (Baum, Brod, Fuchs, Kisch, Kornfeld, Urzidil, and Pick himself—a veritable Prague circle) to his anthology of Prague German writing: see Oskar Wiener, ed., *Deutsche Dichter aus Prag: Ein Sammelbuch* (Leipzig, 1919), 6.

18. Otto Pick to Otokar Theer, 6 August 1912, Fond O. Theer, PNP.

19. Otto Pick to Otokar Theer, 9 August 1912, Fond O. Theer, PNP.

20. Martin Buber Archives [MS Var 350], file 80, 80.15 (8 April 1913), JNUL. The volume was a collection of translations that had been published in part in *Simplizissimus* and Kraus's *Die Fackel.*

21. *Saturn* 3 (June 1913).

22. Paul Reimann makes the valuable point that literary innovation in late nineteenth-century Europe comes increasingly from the previously (and geographically?) "peripheral" countries, and that a decisive moment occurs when these are translated into the major Western European languages. Reimann explicitly recognizes the role of the Prague translators in bringing the "periphery" to the center. See "Die Prager deutsche Literatur im Kampf um einen neuen Humanismus," in Goldstücker, *Weltfreunde,* 11–12.

23. Fond Stanislav Lom, 9 February 1917, PNP.

24. Including the Inselverlag in Leipzig, the Austrian journal *Donauland,* and the Wiener Burgtheater. Fond Stanislav Lom, 11 March and 26 June 1917, PNP.

25. The status of German among these very writers is exceedingly difficult to judge in light of the complex history of the emergence of literary Czech in the Habsburg Empire. While intellectuals were passionately engaged in establishing Czech as a *Kultursprache* since the early nineteenth century, it is well known that they continued to use German even among themselves in certain contexts; many of the early Czech renaissance figures (or national "awakeners"—*buditelé,* as they are known) spoke German primarily, even at home and in their private cor-

respondence and diaries. In view of the intimate relationship of Czech and German in high cultural Czech circles, it is difficult to ascribe a meaning to language choice, even as late as World War I. See D. Sayer, "The Language of Nationality, 190–95, and *Coasts of Bohemia,* 107–18.

26. See the discussion of Werfel's "Glosse zu einer Wedekind-Feier" in chapter 4.

27. "[. . .] diese süße Arbeit," Fond Stanislav Lom, 19 February 1917, PNP.

28. *Selbstwehr* 11, no. 48 (7 December 1917): 2.

29. This is what Vladimír Macura has called "culture as translation," exploring the example of the Czech renaissance of the earlier nineteenth century. He cites Jan Evangelista Purkyně's remarkable introductory comment to his own translations of Schiller: "If the Germans, Italians and Hungarians try to denationalize both our common people and our higher classes, let us use a more noble way of retaliation, taking possession of anything excellent they have created in the world of the mind." See V. Macura, "Culture as Translation," in *Translation, History, and Culture,* ed. Susan Bassnet and André Lefevere (London, 1990), 69.

30. Otto Pick, *Stunden mit Otokar Březina* (Prague, 1929), 14. This rather arcane edition is reprinted from the *Prager Presse,* 17 February 1924.

31. "Ein großer Mystiker in unserer Zeit: Otokar Březina," *Die literarische Welt,* 12 October 1928, 1.

32. George Steiner, *After Babel: Aspects of Language and Translation* (London, 1975), 362. While Steiner's comments are inspired by his reading of Derrida's *Margins of Philosophy,* the depth of his misreading of a deconstructive approach to translation is impressive. Cf. Joseph F. Graham, ed., *Difference in Translation* (Ithaca, N.Y., 1985).

33. "Die deutsche Sprache machte mir Schwierigkeiten [. . .] Ich besuchte häufig das deutsche Theater, las deutsche Bücher, faßte leise den Vorsatz, meinen Freunden zu zeigen, was es Schönes in der tschechischen Literatur gebe, indem ich es ins Deutsche übersetzte." London, 1940, cited without reference in Jürgen Serke, *Böhmische Dörfer,* 249–50. Fuchs's work as a critic of modern Czech painting is given credit above his translation work in Paul Reimann's essay in Goldstücker, *Weltfreunde,* 18.

34. Salus predictably tried to steer the young poet away from "*Stimmungskunst,*" by which he meant symbolist and other aestheticist tendencies. Hugo Salus to Rudolf Fuchs, 12 October 1909, Fond Rudolf Fuchs, PNP.

35. The two volumes were *Der Meteor* (Heidelberg, 1913), published by the press of the expressionist journal *Saturn,* and *Karawane* (Leipzig, 1919), published by the friend of Prague expressionists Kurt Wolff.

36. Including, as late as 1917, the printing of Fuchs's spiritual poem "Abend" in an issue stressing Jewish support of the monarchy. *Selbstwehr* 11, no. 1 (5 January 1917).

37. Willy Haas was most moved by Fuchs's three-part poem "Juden" in *Karawane.* Willy Haas to Rudolf Fuchs, n.d. [1924], Fond Fuchs, PNP.

38. With a preface by Franz Werfel, published by Kurt Wolff (Leipzig, 1916).

39. This judgment is only lightly veiled in the Communist F. C. Weiskopf's summary, written in 1938: "Das nationale und soziale Elend der Beskidenbauern

und Bergleute wird laut in diesen volksliedhaften Liedern: der Trotz und Haß gegen fremde Grubenherren, habsburgiesche Erzherzöge, germanisierende Lehrer, polonisierende Pfarrer, brutale Herrschaftsförster, raffgierige [suddenly no national adjective] Händler [. . .]" See F. C. Weiskopf, "Petr Bezruč, auf deutsch," in *Gesammelte Werke,* ed. Grete Weiskopf and Stephan Hermlin (Berlin, 1960), 8:277.

40. Thus the irony of the poet's 1927 dedication of a photograph to Fuchs, "Rudolf Fuchs in brüderlicher Liebe!" printed in Serke, *Böhmische Dörfer,* 250; see also the postcard from Josef Čapek, in German, where he justifies Czech antipathy toward "German" writers like Fuchs, reprinted in Fuchs, *Die Prager Aposteluhr,* 334.

41. Willy Haas, "Otto Pick: Ein Blatt des Gedenkens," *Stifter Jahrbuch* 3 (1953): 68.

42. Immediately after his death, the volume *Ein wissender Soldat* (London, 1942) was published.

43. See Rudolf Fuchs, *Ein Erntekranz aus hundert Jahren tschechischer Dichtung* (Munich, 1926), 5.

44. Serke, *Böhmische Dörfer,* 248–50.

45. *Der Prager Kreis,* 230.

46. Cf. Kornfeld to Fuchs, 20 October 1918; Wolff to Fuchs, 26 January 1922; and Zweig to Fuchs, 3 March 1922, Fond Rudolf Fuchs, PNP.

47. Paul Kornfeld, *Aufruhr im Mansfelder Land* (Berlin, 1928).

48. *Die Prager Aposteluhr,* 29.

49. See, e.g., E. E. Kisch to Paul Kisch, 16 November 1911 and 15 October 1912, Fond Friedrich Kisch, PNP. On Kisch's intention to translate *Švejk,* see Jarmila Mečasová, in *Kisch-Kalender,* ed. F. C. Weiskopf (Berlin, 1955), 137. Kisch's sensitivity to the problematic of translation comes through in a charming passage from *Aus Prager Gassen und Nächten:* "Manchmal ißt man vielleicht auch eine 'drštková polévka' dazu, was laut Ranks Wörterbuch deutsch "Kuttelflecksuppe" heißt. Na ja, Ranks Wörterbuch ist eben kein Kochbuch, und so kann darin nicht verzeichnet sein, welche Fülle geheimnisvoller Ingredienzien eine kommune Kuttelflecksuppe zu einer Prager 'drštková' stempelt." *GW,* 2:193.

50. E. E. Kisch to Antonin Macek, 13 June 1917, Fond Friedrich Kisch, PNP.

51. See *Aktion, Sonderheft "Böhmen"* (May 1916). The Prague-Jewish role in this crucial moment of German recognition of Czech culture was not missed by *Selbstwehr;* see vol. 10, no. 19 (19 May 1916): 4.

52. Pavel Petr referred to these idiosyncrasies of the translation as "Slavisms." See Pavel Petr, "Die deutsche Übersetzung der *Abenteuer des braven Soldaten Schwejk,*" parts 1 and 2, *Philologica Pragensia* 4, no. 3 (1961): 160–73; no. 4 (1961): 231–41; F. C. Weiskopf, *Gesammelte Werke,* 8:185–88; and Willy Haas, "Německé bidylko," *Literární noviny* (1 November 1935): 2. Weiskopf, in the tradition of Kisch, points out that the untranslatability of the slang is identical to the impossibility of translating the shared vocabulary of Prague mythology (such as the figure Babinsky and others recounted by Kisch's blind singer Methodius); Haas, on the other hand, lets the success or failure of included "Praguisms" rest on whether they were intended by the translator for effect or

remain as unconscious remnants of her Prague German origins. The translator
was Grete Reiner.

53. See Demetz's afterword to *Der Prager Kreis*, 246.

54. Zdeněk Landes, "Künden tschechischer Kunst," in Weltsch, *Dichter-Denker-Helfer*, 89.

55. Ibid.

56. Ibid., 92.

57. Felix Weltsch and Max Brod, *Anschauung und Begriff: Grundzüge eines Systems der Begriffsbildung* (Leipzig, 1913), 225.

58. Ibid.

59. A contemporary review of Brod's play *Die Retterin* cites *Anschauung und Begriff* as a scholarly explication of what any reader will sense in the play: "das heisse Ringen um die Unmittelbarkeit des Herzens und des Erlebens . . . " Review by Joseph Sprengler, *Die schöne Literatur* 16, no. 20 (25 September 1915): 274–75.

60. C. Valerius Catullus, *Gedichte: Vollständige Ausgabe, Deutsch von Max Brod, mit teilweiser Benützung der Übersetzung von R. W. Kamler* (Munich, 1914), 10.

61. Ibid., 11.

62. Friedrich Nietzsche, *Die fröhliche Wissenschaft*, in *Sämtliche Werke: Kritische Studienausgabe in 15 Bänden*, ed. Giorgio Colli and Mazzino Montinari (Munich, 1988), 3:343-651; see 438–39. "In-corporation" because the mode of translation is determined by how one seeks to incorporate (*Einzuverleiben*) past times and books; "conquest," as the French and especially Roman example teaches: "In der Tat, man eroberte damals, wenn man übersetzte . . . " The excerpt is included in English in *Translating Literature: The German Tradition from Luther to Rosenzweig*, ed. André Lefevere (Amsterdam/Assen, 1977), 96.

63. Max Brod, "Tschechisches Opernglück," *Schaubühne*, 15 November 1916.

64. The longish story of the collaboration has been documented in many places, including Brod's memoirs, but perhaps most faithfully and clearly in Charles Susskind, *Janáček and Brod* (New Haven, 1985).

65. See Janáček to the Universal Edition, telegram and letter, nos. 3 and 34, 3.XII.[1916], *Leoš Janáček: Briefe an die Universal Edition*, ed. Ernst Hilmar (Tutzing, 1988).

66. Max Brod, *Prager Sternenhimmel; Musik- und Theatererlebnisse der zwanziger Jahre* (Vienna, 1966), 31.

67. See "Über Janáček's Wortmelodie," in Max Brod, trans., *Jenufa (Ihre Ziehtochter)*, by Gabriele Preiß (Vienna, 1918), i–iii.

68. Ibid., ii.

69. Ibid., iii.

70. Brod, *Prager Sternenhimmel*, 36: "Zu wenig beachtet wurde folgender Satz des Vorwortes: 'Das Studium der Sprachmelodie ist natürlich nur Grundlage, Material, nicht etwa Inhalt der Kunst.' "

71. Susskind, *Janáček and Brod*, 24.

72. Brod, *Prager Sternenhimmel*, 34–35.

73. Brod to Janáček, 13 December 1916, Janáček and Brod, *Korespondence Leoše Janáčka s Maxem Brodem* (Prague, 1954), 18.

74. See Susskind, *Janáček and Brod,* 47, and Jaroslav Vogel, *Leoš Janáček: His Life and Works* (London, 1962), 309. Janáček's position is made clearest in his appeal to the publisher on 30 March 1917; see *Briefe an die Universal Edition,* 37. Brod's agreement with Janáček in this regard is forcefully expressed in the letters of 11 March 1917 and 28 March 1917; see Janáček and Brod, *Korespondence,* 23–24.

75. Janáček and Brod, *Korespondence,* see pp. 24, 30, 33–35, 37–38.

76. See Susskind, *Janáček and Brod,* 49; also *Briefe an die Universal Edition,* 77–79.

77. Brod to Janáček, 3 February 1918, Janáček and Brod, *Korespondence,* 42.

78. Brod, *Prager Sternenhimmel,* 33–34.

79. Ibid., 22.

80. "Als ich das Heft aus dem großen Kouvert zog, war ich fast enttäuscht. Ich wollte von Ihnen hören und nicht die allzu gut bekannte Stimme aus dem alten Grabe. Warum mischte sie sich zwischen uns? Bis mir dann einfiel, daß sie auch zwischen uns vermittelt hatte." Franz Kafka, *Briefe an Milena,* erweiterte Neuausgabe [hereafter *BM*], ed. Jürgen Born and Michael Müller (Frankfurt am Main, 1983), 8–9. Parenthetical page numbers in the text refer to this edition. All English translations adapted from Franz Kafka, *Letters to Milena,* trans. with intro. by Philip Boehm (New York, 1990).

81. *BM,* 9. "Im übrigen aber ist es mir unbegreiflich, daß Sie diese große Mühe auf sich genommen haben, und tief rührend, mit welcher Treue Sie es getan haben, Sätchen auf und ab, einer Treue, deren Möglichkeit und schöne natürliche Berechtigung, mit der Sie sie üben, ich in der tschechischen Sprache nicht vermutet habe. So nahe deutsch und tschechisch?"

82. Jaroslav Dresler's comments on these errors are cited in Ota Filip, "Wer war Milena?" *Die Zeit,* 14 January 1983, 21.

83. See especially the outstanding article by Lori Chamberlain, "Gender and the Metaphorics of Translation," *Signs* 13 (1988): 454–72. Cf. Barbara Godard, "Theorizing Feminist Discourse/Translation," in *Translation, History, and Culture,* ed. Susan Bassnet and André Lefevere (London, 1990), 87–96.

84. Chamberlain, "Gender and the Metaphorics," 454.

85. "Es ist so schön, daß ich Ihren Brief bekommen habe, Ihnen mit dem schlaflosen Gehirn antworten muß. Ich weiß nichts zu schreiben, ich gehe nur hier zwischen den Zeilen herum, unter dem Licht Ihrer Augen, im Atem Ihres Mundes wie in einem schönen glücklichen Tag, der schön und glücklich bleibt, auch wenn der Kopf krank ist, müde und man Montag wegfährt über München" (34).

86. As Mark Anderson has noted, "[t]he 'condition of possibility' structuring the letters is Kafka's isolation." M. Anderson, "Unsigned Letters to Milena Jesenská," in *Reading Kafka,* 244; the same point holds for his earlier correspondence with Felice Bauer, as spotted early by Elias Canetti in *Der andere Prozeß* (TK, 1969).

87. "Siehst Du, Du brauchst eine Feder, warum haben wir die Zeit in Wien

nicht besser ausgenützt? Warum blieben wir z. B. nicht immerfort in dem Papier-
laden, es war doch so schön dort und wir waren einander so nah" (151). Milena's report on the post office visit is in her letter to Max Brod of August 1920,
first published by Brod in his Kafka biography and since in a number of volumes
including *BM*, 363–64.

88. This theme was already at the center of Elias Canetti's early essay on the
correspondence with Felice. See *Der andere Prozeß.*

89. " . . . *nechápu*. Ein fremdartiges Wort im Tschechischen und gar in Ihrer
Sprache, es ist so streng, teilnahmslos, kaltäugig, sparsam und vor allem nußk-
nackerhaft, dreimal drachen im Wort die Kiefer aufeinander oder richtiger: die
erste Silbe macht einen Versuch die Nuß zu fassen, es geht nicht, dann reißt
die zweite Silbe den Mund ganz groß auf, nun paßt schon die Nuß hinein und
die dritte Silbe endlicht knackt, hören Sie die Zähne? Besonders dieses endgiltige
Schließen der Lippen am Schluß verbietet dem andern jede andere weitere gegen-
teilige Erklärung, was ja allerdings manchmal recht gut ist z. B. wenn der andere
so schwätzt wie jetzt ich." *BM*, 28.

90. "Und dann redet noch Milena von Ängstlichkeit, gibt mir einen Stoß vor
der Brust oder fragt, was im Tschechischen an Bewegung und Klang ganz das-
selbe ist: jste žid? Sehen Sie nicht, wie im 'jste' die Faust zurückgezogen wird,
um [. . .] Muskelkraft anzusammeln? Und dann im 'žid' den freudigen, un-
fehlbaren, vorwärts fliegenden Stoß?" *BM*, 28.

91. *BM*, 60.

92. See Walter Benjamin, "Die Aufgabe des Übersetzers," in *Gesammelte
Schriften*, vol. 4, part 1, werkausgabe 10 (Frankfurt am Main, 1980), 9–21.
Translations from "The Task of the Translator," in Walter Benjamin, *Illumina-
tions*, 79 and passim.

93. "The Task of the Translator," 76. "Die Übersetzung aber sieht sich nicht
wie die Dichtung gleichsam im innern Bergwald der Sprache selbst, sondern außerhalb desselben, ihm gegenüber und ohne ihn zu betreten ruft sie das Original
hinein, an dem jenigen einzigen Orte hinein, wo jeweils das Echo in der einen den
Widerhall eines Werkes der fremden Sprache zu geben vermag." *Gesammelte
Schriften*, vol. 4, part 1:16.

94. The paragraph-long parenthetical clause after the name "Milena": "(was
für ein reicher schwerer Name vor Fülle kaum zu heben und gefiel mir anfangs
nicht sehr, schien mir ein Grieche oder Römer nach Böhmen verirrt, tschechisch
vergewaltigt, in der Betonung betrogen und ist doch wunderbar in Farbe und
Gestalt eine Frau, die man auf den Armen trägt aus der Welt, aus dem Feuer ich
weiß nicht und sie drückt sich willig und vertrauend dir in die Arme, nur der
starke Ton auf dem i ist arg, springt dir der Name nicht wieder fort? Oder ist das
vielleicht nur der Glücksprung, den du selbst machst mit deiner Last?)." *BM*, 59.

95. "Du schreibst: "Ano máš pravdu, mám ho ráda. Ale F., i tebe mám
ráda"—ich lese den Satz sehr genau, jedes Wort, besonders beim i bleibe ich
stehn, es ist alles richtig, Du wärst nicht Milena wenn es nicht richtig wäre
und was wäre ich wenn Du nicht wärest und es ist besser daß Du das in Wien
schreibst als daß Du es in Prag sagtest, alles das verstehe ich genau, vielleicht
besser als Du und doch, aus irgendeiner Schwäche kann ich mit dem Satz nicht

fertig werden, es ist ein endloses Lesen und ich schreibe ihn schliesslich hier noch einmal auf, damit auch Du ihn siehst und wir ihn zusammenlesen, Schläfe an Schläfe." *BM,* 112.

96. This passage seems to me to operate in a provocatively parallel way to a verse from the Carmina Burana:

sum presentialiter	I am with you
absens in remota,	even when I am far away.
quisquis amat taliter,	Whosoever loves this much
volvitur in rota.	is turned on the wheel.

The last line has also been translated as "knows the torture of the wheel."

97. Kafka to Brod, early May 1921, *Briefe,* 322.

98. See Hannelore Rodlauer, " 'Ansichten eines Exterritorialen': Albert Ehrenstein und Franz Kafka," in *Expressionismus in Österreich,* 225–52.

99. "Sie wissen ja, wie ich Briefe hasse. Alles Unglück meines Lebens [. . .] kommt, wenn man will, von Briefen oder von der Möglichkeit des Briefeschreibens her. Menschen haben mich kaum betrogen, aber Briefe immer undzwar auch hier nicht fremde, sondern meine eigenen. [. . .] Die leichte Möglichkeit des Briefeschreibens muß—bloß teoretisch angesehn—eine schreckliche Zerrüttung der Seelen in die Welt gebracht haben. Es ist ja ein Verkehr mit Gespenstern undzwar nicht nur mit dem Gespenst des Adressaten, sondern auch mit dem eigenen Gespenst, das sich einem unter der Hand in dem Brief, den man schreibt, entwickelt oder gar in einer Folge von Briefen, wo ein Brief den andern erhärtet und sich auf ihn als Zeugen berufen kann. Wie kam man nur auf den Gedanken, daß Menschen durch Briefe mit einander verkehren können!" *BM,* 301–2.

CONCLUSION

1. Kafka, quoted in Hannah Arendt, *Between Past and Future: Eight Exercises in Political Thought* (New York, 1968), 7.

2. Ibid., 9.

3. F. X. Šalda, review of *The Redemption of Tycho Brahe,* by Max Brod (1916), cited in J. P. Stern, *The Heart of Europe: Essays on Literature and Ideology* (Oxford, 1992), 71. Cf. the discussion of Arne Novák's comparable judgment in chapter 6.

4. The work that has done the most to demonstrate this point in reference to Kafka is Sander Gilman's recent study, *Kafka, the Jewish Patient.* Coming to terms with what Gilman sees as the "internalization" of hostile discourses is a difficult matter, and one that I have tried to address throughout this book.

5. Homi K. Bhabha, "Introduction: Narrating the Nation," in *Nation and Narration,* ed. Homi K. Bhabha (New York, 1990), 4.

6. Ibid.

7. One fascinating proposal, to which I am indebted, is found in Jonathan Boyarin and Daniel Boyarin, "Diaspora and the Ground of Jewish Identity," *Critical Inquiry* 19 (summer 1993): 693–725.

8. Kafka to Felice Bauer, 7 October 1916, *LF,* 517.

9. Cf. Terry Eagleton, "Nationalism: Irony and Commitment," in *National-ism, Colonialism, and Literature,* ed. Terry Eagleton, Fredric Jameson, and Edward Said (Minneapolis, 1990).

10. Benedict Anderson, *Imagined Communities: Reflections on the Origins and Spread of Nationalism* (London, 1983, 1991); see pp. 9–12.

11. See Walter Benjamin, *Gesammelte Schriften,* vol. 5, part 1:566–67; cf. ibid., vol. 5, part 2, 1034–35.

12. David Harvey, *The Condition of Postmodernity: An Enquiry into the Origins of Cultural Change* (Oxford, 1989). The "origins" referred to in the title are the late-capitalist conditions producing this subjective experience of time-space compression under which modernist culture, in the first place, and post-modernist culture, in an even sharper way, came to be produced. "Time-space compression" implies the shrinkage of each of these realms as well as there con-fusion with one another (see 201–326). A similarly ambitious thesis on the re-lationship of modernism to modernity is argued in Stephen Kern, *The Culture of Time and Space, 1880–1918* (London, 1983).

13. Harvey, *The Condition of Postmodernity;* see 284 and 306. The implicit contrast of modernism and postmodernism on which the argument depends re-calls the rigid schema of binaries (narrative vs. antinarrative, master code vs. idio-lect, determinacy vs. indeterminacy, etc.) offered in I. Hassan, "The Culture of Postmodernism," *Theory, Culture, and Society* 2/3 (1985), 123–24, reproduced in Harvey, *The Condition of Postmodernism,* 43. More persuasive than this tax-onomy is Hassan's claim, cited in my first chapter, that these terms are in dialec-tical tension with one another (at the turn of the last century as well as the pres-ent one).

14. Lefebvre, *The Production of Space,* 25.

15. Robert Musil, "Der deutsche Mensch als Symptom" (1923), in Robert Musil, *Gesammelte Werke,* ed. Adolf Frisé (Reinbek bei Hamburg, 1978), 8: 1353–1400. Translations adapted from Robert Musil, *Precision and Soul,* ed. and trans. Burton Pike and David S. Luft (Chicago, 1990), 150–92. See my dis-cussion in "Beyond the Aesthetic Garden."

Bibliography

ARCHIVAL COLLECTIONS

CZECH REPUBLIC

Archiv Statního Židovského Muzea (Archive of the State Jewish Museum), Prague. Oskar Baum Collection: clippings, manuscripts, correspondence.

Archiv Univerzity Karlovy (Charles University Archive), Prague. Lese- und Redehalle der deutschen Studenten in Prag: Protokollbücher der Sektion für Literatur und Kunst; Rapportbücher des Ausschusses; Laufende Korrespondenz; Bedenkbücher; Jahresberichte.

Památník Národního Písemnictví, Literární Archiv (Memorial for National Literature, Literary Archives), Prague-Strahov. Correspondence and manuscripts of Prague authors in collections Rudolf Fuchs, Bedřich Kisch, Stanislav Lom, Antonin Macek, Pavel Eisner, Otto Pick, Alexander Eliasberg Samojlovič, Fraňa Šrámek, Sfinx, Otokar Theer, and others. Uncatalogued papers of E. E. Kisch including student notebooks and student newspapers.

GERMANY

Akademie der Künste (Academy of Arts), Berlin. Clippings, manuscripts, theater program notes, correspondence, and diary pages in Paul Kornfeld Collection; miscellaneous correspondence of other Prague authors in various collections.

Deutsches Literaturarchiv—Schiller-Nationalmuseum (German Literary Archives—Schiller National Museum), Marbach am Neckar. Diaries of Paul Kornfeld; correspondence Franz Werfel–Gertrude Spirk; correspondence Franz Werfel–Paul Zech; varied correspondence and manuscripts of other Prague German authors. Bibliographic catalogue for authors.

Staatsbibliothek Preußischer Kulturbesitz (State Library of Prussian Cultural

Heritage), Berlin. Autobiographical sketches in collections Carl Busse and Brümmer; author-publisher correspondence in papers of Axel Juncker and in Ullstein papers; correspondence with Herwarth Walden, Sturm-Archiv; lengthy Max Brod correspondence in papers of Auguste Hauschner. Central catalogue of German archival collections.

ISRAEL

Central Zionist Archives, Jerusalem. Relevant materials catalogued under Bar Kochba; Prague Zionism; Leo Herrmann; Robert Weltsch; Siegfried Kaznelson.
Jewish National and University Library (Manuscripts Division, Givat Ram), Jerusalem. Shmuel Hugo Bergman [Hugo Bergmann] Archives (Arc 4° 1502): correspondence, diaries, clippings, manuscripts. Copies of mimeographed newsletter *Bar-Kochba Zirkular*. Martin Buber Archives (Ms. Var. 350): correspondence with Prague writers; Felix Weltsch Archives (Ms. Var. 418): manuscripts, poetry manuscripts by Heinrich Weltsch, correspondence, personal records, and effects.

UNITED STATES

Leo Baeck Institute, New York. Unpublished memoirs of Else Fanta Bergmann and Egon Basch.

CONTEMPORARY JOURNALS AND NEWSPAPERS

Die Aktion. Expressionist journal. Berlin.
Arkadia: Jahrbuch für Dichtkunst. Literary journal edited by Max Brod, published by Kurt Wolff. Leipzig, 1913.
Bohemia [Deutsche Zeitung Bohemia]. German-liberal daily. Prague. Various issues, 1900–1918.
Der Brenner: Halbmonatsschrift. German expressionist journal. Innsbruck.
Deutsche Arbeit: Monatschrift für das geistige Leben der Deutschen in Böhmen. German-national cultural journal. Prague, 1901–1918.
Die Deutsche Hochschule: Blätter für deutschnationale [und] freisinnige Farbenstudenten in Österreich. German-national and liberal student periodical; primarily Jewish editorship and readership. Vienna and Leipzig, 1910–1918.
Herder-Blätter. Literary journal of young Prague German-speaking Jewish writers. Prague, 1911–1912 (4 issues). Reprint, Hamburg: Freie Akademie der Künste, 1962.
Der Jude: Eine Monatsschrift. Monthly periodical, edited by Martin Buber. Berlin and Vienna, 1916–1918.
Die neue Rundschau. German periodical. Berlin, 1908–1918.
Prager Tagblatt. German-liberal daily; primarily Jewish readership and editorship. Prague. Various issues, 1900–1918.
Saturn: Eine Monatsschrift. German expressionist monthly. Heidelberg, 1911–1919. Reprint, Nendeln/Liechtenstein: Kraus, 1969.

Selbstwehr: Unabhängige jüdische Wochenschrift. Jewish-national weekly. Prague, 1907–1918.

Der Sturm. Expressionist journal. Berlin, 1911–1918.

Wir: Deutsche Blätter für Kunst. Aestheticist journal, edited by Paul Leppin. Prague, 1906 (2 issues).

CONTEMPORARY BOOKS, PAMPHLETS, AND ARTICLES

Adámek, Karel. *Slovo o Židech* [A word on the Jews]. Chrudim, 1899.

Ahad Ha'am [Asher Ginsberg]. *Ahad Ha-am: Essays—Letters—Memoirs.* Edited by Leon Simon. Philosophia Judaica, edited by S. Hugo Bergman. Oxford: East and West Library, 1946.

Bachmann, Hermann, ed. *Deutsche Arbeit in Böhmen: Kulturbilder.* Berlin: Concordia Deutsche Verlags-Anstalt, 1900.

Bath-Hillel. "Mauthner der Jude." *Neue Jüdische Monatshefte* (Berlin and Munich) 3, no. 6 (25 December 1918): 134–36.

Baum, Oskar. *Die böse Unschuld: Ein jüdischer Kleinstadtroman.* Frankfurt am Main: Rütten & Loening, 1913.

———. "Fanatismus der Verachtung." *Der Sturm* 7 (1917): 52–53.

———. *Ein Schicksal: Erzählungen.* Heidelberg: Saturn, 1913.

———. *Die Tür ins Unmögliche.* Munich and Leipzig: Kurt Wolff, 1919.

———. *Uferdasein: Abenteuer und Tägliches aus dem Blindenleben von heute.* Berlin, Stuttgart, and Leipzig: Axel Juncker, 1908.

———. *Zwei Erzählungen.* Leipzig: Kurt Wolff, 1918.

Beradt, Martin, and Lotte Bloch-Zavřel, eds. *Briefe an Auguste Hauschner.* Berlin: Rowohlt, 1928.

Bergmann, Hugo. "Der Babel der Kleinvölker: Prager Brief." *Jüdische Zeitung,* no. 22 (1907): 9.

———. "Bialiks neue Lieder." *Die Welt* 14, no. 49:1296–97.

———. "Büchertisch." *Jüdische Volksstimme* (Brünn), 20 September 1907.

———. "Einiges über das Jüdische 'Jargon.'" *Unsere Hoffnung* 1, no. 9 (1904): 292–96.

———. "Das hebräische Buch und die deutschen Zionisten." *Der Jude* 4 (1919–1920): 287–88.

———. *Jawne und Jerusalem: Gesammelte Aufsätze.* Berlin: Jüdischer Verlag, 1919.

———. *Die Judenfrage und ihre Lösungsversuche: Zur Aufklärung der Studentenschaft.* Prague: Verein jüdischer Hochschüler "Bar Kochba," 1903.

———. "Jüdische Schulfragen." *Revue der israelitischen Kultusgemeinden in Böhmen,* October 1903.

———. "Ein neues Buch von Scholem Asch." *Die Welt* 11, no. 30 (1907): 14–15.

———. *Das philosophische Werk Bernard Bolzanos: Mit Benutzung ungedruckter Quellen kritisch untersucht.* Halle: Niemeyer, 1909.

———. *Tagebücher und Briefe von Schmuel Hugo Bergman.* Edited by Miriam Sambursky. 2 vols. Königstein/Ts.: Jüdischer Verlag bei Athenäum, 1985.

———. "Über die Bedeutung des Hebräischen für die jüdische Studenten." *Unsere Hoffnung* 1, no. 3 (1904): 85–88.

———. "Unsere Stellung zum Jiddischen." *Die Welt* 18, no. 27 (1914): 705–6.

———. "Das Wesen des Judentums." *Jüdische Volksstimme,* 15 March 1905.

———. "Zum IV. österreichischen Parteitag." *Jüdische Volksstimme,* 15 July 1905.

———. "Die zwei Gedichte von J. L. Perez." *Selbstwehr,* no. 6 (1907): 5.

———, ed. *Worte Mosis. Die Weisheit der Völker,* no. 18. Minden, Westphalia: J. C. C. Bruns, 1913.

Bezruč, Petr [Vladimír Vašek]. *Schlesische Lieder.* Translated by Rudolf Fuchs, with an introduction by Franz Werfel. Leipzig: Kurt Wolff, 1916.

"Bohemia": Israelitische Humanitätsverein. *Festschrift.* Prague, 1913.

Březina, Otokar [Vaclav Jebavý]. *Hymnen.* Translated by Otto Pick. Leipzig: Kurt Wolff, 1919.

Brod, Max. *Abschied von der Jugend: Roman.* Berlin: Axel Juncker, 1911.

———. *Arnold Beer: Roman.* Berlin: Axel Juncker, 1912.

———. *Der Bräutigam: Novelle.* Berlin: Axel Juncker, 1913.

———. "Brief an eine Schülerin nach Galizien." *Der Jude* 1 (1916–1917): 124–25.

———. *Diesseits und Jenseits.* Winterthur: Mondial, 1947.

———. "Erfahrungen im ostjüdischen Schulwerk." *Der Jude* 1 (1916–1917): 32–36.

———. *Die erste Stunde nach dem Tod: Novelle.* Munich: Kurt Wolff, 1916.

———. *Erziehung zur Hetäre: Novellen.* Berlin: Axel Juncker, 1909.

———. *Experimente: Novellen.* Berlin: Axel Juncker, 1907.

———. "Franz Werfels 'christliche Sendung.'" *Der Jude* 1 (1916–1917): 717–24.

———. *Gedichte des Catullus.* Munich: Georg Müller, 1913.

———. *Das gelobte Land: Lyrik.* Munich: Kurt Wolff, 1918.

———. "Grenzen der Politik." *Der Jude* (1917).

———. *Das große Wagnis: Roman.* Munich: Kurt Wolff, 1919.

———. *Heidentum, Christentum, Judentum.* Munich: Kurt Wolff, 1921.

———. *Die Höhe des Gefühls: Lyrik und Szenen.* Berlin: Axel Juncker, 1913.

———. *Im Kampf um das Judentum.* Vienna: R. Löwit, 1920.

———. *Jüdinnen: Roman.* Berlin: Axel Juncker, 1911.

———. *Die Königin Esther: Drama.* Munich: Kurt Wolff, 1918.

———. *Die Retterin: Schauspiel.* Munich: Kurt Wolff, 1914.

———. *Schloß Nornepygge: Roman.* Berlin: Axel Juncker, 1908.

———. *Sozialismus im Zionismus.* Vienna: R. Löwit, 1920.

———. *Tagebuch in Versen: Lyrik.* Berlin: Axel Juncker, 1910.

———. "Technische Kritik." *Saturn* 2, no. 11 (November 1912): 239–41.

———. *Tod den Toten! Novellen.* Berlin: Axel Juncker, 1906.

———. *Ein tschechisches Dienstmädchen: Roman.* Berlin: Axel Juncker, 1909.

———. *Über die Schönheit häßlicher Bilder: Essays.* Munich: Kurt Wolff, 1913.

———. "Versuch einer neuen Metrik." *Der Sturm* 3, no. 58 (1912).

———. "Die Wallfahrt zu Orazio." *Der Sturm* 2, no. 17 (1911): 333–34.

———. *Weg des Verliebten: Lyrik.* Berlin: Axel Juncker, 1907.

———. *Weiberwirtschaft.* Leipzig and Vienna: Kurt Wolff, 1917.

————, trans. *Jenufa (Ihre Ziehtochter)*, by Gabrielle Preiss. Vienna and Leipzig: Universal-Edition, 1918.

Brod, Max, and Hans-Joachim Schoeps. *Im Streit um Kafka und das Judentum: Der Briefwechsel zwischen Max Brod und Hans-Joachim Schoeps*. Edited by Julius H. Schoeps. Königstein: Jüdischer Verlag bei Athenäum, 1985.

Brod, Max, and Felix Weltsch. *Zionismus als Weltanschauung*. Mähr-Ostrau: Dr. R. Färber Verlag, 1925.

Buber, Martin. *Briefwechsel aus sieben Jahrzehnten*. Edited by Grete Schaeder. Vol. 1, *1897–1918*. Heidelberg: Lambert Schneider, 1972.

————. *Drei Reden über das Judentum*. Frankfurt am Main: Rütten & Loening, 1916.

————. "Ekstase und Bekenntnis." In *Ekstatische Konfessionen*, xvi–xviii. Jena: Diedrichs, 1909. Reprinted in Otto F. Best, *Theorie des Expressionismus* (Stuttgart: Reclam, 1976), 94–96.

————. "Die Losung." *Der Jude* 1 (1916–1917): 1–3.

————. "Vorbemerkungen über Franz Werfel." *Der Jude* 2 (1917–1918): 109 ff.

Čapek, Karel. *Kreuzwege*. Translated by Otto Pick. Der jüngste Tag, vol. 64. Leipzig: Kurt Wolff, 1919.

Charmatz, Richard. *Deutsch-österreichische Politik: Studien über den Liberalismus und über die auswärtige Politik Österreichs*. Leipzig: Duncker & Humblot, 1907.

Dilthey, Wilhelm. *Von deutscher Dichtung und Musik: Aus den Studien zur Geschichte des deutschen Geistes*. Leipzig and Berlin: B. G. Teubner, 1933.

Dvořák, Arno. *Der Volkskönig: Drama in 5 Akten*. Translated by Maz Brod. Leipzig: Kurt Wolff, 1914.

Festschrift der Lese- und Redehalle der deutschen Studenten in Prag anlässlich des 150.-semestrigen Sitzungsfestes, 1848–1923. Prague: Lese- und Redehalle der deutschen Studenten in Prag, 1923.

Fischel, Alfred. *Das österreichische Sprachenrecht: Eine Quellensammlung*. Brunn: Friedr. Irrgang, 1910.

————, ed. and trans. *Ein Erntekranz aus hundert Jahren tschechischer Dichtung*. Munich: Kurt Wolff, 1926.

Fuchs, Rudolf. *Karawane: Gedichte*. Leipzig: Kurt Wolff, 1919.

————. *Der Meteor: Gedichte*. Heidelberg: Saturn, 1913.

————. *Die Prager Aposteluhr: Gedichte, Prosa, Briefe*. Edited by Ilse Seehase. Halle and Leipzig: Mitteldeutscher Verlag, 1985.

————. *Ein wissender Soldat: Gedichte und Schriften aus dem Nachlaß*. London: "Einheit," 1943.

Fünfzig Semester "Barissia": Festschrift herausgegeben anlässlich des 50-semestrigen Stiftungsfestes der jüdisch-akademischen Verbindung "Barissia." Prague: "Barissia," 1928.

Hauschner, Auguste. *Die Familie Lowositz*. 2 vols. Berlin: Fleischel, 1908–1910.

————. *Die Siedlung*. Berlin: Fleischel, 1918.

Herder-Blätter: Faksimileausgabe zum 70. Geburtstag von Willy Haas. Hamburg: Freie Akademie der Künste, 1962.

Hiller, Kurt. *Die Weisheit der Langeweile*. Leipzig: Kurt Wolff, 1913.

————, ed. *Der Kondor*. Heidelberg: R. Weissbach, 1912.

————. *Das Ziel: Jahrbücher für geistige Politik*. Munich: Kurt Wolff, 1916.

Janowitz, Franz. *Auf der Erde: Gedichte*. Munich: Kurt Wolff, 1919.

Janáček, Leoš. *Briefe an die Universal Edition*. Edited by Ernst Hilmar. Tutzing: Hans Schneider, 1988.

Janáček, Leoš, and Max Brod. *Korespondence Leoše Janáčka s Maxem Brodem*. [Janáčkuv archiv 9.] Prague, 1954.

Das jüdische Prag: Eine Sammelschrift. Prague: Selbstwehr, 1917.

Kafka, Franz. *Betrachtung*. Leipzig: Ernst Rowohlt, 1913.

————. *Briefe, 1902–1924*. Edited by Max Brod. New York: Schocken, 1959. Translated by Richard Winston and Clara Winston under the title *Letters to Friends, Family, and Editors* (New York: Schocken, 1977).

————. *Briefe an Felice und andere Korrespondenz aus der Verlobungszeit*. Edited by Erich Heller and Jürgen Born. Translated by James Stern and Elisabeth Duckworth under the title *Letters to Felice* (New York: Schocken, 1973).

————. *Briefe an Milena*. Erweiterte und neu geordnete Ausgabe. Edited by Jürgen Born und Michael Müller. Frankfurt am Main: S. Fischer, 1983. Translated by Philip Boehm under the title *Letters to Milena* (New York, 1990).

————. *Dearest Father*. Translated by Ernst Kaiser and Eithne Wilkins. New York: Schocken, 1954.

————. *Der Heizer: Ein Fragment*. Leipzig: Kurt Wolff, 1913.

————. *Nachgelassene Schriften und Fragmente in der Fassung der Handschrift*. Edited by Hans-Gerd Koch, Michael Müller, and Malcolm Pasley. 4 vols. New York and Frankfurt am Main: S. Fischer, 1992.

————. *Tagebücher in der Fassung der Handschrift*. Edited by Hans-Gerd Koch, Michael Müller, and Malcolm Pasley. 2 vols. New York and Frankfurt am Main: S. Fischer, 1990.

————. *Das Urteil*. Der jüngste Tag, vol. 34. Leipzig: Kurt Wolff, 1916.

————. *Die Verwandlung*. Der jüngste Tag, vol. 22/23. Leipzig: Kurt Wolff, 1915.

————. "Zwei Tiergeschichten." *Der Jude* 2 (1917–1918). "Schakale und Araber": 488–90; "Ein Bericht für eine Akademie": 559–65.

Kisch, Egon Erwin. *Briefe an den Bruder Paul und an die Mutter, 1905–1936*. Edited by Josef Poláček with Fritz Hofman. Berlin and Weimar: Aufbau, 1978.

————. *Der freche Franz und andere Geschichten*. Berlin: Hugo Steinitz, 1906.

————. *Gesammelte Werke in Einzelausgaben*. Ed. Bodo Uhse, Gisela Kisch, Fritz Hofmann, and Josef Poláček. 12 vols. Vol. 1, *Der Mädchenhirt/Schreib das auf, Kisch!/Komödien*. Vol. 2, *Aus Prager Gassen und Nächten/Prager Kinder/Die Abenteuer in Prag*. Vol. 3, *Prager Pitaval/Späte Reportagen*. Vol. 4, *Zaren, Popen, Bolschewiken/Asien gründlich verändert/China geheim*. Vol. 5, *Paradies Amerika; Landung in Australien*. Vol. 6, *Der rasende Reporter/Hetzjagd durch die Zeit/Wagnisse in aller Welt/Kriminalistisches Reisebuch*. Vol. 7, *Geschichten aus sieben Ghettos/Eintritt verboten/Nachlese*. Vol. 8, *Marktplatz der Sensationen/Entdeckungen in Mexiko*. Vol. 9, *Mein Leben für die Zeitung 1906–1925*. Vol. 10, *Mein Leben für die Zeitung*

1926–1947. Vol. 11, *Läuse auf dem Markt/Vermischte Prosa.* Vol. 12, *Der freche Franz/Vom Blütenzweig der Jugend/Nachgelassenes und Verstreutes.* Berlin and Weimar: Aufbau-Verlag, 1960–1993.

———. *Der Mädchenhirt.* Berlin: Erich Reiss, 1914.

———. *Soldat im Prager Korps.* Leipzig and Prague: K. André, 1922.

———. *Vom Blütenzweig der Jugend: Gedichte.* Dresden: E. Pierson's, 1905 [1904].

Knoll, Philipp. *Beiträge zur heimischen Zeitgeschichte.* Prague: J. G. Calve'sche k. u. k. Hof- und Universitäts-Buchhandlung, 1900.

———. *Das Deutschthum in Böhmen: Vortrag, gehalten am 8 November 1885 zu Dresden vor der II. Hauptversammlung des Landesverbandes Sachsen des Allgemeinen Deutschen Schulvereins.* Dresden: E. Blochmann und Sohn, 1885.

———. *Über das Deutschthum in Prag und seine augenblickliche Lage: Vortrag gehalten am 20. März 1883 im Deutschen Vereine in Prag.* Prague: Deutscher Verein, 1883.

———. *Vortrag über die Prager Universitätsfrage: Gehalten am 12. März 1881 im Deutschen Vereine in Wien.* Vienna, 1881.

Kohn, Hans. "Prager Dichter." *Selbstwehr* 7, no. 23 (6 June 1913): 1–3.

Kornfeld, Paul. "Die Begegnung." *Die neue Rundschau* 28 (1917): 355–66.

———. "Der beseelte und der psychologische Mensch." *Das junge Deutschland* 1 (1918): 1–13.

———. *Himmel und Hölle* excerpt prepublished, *Der Anbruch* 1, no. 6 (1918): 3.

———. *Himmel und Hölle: Eine Tragödie in fünf Acten und ein Epilog.* Berlin: S. Fischer, 1919.

———. "Legende." *Die weissen Blätter* 4, no. 1 (1917): 105–70.

———. *Legende.* Berlin: S. Fischer, 1917.

———. "Metapolitik." *Der Anbruch* 1, no. 4 (1918): 3.

———. "Mission der Kunst." *Der Anbruch* 1, no. 6 (1918): 2.

———. *Revolution mit Flötenmusik und andere kritische Prosa, 1916–1932.* Edited by Manon Maren-Grisebach. Heidelberg: Schneider, 1977.

———. *Die Verführung.* Berlin: S. Fischer, 1916.

———. "Zwei Gedichte in Prosa" ("Gebet" and "Schweigend ist der Mensch größer denn sprechend"). *Daimon* 1 (1918): 47–50.

Kraft, Paul. "Literarische Neuerscheinungen: Franz Werfel, *Wir sind.*" *Die Aktion* 3, no. 26 (25 June 1913): 643–44.

Kraus, Karl. "Heine und die Folgen." *Die Fackel,* August 1911.

———. *Die Sprache.* Vienna: Verlag "Die Fackel," 1937.

Laforgue, Jules. *Pierrot, der Spaßvogel: Lyrik.* Translated by Max Brod with Franz Blei. Berlin: Axel Juncker, 1909.

Landauer, Gustav, and Fritz Mauthner. *Gustav Landauer–Fritz Mauthner Briefwechsel, 1890–1919.* Edited by Hanna Delf and Julius H. Schoeps. Munich: C. H. Beck, 1994.

Leppin, Paul. *Daniel Jesus: Ein Roman.* Berlin: J. Hegner, 1905.

———. *Severins Gang in die Finsternis: Ein Prager Gespensterroman.* Munich: Delphin, 1914.

Lukács, Georg von. *Die Seele und die Formen: Essays.* Berlin: Egon Fleischel,
    1911. Reprint, Neuwied and Berlin: Luchterhand, 1971.

Mauthner, Fritz. *Beiträge zu einer Kritik der Sprache.* Reprint of 3d ed., 3 vols.,
    Hildesheim: Olms, 1969.

———. *Die böhmische Handschrift.* Constance: Reuß & Itta, 1916.

———. *Der letzte Deutsche von Blatna: Erzählung aus Böhmen.* Berlin and Vi-
    enna: Ullstein, 1913.

———. *Muttersprache und Vaterland.* Leipzig: Dürr and Weber, 1920.

———. *Schmock oder die litterarische Karriere der Gegenwart.* Berlin: F. & P.
    Lehmann, 1888.

Meyrink, Gustav. *Der Golem: Roman.* Leipzig: Kurt Wolff, 1915.

———. "Prag: Eine optimistische Schilderung in vier Bildern von Gustav Mey-
    rink." *März* 1, no. 4 (February 1907): 350–55.

Novák, Arne. "Pražský roman?" *Venkov* 12, no. 86 (12 April 1917): 3.

Ortsrat Prag des deutschen Volksrates für Böhmen. *Prag als deutsche Hoch-
    schulstadt.* Prague: Verlag des Ortsrats Prag, 1911.

Pfemfert, Franz, ed. *Jüngste tschechische Lyrik: Eine Anthologie.* Berlin: Die
    Aktion, 1916.

Pick, Otto. *Freundliches Erleben: Gedichte.* Berlin: Axel Juncker, 1912.

———. "Die kulturelle Annäherung zwischen Deutschen und Čechen." *Union*
    58, no. 195 (15 July 1918): 2.

———. *Die Probe: Novellen.* Heidelberg: Saturn, 1913.

———. *Stunden mit Otokar Březina.* Prague: Orbis, 1929.

———, ed. *Deutsche Erzähler aus der Tschechoslowakei: Ein Sammelbuch.* Vi-
    enna and Leipzig, 1919.

Pinès, Meyer. *Histoire de la littérature judéo-allemande.* Paris: Jouve, 1910.

Pinthus, Kurt, ed. *Menschheitsdämmerung: Ein Dokument des Expressionis-
    mus.* Berlin: Rowohlt, 1920.

Plener, Ernst [Freiherr von]. *Eine Kreisordnung für Böhmen.* [Sonder-Abdruck
    aus der Zeitschrift für Volkswirtschaft, Socialpolitik und Verwaltung, Jg.
    1899, 3. Heft.] Vienna and Leipzig: Wilhelm Braumüller, 1900.

———. *Reden, 1873–1911.* Stuttgart and Leipzig: Deutsche Verlags-Anstalt,
    1911.

Popper-Lynkeus, Josef. *Gespräche: Mitgeteilt von Margit Ornstein und Hein-
    rich Löwy.* Vienna: 1924.

Prager Schulerhaltungs-Verein. *Prager deutsche Worte: Individuelle Meinungs-
    äußerungen deutschen* [sic] *Bewohner Prags über locale Verhältnisse am
    Ende des 19. Jahrhunderts.* Prague: Prager Schulerhaltungs-Verein, 1900.

Rauchberg, Heinrich. *Die Bedeutung der Deutschen in Österreich.* Dresden:
    Zahn & Jaensch, 1908.

———. *Der nationale Besitzstand in Böhmen.* Im Auftrage der Gesellschaft zur
    Forderung Deutscher Wissenschaft, Kunst und Literatur in Böhmen. 2 vols.
    Leipzig: Duncker & Humblot, 1905.

———. *Das Zahlenverhältnis der Deutschen und der Tschechen in Böhmen.*
    Munich: G. D. W. Callwey, 1902 [?].

Ritschel, Augustin. "Das Prager Deutsch." In *Phonetische Studien: Zeitschrift
    für wissenschaftliche und praktische Phonetik* 6 (1893): 129–33.

Ruest, Anselm. "Der Max Brod-Abend." *Die Aktion 1*, no. 45 (12 December 1911): 1425–26.

Samassa, Paul. *Der Völkerstreit im Habsburgerstaat.* Leipzig: Dieterich, 1910.

Sauer, August. *Kulturpolitische Reden und Schriften.* Edited by Josef Pfitzner. Reichenberg: Sudetendeutscher Verlag Franz Kraus, 1928.

Schopenhauer, Arthur. *Die Welt als Wille und Vorstellung.* Edited by Julius Frauenstädt. Leipzig: 1923.

Srb, Jan. *Obcovací řeč jako prostředek sesilující národní državu německou v zemích koruny české zvlášť a v Rakousku vůbec* [Everyday language as a means of strengthening the national position of Germans in Czech lands in particular and in Austria generally]. Prague, 1909.

Stauf von der March, Ottokar. *Zum Kampf um die Erhaltung des Deutschtums.* Staatspolitische Aufklärungsschrift no. 16. Berlin: Deutschnationale Schriftenvertriebsstelle, 1920.

———, ed. *Die Juden im Urteil der Zeiten: Eine Sammlung jüdischer und nichtjüdischer Urteile.* Munich: Deutscher Volksverlag, 1921.

Steiner, Max. *Die Rückständigkeit des modernen Freidenkertums: Eine kritische Untersuchung.* Berlin: Ernst Hofmann & Co., 1905.

———. *Die Welt der Aufklärung: Nachgelassene Schriften.* Edited by Kurt Hiller. Berlin: 1912.

Strobl, Carl Hans. *Tschechen.* Leipzig: Dürr & Weber, 1920.

———. *Die Vaclavbude: Eine Prager Studentengeschichte.* Reprint with new preface, Karlsbad and Leipzig: A. Kraft, 1943.

———. *Das Wirtshaus "Zum König Przemysl": Eine Prager Geschichte.* Leipzig: L. Staackmann, 1913.

Šrámek, Fráňa. *Erwachen: Ein Akt.* Translated by Otto Pick. Heidelberg: Saturn, 1913.

———. *Flammen: Novellen von Fráňa Šrámek.* Edited and translated by Otto Pick. Leipzig: Ernst Rowohlt, 1912.

Teweles, Heinrich. *Der Kampf um die Sprache: Linguistische Plaudereien.* Leipzig: Carl Reißner, 1884.

Utitz, Emil. *Die Funktionsfreuden in ästhetischen Verhalten.* Halle: M. Niemeyer, 1911.

———. *Die Gegenständlichkeit des Kunstwerks.* Berlin: Reuther & Reichard, 1917.

———. *Die Grundlagen der jüngsten Kunstbewegung.* Stuttgart: Ferdinand Enke, 1913.

———. *Grundzüge der ästhetischen Farbenlehre.* Stuttgart: Ferdinand Enke, 1908.

———. *Was ist Stil?* Stuttgart: Ferdinand Enke, 1911.

Verein jüdischer Hochschüler Bar-Kochba in Prag. *Neue Wege: Fest-schrift herausgegeben anläßlich des zehn-jährigen Bestandes des Vereines "Bar Kochba" in Prag.* Prague: Bar Kochba Verein, 1903.

———. *Vom Judentum: Ein Sammelbuch.* Leipzig: Kurt Wolff, 1913.

Weininger, Otto. *Geschlecht und Charakter.* Vienna: Braunmüller, 1903.

Weiskopf, F[ranz] C[arl]. *Gesammelte Werke.* Edited by Grete Weiskopf and Stephan Hermlin. Berlin: Dietz, 1960.

————. *Über Literatur und Sprache.* Berlin: Dietz, 1960.

Weltsch, Felix. *Nationalismus und Judentum.* Berlin: Welt, 1920.

————, ed. *Jüdischer Almanach auf das Jahr 5695.* Prague: Selbstwehr, 1935.

Weltsch, Felix, and Max Brod. *Anschauung und Begriff: Grundzüge zu einem System der Begriffsbildung.* Leipzig: Kurt Wolff, 1913.

Werfel, Franz. "Absage an den Expressionismus." *Wiener Mittagspost,* May 1920, 3. Reprinted in *Zwischen Oben und Unten,* edited by Adolf Klarmann (Munich and Vienna: Langen Müller, 1975), 591–92.

————. "Aphorismus zu diesem Jahr." *Die Aktion* 4 (1914): 902–5.

————. *Barbara oder die Frömmigkeit.* Vienna: Paul Zsolnay, 1929.

————. "Begegnung mit Rilke." *Das Tagebuch* 8 (1927): 140–44.

————. *Der Besuch aus dem Elysium: Drama.* Prague: Verlag der Herderblätter, 1912.

————. "Brief an einen Staatsmann." In *Das Ziel: Aufrufe zum tätigen Geist,* edited by Kurt Hiller, 91–98. Munich and Berlin: Georg Müller, 1916. Reprinted in *Zwischen Oben und Unten,* edited by Adolf D. Klarmann (Munich and Vienna: Langen Müller, 1975), 210–16.

————. "Die christliche Sendung." *Die Neue Rundschau* 28 (1917): 92–105.

————. *Einander: Oden, Lieder, Gestalten.* Munich: Kurt Wolff, 1915.

————. "Ex Abrupto." *Die Aktion* 6 (26 October 1916): 602.

————. "Fragment Gegen das Männergeschlecht." *Der Friede* 2, no. 48–49 (23 December 1918): 530–32.

————. *Gedichte: Aus den Jahren 1908–1945.* Los Angeles: Pacific Press, 1946.

————. *Der Gerichtstag.* Munich: Kurt Wolff, 1919.

————. *Gesänge aus den drei Reichen: Ausgewählte Gedichte.* Munich: Kurt Wolff, 1917.

————. "Glosse zu einer Wedekind-Feier." *Prager Tagblatt,* 18 April 1914.

————. "Ein grosser Mystiker in unserer Zeit: Otokar Březina." *Die literarische Welt,* 12 October 1928, 1. Reprinted in *Zwischen Oben und Unten,* edited by Adolf D. Klarmann (Munich and Vienna: Langen Müller, 1975), 427.

————. *Das Lyrische Werk.* Edited by Adolf Klarmann. Frankfurt am Main: A. Fischer, 1967.

————. *Nicht der Mörder, der Ermordete ist schuldig.* Munich: Kurt Wolff, 1919.

————. "Otto Pick zum 50. Geburtstag." *Die Brücke-Most* 4 (21 May 1937): 21. Reprinted in *Zwischen Oben und Unten,* edited by Adolf D. Klarmann (Munich and Vienna: Langen Müller, 1975), 454.

————. "Prag als Literaturstadt." *Prager Tagblatt,* 3 June 1922, 6.

————. "Rede an die Arbeiter von Davos" (May 1918 introduction to reading). *Europäische Heften* 1 (11 October 1934): 413–16. Reprinted in *Zwischen Oben und Unten,* edited by Adolf D. Klarmann (Munich and Vienna: Langen Müller, 1975), 531–34.

————. "Sonderheft Franz Werfel." *Der Neue Daimon* (Vienna), 1919.

————. "Die Stagione: Eine Novelle" (written in Leipzig, 1912; published with an introduction by Eduard Goldstücker). *Germanistica Pragensia* 4 (1966) [= *Acta Universitatis Carolinae: Philologica* 5]: 75–83. Reprinted (without

Goldstücker's introduction) in *Zwischen Oben und Unten,* edited by Adolf
D. Klarmann (Munich and Vienna: Langen Müller, 1975), 821–31.

———. "Substantiv und Verbum: Notiz zu einer Poetik." *Die Aktion,* nos. 1–2
(1917).

———. *Die Troerinnen.* Munich: Kurt Wolff, 1915.

———. "Ein Ulan." *Das Zeit-Echo,* no. 3 (1914): 26–27. Reprinted in *Zwischen Oben und Unten,* edited by Adolf D. Klarmann (Munich and Vienna:
Langen Müller, 1975), 204.

———. *Die Versuchung: Ein Dialog.* Munich: Kurt Wolff, 1913.

———. "Warum haben Sie Prag verlassen?" *Prager Tagblatt,* 4 June 1922. Reprinted in Kurt Krolop, "Hinweis auf eine verschollene Rundfrage, 'Warum
haben Sie Prag verlassen?'" *Germanistica Pragensia* 4 (1966) [= Acta Universitatis Carolinae: Philologica 5]: 47–62.

———. *Der Weltfreund: Gedichte.* Munich: Kurt Wolff, 1911.

———. *Wir sind: Neue Gedichte.* Munich: Kurt Wolff, 1913.

———. Response in *Die Zukunft der deutschen Bühne: Fünf Vorträge und eine
Umfrage.* Berlin: Oesterheld, 1917. Also in *Zwischen Oben und Unten,* 590–
91.

———. *Zwischen Oben und Unten: Prosa-Tagebücher-Aphorismen-Literarische
Nachträge.* Edited by Adolf Klarmann. Munich and Vienna: Langen Müller,
1975.

Wiener, Oskar, ed. *Deutsche Dichter aus Prag: Ein Sammelbuch.* Leipzig and
Vienna, 1919.

Wiener, Oskar, and Johann Pilz, eds. *Der Heimat zum Gruss: Ein Almanach
deutscher Dichtung und Kunst aus Böhmen.* Berlin: Prometheus, 1914.

SECONDARY BOOKS AND ARTICLES, MEMOIRS

Ackermann, Johannes. "Prager deutsche Gesellschaft gestern und heute." *Die
Brücke* 3, no. 24 (7 August 1936): 11–13.

Adalbert Stifter Verein. *Franz Werfel zwischen Prag und Wien: Ausstellung des
Adalbert Stifter Vereins.* Munich: Adalbert Stifter Verein, 1990.

Adler, Friedrich. "Prager deutsche Dichter." *Urania: Monatsschrift für moderne
Bildungspflege* 6, no. 2 (February 1929): 29–31.

Adler-Rudel, Shalom. *Ostjuden in Deutschland, 1880–1940.* Schriftenreihe
wissenschaftlicher Abhandlungen des Leo Baeck Instituts, no. 1. Tübingen:
J. C. B. Mohr, 1959.

Adorno, Theodor W. *Prisms.* Translated by Samuel and Shierry Weber. London:
Neville Spearman, 1967.

Amann, Klaus, and Armin A. Walker, eds. *Expressionismus in Österreich: Die
Literatur und die Künste.* Literatur in der Geschichte/Geschichte in der Literatur, no. 30. Vienna, Cologne, and Weimar: Böhlau, 1994.

Anders, Günther. *Kafka, pro und contra: Die Prozess-Unterlagen.* Munich:
C. H. Beck, 1951.

Anderson, Benedict. *Imagined Communities: Reflections on the Origins and
Spread of Nationalism.* Rev. ed. London and New York: Verso, 1991.

Anderson, Mark M. "Kafka, Homosexuality, and the Aesthetics of 'Male Culture.'" In *Gender and Politics in Austrian Fiction,* Austrian Studies, no. 7, ed. Ritchie Robertson and Edward Timms, 79–99. Edinburgh: Edinburgh University Press, 1996.

———. *Kafka's Clothes: Ornament and Aestheticism in the Habsburg* Fin-de-Siècle. Oxford: Clarendon, 1992.

———, ed. *Reading Kafka: Prague, Politics, and the* Fin de Siècle. New York: Schocken, 1989.

Anz, Thomas, and Michael Stark, eds. *Expressionismus: Manifeste und Dokumente zur deutschen Literatur, 1910–1920.* Stuttgart: Metzler, 1981.

Arendt, Hannah. *Between Past and Future: Eight Exercises in Political Thought.* New York: Viking, 1968.

Arlt, Gustave O. "Franz Werfel, 1890–1945: In Memoriam." *Monatshefte* 37 (1945): 506–9.

Aschenbrenner, Viktor. *Blütezeiten der Kultur in Böhmen, Mähren und Schlesien.* Beiträge des Witikobundes zu Fragen der Zeit, no. 13. Munich: Witikobund, 1964.

Aschheim, Steven E. *Brothers and Strangers: The East European Jew in German and German Jewish Consciousness, 1800–1923.* Madison: University of Wisconsin Press, 1982.

———. "The East European Jew and German Jewish Identity." *Studies in Contemporary Jewry* 1 (1984).

Ash, Timothy Garton. *The Uses of Adversity: Essays on the Fate of Central Europe.* New York: Random House, 1989.

Avineri, Shlomo. *The Making of Modern Zionism.* New York: Basic Books, 1981.

Bab, Julius. "Franz Werfel." *März: Eine Wochenschrift* 3 (1916): 164–70.

Bacher, F[ranz] B. "Die Klasse Beda Wysoký, Erinnerungen an die Piaristen-Schule." *Deutsche Zeitung Bohemia* 105, no. 116 (15 May 1932): 14.

Baioni, Giuliano. *Kafka: Letteratura ed ebraismo.* Turin: Giulio Einaudi, 1984.

Beck, Evelyn Torton. *Kafka and the Yiddish Theater: Its Impact on His Work.* Madison, Milwaukee, and London: University of Wisconsin Press, 1971.

Benjamin, Walter. *Gesammelte Schriften: Unter Mitwirkung von Theodor W. Adorno und Gershom Scholem.* Ed. Rolf Tiedemann and Hermann Schweppenhäuser. 7 vols. Frankfurt am Main: Suhrkamp, 1972–1989.

———. *Illuminations.* Edited by Hannah Arendt. Translated by Harry Zohn. New York: Schocken, 1968.

———. *Reflections.* Edited by Peter Demetz. Translated by Edmund Jephcott. New York: Schocken, 1978.

Bensmaïa, Réda. "The Kafka Effect." Translated by Terry Cochran. Foreword to *Kafka: Toward a Minor Literature,* by Gilles Deleuze and Félix Guattari. Minneapolis: University of Minnesota Press, 1986.

Berend, Ivan T. *The Crisis Zone of Europe: An Interpretation of East-Central European History in the First Half of the Twentieth Century.* Cambridge: Cambridge University Press, 1986.

Bergman, S. H. [Hugo Bergmann]. "Erinnerungen an Franz Kafka." *Universitas,* no. 27 (1972): 739–50.

Bernheimer, Charles. *Flaubert and Kafka: Studies in Psychopoetic Structure.* New Haven and London: Yale University Press, 1982.

Bettelheim, Bruno. *The Informed Heart.* New York: Free Press, 1960.

Bhabha, Homi K. *Nation and Narration.* London and New York: Routledge, 1990.

Bial, David. *Power and Powerlessness in Jewish History.* New York: Schocken, 1986.

Binder, Hartmut. *Franz Kafka: Leben und Persönlichkeit.* Stuttgart: Alfred Kröner, 1979.

———. "Franz Kafka and the Zionist Weekly *Selbstwehr,*" *Leo Baeck Institute Yearbook* 12 (1967): 135–48.

———. "Kindheit in Prag: Kafkas Volksschuljahre." Edited by Erik Carlquist. In *Humanismen som salt och styrka: Bilder och betraktelser tillagnade Harry Jarv,* 63–115. Stockholm: Atlantis, 1987.

———, ed. *Kafka-Handbuch.* 2 vols. Stuttgart: Alfred Kröner, 1979.

Binder, Hartmut, and Ernst Edmund Kiel, eds. *Franz Kafka und die Prager deutsche Literatur: Deutungen und Wirkungen.* Bonn: Kulturstiftung der Deutschen Vertriebenen, 1988.

Birnbaum, Solomon A. "Der Mogel." *Zeitschrift für deutsche Philologie* 74 (1955).

Blei, Franz. *Erzählung eines Lebens.* Leipzig: P. List, 1930.

Bondy, Fritz [N. O. Scarpi, pseud.]. *Liebes altes Prag: Rückblicke eines gar nicht zornigen alten Mannes.* Zurich and Stuttgart, 1968.

Borman, Stuart. "The Prague Student Zionist Movement, 1896–1940." Ph.D. diss., University of Chicago, 1972.

Born, Jürgen, ed., with Martina Dickert and Klaus Peter Wahner. *Deutschsprachige Literatur aus Prag und den böhmischen Ländern, 1900–1925: Chronologische Übersicht und Bibliographie.* 2d ed. Munich, London, New York, and Paris: K. G. Saur, 1993.

Bosl, Karl, ed. *Handbuch der Geschichte der böhmischen Länder.* Stuttgart: A. Hiersemann, 1970.

Botstein, Leon. *Judentum und Modernität: Essays zur Rolle der Juden in der deutschen und österreichischen Kultur, 1848–1938.* Vienna: Bahlan, 1991.

Boyarin, Daniel. *Unheroic Conduct: The Rise of Heterosexuality and the Invention of the Jewish Man.* Berkeley and Los Angeles: University of California Press, 1997.

Boyarin, Jonathan, and Daniel Boyarin. "Diaspora, Generation, and the Ground of Jewish Identity." *Critical Inquiry* 19 (summer 1993): 693–725.

Boyer, John W. *Culture and Political Crisis in Vienna: Christian Socialism in Power, 1897–1918.* Chicago and London: University of Chicago Press, 1995.

———. *Political Radicalism in Late Imperial Vienna: Origins of the Christian Social Movement, 1848–1897.* Chicago and London: University of Chicago Press, 1981.

"Der Brennerverlag: Eine Gesamtbibliographie, 1910–1954." In *Nachrichten aus dem Kösel-Verlag: Sondernummer "Der Brenner" 1965.* Munich: Kösel, 1965.

Breycha-Vautier, Arthur, ed. *Sie trugen Österreich mit sich in die Welt: Eine*

Auswahl aus den Schriften der Österreichischen Emigration. Vienna: Öster-reichische Staatsdruckerei, 1962.

Brix, Emil, and Wolfgang Mantl, eds. *Liberalismus: Interpretation und Per-spektiven.* Vienna, Cologne, and Graz: Böhlau, 1996.

Brod, Leo. "Prager Piaristen-Schule." *Im Herzen Europas* 6, no. 12 (December 1963): 6–8.

———. "Ein vergessener Prager Dichter: Paul Kornfeld." *Sudetenland* 27 (1985): 79.

Brod, Max. "Aus Kafkas Freundekreis." *Wort in der Zeit* 10, no. 6 (June 1964): 4–7.

———. "Prager Dichterschule?" *Der Friede* 2, no. 33 (6 September 1918): 168.

———. *Der Prager Kreis.* Stuttgart, Berlin, Cologne, and Mainz: W. Kohlhammer, 1966. Reprint with an afterword by Peter Demetz, Suhrkamp Taschenbuch 547 (Frankfurt am Main: Suhrkamp, 1979).

———. *Prager Sternenhimmel: Musik- und Theatererlebnisse der zwanziger Jahre.* Vienna and Hamburg: Paul Zsolnay, 1966.

———. *Prager Tagblatt: Roman einer Redaktion.* Frankfurt am Main: Fischer, 1968.

———. Review of *Der pünktliche Eros,* by Paul Leppin. *Die literarische Welt* 3, no. 12 (1927): 7.

———. *Streitbares Leben, 1884–1968.* Munich: Kindler, 1960.

———. "Verkehr mit Dichtern," *Prager Tagblatt,* 21 December 1924, 17.

———. "Wie ich Franz Werfel entdeckte." *Prager Montagsblatt,* no. 52, "Jubiläumsnummer: 60 Jahre," 27 December 1937.

Bronner, Stephen Eric, and Douglas Kellner, eds. *Passion and Rebellion: The Expressionist Heritage.* South Hadley, Mass.: Bergin, 1983.

Bronsen, David, ed. *Jews and Germans from 1860 to 1933: The Problematic Symbiosis.* Heidelberg: Carl Winter, 1979.

Bruce, Iris. "'Aggadah Raises Its Paw against Halakha': Kafka's Zionist Critique in 'Forschungen eines Hundes.'" *Journal of the Kafka Society of America* 16, no. 1 (June 1992): 4–18.

Bruckmüller, Ernst, Ulrike Döcker, Hannes Stekl, and Peter Urbanitsch, eds. *Bürgertum in der Habsburgermonarchie.* Vienna and Cologne: Böhlau, 1990.

Bürger, Christa, Peter Bürger, and Jochen Schulte-Sasse, eds. *Naturalismus/Ästhetizismus.* Hefte für Kritische Literaturwissenshaft, vol. 1. Frankfurt am Main: Suhrkamp, 1979.

Bürger, Peter. *Theory of the Avant-Garde.* Translated by Michael Shaw. Minneapolis: University of Minnesota Press, 1984.

Busek, Erhard, and Emil Brix. *Projekt Mitteleuropa.* Vienna: Ueberreuter, 1986.

Canetti, Elias. *Der andere Prozeß.* Carl Hauser, 1969.

Castle, Eduard. *Geschichte der deutschen Literatur in Österreich-Ungarn im Zeitalter Franz Josefs I.* 2 vols. Vienna: Carl Fromme, 1937.

Cohen, Arthur A. "Kafka's Prague." *Partisan Review* 48, no. 4 (1981): 552–63.

Cohen, Gary B. "Jews in German Society: Prague, 1860–1914." *Central European History* 10 (March 1977): 28–54.

———. *The Politics of Ethnic Survival: Germans in Prague, 1861–1914.* Princeton, N.J.: Princeton University Press, 1981.

Cysarz, Herbert. *Prag im deutschen Geistesleben: Blicke durch ein Jahrtausend.* Mannheim-Sandhofen: Kessler, 1961.

Danès, Jean-Pierre. "Situation de la littérature allemande à Prague à l'époque de Kafka." *Études germaniques* 39, no. 2 (April–June 1984): 119–39.

Davidheiser, James C. "The Quest for Cultural and National Identity in the Works of Franz Werfel." *Perspectives on Contemporary Literature* 8 (1982): 58–66.

Deleuze, Gilles, and Félix Guattari. *Kafka: Toward a Minor Literature.* Translated by Dana Polan. Minneapolis: University of Minnesota Press, 1986.

Demetz, Peter. "Noch einmal, Prager Deutsch." *Literatur + Kritik* 1, no. 6 (September 1966): 58–59.

———. *Prague in Black and Gold: Scenes from the Life of a European City.* New York: Hill and Wang, 1997.

———. *René Rilkes Prager Jahre.* Düsseldorf: E. Diedrichs, 1953.

Deutsch, Julius. *Ein weiter Weg: Lebenserinnerungen.* Zurich: Amalthea, 1960.

Eagleton, Terry. *The Ideology of the Aesthetic.* Cambridge, Mass.: Basil Blackwell, 1990.

Eagleton, Terry, Fredric Jameson, and Edward Said. *Nationalism, Colonialism, and Literature.* Minneapolis: University of Minnesota Press, 1990.

Eder, Karl. *Der Liberalismus in Altösterreich: Geisteshaltung, Politik und Kultur.* Wiener Historische Studien, no. 3. Vienna and Munich: Herold, 1955.

Einstein, Siegfried. "Wer wird in diesem Jahr den Schofar blasen? Sieben jüdischen Dichtern deutscher Sprache zum Gedanken." *Mannheimer Hefte,* no. 3 (1969): 23–30.

Eisner, Pavel. *Franz Kafka and Prague.* Translated by Lowry Nelson and Rene Wellek. New York: Arts, 1950.

———. *Milenky: Německý básník a Česká žena* [Beloveds: German writers and the Czech woman]. Prague: Helios, 1930.

Engerth, Ruediger, ed. *Im Schatten des Hradschin: Kafka und sein Kreis.* Graz, Vienna, and Cologne: Stiasny, 1965.

Fischer, J. M. *Fin-de-siècle: Kommentar zu einer Epoche.* Munich: Winkler, 1978.

Foucault, Michel. "L'ordre du discours." In *Die Ordnung des Diskurses,* edited and translated by Wolfgang Lepenies and Henning Ritter. Munich: Ullstein, 1974.

Frank, E. "Auguste Hauschner und Ihr Kreis." *Sudetenland* 10 (1968).

Frankel, Jonathan. *Assimilation and Community: The Jews in Nineteenth-Century Europe.* Cambridge and New York: Cambridge University Press, 1992.

———. *Prophecy and Politics: Socialism, Nationalism, and the Russian Jews, 1862–1917.* Cambridge and New York: Cambridge University Press, 1981.

Franz, Georg. *Liberalismus: Die deutschliberale Bewegung in der Habsburgischen Monarchie.* Munich: Georg D. W. Callwey, 1955.

Frýd, Norbert. "Die deutschen Dichter Prags: Vom Ende einer Insel." *Im Herzen Europas* 2, no. 3 (March 1959): 4–6.

Gates, Henry Louis, Jr., ed. *Race, Writing, and Difference.* Chicago: University of Chicago Press, 1986.

Gay, Peter. "Encounter with Modernism: German Jews in German Culture, 1888–1914." *Midstream,* February 1975.

Gelber, Mark. "Antisemitism, Indifferentism, the Holocaust, and Zionism: The Cases of Thomas Mann and Max Brod." In *Holocaust Studies Annual, 1990: General Essays,* edited by Sanford Pinsker and Jack Fischel. Garland Reference Library of Social Science, no. 631. New York: Garland, 1990.

———. *Von Franzos zu Canetti: Jüdische Autoren aus Österreich: Neue Studien.* Tübingen: Niemeyer, 1996.

Gesellschaft zur Förderung deutscher Wissenschaft, Kunst und Literatur in Böhmen. *Bibliothek deutscher Schriftsteller aus Böhmen.* 50 vols. Prague: Tempsky, 1894.

Gierach, Erich, ed. *Sudetendeutsche Lebensbilder.* Reichenberg: Gebrüder Stiepel, 1934.

Gilman, Sander L. *Franz Kafka, the Jewish Patient.* New York and London: Routledge, 1995.

———. *Jewish Self-Hatred: Anti-Semitism and the Hidden Language of the Jews.* Baltimore and London: Johns Hopkins University Press, 1986.

———. "The Rediscovery of Eastern Jews: German Jews in the East, 1890–1918." In *Jews and Germans from 1860 to 1933: The Problematic Symbiosis,* edited by David Bronsen. Heidelberg: Winter, 1979.

Gluck, Mary. *Georg Lukács and His Generation.* Cambridge: Harvard University Press, 1985.

Goldstücker, Eduard. "Franz Werfel, Prag und Böhmen." In *Bild und Gedanke: Festschrift für Gerhart Baumann zum 60. Geburtstag,* edited by Günter Schnitzler, Gerhard Neumann, and Jürgen Schroder, 402–9. Munich: Fink, 1980.

———. "Die Prager deutsche Literatur." In *E. E. Kisch/F. C. Weiskopf: Leben und Werk,* Schriftsteller der Gegenwart, no. 2, 6–18. Berlin: Volk und Wissen, 1963.

———. "Ein Unbekannter Brief von Franz Werfel." In *Austriaca: Beiträge zur österreichischen Literatur.* Tübingen: Max Niemeyer, 1975.

———. "Zum Profil der Prager deutschen Dichtung um 1900." *Philologica Pragensia* 5, no. 3 (July 1962): 130–35.

———, ed. *Weltfreunde: Konferenz über die Prager deutsche Literatur.* Prague: Academia, Verlag der Tschechoslowakischen Wissenschaften, 1967.

Goldstücker, Eduard, et al., eds. *Franz Kafka aus Prager Sicht.* Berlin: Voltaire, 1966.

Grimm, Günter E. *Im Zeichen Hiobs: Jüdische Schriftsteller und deutsche Literatur im 20. Jahrhundert.* Königstein/Ts.: Athenäum, 1985.

Gross, Ruth V., ed. *Critical Essays on Franz Kafka.* Boston: G. K. Hall, 1990.

Grözinger, Karl Erich, Stéphane Mosès, and Hans Dieter Zimmermann, eds. *Kafka und das Judentum.* Frankfurt am Main: Jüdischer Verlag bei Athenäum, 1987.

Haas, Willy. "Der junge Max Brod." *Tribüne: Zeitschrift zum Verständnis des Judentums* 3, no. 10 (1964): 1075–76.

———. *Die literarische Welt: Erinnerungen.* Munich: P. List, 1958.

———. "Otto Pick: Ein Blatt des Gedenkens." *Stifter Jahrbuch* 3 (1953): 67–71.

———. "Die Prager deutsche Gesellschaft vor dem Weltkrieg." *Prager Montagsblatt*, no. 52, "Jubiläumsnummer 60 Jahre," 27 December 1937: 1–2.

Hamann, Richard, and Jost Hermand. *Stilkunst um 1900*. Munich, 1973.

Hamšik, Dušan, and Alexey Kusák. *O zuřivém reporéru E. E. Kischovi* [Of the roving reporter E. E. Kisch]. Prague, 1962.

Harvey, David. *The Condition of Postmodernity*. Oxford, 1990.

Havránek, Jan. "The Development of Czech Nationalism." *Austrian History Yearbook* 3 (1967).

Heidegger, Martin. *Poetry, Language, Thought*. Edited and translated by Albert Hofstadter. New York: Harper & Row, 1971.

———. *Sein und Zeit*. Tübingen: Niemeyer, 1957. Translated by John Macquarrie and Edward Robinson under the title *Being and Time* (New York: Harper & Row, 1962).

———. *Der Ursprung des Kunstwerkes*. Stuttgart: Reclam, 1967.

Heneka, A., ed. *A Besieged Culture: Czechoslovakia Ten Years after Helsinki*. Translated by Joyce Dahlberg. Stockholm: Charta 77 Foundation, 1985.

Hever, Hannan. "Hebrew in an Israeli Arab Hand: Six Miniatures on Anton Shammas's *Arabesques*." *Cultural Critique* 7 (fall 1987).

Höbelt, Lothar. *Kornblume und Kaiseradler: Die deutschfreiheitlichen Parteien Altösterreichs, 1882–1918*. Vienna: Verlag für Geschichte und Politik; Munich: R. Oldenbourg, 1993.

Horwath, Peter. "The Erosion of 'Gemeinschaft': German Writers of Prague, 1890–1924." *German Studies Review* 4, no. 1 (February 1981): 9–37.

Huebner, Friedrich Markus. *Europas neue Kunst und Dichtung*. Berlin: E. Rowohlt, 1920.

Hyršlová, Kvetuše. "Zur Frage der Heimat im Werke Franz Werfels." *Zeitschrift für Slawistik* 3 (1958): 727–36.

Iggers, Wilma Abeles. "The Flexible National Identities of Bohemian Jewry." *East Central Europe* 7, no. 1 (1980): 39–48.

———. *Karl Kraus: A Viennese Critic of the Twentieth Century*. The Hague: Martinus Nijhoff, 1967.

———. *Women of Prague: Ethnic Diversity and Social Change from the Eighteenth Century to the Present*. Providence and Oxford: Berghahn, 1995.

———, ed. *Die Juden in Böhmen und Mähren: Ein historisches Lesebuch*. Munich: C. H. Beck, 1986.

International Organization of Journalists. *Egon Erwin Kisch, 1885–1948: Erinnerungen zum 90. Geburtstag*. Prague: International Organization of Journalists, 1975.

Jacobi, Jutta. *Journalisten im literarischen Text*. Frankfurt am Main, 1989.

Jameson, Fredric. *Postmodernism; or, The Cultural Logic of Late Capitalism*. Durham: University of North Carolina Press, 1984.

Janik, Allan, and Stephen Toulmin. *Wittgenstein's Vienna*. New York: Simon and Schuster, 1973.

JanMohamed, Abdul R., and David Lloyd. "Introduction: Toward a Theory of

Minority Discourse." Parts 1 and 2. *Cultural Critique* 6 (spring 1987): 5–12; 7 (fall 1987): 5–17.

———. *The Nature and Context of Minority Discourse.* New York: Oxford University Press, 1990.

Janouch, Gustav. *Gespräche mit Kafka: Erinnerungen und Aufzeichnungen.* Frankfurt am Main: S. Fischer, 1951.

Jindra, Zdeněk, and J. Křížek. *Beiträge zur neuesten Geschichte der Mitteleuropäischen Völker.* Prague: Československá historická společnost, 1960.

Johnston, William M. *The Austrian Mind: An Intellectual and Social History, 1848–1938.* Berkeley and Los Angeles: University of California Press, 1972.

———. "Prague as a Center of Austrian Expressionism versus Vienna as a Center of Impressionism." *Modern Austrian Literature* 6, no. 3/4 (1973): 176–81.

"Das Judentum in der Sudetendeutschen Literatur." *Prager Presse,* 27 July 1933.

Judson, Pieter M. *Exclusive Revolutionaries: Liberal Politics, Social Experience, and National Identity in the Austrian Empire, 1848–1914.* Ann Arbor: University of Michigan Press, 1996.

———. "Inventing Germans: Class, Nationality, and Colonial Fantasy at the Margins of the Hapsburg Monarchy." *Social Analysis* 33 (1993).

———. " 'Not Another Square Foot!' German Liberalism and the Rhetoric of National Ownership in Nineteenth-Century Austria." *Austrian History Yearbook* 22 (1991): 83–88, 91–95.

———. " 'Whether Race or Conviction Should Be the Standard': National Identity and Liberal Politics in Nineteenth-Century Austria." *Austrian History Yearbook* 22 (1991): 76–95.

Jungk, Peter Stephan. *Franz Werfel: A Life in Prague, Vienna, and Hollywood.* Translated by Anselm Hollo. New York: Fromm, 1991.

Kahn, Lothar. *Mirrors of the Jewish Mind: A Gallery of Portraits of European Jewish Writers of Our Time.* New York: Thomas Yoseloff, 1968.

Kayser, Werner, and Horst Gronemeyer, eds. *Max Brod.* Hamburger Bibliographien, vol. 12. Hamburg: Hans Christians, 1972.

Kempf, Franz. "Kafka und der Expressionismus: 'Die Verwandlung.' " *Seminar: A Journal of Germanic Studies* 26, no. 4 (November 1990): 327–41.

Kestenberg-Gladstein, Ruth. *Neuere Geschichte der Juden in den böhmischen Ländern.* Tübingen: Mohr, 1969.

Keith, Michael, and Steve Pile, eds. *Place and the Politics of Identity.* London, 1993.

Kieval, Hillel Joseph. *The Making of Czech Jewry: National Conflict and Jewish Society in Bohemia, 1870–1918.* Studies in Jewish History. New York and Oxford: Oxford University Press, 1988.

———. "Pursuing the Golem of Prague: Jewish Culture and the Invention of a Tradition." *Modern Judaism* 17 (February 1997): 1–23.

Kisch, Bruno. *Wanderungen und Wandlungen: Die Geschichte eines Arztes im 20. Jahrhundert.* Cologne: Greven, 1966.

Kisch, Egon Erwin. *Marktplatz der Sensationen: Entdeckungen in Mexiko.* Berlin: Aufbau, 1947.

Kisch, Paul. "Deutsche Erzähler aus der Tschechoslowakei." *Deutsche Zeitung Bohemia* 96, no. 31 (8 February 1923): 3–4.

Klaar, Alfred. "Die deutschböhmische Literatur in den letzten 60 Jahren." *Deutsche Arbeit* 8, no. 3 (December 1908): 212–25.

Klarmann, Adolf D. "Franz Werfel's Eschatology and Cosmogony." *Modern Language Quarterly* 7 (1946): 385–410.

———. "Gottesidee and Erlösungsproblem beim jungen Werfel." *Germanic Review* 14 (1939).

Kohn, Hans. *Living in a World Revolution: My Encounters with History.* New York: Trident Press, 1964.

———. "Prager Dichter." *Selbstwehr* 6, no. 51 (20 December 1912): 2–3.

Kopetz, Heinrich Ritter von. *Plaudereien eines alten Pragers.* Prague, 1905.

Kořalka, Jiří. "Nationale und regionale Identität der Tschechen und der Deutschen in den böhmischen Ländern." *brücken: Germanistisches Jahrbuch* (1991/1992), Neue Folge 1:9–17.

———. "Das Nationalitätenproblem in den böhmischen Ländern, 1848–1918." *Österreichische Osthefte* 5 (1963): 1–12.

Körner, Josef. "Dichter und Dichtung aus dem deutschen Prag." *Donauland: Illustrierte Monatsschrift* 1, no. 7 (September 1917): 777–88.

Křen, Jan. *Die Konfliktgemeinschaft: Tschechen und Deutsche, 1780–1918.* Translated by Peter Heumos. Veröffentlichungen des Collegium Carolinum, vol. 71. Munich: R. Oldenbourg, 1996.

Krojenker, Gustav, ed. *Juden in der deutschen Literatur: Essays über zeitgenössische Schriftsteller.* Berlin: Welt-Verlag, 1922.

Krolop, Kurt. "Ein Manifest der Prager Schule." *Philologica Pragensia* 7, no. 4 (1964): 329–36.

———. "Das 'Prager Erbe' und 'das Österreichische.'" *Zeitschrift für Germanistik* 4 (1983): 168–78.

———. "Zur Geschichte und Vorgeschichte der Prager deutschen Literatur." In *Weltfreunde: Konferenz über die Prager deutsche Literatur,* ed. Eduard Goldstücker, 47–96. Prague: Academia, Verlag der Tschechoslowakischen Wissenschaften, 1967.

Krolop, Kurt, and Hans Dieter Zimmermann, eds. *Kafka und Prag.* Colloquium im Goethe-Institut Prag, 24.–27. November 1992. Berlin and New York: Walter de Gruyter, 1994.

Krywalski, Diether. "Die deutsche Prager Literatur nach der Jahrhundertwende." *Sudetenland* 31 (1989): 229–35; 314–31.

Kukula, Richard. *Erinnerungen eines Bibliothekars.* Weimar: Straubling & Müller, 1925.

Langer, František. *Byli a bylo* [They were and it was]. Prague: Československý Spisovatel, 1963.

Le Rider, Jacques. *Modernity and Crises of Identity: Culture and Society in Fin-de-Siècle Vienna.* Translated by Rosemary Morris. New York: Continuum, 1993.

Lefebvre, Henri. *The Production of Space.* Translated by Donald Nicholson-Smith. Oxford and Cambridge, Mass., 1991.

Leppin, Paul. "Prager Literatur vor drei Jahrzehnten." *Prager Presse* 4, no. 261, Beilage "Dichtung und Welt," no. 38 (21 September 1924): 2–3.

———. "Schriftstellerkolonier VIII: Prag." *Das literarische Echo* 21, no. 5 (1 December 1918): 273–76.

Lessing, Theodor. *Der jüdische Selbsthaß.* Berlin: Zionistischer Bücher-Bund, 1930.

Lethen, Helmut. *Verhaltenslehren der Kälte: Lebensversuche zwischen den Kriegen.* Frankfurt am Main: Suhrkamp, 1994.

Lidtke, Vernon L. "Naturalism and Socialism in Germany." *American Historical Review* 79 (February 1974): 14–37.

Loesberg, Jonathan. *Aestheticism and Deconstruction: Pater, Derrida, and De Man.* Princeton, N.J.: Princeton University Press, 1991.

Löwy, Michael. *Rédemption et utopie: Le Judaïsme libertaire en Europe centrale: Une étude d'affinité élective.* Paris: Presses Universitaires de France, 1988.

Luz, Ehud. *Parallels Meet: Religion and Nationalism in the Early Zionist Movement (1882–1904).* Translated by Lenn J. Schramm. Philadelphia: Jewish Publication Society, 1988.

Magris, Claudio. "Der habsburgische Mythos in der österreichischen Literatur." *Literatur + Kritik* 1, no. 3 (June 1966): 1–9. Offprint, Salzburg: O. Müller, 1966.

———. "Prag als Oxymoron." *Neohelicon: Acta Comparationis Litterarum Universarum* 7, no. 2 (1979–80): 11–65.

———. *Der unauffindbare Sinn: Zur österreichischen Literatur des 20. Jahrhunderts.* Klagenfurt: Carinthia, 1978.

———. *Weit von wo: Verlorene Welt des Ostjudentums.* Vienna: Europaverlag, 1974.

Mahler-Werfel, Alma. *Mein Leben.* Frankfurt am Main: Fischer, 1960.

Mann, Thomas. "Gruß an Prag." *Prager Tagblatt,* 22 January 1935, 3. Reprinted in *Vollendung und Größe Thomas Manns,* edited by Georg Wenzel (Halle/Salle, 1967).

Maren-Grisebach, Manon. "Weltanschauung und Kunstform im Frühwerk Paul Kornfelds." 1960. German Literary Archives—Schiller National Museum, Marbach am Neckar.

Massey, Doreen. *Space, Place, and Gender.* Minneapolis: University of Minnesota Press, 1994.

Mauthner, Fritz. *Erinnerungen.* Vol. 1, *Prager Jugendjahre.* Munich: Georg Müller, 1918.

Mayer, Hans. *Der Widerruf: Über Deutsche und Juden.* Frankfurt am Main: Suhrkamp, 1994.

Mayer, Sigmund. *Ein jüdischer Kaufmann, 1831 bis 1911: Lebenserinnerungen.* Berlin and Vienna: Benjamin Harz, 1926.

Mehlman, Jeffrey. "Portnoy in Paris." *Diacritics* 2, no. 4 (winter 1972): 21.

Mendes-Flohr, Paul. *Divided Passions: Jewish Intellectuals and the Experience of Modernity.* Detroit: Wayne State University Press, 1991.

Methlagl, Walter, Eberhard Sauermann, and Sigurd Paul Scheichl, eds. *Untersuchungen zum Brenner.* Salzburg: Müller, 1981.

Moi, Toril. *Sexual/Textual Politics: Feminist Literary Theory*. London and New York: Methuen, 1985.
Mosse, George L. *German Jews beyond Judaism*. The Modern Jewish Experience series. Cincinnati: Hebrew Union College, 1985.
——. *Germans and Jews: The Right, the Left, and the Search for a "Third Force" in pre-Nazi Germany*. New York: Grosset & Dunlap, 1971.
——. *Nationalism and Sexuality: Middle-Class Morality and Sexual Norms in Modern Europe*. Madison: University of Wisconsin Press, 1988.
——. *The Nationalization of the Masses: Political Symbolism and Mass Movements in Germany from the Napoleonic Wars through the Third Reich*. Ithaca, N.Y.: Cornell University Press, 1991.
Mühlberger, Josef. *Geschichte der deutschen Literatur in Böhmen, 1900–1939*. Munich and Vienna: Langen Müller, 1981.
Münch, Hermann. *Böhmische Tragödie*. Braunschweig: G. Westermann, 1949.
Muneles, Otto. *Bibliographic Survey of Jewish Prague*. Prague: Orbis, 1952.
Németh, André. *Kafka ou le mystère juif*. Paris, 1947.
Österreichische Franz-Kafka-Gesellschaft Wien-Klosterneuburg. *Prager deutschsprachige Literatur zur Zeit Kafkas*. Vienna: Braunmüller, 1989.
Otten, Karl. *Ahnung und Aufbruch: Expressionistische Prosa*. Darmstadt und Neuwied: Luchterhand, 1977.
——. "Paul Kornfeld. Biographischer und bibliographischer Hinweis." In Karl Otten, *Das leere Haus*, 643–44. Stuttgart: Cotta, 1959.
Otto Pick zum 50. Geburtstag. Prague: Orbis, 1937.
Parker, Andrew, Mary Russo, Doris Sommer, and Patricia Yaeger, eds. *Nationalisms & Sexualities*. New York and London: Routledge, 1992.
Pawel, Ernst. *The Nightmare of Reason: A Life of Franz Kafka*. New York: Farrar, Straus, Giroux, 1984.
Pazi, Margarita. "Franz Kafka und Ernst Weiß." *Modern Austrian Literature 6*, no. 3/4 (1973): 52–92.
——. *Fünf Autoren des Prager Kreises*. Frankfurt am Main, Berne, and Las Vegas: Peter Lang, 1978.
——. *Max Brod: Leben und Persönlichkeit*. Bonn: H. Bouvier, 1970.
——. "Der 'Prager Kreis'—Judentum und zionistischer Gedanke." *Emuna Israel-Forum: Vereinigte Zeitschriften über Israel und Judentum*, no. 2 (1977): 46–51.
——. "'Smither kauft Europa': Über eine unbekannte Komödie Paul Kornfelds." *Orbis Litterarum* (Copenhagen) 29 (1974): 133–59.
——. "Zu Paul Kornfelds Leben und Werk: Tagebücher aus seiner Frankfurter Zeit, 1914–1921." *Jahrbuch der deutschen Schillergemeinschaft* 27 (1983): 59–85.
——, ed. *Max Brod, 1884–1984: Untersuchungen zu Max Brods literarischen und philosophischen Schriften*. New York: P. Lang, 1987.
Peck, Jeffrey M. "Methodological Postscript: What's the Difference? Minority Discourse in German Studies." *New German Critique*, no. 46 (winter 1989): 203–8.
Petr, Pavel. "Die deutsche Übersetzung der *Abenteuer des braven Soldaten*

Schwejk." Parts 1 and 2. *Philologica Pragensia* 4, no. 3 (1961): 160–73; no. 4 (1961): 231–41.

Pick, Otto. "Über deutsche Dichtung in der Tschechoslowakei." *Die Provinz* 1, no. 7/8 (October 1924): 204–8.

———. *Um das Deutsche Theater in Prag.* Prague: Verlag Prag II, 1931.

———. "Zwanzig Jahre deutsches Schrifttum in Prag." *Witiko: Zeitschrift für Kunst und Dichtung* 2, no. 3 (June 1929): 116–20.

Plener, Ernst [Freiherr von]. *Erinnerungen.* 2 vols. Stuttgart and Leipzig: Deutsche Verlags-Anstalt, 1921.

Poláček, Josef. "Egon Erwin Kisch, 1914–1920: Bausteine einer Biographie." *Philologica Pragensia* 10, no. 3 (1967): 129–46.

———. "Der junge Kisch." *Philologica Pragensia* 8, no. 1 (1965): 26–44; and 9, no. 3 (1966): 236–52.

———. "Zu zwei Fragen der Egon-Erwin-Kisch-Forschung." *Germanistica Pragensia* 6 (1972) [= Acta Universitatis Carolinae: Philologica 5]: 61–74.

Politzer, Heinz. "Das Mütterchen hat Krallen: Prag und die Ursprünge Rainer Maria Rilkes, Franz Kafkas und Franz Werfels." *Literatur + Kritik* 8 (1 February 1974). Translated under the title "Prague and the Origins of Rainer Maria Rilke, Franz Kafka, and Franz Werfel," *Modern Language Quarterly* 16 (1955): 49–62.

———. "Vom geheimen Prag." *Die Sammlung* 2 (1934/1935): 576–79.

Portheim, Gustav von. "Aus meinen Erinnerungen." *Deutsche Arbeit* 7 (1907/1908): 714–23.

Povejšil, Jaromír. "Ein Kennzeichen des Prager Deutsch." *Philologica Pragensia* 5, no. 4 (1962): 207–10.

Prager deutsche Literatur vom Expressionismus bis zu Exil und Verfolgung: Ausstellungsbuch erarbeitet und herausgegeben von Ernest Wichner und Herbert Wiesner. Texte aus dem Literaturhaus Berlin, no. 2. Berlin: Literaturhaus, 1995.

Preidel, Helmut. *Germanen in Böhmens Frühzeit.* Karlsbad-Drahowitz and Leipzig: Adam Kraft, 1938.

———. *Die germanischen Kulturen in Böhmen und ihre Träger.* 2 vols. Kassel-Wilhelmshöhe: J. Stauda, 1930.

———, ed. *Die Deutschen in Böhmen und Mähren: Ein historischer Rückblick.* Gräfeling bei München: E. Gans, 1952.

Raabe, Paul. *Die Zeitschriften und Sammlungen des literarischen Expressionismus.* Stuttgart: Metzler, 1964.

———, ed. *Expressionismus: Aufzeichnungen und Erinnerungen der Zeitgenossen.* Olten: Walter Verlag, 1965.

———. *Ich schneide die Zeit aus: Expressionismus und Politik in Franz Pfemferts "Aktion," 1911–1918.* Munich: Deutscher Taschenbuch Verlag, 1964.

Raabe, Paul, ed., with Ingrid Hannich-Bode. *Die Autoren und Bücher des literarischen Expressionismus: Ein bibliographisches Handbuch.* Stuttgart: Metzler, 1985.

Reimann, Paul. *Von Herder bis Kisch: Studien zur Geschichte der deutschösterreich-tschechischen Literaturbeziehungen.* Berlin: Dietz, 1961.

Riese, Utz. "Postmodern Culture: Symptom, Critique, or Solution to the Crisis of Modernity? An East German Perspective." *New German Critique,* no. 57 (fall 1992): 157–69.

Riff, Michael A. "Czech Antisemitism and the Jewish Response before 1914." *Wiener Library Bulletin* 29, no. 39/40 (1976).

Ripellino, Angelo Maria. *Praga magica.* Turin: Einaudi, 1973.

Ritter, Harry. "Austro-German Liberalism and the Modern Liberal Tradition." *German Studies Review* 7, no. 2 (May 1984): 227–48.

Robert, Marthe. *As Lonely As Franz Kafka.* New York: Harcourt Brace Jovanovich, 1982.

Robertson, Ritchie. "In Search of the Historical Kafka: A Selective Review of Research, 1980–92." *Modern Language Review* 89 (January 1994): 107–37.

———. *Kafka: Judaism, Politics, and Literature.* New York: Oxford University Press, 1985.

———. "National Stereotypes in Prague German Fiction." *Colloquia Germanica, Internationale Zeitschrift für Germanische Sprach- und Literaturwissenschaft* 22, no. 2 (1989): 116–36.

———. "Western Observers and Eastern Jews: Kafka, Buber, Franzos." *Modern Language Review* 83 (January 1988): 87–105.

Robertson, Ritchie, and Edward Timms, eds. *Gender and Politics in Austrian Fiction.* Austrian Studies, no. 7. Edinburgh: Edinburgh University Press, 1996.

Rolland, Romain. *Zwischen den Völkern: Aufzeichnungen und Dokumente aus den Jahren 1914–1919.* Stuttgart: Deutsche Verlags-Anstalt, 1955.

Rosenfeld, Otto. "Prag, eine literarische Stadt." *Deutsche Zeitung Bohemia* 90, no. 320 (21 November 1917), morning edition, 3–4.

Rosenheim, Richard. *Die Geschichte der Deutschen Bühnen in Prag, 1883–1918: Mit einem Rückblick, 1783–1883.* Prague: Heinr. Mercy Sohn, 1938.

Roth, Michael S. *The Ironist's Cage: Memory, Trauma, and the Construction of History.* New York: Columbia University Press, 1995.

Rubinstein, William C. "Kafka's 'Jackals and Arabs.'" *Monatshefte* 59 (1967): 13–18.

Said, Edward W. *Culture and Imperialism.* New York: Knopf, 1993.

———. *Orientalism.* New York: Pantheon, 1978. Afterword in Vintage Edition (New York, 1994).

Sauer, August. "Zur Prager Literaturgeschichte." *Deutsche Arbeit* 6, no. 7 (April 1907): 452–55.

Sayer, Derek. *The Coasts of Bohemia: A Czech History.* Princeton, N.J.: Princeton University Press, 1998.

———. "The Language of Nationality and the Nationality of Language: Prague, 1780–1920." *Past and Present* 153 (November 1996): 164–210.

Schlenstedt, Dieter. *Egon Erwin Kisch: Leben und Werk.* Schriftsteller der Gegenwart, no. 11. Berlin: Volk und Wissen, 1985.

———. *Die Reportage bei Egon Erwin Kisch.* Berlin: Rütten & Loening, 1959.

Schlögel, Karl. "Die Mitte liegt im Osten: Die Deutschen und Mitteleuropa." *Die Zeit,* 18 April 1986, 19 f.

Schluderpacher, Carl, ed. *Prager Theaterbuch: Gesammelte Aufsätze über Deutsche Bühnenkunst.* Prague: G. Fanta, 1924.

Schneider, Karl Ludwig, and Roger Bauer. "La théorie du drame expressionniste et sa mise en oeuvre chez Paul Kornfeld." In *L'expressionnisme dans le théâtre européen*, edited by Denis Bablet and Jean Jacquot, 111–18. Paris: Centre National de la Recherche Scientifique, 1984.

Scholem, Gershom. *Major Trends in Jewish Mysticism*. Reprint, New York: Schocken, 1961.

Schone, Albrecht, Walter Rolle, and Hans-Peter Bayerdorfer, eds. *Auseinandersetzungen um jiddische Sprache und Literatur: Jüdische Komponenten in der deutschen Literatur—die Assimilationskontroverse*. Tübingen: Niemeyer, 1986.

Schorske, Carl E. *Fin-de-Siècle Vienna: Politics and Culture*. New York: Knopf, 1980.

———. *Thinking with History: Explorations in the Passage to Modernism*. Princeton, N.J.: Princeton University Press, 1998.

Schumann, Wolfgang. "Deutsch-österreichische Dichtung unsrer Zeit." *Deutsche Arbeit* 12, no. 1 (October 1912): 16–23, 87–93.

Schwanzer, Viliam. "Störungen in der deutschen Sprachstruktur durch Isolation und Einwirkungen des Slawischen." *Zeitschrift für deutsche Philologie* 87, no. 1 (1968): 86–96.

Seliger, Helfried W., ed. *Der Begriff "Heimat" in der deutschen Gegenwartsliteratur*. Munich: iudicium, 1987.

Serke, Jürgen. *Böhmische Dörfer: Wanderungen durch eine verlassene literarische Landschaft*. Vienna and Hamburg: Paul Zsolnay, 1987.

Seton-Watson, Hugh. *Nations and States: An Enquiry into the Origins of Nations and the Politics of Nationalism*. London: Methuen, 1977.

Seton-Watson, R. W. *A History of the Czechs and Slovaks*. London, 1943.

Shohetman, Baruch, ed. *Kitvei Shmuel Hugo Bergman: Bibliografiya, 1903–1967* [The writings of Shmuel Hugo Bergman (Hugo Bergmann): Bibliography, 1903–1967]. Jerusalem: Magnus Press, 1968.

Siegel, Christian Ernst. *Egon Erwin Kisch: Reportage und politischer Journalismus*. Bremen: Carl Schünemann, 1973.

Skála, Emil. "Das Prager Deutsch." *Zeitschrift für deutsche Sprache* 22, no. 1/2 (1966): 84–91.

Sloterdijk, Peter. *Weltfremdheit*. Frankfurt am Main: Suhrkamp, 1993.

Sokel, Walter Herbert. *The Writer in Extremis: Expressionism in Twentieth-Century German Literature*. Stanford, Calif.: Stanford University Press, 1959.

———, ed. *Anthology of German Expressionist Drama: A Prelude to the Absurd*. Ithaca, N.Y.: Cornell University Press, 1963.

Soler Alvarez, Fernando. "Kafka y Checoslovaquia o el poeta y su tierra." *Quimera: Revista de Literatura*, no. 34 (December 1983): 28–34.

Spector, Scott. "Another Zionism: Hugo Bergmann's Circumscription of Spiritual Territory." *Journal of Contemporary European History*, January 1999.

———. "Auf der Suche nach der Prager deutschen Kultur: Deutsch-jüdische Dichter in Prag von der Jahrhundertwende bis 1918." In *Deutsche im Osten: Geschichte, Kultur, Erinnerungen*, edited by Deutsches Historisches Museum Berlin. Munich and Berlin: Koehler & Amelang, 1994.

————. "Beyond the Aesthetic Garden: Politics and Culture on the Margins of *Fin-de-Siècle Vienna.*" *Journal of the History of Ideas,* October 1998.

————. "From Big Daddy to Small Literature: On Taking Kafka at His Word." In *Evolving Jewish Identities in German Culture: Borders and Crossings,* edited by Linda E. Feldman and Diana Orendi. Westport, Conn.: Prager, 1998.

————. "Die Konstruktion einer jüdischen Nationalität—die Prager Wochenschrift 'Selbstwehr.'" *brücken: Germanistisches Jahrbuch* (1991/1992), Neue Folge 1.

————. "Workshop Nationen: Otto Picks Vermittlungsräume." *Das Jüdische Echo: Zeitschrift für Kultur & Politik* (Vienna) 45.

Stach, Reiner. *Kafkas erotischer Mythos: Eine ästhetische Konstruktion des Weiblichen.* Frankfurt am Main: Fischer, 1987.

Steiman, Lionel B. *Franz Werfel: The Faith of an Exile: From Prague to Beverly Hills.* Waterloo, Ontario: Wilfrid Laurier University, 1985.

Steinberg, Michael P. *The Meaning of the Salzburg Festival: Austria as Theater and Ideology, 1890–1938.* Ithaca, N.Y.: Cornell University Press, 1990.

————. "'Fin-de-Siècle Vienna' Ten Years Later: 'Viel Traum, Wenig Wirklichkeit.'" *Austrian History Yearbook* 22 (1991): 151–62.

Stekl, Hannes, Peter Urbanitsch, Ernst Bruckmüller, and Hans Heiss, eds. *"Durch Arbeit, Besitz, Wissen und Gerechtigkeit."* Vol. 2 of *Bürgertum in der Habsburgermonarchie.* Vienna, Cologne, and Weimar: Böhlau, 1992.

Stern, Desider. *Werke von Autoren jüdischer herkunft in deutscher Sprache: Eine Bio-Bibliographie.* Munich: Frühmorgen and Holzmann, 1969.

Stern, J. P. *The Heart of Europe: Essays on Literature and Ideology.* Oxford and Cambridge, Mass.: Blackwell, 1992.

————. "'Words Are Also Deeds': Some Observations on Austrian Language Consciousness." *New Literary History* 12 (1981): 509–28.

————, ed. *The World of Franz Kafka.* New York: Holt, Rinehart and Winston, 1980.

Stölzl, Christoph. *Kafkas böses Böhmen: Zur Sozialgeschichte eines Prager Juden.* Munich: edition text + kritik, 1975.

————. "Zur Geschichte der böhmischen Juden in der Epoche des modernen Nationalismus." *Bohemia: Jahrbuch des Collegium Carolinium* 14 (1973): 179–221; 15 (1974): 129–57.

Strobl, Karl Hans. *Heimat im frühen Licht: Jugenderinnerungen aus deutschem Ostland.* Budweis and Leipzig, 1942.

Sudhoff, Dieter. "Der Dichter des Tages oder Die Last der Welt: Über Leben und Werk von Franz Janowitz" In Klaus Amann and Armin A. Wallas, eds., *Expressionismus in Österreich: Die Literatur und die Künste,* Literatur in der Geschichte/Geschichte in der Literatur, vol. 30, 253–74. Vienna, Cologne, and Weimar: Böhlau, 1994.

Susskind, Charles. *Janáček and Brod.* New Haven and London: Yale University Press, 1985.

Suttner, Bertha von. *Die Waffen nieder!* Dresden: Pierson, 1906.

Szporluk, Roman. *The Political Thought of Tomáš G. Masaryk.* New York: Columbia University Press, 1981.

Teweles, Heinrich. *Theater und Publikum*. Prague: Gesellschaft Deutscher Bü-
cherfreunde in Böhmen, 1927.

Theweleit, Klaus. *Männerphantasien*. Reinbek bei Hamburg: Rowohlt Taschenbuch Verlag, 1980.

Timms, Edward. "Musil's Vienna and Kafka's Prague: The Quest for a Spiritual
City." In *Unreal City: Urban Experience in Modern European Literature and
Art*, edited by Edward Timms and David Kelley, 247–63. New York: St. Mar-
tin's Press, 1985.

Tomberg, Friedrich. "Kafkas Tiere." *Das Argument* 6, no. 1 (1964).

Tramer, Hans. "Die Dreivölkerstadt Prag." In *Robert Weltsch zum 70. Geburtstag von seinen Freunden*, 138–203. Tel Aviv: Bitaon, 1961. Translated under the title "Prague—City of Three Peoples," *Leo Baeck Institute Yearbook*
9 (1964).

———, ed. *Robert Weltsch zum 70. Geburtstag von seinen Freunden*. Tel Aviv:
Bitaon, 1961.

Trost, Pavel. "Franz Kafka und das Prager Deutsch." *Germanistica Pragensia* 3
(1964) [= Acta Universitatis Carolinae: Philologica 1]: 29–37.

———. "Die Mythen vom Prager Deutsch." *Zeitschrift für Deutsche Philologie*
100, no. 3 (1981): 381–90.

———. "Prager Deutsch und Baltendeutsch." *Germanistica Pragensia* 5 (1968)
[= Acta Universitatis Carolinae: Philologica 5]: 17–20.

———. "Und wiederum: Prager Deutsch." *Literatur + Kritik* 1, no. 9/10 (December 1966): 107–8.

Unseld, Joachim. *Franz Kafka: Ein Schriftstellerleben*. Munich and Vienna: Karl
Hanser, 1982.

Urzidil, Johannes. *Da geht Kafka*. Munich: Deutscher Taschenbuch Verlag, 1966.

———. "Deutsche Literatur in der Tschechoslowakei." *Deutsche Zeitung Bohemia* 101 (2 February 1929): 31–32.

———. *Goethe in Böhmen*. Zurich and Stuttgart: Artemis, 1962.

———. *Prager Triptychon*. Munich: A. Langen and G. Müller, 1960.

———. *Die verlorene Geliebte*. Munich: A. Langen and G. Müller, 1956.

Utitz, Emil. *Egon Erwin Kisch: Der klassische Journalist*. Berlin, 1956.

———. *Die Kultur in der Epoche des Weltkrieges*. Stuttgart: Ferdinand Enke,
1927.

Veselá, Gabriela. "E. E. Kisch und der deutschsprachige Prager erotische Roman." *Philologica Pragensia* 28, no. 4 (1985): 202–15.

Vogel, Jaroslav. *Leoš Janáček: His Life and Works*. London: P. Hamlyn, 1962.

Wagenbach, Klaus. *Kafka: Eine Biographie seiner Jugend, 1883–1912*. Berne:
Francke, 1958.

Wallas, Armin A., ed. *Texte des Expressionismus: Der Beitrag jüdischer Autoren
zur österreichischen Avantgarde*. Linz: Edition Neue Texte, 1988.

Weiß, Ernst, Paul Kornfeld, and Gustav Meyrink. "Prag als Literaturstadt."
Prager Tagblatt, 2 June 1922, 6.

Weltsch, Felix. "The Rise and Fall of the Jewish-German Symbiosis: The Case of
Franz Kafka." *Leo Baeck Institute Yearbook* 1 (1956).

———. Review of *Tycho Brahes Weg zu Gott*, by Max Brod. *Die Schaubühne*
12, no. 21 (24 March 1917).

————, ed. *Dichter-Denker-Helfer: Max Brod zum 50. Geburtstag*. Mährisch-Ostrau: Keller & Co., 1934.

Weltsch, Robert. *Max Brod and His Age*. Leo Baeck Memorial Lecture no. 13. New York: Leo Baeck Institute, 1970.

Wertheimer, Jack L. *Unwelcome Strangers: East European Jews in Imperial Germany*. New York and Oxford: Oxford University Press, 1987.

Wiegler, Paul. "Prager Autorenabend." *Bohemia* 85, no. 337 (December 1912): 12.

Wiener, Oskar. *Alt-Prager Guckkasten: Wanderungen durch das romantische Prag*. Prague, Vienna, and Leipzig: A. Haase, 1922.

Winter, Eduard. *Frühliberalismus in der Donaumonarchie: Religiöse, nationale und wissenschaftliche Strömungen von 1790–1868*. Beiträge zur Geschichte des religiösen und wissenschaftlichen Denkens, vol. 7. Berlin: Akademie, 1968.

Wiskemann, Elizabeth. *Czechs and Germans*. New York: Oxford University Press, 1938.

Wolkan, Rudolf. *Geschichte der deutschen Literatur in Böhmen und in den Sudetenländern*. Aussig: V. Stada Verlag, 1925.

Wurghaft, Lewis D. *The Activists: Kurt Hiller and the Politics of Activism on the German Left, 1914–1933*. Philadelphia: American Philosophical Society, 1977.

Wyatt, Frederick. "Der frühe Werfel bleibt: Sein Beitrag zu der expressionistischen Gedichtsammlung." In *Literaturpsychologische Studien und Analysen,* edited by Walter Schonau, 249–74. Amsterdam: Rodopi, 1983.

Yaeger, Patricia, ed. *The Geography of Identity*. Ann Arbor: University of Michigan Press, 1996.

Zimmermann, Hans Dieter. *Der babylonische Dolmetscher: Zu Franz Kafka und Robert Walser*. Frankfurt am Main: Suhrkamp, 1985.

Zipperstein, Steven J. *Elusive Prophet: Ahad Ha'am and the Origins of Zionism*. Berkeley and Los Angeles: University of California Press, 1993.

Žižek, Slavoj. *The Metastases of Enjoyment: Six Essays on Woman and Causality*. London and New York: Verso, 1994.

————. *Tarrying with the Negative*. London and New York: Routledge, 1993.

Zweig, Stefan. *The World of Yesterday*. New York: Viking, 1943.

Index

Text:	10/13 Sabon
Display:	Sabon
Composition:	G & S Typesetters, Inc.
Printing and binding:	Thomson-Shore, Inc.

AEE-1486

WITHDRAWN